Middle East Historiographies

Middle East Historiographies

NARRATING THE TWENTIETH CENTURY

Edited by

Israel Gershoni

Amy Singer

Y. Hakan Erdem

UNIVERSITY OF WASHINGTON PRESS Seattle and London

University of Washington Press

PO Box 50096, Seattle, WA 98145

www.washington.edu/uwpress

Library of Congress Cataloging-in-Publication Data

Middle east historiographies: narrating the Twentieth Century /
edited by Israel Gershoni, Amy Singer, Y. Hakan Erdem.

p. cm.

Includes bibliographical references and index.

ISBN 0-295-98604-2 (pbk. : alk. paper)

1. Middle East—Historiography.

2. Middle East—History—20th century.

I. Gershoni, I.   II. Singer, Amy.   III. Erdem, Y. Hakan.

DS61.6M534 2006   956.04072—dc22   2006005089

Contents

ACKNOWLEDGMENTS VII

PART I: THE STATE OF THE ART

Introduction 3
ISRAEL GERSHONI AND AMY SINGER

1 / The Historiography of the Modern Middle East:
Transforming a Field of Study 19
R. STEPHEN HUMPHREYS

PART II: COLONIALISM AND NATIONALISM

2 / The Historiography of World War I and the
Emergence of the Contemporary Middle East 39
CHARLES D. SMITH

3 / Twentieth-Century Historians and Historiography
of the Middle East: Women, Gender, and Empire 70
JULIA CLANCY-SMITH

4 / Reading Genocide: Turkish Historiography on the
Armenian Deportations and Massacres of 1915 101
FATMA MÜGE GÖÇEK

PART III: NARRATIVES OF CRISIS

5 / The Theory of Crisis and the Crisis in a Theory:
Intellectual History in Twentieth-Century
Middle Eastern Studies 131
ISRAEL GERSHONI

6 / The Historiography of Crisis in the
Egyptian Political Economy 183
ELLIS GOLDBERG

PART IV: EMERGING VOICES

7 / On Gender, History, . . . and Fiction 211
MARILYN BOOTH

8 / Will That Subaltern Ever Speak? Finding African
Slaves in the Historiography of the Middle East 242
EVE M. TROUTT POWELL

9 / Muslim Religious Extremism in Egypt:
A Historiographical Critique of Narratives 262
JUAN R. I. COLE

10 / Audiovisual Media and
History of the Arab Middle East 288
WALTER ARMBRUST

GLOSSARY 315

CONTRIBUTORS 317

INDEX 321

Acknowledgments

This book is the second volume of a collaborative project sponsored by the Institute for Advanced Studies at the Hebrew University of Jerusalem, Boğaziçi University (Istanbul), and the Chaim Herzog Center for Middle East Studies and Diplomacy at Ben Gurion University of the Negev. We extend our sincere thanks to these institutions for their financial support and encouragement. In particular, we recognize the hospitality of Boğaziçi University and the Boğaziçi University Foundation (BUVAK) in hosting the workshop "Twentieth-Century Historians and Historiographies of the Middle East," from which the present collection evolved.

For their intellectual contributions, their insights and critiques, our thanks go to the authors included in this volume and to the other participants in the workshop: Iris Agmon, Beth Baron, Joel Beinin, Halil Berktay, Selçuk Esenbel, Haim Gerber, Joel Gordon, Jane Hathaway, Gün Kut, Afsaneh Najmabadi, İlber Ortaylı, Şevket Pamuk, Ilan Pappe, Leslie Peirce, Haggai Ram, André Raymond, Yezid Sayigh, Tal Shoval, Dror Ze'evi, and Sami Zubaida. A separate collection of articles on Ottoman historians and historiographies was published as a special issue of *Mediterranean Historical Review* (vol. 19, no. 1, [2004]), including the contributions by Peirce, Hathaway, Raymond, and Ze'evi.

We have incurred many personal debts to people who provided intellectual and material support over the course of this project: Ariel Weiss; B. Z. Kedar, head of the Institute for Advanced Studies; and Dror Ze'evi, former director of the Herzog Center. Geoffrey Harpham, president and director, and Kent Mullikin, deputy director of the National Humanities Center (Research Triangle Park, North Carolina), provided a supportive environment in the final stages of preparing the volume. The staffs of these institutions, particularly Pnina Feldman at the Institute for Advanced Studies, Dvora Kremer at the Herzog Center, Lois Whittington at the National Humanities Center, and Ayala Lavie at Tel Aviv University, helped us to manage the administrative aspects of this endeavor as painlessly as possible.

Our sincere thanks are offered to Ursula Woköck, Susynne McElrone, Avi Mor, and Sylvie Kraus at Tel Aviv University for their sound editorial advice and production assistance. Karen Carroll provided meticulous and ongoing editorial assistance at the National Humanities Center.

This volume has benefited greatly from the professional guidance of the editorial staff at the University of Washington Press. Our sincere thanks to Michael Duckworth, Mary Ribesky, and Jane Lichty for helping to bring this project to print.

PART I

The State of the Art

Introduction

ISRAEL GERSHONI AND AMY SINGER

The twentieth century witnessed profound transformations in the study of Islamic and Middle Eastern history. The emergence of the post-Ottoman Middle East after World War I prompted the beginnings of a systematic academic study of the region. Yet during the interwar era the field developed unevenly, and it was only after World War II that the profession bloomed. Since then it has become a thriving academic discipline, one that continues to evolve and expand. In the West, particularly in Europe and America, and in the Middle East, this growth has found expression in the continuous establishment of university departments, research centers, institutions, schools, programs, and chairs devoted to the study of the modern Middle East.

The transformation in Middle Eastern studies was both quantitative and qualitative, theoretical and practical. On the quantitative level, the field of inquiry expanded over the course of the century from a relatively narrow focus on diplomatic and political histories, and cultural history that was to a large extent Orientalist in perspective, to include many more diverse historical aspects of Middle Eastern societies and cultures. Among these are political, economic, social, legal, institutional, cultural, religious, intellectual, and gender histories. To the histories of governing elites and intellectual luminaries were added histories of the lives of women and nonelite groups such as workers, peasants, and slaves. Similarly, the focus on texts and discourse analysis produced by the learned elite culture was broadened to include texts, voices, images, and discourses of the popular, oral, printed, visual, and cinematic cultures. To the focus on colonialism and colonialist policies was added the study of local responses to colonialism, particularly

3

nationalism. Alongside general histories of the region, which encompassed entire societies and cultures of the Middle East in the context of globalization, the global market, capitalism, science, and technology, there emerged specific studies of particular nations searching for their distinct identities and preserving their own indigenous cultures.

The growing multiplicity of historical investigations was documented and disseminated through industrious publication projects. In addition to the increase in the publication of scholarly monographs and books, collections of articles, and other works, the twentieth century also witnessed a parallel expansion in the scope and number of professional journals, recently further expanded through the advent of electronic publication. Academic conferences and workshops, as well as the growth in size and number of professional organizations, have also given dynamic expression to these developments.

The expanding scope of investigations in Middle Eastern studies has been effected and affected by qualitative changes as well. Scholars now make more extensive use of locally produced source material: Middle Eastern archives, literary productions and other written texts, and visual and audio material. Simultaneously the use of foreign sources, mainly British, French, Italian, Russian, German, and American, has also increased dramatically. Equally important has been the proliferation of methodologies employed to examine these sources. The humanities and social sciences—political science, political economy, sociology, anthropology, history, literary criticism, cultural studies, subaltern studies, and gender studies—have all supplied insights; various theoretical frameworks have been explored, adopted, and adapted, including post-structuralism, postmodernism, postcolonialism, dependency, and world-economy theories.

Nevertheless, while Middle Eastern studies now cover a richer terrain, the study of the profession itself has been relatively neglected. There is, however, an ever-present need for professional introspection and self-reflection: to give serious attention to what the research has chosen to include and exclude, to examine what has been accomplished and what has been overlooked, to situate previous research with respect to the state of the art when it was produced, to become more consciously aware of shifts in research approaches and methods, and to examine critically the evolving state of the art and suggest new directions for further inquiry.

To be sure, the profession has never been completely lacking in self-reflection, voiced through historiographical discussions and rethinkings of the state of the art. Bernard Lewis and Peter Malcolm Holt were, in the late

1950s, the first to discuss historiographical issues that emerged in the profession after World War II. Their edited collection, published in the early 1960s, presented works of major scholars of Islamic and Middle Eastern studies on a wide variety of subjects of then-current interest. It was based on the assumption that "the development of Western historiography on the Muslim peoples has received little attention."[1] However, only a relatively small part of the collection was devoted to a discussion of "Modern Middle Eastern Historical Writing." From the 1970s until his death in the early 1990s, Albert Hourani, one of the contributors to Lewis and Holt's pioneering collection, continued to produce important essays on historiographical issues in Middle Eastern studies. He was at the forefront of a growing group of academics who expressed awareness of the need to record historiographical shifts, and his dedication to describing and understanding the contemporary state of Middle Eastern historiography, while defining new directions for future research, demonstrated his academic leadership. In several of his historiographical studies, Hourani presented in meticulous detail the "present state of Islamic and Middle Eastern historiography." He continuously encouraged historians to be more critically aware of the workings of their profession in order to understand better the question, "How should we write the history of the Middle East?"[2]

Edward Said's *Orientalism* (1978) shook the profession to its roots and triggered a profound rethinking of Middle Eastern studies, including its historiography. Even those who were less enthusiastic about *Orientalism*'s line of argumentation had to admit that the work forced a reevaluation of the profession, thereby giving impetus to new directions and methods in research. From the 1990s, a number of historiographical studies on specific topics further contributed to this process of professional self-reflection.[3] Yet, a real lacuna still exists: the considerable developments in Middle Eastern studies accomplished through the examination of *history* were realized primarily in the absence of a thorough discussion of *historiography*.

The present collection of essays strives to locate itself at the intersection of self-reflection and historiography. The end of the twentieth century and the beginning of the twenty-first appear to us as a uniquely appropriate moment for reflection on the profession as it has developed. We asked a group of prominent scholars in our field to convene to rethink historiographical issues and examine critically the state of the art of our field. Istanbul, with its distinct historical view on the Middle East, was selected as an appropriate venue for such discussion and reassessment. We asked the scholars to reflect on how the histories of the modern Middle East have been narrated and how they contributed to the shaping and reshaping of Middle Eastern studies and its various branch disciplines. More specifically, we asked them to consider old and new, hegemonic and subversive, and official and vernacular narratives that have become wholly or partly canonized in the profession. We encouraged them to deal critically with these histories and historiographies. Our interest was threefold: to understand the methods through which Middle Eastern studies have developed, to identify the specific agents who created these methods, and to define more clearly the nature of the ensuing historiographical developments. It was an experiment in self-reflection and self-awareness.

The group of scholars who were invited to the workshop included historians, sociologists, anthropologists, literary critics, and political scientists from the Middle East, Turkey, Arab countries, and Israel and from France, England, Canada, and the United States. The group was selected, first and foremost, because each member is an authority in the field and, second, because each has an acute awareness of the need to rethink and reshape paradigms and narratives in Middle Eastern historiography. As a group, therefore, they were able to reassess and, if necessary, deconstruct old, outmoded paradigms and narratives. In particular, they brought to the workshop the knowledge and energy to effect a sharp revision of the Orientalist paradigms and narratives that dominated Middle Eastern historiography during a large portion of the twentieth century, offering possibilities for new histories and historiographies. The deconstruction of Orientalist paradigms was not meant to be a total destruction, but a serious reexamination of them and an attempt to suggest new alternatives. The idea of historiographical revisionism was also based on an attempt on the part of this group of scholars to recover and reconstruct "internal voices" that sprang from the Middle Easterners' self-views of their own histories.

Discussants and commentators added a crucial dimension to the proceedings. The fruits of their insights were incorporated into the essays published in this volume, which represent, beyond their authors, the overall critical atmosphere produced at the workshop by the collectivity of its participants. It is important to emphasize that the workshop convened a large group of scholars. Naturally, only some contributions could be published here. Four papers addressing the Ottoman period appeared separately in a special issue of *Mediterranean Historical Review* (vol. 19, no. 1 [2004]).

Needless to say, such historiographical examination is, by nature, partial and not exhaustive. It does not pretend to embrace or to represent the entire scope of developments and changes in the field. Of necessity, it is limited to representative historiographical subjects that characterized Middle Eastern studies during the twentieth century. Within these selective areas we asked participants to identify major paradigms and narratives and to analyze how they contributed to the formation of conceptual and practical frameworks for narrating histories of the Middle East. We limited the discussion to historiographies examining the development of the modern Middle East from World War I onward. Egypt, because of its historiographically thick description, seemingly thicker than those of other Arab Middle East countries, is a focus of special attention; additional foci include other Arab polities, societies, and cultures, including those from the Maghreb and the Mashreq. Turkey receives specific treatment. Local Arab and Turkish histories and historiographies by Egyptian, Palestinian, Syrian, Maghrebi, and Turkish authors in their own languages are examined in the essays included in this collection; however, primary attention is given to Western historiographies of the Middle East, particularly studies written in English and French.

The individual essays discuss modes of narrating history applied by individual historians or historical schools, or suggested by various historical paradigms and more specific narratives. Each essay presents an aspect or aspects of more traditional historiographies as well as revisionist studies. Simultaneously, each points to flaws and misconceptions of commonly accepted historiographical narratives and suggests alternative ways to rewrite these histories. Together, they cover four interrelated topics. The first is general historiography, which considers the Middle East from a regional perspective. The second is a treatment of national historiographies and national narratives, in part intersecting considerations of the regional impact of colonialism. The third includes "historiographies of crises" in economic and intellectual histories. The fourth is an examination of historiographies that, until fairly recently, were relatively ignored in the historiography of the Middle East, focusing in particular on popular culture and traditionally disadvantaged and subaltern groups.

Following the introduction, R. Stephen Humphreys continues the first part of this collection with an analysis of twentieth-century Middle Eastern historiography. As a former president of the Middle East Studies Association of North America and a former editor of the *International Journal of Middle East Studies*, Humphreys has a broad appreciation and overview of the field. Focusing on the historians who shaped the contours of the field and the personal and sociopolitical biographical factors that influenced their choices of topic and approach, Humphreys organizes for us an analytical framework that addresses the reasons behind the directions and developments of Middle Eastern studies over the past century. As he demonstrates, these reasons most often remained unexamined, as scholars concentrated on "what happened." Yet changes of theory and method are key for understanding the historiographical corpus and its dimensions, as explored in the following essays. Humphreys shows that sociopolitical developments, changes of method and theory, and external forces consistently attracted more focused analysis than did factors shaping the selection of subject matter and approach. Yet it is these latter elements that are the key to understanding historiographical evaluations of the field.

Charles D. Smith focuses on World War I, a key historiographical chapter in the formation of the modern Middle East. The encounter during these years between British and French imperialisms and the Ottoman Empire, in particular regarding its Arab lands, and between these forces and Arab and Jewish nationalisms in Palestine, determined the shape of the Middle East that emerged after the war. Superpower interests and imperial actions; emerging Arab, Turkish, and Jewish nationalisms; and the series of conflicting treaties and alliances regarding the Middle East between Britain and France, Britain and Zionists, and Britain and Arab nationalists—and contested historiographical interpretations of them—have constructed a labyrinth of narratives through which historians have been trying to find their way for years. The result has been a wealth of literature, sometimes contradictory, much of it a response to George Antonius's classic, *The Arab Awakening* (1938).

On one level, Smith presents a critical and comparative analysis of the development over the twentieth century of these highly charged historiographies, focusing on works published in English and French. He reexamines the strength of their documentary evidence and traces their development of lines of argumentation. Identifying the motivations for various imperialist, Arab-nationalist, Turkish-nationalist, and Zionist narratives, and highlighting more recent, revisionist research, he underlines the importance of these works and suggests reasons for their historical inaccuracies. Going beyond this, Smith examines this period and the corpus of literature about it in light of insights suggested by other fields, in particular studies of nationalism, ethnicity, conflict, political economy, and subaltern groups. He emphasizes the importance of reintroducing the Ottoman dimension of the story into the historical narrative and studying the Middle East from a nonexceptionalist perspective. And he shows the theoretical and practical potential to be derived from comparison between the Ottoman Empire and the other multiethnic empires that collapsed during World War I. Moreover, through his historiographical review, Smith clearly demonstrates the continuing currency of the historical and historiographical debates over this period.

Julia Clancy-Smith examines the historiographies that narrated colonialism and imperialism in the Middle East, both in the Mashreq and the Maghreb. At the center of her discussion are the mutual relations between British and French colonialisms and colonizers and Middle Eastern colonized societies. Clancy-Smith attempts to balance the historiographical discussion, which has traditionally focused primarily on British imperialism, with a thorough discussion of historiographies of French imperialism. She particularly criticizes the traditional tendency to study the "colonizer," the imperialist or the colonialist, and the "colonized," the native or the nationalist, as exclusive categories. In doing so, she exposes the essentialist nature of this historiographical dichotomy and calls for a more sensitive and complex reading of the blurred borders where colonizer and colonized intersect, the space in which the colonial experience was mutually negotiated.

Following lines of investigation suggested by recent works, Clancy-Smith proposes a more complex framework for the study of imperialism and colonialism, disentangling these concepts from the study of nationalism. She emphasizes in particular the value of relocating the discussion on imperialism within women's and gender studies and postcolonial and subaltern studies. As some young Tunisian historians have demonstrated, this allows the historian to step outside of the "*nationalist* narrative" and reintegrate the histories of minorities, women, and marginal colonial "others" into a more complete *national* narrative. These neocolonial studies, as Clancy-Smith characterizes them, reflect, in her view, a historiographical sea change occurring in colonialism studies and suggest the need for further paradigm shifts in our understanding of the colonial moment.

The third essay in part 2 deals with national historiography and nationalist narratives. One particularly critical case occupied a prominent place in twentieth-century Middle Eastern historiography and remains controversial at the beginning of the twenty-first: the massacre of Armenians and their expulsion from the Ottoman Empire during World War I, considered here in light of Ottoman and Turkish historiographical treatment of this tragic chapter in history. Fatma Müge Göçek's thought-provoking article suggests reasons why official Turkish histories throughout the twentieth century were constructed as a denial of the relocations and massacres of Armenians in

1915. Her in-depth, critical historiographical analysis of a broad corpus of works assesses each in relation to time, the changing contexts of political circumstances in Turkey, the continuing evolution of Turkish nationalism, and the growth and expansion of civil society in the Turkish state. Göçek divides twentieth-century historical literature on the subject along two main lines, both of which follow a narrative of denial, absolve the state of blame, and point to the Armenian victims as a subversive element in Ottoman society. The first line, which she identifies as the Ottoman investigative narrative, was created primarily through the use of memoirs, contemporary accounts, and Ottoman documents pertaining to Ottoman Armenians that were published either by the Turkish state or by opposing political groups. The second, the Republican defensive narrative, was, as Göçek identifies it, a nationalist narrative constructed through a selective reading of history, intended to legitimize further the Turkish master nationalist narrative. Göçek identifies two main sources for these historiographical narratives: current or former state officials who consider it incumbent on them to support the Turkish nation-state's official narrative, and academic researchers at state universities who, as she shows, are subject to professional sanction and other pressures for challenging this narrative. Both narratives, as Göçek demonstrates, continued to be reproduced in the last decade of the century.

Göçek deconstructs the Ottoman investigative and Republican defensive narratives from a historical sociological perspective informed by nationalism studies and as a study of power relationships suggested by gender studies and race theory. She shows how the official view equating the Turkish state with the Turkish nation has served to silence alternative and minority voices in Turkish society. Göçek then points to the beginnings, in the last years of the twentieth century, of a third narrative line of investigation, which she terms a postnationalist critical narrative. This narrative has developed primarily in academic works that approach Turkish society as a mosaic of ethnicities and religions, and attempt to give voice and face to the plurality of elements in Turkish society, Armenians among them, who have been historically silenced. It can also be found in Turkish-Armenian literary works from the first part of the twentieth century that, in recent years, have begun to appear in Turkish translation, and a number of studies specifically on the events of 1915. The academic authors in this group, as defined by Göçek, are distinguished by their institutional independence from the state; the absence in their works of the converse line of investigation, found in the other two narratives, that works to prove an assumption rather than investigate a question; and their willingness to reflect critically on what

Turkish identity includes and should include. Göçek views in this third metanational narrative the beginnings of postnationalism in Turkey, in a climate that she sees as favorable to critical analysis of events in Turkish history. In her view, though, nationalist rhetoric continues to present a major obstacle to this transition, which leads her to suggest a nonnationalist reconceptualization of the periodization of nationalism in studies on Turkey. A main feature of this alternate framework is the location of Mustafa Kemal's entrance into Anatolia in 1919 as a later stage—and not the founding moment—of Turkish nationalism.

The third part of this collection, historiographies of crisis, discusses historiographical narratives that view the Middle East's encounter with Western ideas and practices as one leading to crisis and failure for Middle Eastern cultures and economies. Israel Gershoni and Ellis Goldberg identify and deconstruct well-established narratives that have become conceptual frameworks for the understanding and writing of twentieth-century Middle Eastern history, in the fields of intellectual history and economic history, respectively. Both focus on the modern history of Egypt and its historiographical representation. Israel Gershoni analyzes the evolution of intellectual history in Middle Eastern studies over the course of the twentieth century. He identifies what he defines as a "narrative of crisis" that assumes (more than it proves) that the modernist intellectual movement in the Middle East was assigned the task of importing and implementing European scientific culture to Middle East societies and cultures, and that it failed. According to the narrative, this failure plunged modernist intellectuals into a severe crisis from which they never recovered, and this was reflected both in their retreat from Western ideals and principles to which they had previously adhered and by the parallel growth of their "apologetic writings" on Islam, focusing on Islamic heroes and events of the seventh century. This "failure" of the intellectuals was identified by historians as a central factor leading to the dramatic reactionary reassertion of Islamic values and norms that gave birth to the Mahdist, fundamentalist Islamic movement that came to dominate the cultural arena.

Gershoni demonstrates that from the early 1950s an alternative scholarly narrative emerged to counter the "crisis narrative." In these revisionist interpretations the intellectuals' shift is seen not as a crisis but rather as a shifting of gears—a calculated, functional ideational move on the part of intellectuals to writing on Islamic subjects in modernist fashion that did not involve abandonment of Western values and norms of science, rationalism, and progress. The *Islamiyyat* project of the intellectuals was intended to reconstruct Islamic history and culture in new, modernist contours. Gershoni traces the development of this counternarrative throughout the second half of the century. His deconstruction of the historiography of the crisis narratives, and the environment in and motives for which they were written, provides an important road map for understanding the Orientalist ebbs and flows that created theories of crisis.

During the first two decades of the twentieth century, yields of Egypt's primary export crop, cotton, experienced a steady decline. This agricultural and ecological crisis, as it has been defined, has constituted a fundamental basis for understanding Egypt's political economy in the British imperial era and is the subject of Ellis Goldberg's case study. Since first proffered by Charles Issawi in his classic, mid-twentieth-century history of Egyptian political economy, this narrative of crisis has been attributed to the demanding, domestic, economic interests of colonial Britain and its textile industry on the one hand and the self-interested, structurally weak Egyptian government on the other. Searching beyond the boundaries of the narrative, Goldberg reexamines the major shift in agricultural trends in these decades, namely, the successful introduction of an extra-long-staple cotton plant, Sakellaridis, with a lower per-plant yield but a higher tolerance for increased-density planting. Dismantling the ecological fallacy of declining yields, and reassessing Egyptian farmers' economic and efficiency-related crop-management decisions alongside the contemporary, domestic agricultural discourse, Goldberg is able to deconstruct this theory of crisis. His suggestion that the origins of this crisis narrative are to be found in a variety of interest-based arguments that have been applied, alternatively, to bolster particular political, institutional, colonial, and anticolonial arguments paves the way for a reassessment of the influence of colonialism on the early twentieth-century Egyptian political economy.

The fourth section in this collection brings to the fore subjects that are relatively new to Middle Eastern historical studies: gender studies, the history of slaves and slavery, and the study of popular, visual culture. In addition, the historical study of radical Islam has, since the 1970s, been significantly reshaped by the incorporation of insights drawn from other social science disciplines. This interdisciplinary approach, which draws in particular from sociology and anthropology, has altered, and considerably enriched, the historiography of this fundamentalist Islamic expression.

While the historiography of women's studies and gender history of Middle Eastern societies is most often focused on the wealth of research that has appeared since the 1960s in European languages, Marilyn Booth turns our attention to relatively neglected but significant peripheries of these academic fields. Her three-pronged approach focuses not only on the rich corpus of literature on women's studies, gender history, and gender-sensitive histories of the Middle East in European languages—with specific reference to the developments and theories that shaped these fields' main contours over the century, potential pitfalls of current research trends, and needed lines of investigation—but also on nontraditional, indigenous sources for the turn-of-the-twentieth-century discourse on women and gender roles in the Arab Middle East, as well as on contributions of recent and current work on these topics produced in Middle Eastern languages.

Booth analyzes historiographical questions central to the field, giving special attention to the compatibility or incompatibility of feminism with Islam, a public and academic debate that in her view is often misleadingly polarized. This debate, ongoing since the late nineteenth century, is often traced to Qasim Amin and his 1899 work *Tahrir al-mar'a* (Liberating the Woman). Booth, however, points to lesser-known, female contemporaries of Amin who were active in this debate and focuses in particular on the case of writer and novelist Zaynab Fawwaz. Through a detailed analysis of one of Fawwaz's novels, published the same year as Amin's treatise, Booth draws out its bold feminist argument, which would have been rejected by Egyptian society (and publishers) of the time if presented in a straightforward, nonfictional form. Through an analysis of this novel and its characters, Booth makes a powerful argument for the value of nontraditional written sources such as fiction for their important historical insight into the history of women and women's thought in the Middle East. She also points to the political dimension of women's studies and gender history in the region. Political struggles, political interests of state and nonstate actors, and periods of political crisis have been important, she argues, in shaping academic approaches to and research on women in the region. The publication, or republication, of biographies of Muslim women and historical narratives of early Islamic figures and events has been and is used alternately by both feminists and traditionalists to advance opposing views on the proper role for women in Muslim societies. In fact, a central underlying theme of Booth's research is that the historical discourses on gender and women's roles in the Middle East—particularly how gender as a socially constructed concept has been and is expressed and understood by women—need to be researched within, and not alongside, the more general field of Middle Eastern history, since the dynamics of gender in Middle Eastern societies continue to be both political and controversial.

Eve M. Troutt Powell examines historiographies of African slavery and slaves in the Middle East and other parts of the Islamic world. Troutt Powell focuses particularly on how twentieth-century historians negotiated the study of African slavery in the Middle East. Obviously, a crucial point here is the ability of historians to reconstruct the authentic voice of the slaves, a particularly difficult task in the case of Middle Eastern slavery, since this subaltern discourse was seldom recorded. Troutt Powell considers, in particular, how individual scholars have contributed to the expression, muting, or confounding of slaves' thoughts and voices. She shows how divergent constructions of race in Africa, the Middle East, Great Britain, and the United States have affected and distorted this historiography, and she traces its development over the century in light of the influences of these various perspectives.

Simultaneously, Troutt Powell reviews alternative methods for recovering and comprehending the muted voice of African slaves in the Middle East. She emphasizes the importance of studying slaves' experiences of living through slavery, within the framework of the particular societies in which they were enslaved (and in which they often remained after gaining their freedom). From this perspective, she recognizes and highlights the importance of revisionist research on diverse topics such as the reasons for slaves' adoption of Islam alongside their continued observance of their homeland traditions, the dynamics of the close relations between slave and master in the elite Ottoman household, slaves' self-reorganization into quasi-ethnic and quasi-kinship categories within these societies after manumission, and alternative expressions, including naming and song. These alternative avenues of research, as Troutt Powell clearly shows us, exemplify the possibility of activating and humanizing the history of slaves, of extracting them further from their silence, and giving concrete faces to the faceless, as active historical subjects and objects.

Muslim fundamentalist groups received much academic attention from historians and social scientists in the final decades of the twentieth century. Juan R. I. Cole turns a critical eye to both the historical subject within its environment and the researcher within his. His broad-based, historically informed historiographical analysis of works published in the 1980s and 1990s on Egyptian Muslim fundamentalist groups not only brings to light historical inaccuracies found in this research but also challenges the very conceptual and methodological frameworks applied in the academic reconstruction of these contemporary histories. Historiographically, Cole focuses specifically on two recent influential academic works on Islamic fundamentalist groups in Egypt: Gilles Kepel's *Le Prophète et Pharaon* (1984), published in translation as *Muslim Extremism in Egypt: The Prophet and the Pharaoh* (1985), and Denis Sullivan and Sana Abed-Kotob's *Islam in Contemporary Egypt: Civil Society vs. the State* (1999). Cole particularly challenges in these works the reading of the development, role, and influence of Muslim fundamentalist groups within Egyptian society. He identifies in them a tendency to view these groups as one legitimized expression within the discourse of mainstream Islam on the one hand and within pluralistic, Egyptian civil society on the other. Both are, in his evaluation, derived from inaccurate readings of history, and Orientalist analyses that essentialize Islam and erroneously normalize extremist fundamentalism within it.

Cole deconstructs the academic paradigms developed in these works into what he identifies as structuralist-, Marxist-, and third world-theory-influenced components, and he analyzes the efficacy of these theoretical frameworks for understanding Egyptian, Muslim fundamentalist groups. Ultimately, he finds these frameworks inadequate and shows how they tend to reduce Muslim fundamentalism essentially to an expression of class struggles within Muslim society, a reaction to oppression on the part of the state, or a protest that is anti-imperialist/anti-Western or socioeconomic in nature. He is critical of the tendency to view Islamic fundamentalism as an essentialist phenomenon with a unique grammar and lexicon logical only within the specific framework of "the Muslim cultural tradition." He also problematizes the historiographical attempt to locate this phenomenon in the public sphere of open, pluralistic civil society. Cole views these perspectives as falling prey to an uncritical analysis of fundamentalist ideology and discourse and a reductionist definition of pluralistic society, which confuses the presence of multiple voices within society with true civic pluralism. He proposes, instead, a more comparative approach for analyzing Muslim fundamentalist groups, suggesting that Islamic fundamentalism should be de-essentialized and located along the axis of other fundamentalisms, Christian and Jewish. He emphasizes the need to make more extensive use of the Weberian tradition in the sociology of religions, in particular viewing Muslim fundamentalist groups as members of "New Religious Movements," or sects and cults, offshoots instead of natural outgrowths of an essential "Islam." Cole fills out this alternative conceptual framework with both neglected historical sources and alternative, contemporary sources and offers an important rereading of this current and controversial subject.

In the final article of this volume, Walter Armbrust explores mass media in the Arab Middle East in relation to our historical understanding of Arab and Pan-Arab cultural and societal transformations over the twentieth century. As Armbrust points out, mass media are both the agents and products of these transformations and cannot, nor should not, be understood in isolation from them. Thus researching mass media—how they have developed and been deployed and employed by both internal and external forces in the Middle East—is fruitful not only for what it reveals about Middle Eastern cultures, societies, societal organization, and politics but also for our understanding of broader issues of historical interest, such as colonialism, nationalism, and modernities, and how these concepts and realities have been expressed, disseminated, consumed, understood, and reacted to in the Middle East. Research on Middle Eastern mass media was almost nonexistent until the early 1980s, but since then, and particularly in the closing years of the twentieth century, the corpus of literature on mass media subjects has expanded literally in leaps and bounds. Armbrust organizes the multiplicity of recent research within thematic frameworks and posits useful theoretical perspectives for approaching the study of Middle Eastern mass media.

Armbrust begins with an analysis of the gradual shift in the Arab Middle East from the dominance of auditional modes of information dissemination to silent reading practices, inspiring and inspired by the introduction of the printing press to the Middle East and the development of an Arabic-language print media from the late nineteenth century. He points to this shift, and the accompanying change in the social deployment of sensory practices in the modern period, as the beginning of the transformation in the Middle East from an audiocentric to a visualist-centered culture and means of expression. Significantly, as Armbrust makes us aware, this shift occurred in the Arab world parallel to the development of indigenous audiocentric practices—the phonograph and the almost simultaneous introduction of radio broadcast and film. Egypt, the undisputed cultural leader of the Arab Middle East for most of the twentieth century, provides a natural basis for Armbrust's observations, and he traces the various Arabic-language mass media that developed in the twentieth century, from the phonograph record in the beginning of the century to the music video at its close, through the case of Egypt. Music has often served as a sounding board for debates about cultural authenticity in the face of colonialism, and music along with the various media in which it has been central therefore form important foci of his research. Armbrust uses the multimedia fame of Umm Kulthum and Muhammad 'Abd al-Wahhab, singers whose voices and stardom in the music world catapulted them to the top of the film industry, to explore the construction and dissemination of national culture in Egypt and the Arab world through mass media. His historical overview of the development of the media that helped make these and other Arab superstars famous sets forth a useful historiographical framework for future study in this new and burgeoning important subfield of Middle Eastern history.

In summary, the contributions to this collection take part in a common effort to rethink and reevaluate central historiographical issues in the writing of the history of the twentieth-century Middle East. As noted earlier, these chapters represent only a handful of the problems and dilemmas associated with the construction and narration of this history. Many of its topics await future consideration and debate. The profound quantitative and qualitative transformations in Middle Eastern studies and Middle Eastern historiography over the twentieth century were so diverse and far-reaching that a slim volume such as this one can only hope to illuminate some of the directions in which the field developed and can further evolve. Nonetheless, the subjects of study debated in this collection problematize and reconceptualize themes that are, in our estimation, of central importance in our field. Beyond their specific, individual contributions, we hope these chapters will inform and inspire further historiographical rethinking, as well as clarify the existing map of the profession. Indeed, we would like to believe that this collection can make a humble contribution to the rethinking and reevaluation of the agenda of modern Middle Eastern studies.

NOTES

1. Bernard Lewis and P. M. Holt, eds., *Historians of the Middle East* (London: Oxford University Press, 1962), quotation from 4.

2. Albert Hourani, "The Present State of Islamic and Middle Eastern Historiography," in *Europe and the Middle East* (London: Macmillan, 1980), 161–96; Hourani, "How Should We Write the History of the Middle East?" *International Journal of Middle East Studies* 23 (1991): 125–36. Also see Albert Hourani, *A History of the Arab Peoples* (Cambridge, MA: Harvard University Press, 1991); Hourani, "Patterns of the Past," in *Paths to the Middle East: Ten Scholars Look Back*, ed. Thomas Naff (Albany: State University of New York Press, 1993), 27–56; Albert Hourani, Philip S. Khoury, and Mary C. Wilson, eds., *The Modern Middle East* (Berkeley and Los Angeles: University of California Press, 1993); and Nancy Elizabeth Gallagher, *Approaches to the History of the Middle East* (Reading, UK: Ithaca Press, 1994), 19–45. Also see Donald M. Reid, "*Arabic Thought in the Liberal Age* Twenty Years After," *International Journal of Middle East Studies* 14 (1982): 541–57.

3. See, e.g., the works of Gallagher, Hourani, and Naff published between 1991 and 1994, as cited in the previous note. Also see the special issue of *American Historical Review* devoted to Middle Eastern historiography (vol. 96, no. 5 [1991]); and Edmund Burke III, ed., *Struggle and Survival in the Modern Middle East* (Berkeley and Los Angeles: University of California Press, 1993). One can also include R. Stephen Humphreys, *Islamic History: A Framework for Inquiry*, rev. ed. (Princeton, NJ: Princeton University Press, 1991) as an important survey of Islamic and Middle Eastern historiographies. For the most recent and comprehensive critical study of Middle Eastern historiographies and narratives, see Zachary Lockman, *Contending Visions of the Middle East: The History and Politics of Orientalism* (Cambridge, UK: Cambridge University Press, 2004). For more specific consideration of particular historiographical case studies, see, e.g., regarding Arab nationalism, Rashid Khalidi, "Ottomanism and Arabism in Syria before 1914: A Reassessment," in *The Origins of Arab Nationalism*, ed. Rashid Khalidi, Lisa Anderson, Muhammad Muslih, and Reeva S. Simon (New York: Columbia University Press, 1991), 50–69; Israel Gershoni, "Rethinking the Formation of Arab Nationalism in the Middle East, 1920–1945: Old and New Narratives," *Rethinking Nationalism in the Arab Middle East*, ed. James Jankowski and Israel Gershoni (New York: Columbia University Press, 1997), 3–25. For a specific discussion of the history of women's studies, see, e.g., Lila Abu-Lughod, "Feminist Longings and Postcolonial Conditions," in *Remaking Women, Feminism and Modernity in the Middle East*, ed. Lila Abu-Lughod (Princeton, NJ: Princeton University Press, 1998), 3–31; and Nikki R. Keddie, "Women in the Limelight: Some Recent Books on Middle Eastern Women's History," *International Journal of Middle East Studies* 34 (2002): 553–73.

The Historiography of the Modern Middle East

Transforming a Field of Study

R. STEPHEN HUMPHREYS

As with many subjects, a solid, tradition-minded account of the historians and historiography of the Middle East in the twentieth century best begins with the basic facts of geography and demography. Who wrote this literature? How many historians were there? Where did they live? The answers to these questions are simple enough, but they reveal a complex world of scholarship and politics.

In the closing decades of the nineteenth century and the beginning of the twentieth, the history of the Middle East was written by a very few people—almost all male, and almost all from Western and Central Europe. By the end of twentieth century, historians specializing in the Middle East had become far more numerous (though of course not so numerous as their contemporaries who focused on U.S. or European history). Males still constituted a large majority, but there were many women, as many as a quarter of the total in some countries. As for their place of birth and residence, Europe remained important, but the countries of the Middle East itself had emerged as significant centers of historical writing on the region. The most striking change, however, was that the center of gravity—in terms both of quantity and the perceived importance of the publications produced—had migrated to North America.

This geographical shift correlates nicely with a linguistic shift as well. At the beginning of the twentieth century, the principal languages of research on the Middle East were French and German. A surprising number of major works were produced in Dutch in spite of its limited number of speakers. Only a few publications in Spanish and Italian were to be found, but these included works of the highest distinction. In all this, English was very much the poor cousin, in spite of Britain's imposing presence in Middle Eastern affairs and the vast number of English speakers throughout the world. As for the major literary languages of the Middle East, which presumably ought to have been the major vehicles of historical writing on the region, their status was ambiguous at best—a matter to which we shall return later in this essay.[1]

By the close of the twentieth century, English was simply the paramount language in the field. For certain areas of inquiry French retained a major role, but German had retreated to a distant third, while Dutch had disappeared altogether. On the other hand, Japanese had begun to make an appearance, though few but Japanese scholars themselves had access to scholarship in this language. Middle Eastern languages (which included Hebrew alongside Arabic, Persian, and Turkish) had by now produced a substantial and important literature, but overall their status still remained ambiguous.[2]

What one cannot guess from these geographical and linguistic shifts is the ethnic and national origins or the religious identity of the region's historians. Even at the beginning of the twentieth century language was an uncertain predictor of these things; by the end it was all but useless. English, in particular, but also French and even German have become the preferred scholarly tongues of Arabs, Israelis, Turks, Iranians, South Asians, and many others. Indeed, if the standing of Arabic, Persian, Turkish, and Hebrew as international languages of scholarship has yet to be established, the scholarly rank and importance of those who speak these languages as their mother tongues is not in doubt. In stark contrast to the situation a century ago, they constitute a very significant percentage, and possibly a majority, of historians working on the Middle East. We can say, then, that though the imperial languages still hold sway in this arena, Middle Easterners have in large part reclaimed it as their own.

These dramatic shifts do not represent the slow, imperceptible transformations of the *longue dureé*. On the contrary, and with important exceptions, they are the product of the past four decades. Indeed, they manifested themselves in force only by the mid-1970s, a quarter century ago. Obviously we shall want to know how and why all this happened, but an examination of that question has to be put off until we have looked more closely at the first two-thirds of the twentieth century.

I have stressed the fewness, the maleness, and the Europeanness of historians of the Middle East at the beginning of the past century. Now, this is connected with many things. First, there was the elite character of Euro-

pean universities at that time both as to curriculum and admissions policies. Second, women were simply not admitted to university study until after
World War I, though that fact did not prevent a number of them from
becoming prominent writers and intellectuals. Third, the study of Oriental languages followed the methods developed for Greek and Latin. The very
few students who pursued these languages did so from a philological and
linguistic perspective as part of a curriculum in Semitic or Indo-Iranian studies. Their training directed them toward high culture—languages, literature,
philosophy, theology, and so forth. If they found their way into political
and social history it was largely by instinct and accident, for there was no
field of Middle Eastern history per se. Indeed, in the eyes of many of Europe's
leading thinkers the East had no history—that is, no internally generated
processes of change that could bring about a new order of society, politics,
and culture. Hegel and Marx, to name but two, famously declared that the
contemporary Orient stood outside the processes of history. In the preface
to her *Amurath to Amurath*, Gertrude Bell wrote,

> Conqueror follows upon the heels of conqueror, nations are overthrown
> and cities topple down into the dust, but the conditions of existence are
> unaltered and irresistibly they fashion the new age in the likeness of the old.
> "Amurath an Amurath succeeds" and the tale is told again.
>   Where past and present are woven so closely together, the habitual appre-
> ciation of the divisions of time slips insensibly away. Yesterday's raid and an
> expedition of Shalmaneser fall into the same plane; and indeed what essen-
> tial difference lies between them?[3]

On the other hand, a scholar of Arabic, Persian, or (rarely) Turkish was
free to dabble in many things as the spirit moved him—hence the immense
range of Ignaz Goldziher, Julius Wellhausen, Theodor Nöldeke, Christiaan
Snouck Hurgronje, Max van Berchem, Louis Massignon, and—the last
survivor—H. A. R. Gibb. Genius trumps academic training, and when
scholars like these tried their hand at political and social history, they produced work that still compels our attention and respect. Even so, their publications in this field—apart from Wellhausen's—do not really match the
methodological rigor and sophistication of the best historians of Rome,
Byzantium, or medieval Europe among their contemporaries.[4]
    We can look at this problem from a different but no less important angle.
The year 1900 was the high-water mark of modern European imperialism,
and this obviously had a great impact on those who wrote the history of

the Middle East. I am by no means a sociological determinist, or a fan of the more simplistic formulations of postcolonialism, which can easily degenerate into a kind of politicized solipsism. People are unpredictable and full of surprises. Thus Goldziher, the greatest Orientalist of his age or any other, was not only anti-imperialist and anti-Zionist but also a vigorous advocate of the early Islamic reform movements that he had observed on his sojourn in Damascus and Cairo in the 1870s.[5] E. G. Browne, the founder of Persian studies in Great Britain and still its most eminent figure, was an ardent supporter of the Constitutional Revolution of 1906–9.[6] Other scholars, like Snouck Hurgronje, who had been actively engaged in Dutch colonial policy in the East Indies and wrote some of his most important work as a product of that involvement, turned against colonialism after World War I.[7] But even when we take account of these facts, imperialism inevitably had its impact.

First, it induced a sense of European superiority, not only in material, but even more in intellectual matters. The unquestioned fact of superiority inevitably produced an Olympian gaze among Western scholars of the region; one looked down from on high at the objects of one's study. One could admire or sympathize with them, but in the end they were specimens under a microscope. To change the image, Western scholars could discuss Middle Easterners as if they were not in the same room, or at least could not understand what was being said about them.

Second, I have so far pretended that historical studies on the Middle East circa 1900 formed an undifferentiated whole, from Muhammad down to the present. I have been talking as if this whole period of thirteen hundred years and millions of square miles was dealt with in more or less the same manner by more or less the same body of scholars. But of course that is not the case. Even if certain academic Orientalists (Snouck Hurgronje in particular, but also Browne) were astute and extremely well-informed observers of the contemporary world, it is still true that formal scholarship focused heavily on the first three centuries of Islam. Edward Said and his followers often point to this fact as a manifestation of the Orientalist dogma of the timeless East. The charge is not wholly without merit, but anyone acquainted with the historiography of Europe itself in the nineteenth century would find this focus on the beginnings of Islam to be the most natural thing in the world. In German Romanticism and historicism (*historismus*), the essence of a thing was revealed in its origins; the oak was explained by the acorn. Undeniably, however, a great deal was written about pre-Islamic Arabia, the life of Muhammad, the early conquests, the Umayyads, and the

Abbasid revolution. Then, shortly after 750 C.E., it was as if political and social history had ground to a halt, or at least ceased to have much to teach us: "Amurath an Amurath succeeds." To be honest, Orientalists did pursue studies in law, theology, and philosophy down into a later period, but even in these arenas the death of al-Ghazali in 1111 was taken to mark the end of real intellectual creativity (apart from "exceptional" and hence unexplainable figures like Ibn Rushd and Ibn Khaldun).[8]

Just as striking were the blind spots among historians who studied "mainstream" European topics. For example, a genuinely imposing body of work on the later Roman Empire and Byzantium was never linked to the study of early Islam (save by Carl Becker and Alexander Vasiliev). Likewise, a flood of excellent studies on the Crusades did not inspire much curiosity among either Europeanists or Islamicists about the Muslim side of that complex and long-lived enterprise. (Always there are exceptions; in this case, Max van Berchem, the founder of Arabic epigraphy and perhaps even now its most effective and original exponent.)[9]

Who then wrote the history of the Middle East in later, "post-formative" times? That was, to a very large degree, not the province of academic scholars but of men of affairs. For the most part, naturally enough, they wrote recent and contemporary history, because they explicitly intended their writings to be a guide for policymaking. I cannot trace here the remote origins of this body of work, but it first began to flourish in the second half of the seventeenth century. Paul Rycaut's *Reflections on the Present State of the Ottoman Empire* (which retains its value to a remarkable degree) both exemplifies this trend and stands in a class by itself. Our present arena of concern, the turn of the twentieth century, presents a host of cases: Lord Cromer's *Modern Egypt*, Lord Curzon's *Persia and the Persian Question*, and Sir Edwin Pears's life of Sultan Abdulhamid II. In these works, the Ottoman Empire looms large. Joseph von Hammer-Purgstall (whose history of the Ottoman Empire would be the only one based on Turkish-language sources for more than a century) was a typical figure in that he began his career as a dragoman in the Austrian embassy in Constantinople and retained a close connection to the Hapsburg court throughout his life.

It is in this body of work, and especially in its late nineteenth-century version, that Orientalist attitudes (so called) are most overt and least nuanced. But of course we are here dealing with men who had the habit of command and who felt no need to disguise their attitudes toward indigenous peoples. We should also remember (a point neglected by Said) that the work of academic Orientalists both shared in and, over time, subverted

these attitudes. After all, academic Orientalists always knew at least the literary languages of the Middle East, sometimes to an extraordinary degree,
whereas those who wrote on contemporary issues often possessed only a
casual knowledge (or none at all) of these tongues.

We come then to a third impact of imperialism on historical writing. One
of the most striking facts about the historiography of the Islamic and modern Middle East circa 1900 is that so little of it was written in Arabic, Persian, or Turkish. Moreover, the best of what was produced in these languages
was markedly traditional in its scope and approach. In a profound sense
an ancient, deep-rooted, and incredibly rich historiographic tradition was
losing its voice. We thus face the anomaly of a history largely written by
foreigners for the use and edification of foreigners. As we go past World
War I, we begin to find a few historical works written by Middle Easterners that were both serious and produced within methodological and literary frameworks modeled on those used by European historians. For a long
time, however, such publications were few in number, and quite as likely
to be written in French (or occasionally English) as in a Middle Eastern language. By the 1930s, with the works on Ottoman history of Fuat Köprülü,
İsmail Hakkı Uzunçarşılı, and a few others, the Turks had begun to reclaim
the writing of history for themselves, and in their own language. Elsewhere,
even in Egypt, the process was slower.[10]

Now if we jump ahead a century to the present, we need only reverse
most of these propositions to get a reasonably accurate picture of current
historical scholarship on the Middle East, though of course many nuances
and ironies would escape us. A detailed description of these changes would
be tiresome and not terribly productive; more to the point is to ask when
and how the new picture emerged to replace the old.

First, we should begin by recalling an earlier point—namely, the structures of knowledge and inquiry that existed circa 1900 persisted for a very
long time. Down at least to 1960, we would not need to alter in any fundamental way the tableau I have sketched. The kind of people who entered
the field of Middle Eastern studies was much the same as before, and the
training they received was little changed. The latter point should occasion
little surprise, since most of the leading figures—Gibb, Joseph Schacht, Paul
Wittek, and Philip Hitti, to name only a few—had established their reputations in the 1930s, and the enormous disruptions of the war had slowed
(though not entirely blocked) the emergence of a younger generation. A few
Americans were beginning to enter the field, though they still counted for
little. Women were still conspicuous by their absence. Anne K. S. Lambton,

beyond dispute the most influential student of medieval and modern Iran during the 1950s and 1960s, was undoubtedly an imposing exception to the rule, but in an earlier era so were Gertrude Bell and Margaret Smith. The history of the modern Middle East was still largely the province of journalists and retired diplomats—men with a lot of hands-on knowledge (though not always as much as they liked to think) but with a limited grasp of language, culture, and social structure.

Attitudes toward the religion of Islam were certainly more irenic than they had been a century earlier—due largely, I think, to the work and influence of Massignon and Gibb.[11] By now many scholars were quite ready to recognize its spiritual authenticity, and even its parity with Judaism and Christianity as a form of religious belief and expression. Finally, the French and British Empires were on their way out, and with them went much of the old cultural arrogance. Even so, the traditional Olympian gaze of Orientalism persisted, as empire was replaced by the apparent certainties of modernization theory and social science. Of this tendency the quintessential product is no doubt Daniel Lerner's *The Passing of Traditional Society*, first published in 1958 and widely regarded as a reliable guide to the not-so-distant future.[12]

One last characteristic of the year 1960 requires comment. It was, perhaps even more than 1900, an era of "one field, one master." Most aspects of medieval Islamic history were represented by a sole spokesman, who was often ready to defend his turf quite jealously. The history of Islamic law was led by Joseph Schacht, social and economic history by Claude Cahen, North Africa by Robert Brunschvig, Mamluk studies by David Ayalon, and Islamic Spain by Évariste Levi-Provencal. The burgeoning field of Geniza studies was in effect created by S. D. Goitein, though he was a dedicated and prolific teacher, demanding but not at all jealous. In Ottoman and modern Turkish history, a young Bernard Lewis (also an excellent and productive teacher) had just claimed the front rank with the publication of *The Emergence of Modern Turkey* (1958).

Twenty years later the situation had changed almost beyond recognition.[13] There could no longer be any question of simply touching up the old picture. How shall we account for this abrupt transformation? Many things converged all at once. There was the end of European empire, far advanced but still in process, and still a matter of living memory, in 1960. Rising populist attitudes throughout North America and Europe were making universities an instrument of mass rather than elite education, and this tendency was reinforced by the social turbulence and radical youth movements of the later 1960s—a confluence of two powerful rivers, if you will. The feminist revival of the 1970s initially had an extremely limited impact on university life in general, and the membership of history departments in particular. By 1980, however, it had already set in motion a search for new ways of thinking about the past. Finally, there was a concatenation of apparently disconnected events—Sputnik, Vietnam, feminism, even U.S. immigration reform under Lyndon Johnson—that would collectively have an immense impact on the study of the Middle East. In the United States, at least, 1980 was in every way a world turned upside down. The influence of some of these events and processes is obvious enough, for others it is less so.

The end of European empire in the Middle East between 1945 and 1962, for example, was not a matter merely of changing political power. The process evoked an intense soul-searching among both the former colonizers and the colonized. The former had to reexamine and redefine their attitudes toward the peoples and cultures that they had not only dominated but also deformed and reshaped over the previous century. The latter had to undertake a similar task but from the opposite direction. In very circuitous ways the former colonizers moved toward relativism, then (in an effort to lend a positive conceptual and ethical content to that approach) into multiculturalism. Multiculturalism began with a naive if undeniably enthusiastic effort to remove "Western civilization" as the sole standard of comparison and value, and to proclaim the equal standing of all cultures. Soon enough, and perhaps inevitably, it evolved into a severe critique of Western ideas and institutions as compared with almost any other sociocultural formation that one could name. Among the formerly colonized there was an anguished search for identity, a struggle to recover an autonomous sense of who they were and ought to become. Searches for identity tend to spiral inward as one seeks to plumb the depths, and postcolonialism could sometimes become terribly self-regarding, an obsession with self rather than the lives of others. Since it has become customary either to laud or to excoriate Michel Foucault and Edward Said for these intellectual currents, it needs to be said that they had almost nothing to do with creating them. What they did do was to frame an integrated body of ideas, a language, which could give voice to and even canonize a process that was already well underway by the mid-1970s.

Changes in university education, first in the United States and then increasingly in Europe, likewise had an enormous impact. In large part this was due to the burgeoning number of students from third world countries who were admitted to undergraduate and advanced studies. This policy was a core element of the development project of the times, the creation of a large pool of men (and some women) who could take charge of the modernization of their countries. But of course things take on a life of their own. Some of these students turned to the study of history, and inevitably they brought a distinct agenda of their own with them. Immigration reform in the United States after 1965 (along with related initiatives in Europe at roughly the same time) made it possible for many of these new scholars not only to be educated in the West but also to remain there and take up university teaching positions. The political, economic, and social problems of their home countries often made the choice to remain not merely appealing but almost compulsory. In this way a new history of the Middle East began to emerge, told by Middle Easterners, albeit in Western languages and largely for Western audiences.[14]

In most respects the history produced by Middle Eastern expatriates seemed very similar to that written by Westerners; it addressed the same set of subjects and shared the same world of interpretive concepts and analytic tools. Even the tone and sense of political engagement was not greatly different. That is hardly a surprise, since both groups were taught by the same mentors in the same graduate seminars. More important, both groups were writing in constant dialogue with each other. In a sense, if Middle Eastern scholars needed to show that they commanded all the theoretical and methodological tools of contemporary historical writing, their Western counterparts felt a similar need to demonstrate their own sense of commitment and moral urgency about the people they studied. They were coming to regard themselves as advocates for the Middle East—sometimes in a narrowly partisan manner, but more often in the sense of a warm sympathy for Middle Eastern cultural patterns, values, and perspectives. In this way, the growing presence in Western universities of historians of Middle Eastern background created a climate in which the Olympian gaze of the imperial era was no longer acceptable.

If the rising presence of Middle Easterners had already had a powerful impact on the Western academy by 1980, the same could not really be said of the women's movement. By that time, second-wave feminism had become a significant political force and had already generated a powerful and skillfully focused backlash. However, it had not really affected the academic study of the Middle East in any important way. The number of women graduate students in the humanities and social sciences (including Middle Eastern studies) was rising sharply, but tenure-track teaching positions for women in major universities were still rare and hard-won.

Nor did most women at that time focus particularly on gender-specific topics or approaches. Even in U.S. and British history, women's history was
just beginning to find a solid footing, and more sophisticated variants like
gender studies were still only vaguely imagined.[15]

As the 1980s wore on, the situation in Middle Eastern studies began to
change, although much more visibly in anthropology and sociology than
in history, either medieval or modern. When I completed the final revisions
for my *Islamic History: A Framework for Inquiry* in June 1990, it was still
impossible to prepare a serious chapter on women and gender in the
medieval Islamic world. I knew of important work in progress, but almost
none of it had yet been published. On the other hand, by that time women
were establishing themselves in growing numbers within the academy, and
inevitably many of them would open up new areas of inquiry and bring
new perspectives to bear on old ones. That is precisely what has occurred
over the past decade. Although the medieval period is still badly neglected,
there are by now a number of outstanding works on women and gender in
Ottoman and modern history.[16]

In examining the changes brought to our field by the growing presence
of Middle Easterners and women, we have been considering the sometimes
surprising consequences of long-term processes. Yet dramatic events have
had a powerful and durable impact as well. Sputnik and Vietnam in many
ways symbolize the cold war, but we should not take them for mere surro-
gates of this "long twilight struggle." Sputnik launched not merely the space
race but the National Defense Education Act of 1958, the first major higher
education funding initiative by the federal government to be targeted at
specific fields of study. (The Morrill Act of 1868 and the GI Bill after World
War II provided general financing to support higher education but were not
aimed at narrowly defined areas of teaching and research.) To compete with
rapidly expanding Soviet influence in Asia and Africa, the United States
needed area specialists of its own. Having none, it had to create them, and
that could be done only by paying universities to teach languages that they
could not afford to offer with their own resources.[17]

It is by now an old story that area studies (including Middle Eastern
studies) is an artifact of the cold war, but irony never ceases to work its
wonders. For hardly had area studies taken root when Vietnam became the
front-burner issue in American life. Vietnam created, and still works to create, an American academic establishment that is profoundly alienated from
the idea of government service. In the eyes of many of the scholars trained
under the National Defense Education Act (aka Title VI) in Middle Eastern

studies, to enter the U.S. Department of State or the intelligence services is to sell out the people whom they have studied and with whom (in a post-colonialist way) they have come to identify themselves. The National Defense Education Act was intended to build a cadre of professionals whose expertise would inform government policymaking. Instead it wound up creating a pack of dissidents—a point that has not escaped notice by the American and Israeli Right. Contrary to the professed (and no doubt sincere) beliefs of the latter group, however, this culture of dissent was not the work of professors in Middle Eastern studies, most of who were conservative or at least publicly apolitical in the 1960s. Rather, the culture of dissent was rooted in the experience of Vietnam and the kind of students (returning Peace Corps volunteers, foreign students, etc.) who entered area studies programs.

In underwriting the creation of a large number of U.S. specialists on the Middle East, Title VI also created a substantial number of historians. The process was incremental (not to say glacial) rather than immediate, but in the long run several hundred scholars of the Middle East would identify themselves as historians—sometimes for lack of any plausible alternative, to be sure. This number includes specialists in all periods, but the great majority focus on the nineteenth and twentieth centuries. In short, the modern era is no longer handled, as it was down to the 1950s, exclusively by former diplomats, journalists, and political activists. These groups still participate in the writing of recent and contemporary history and often produce important work, but the modern history of the Middle East is nowadays mainly an academic enterprise.

What is the significance of this dual process of professionalization and growth in scale? On one level, it means that the day of the academic fiefdom is over. In almost every major subfield, there are strong alternative voices. The effect is sometimes harmonious, sometimes quite the opposite, but no one scholar can now present himself or herself as the sole arbiter of what is to be said about a given subject. Or to put the matter in a different light, we now have serious debate instead of *obiter dicta*. And of course the pace of research has picked up markedly. Vast areas remain sketchy or completely unstudied, but at least one has the sense that a comprehensive and carefully detailed picture of the modern Middle East is slowly emerging.

On another level, professionalization encouraged a turn to theory among historians of the modern Middle East—a tendency clearly in evidence by 1980, and one that has become only stronger in the quarter century since. Among historians of the medieval Islamic world, it should be said, the tug of theory has been markedly less, though it is certainly felt to some degree.

The reasons for this lack of interest are complex, but a few points can be noted. First, the topic of "Islamic origins" (i.e., the period from ca. 600 to 800) has reverted to an agenda established by Goldziher, Wellhausen, Leone Caetani, and Henri Lammens at the beginning of the twentieth century. What had seemed a stable consensus was challenged and revitalized by the radical skepticism of two works published in the mid-1970s—John Wansbrough, *Qur'anic Studies,* and Patricia Crone and Michael Cook, *Hagarism*—and by a large cluster of studies produced since. However, this is (to put the matter a bit too simply) a literature based on philology and source criticism. Few if any of the scholars involved in it have explicitly deployed postcolonialism, postmodernism, or "the linguistic turn" in their debates.[18] Second, historians who work in the "middle periods" (i.e., the six centuries from 900 to 1500) are still struggling with such old-fashioned tasks as establishing well-documented political narratives, reconstructing administrative and fiscal institutions, discovering networks of manufacturing and commerce, or working out structures of class and status. In a sense, contemporary theory aims at interrogating, subverting, and decentering "hegemonic discourses." In medieval Islamic history, there are too few such discourses to make a tempting target.[19]

As Suraiya Faroqhi has noted, Ottoman history is similarly conservative in orientation—again, in large part because we are far from resolving the traditional problems of historical research and inquiry.[20] The history of the nineteenth and twentieth centuries is quite a different matter, however. In large part the turn to theory among many younger historians simply reflects broader trends in historical research and writing since 1970. Historians of the Middle East, trained in history departments, would inevitably share the intellectual enthusiasms of their fellow students, all the more as they were desperate to liberate themselves from the shackles of traditional Orientalism as well as from the once-common charge that their field was merely a species of journalism.

One might also suppose that the new interest in theory was encouraged by the very structure of the Middle Eastern studies programs erected under the aegis of Title VI. Their multidisciplinary approach might have seemed mere dilettantism to hard-core sociologists and political scientists, but it did mean that young historians would have some acquaintance with their ways of thinking, and perhaps a desire to emulate the apparent rigor of their theories. Among the social sciences, anthropology has had perhaps the most marked impact, both because of its obvious utility in describing lineage-based social systems, and because of the extraordinary influence of Clifford

Geertz, whose work in Indonesia and Morocco made him (almost) "one of us." As Geertz himself pointed out long ago, anthropology has been a protean if not fickle discipline in recent decades, and as such it has been unable to provide historians with a stable or consistent body of theory.[21] Even so it retains much of its appeal.

In a broader framework, historians of the modern Middle East have been torn between the grand theory that stems from Marx and Max Weber—in particular, the world-systems approach of Immanuel Wallerstein attracted much enthusiasm for many years—and the interpretive strategies deriving from contemporary literary-critical theory, with its roots in Michel Foucault, Roland Barthes, Jacques Derrida, Edward Said, and others.[22] The appeal of grand theory is its claim to have enormous comparative and explanatory power, but its explanations often fall apart under critical scrutiny. Literary-critical theory is a tool of irony—the historian's indispensable frame of mind—but it is of little use in reassembling the structures it so deftly dismantles. We cannot enter into these debates in this essay; suffice it to say that even historians who reject the value of theory cannot simply ignore it. It has become an integral part of their milieu, of the everyday world of academic discourse.

What conclusions are suggested by this very broad overview of a very complex subject? It is obvious that I have made no effort to describe the content of twentieth-century historical scholarship on the Middle East— the range of subjects studied, changing tastes in interpretation, the methodologies that have governed research, or the theories that have driven it.[23] Rather, I have contented myself with a sketch for a "sociology of knowledge," to use what is now almost an antique term. Such a sociology has its uses in understanding why historians write as they do, but I trust that everyone is aware of its limitations. It can identify only the external environment within which historical discourse must take place. No sociology of knowledge can tell us anything about the value of the work produced within the constraints of that environment, or the capacity of gifted individuals to bend those constraints and produce knowledge and insights that continue to inform and challenge for generation after generation.

To put the point a bit more polemically, we need to admit that at least within the guild of professional historians of Islam and the Middle East, "Orientalism" is a very dead horse. It is time to stop beating it. It is a word that is well on the way to losing whatever specificity and analytic value it once had, and it is now hardly more than a term of abuse for scholarship that one dislikes. Insofar as a single word can be taken to characterize the whole vast realm of painting, imaginative literature, official policymaking, and academic scholarship—and the very act of deploying such a global concept seems a quintessentially Orientalist conceit—it can refer only to a particular moment in our intellectual history, with its particular configuration of power relations and cultural confrontations. The study of Islam and the Middle East is no more a timeless and unchanging essence than the Orient itself. The moment that gave rise to Orientalism in this invidious sense has passed, though its effects undoubtedly linger. We need to find new terms, more precise and better attuned to the constantly shifting contours of the field, to describe the theoretical and methodological issues that confront us as we try to interpret and put to use the historical writing bequeathed to us by the twentieth century.

NOTES

1. A full listing of works is out of the question, especially those in German and French. Dutch scholarship was far more prominent in numbers and influence than the size of the country would suggest; Leiden was easily a match for Paris and Tubingen. Dutch scholars even then often published in French (e.g., R. P. A. Dozy and M. J. de Goeje), but many—G. Van Vloten, C. Snouck Hurgronje, J. Wensinck et al.—preferred their native language. Russian is a special case, since Russian scholarship, predictably enough, focused on Turcology and Central Asia, where it was of paramount importance; the oeuvre of V. V. Bartol'd (Wilhelm Barthold) is paradigmatic. Russia did produce an outstanding Arabist in the person of I. I. Krachkovskii. For detailed reviews of how Orientalist scholarship had evolved down to World War I, see Gustav Pfannmueller, *Handbuch der Islam-Literatur* (Berlin: W. de Gruyter, 1923); and J. W. Fueck, *Die arabischen Studien in Europa bis in den Anfang des 20. Jahrhunderts* (Leipzig: O. Harrassowitz, 1955). More briefly, see A. H. Hourani, "Islam in European Thought," in the volume of essays published under the same title (Cambridge: Cambridge University Press, 1991). This essay will of course allude at various points to the seminal and highly revisionist book of Edward Said, *Orientalism* (New York: Vintage Books, 1978). Suffice it to say that Said's approach is literary-critical rather than historical, and that he has explicitly chosen to focus on certain scholarly traditions (British and French) to the exclusion of others (German).

2. Some of these issues are discussed, with references, in R. S. Humphreys, "Modern Arab Historians and the Challenge of the Islamic Past," in *Middle Eastern Lectures* (Tel Aviv: Moshe Dayan Center for Middle Eastern and African Studies, 1995), 1:119–31; Humphreys, "Historiography," *Oxford Encyclopedia of the Modern Islamic*

World, ed. John L. Esposito, 4 vols. (New York: Oxford University Press, 1995), 2:114–20.

3. Gertrude Bell, *Amurath to Amurath* (London: William Heinemann, 1911), vii–viii.

4. Julius Wellhausen's studies on early Islamic history represented a huge methodological advance over the work of his predecessors. His work displays an uncanny understanding of the dynamics of Arabian tribal society and of the social tensions and ideological conflicts that rent the Muslim community during the first Islamic century. Snouck Hurgronje's historical instincts were not so developed, but as an ethnographer of contemporary Islamic societies he was then, and perhaps remains even now, unequalled; see his *Mekka in the Latter Part of the Nineteenth Century*, trans. J. H. Monahan (Leiden: Brill, 1931), and *The Achehnese*, trans. A. W. S. O'Sullivan, 2 vols. (Leiden: Brill, 1906).

5. On Goldziher's career and attitudes, see Lawrence Conrad, "The Near East Study Tour Diary of Ignaz Goldziher," *JRAS*, no. 1 (1990): 105–26; Conrad, "The Dervish's Disciple: On the Personality and Intellectual Milieu of the Young Ignaz Goldziher," *JRAS*, no. 2 (1990): 225–66.

6. A point sufficiently proved by his *History of the Persian Revolution, 1905–1909* (Cambridge: Cambridge University Press, 1910), but also by many other aspects of his life and work; see the memoir by E. Denison Ross, which prefaces the second edition of *A Year amongst the Persians* (Cambridge: Cambridge University Press, 1926); originally published in 1893.

7. See C. Snouck Hurgronje, *Oeuvres choisies; Selected Works*, ed., G.-H. Bousquet and J. Schacht (Leiden: Brill, 1957), xix (biographical sketch by Bousquet).

8. Of this tendency—widely shared among Middle Eastern intellectuals of that period, it should be noted—there are too many examples to cite here. Perhaps most telling is the title of a volume coedited by Robert Brunschvig and G. E. von Grunebaum, *Classicisme et déclin culturel dans l'histoire de l'Islam* (Paris: Editions Besson, 1957).

9. For a brief conspectus of van Berchem's work, see my *Islamic History: A Framework for Inquiry*, rev. ed. (Princeton, NJ: Princeton University Press, 1991), 57; Sheila S. Blair, *Islamic Inscriptions* (New York: New York University Press, 1998), 13–14.

10. There is much less work on the transition from "traditional" to "modern" historical writing in the Middle East than there ought to be. The present state of the discussion is summarized in "Historiography," *Oxford Encyclopedia of the Modern Islamic World*. Egyptian historiography is studied in Jack Crabbs, *The Writing of History in Nineteenth Century Egypt: A Study in National Transformation* (Detroit: Wayne State University Press, 1984). Historical writing is situated within a broad political-

intellectual milieu in the indispensable study of Gilbert Delanoue, *Moralistes et politiques musulmans dans l'Égypte du XIXe siècle*, 2 vols. (Cairo: Institut Français d'Archéologie Orientale du Caire, 1982).

11. Their influence was first analyzed in Jacques Waardenburg, *L'Islam dans le miroir de l'Occident* (The Hague: Mouton, 1967).

12. Daniel Lerner, *The Passing of Traditional Society* (New York: Free Press, 1958).

13. If a single work heralded the change from the old order to the new, it would be Marshall G. S. Hodgson's *The Venture of Islam: Conscience and History in a World Civilization*, 3 vols. (Chicago: University of Chicago Press, 1974)—both a masterful summation of the Orientalist tradition and a profound critique of it. The third volume, dealing with the modern era (since 1500), was left in a quite unfinished state at Hodgson's death, but even as it stands it points to a new way of looking at things. The first stages of the transition are concisely but penetratingly analyzed in A. H. Hourani, "The Present State of Islamic and Middle Eastern Historiography," in Hourani, *Europe and the Middle East* (Berkeley: University of California Press, 1980), 161–96; originally published in Leonard Binder, ed., *The Study of the Middle East: Scholarship in the Humanities and Social Sciences* (New York: John Wiley, 1976). A valuable introduction to the life and work of the scholars who initiated and oversaw the "new order" is Nancy E. Gallagher, *Approaches to the History of the Middle East: Interviews with Leading Middle East Historians* (Reading, UK: Ithaca Press, 1994).

14. The impact of Middle Eastern expatriates on area studies in the United States is broached in R. Stephen Humphreys, "Tradition and Innovation in the Study of Islamic History: The Evolution of North American Scholarship since 1960," in *Islamic Area Studies, Working Papers, no. 1* (Tokyo: Islamic Area Studies Projects, 1998), 7–8, 13–14.

15. Ibid., 8, 11–12, 14.

16. For the medieval period, see Denise Spellberg, *Politics, Gender, and the Islamic Past: The Legacy of 'A'isha bint Abi Bakr* (New York: Columbia University Press, 1994); Leila Ahmed, *Women and Gender in Islam: Historical Roots of a Modern Debate* (New Haven, CT: Yale University Press 1992); Gavin R. G. Hambly, ed., *Women in the Medieval Islamic World* (New York: St. Martin's Press, 1998). (The papers in the last of these three in fact largely focus on the Ottomans, Safavis, and Mughals.) The Ottoman period has been most fully explored in the works of Leslie Peirce (*The Imperial Harem* [Oxford: Oxford University Press, 1993]; *Morality Tales: Law and Gender in the Ottoman Court of Aintab* [Berkeley and Los Angeles: University of California Press, 2003]) and Judith E. Tucker (*Women in Nineteenth-Century Egypt* [Cambridge: Cambridge University Press, 1985]; *In the House of the Law: Gender and Islamic Law in Ottoman Syria and Palestine* [Berkeley and Los Angeles: Uni-

versity of California Press, 1998]). We owe the first serious archival studies to the late Ronald Jennings, "Women in Early Seventeenth-Century Ottoman Judicial Records: The Sharia Court of Anatolian Kayseri," *JESHO* 18 (1975): 53–114.

17. Binder, *Study of the Middle East.*

18. John Wansbrough, *Qur'anic Studies: Sources and Methods of Scriptural Interpretation* (Oxford: Oxford University Press, 1977); Wansbrough, *The Sectarian Milieu: Content and Composition of Islamic Salvation History* (Oxford: Oxford University Press, 1978); Patricia Crone and Michael Cook, *Hagarism: The Making of the Islamic World* (Cambridge: Cambridge University Press, 1977). The extensive literature on this field cannot be reviewed here. The current state of the field is fairly represented in F. M. Donner, *Narratives of Islamic Origins: The Beginnings of Islamic Historical Writing* (Princeton, NJ: Darwin Press, 1998), and Harald Motzki, ed., *The Biography of Muhammad: The Issue of the Sources* (Leiden: Brill, 2000). Donner and Motzki would regard themselves as counterrevisionists, but their arguments and conclusions are in fact fairly radical.

19. One can overstate this point, of course. The social science theory and method of the 1960s and 1970s certainly did find a following. Ira Lapidus, *Muslim Cities in the Later Middle Ages* (Cambridge, MA: Harvard University Press, 1977), based his influential analysis on the sociology of Talcott Parsons and Edward Shils. Fred M. Donner, *The Early Islamic Conquests* (Princeton, NJ: Princeton University Press, 1981), draws both on ethnographic descriptions of Arabian tribal life and on theories of segmentary lineage structures. Carl M. Petry, *The Civilian Elite of Cairo in the Later Middle Ages* (Princeton, NJ: Princeton University Press, 1981), constructed a quantitative analysis of the scholars and bureaucrats of Cairo in the fifteenth century.

20. Suraiya Faroqhi, *Approaching Ottoman History: An Introduction to the Sources* (Cambridge: Cambridge University Press, 1999), esp. 1–26. Again, feminist analysis forms a limited but important exception; see n. 16 above.

21. Clifford Geertz, "Blurred Genres: The Refiguration of Social Thought," *American Scholar* 49 (1980): 165–79; and Geertz, *After the Fact: Two Countries, Four Decades, One Anthropologist* (Cambridge, MA: Harvard University Press, 1995), esp. chap. 5, "Disciplines," 96–135. Dale Eickelman, *The Middle East: An Anthropological Approach* (Englewood Cliffs, NJ: Prentice Hall, 1981; 4th rev. ed., 1999), shows the many levels on which historical research has been, or could be, informed by anthropological perspectives, both descriptive and theoretical.

22. The pioneer work in this latter vein was probably Timothy Mitchell, *Colonising Egypt* (Cambridge: Cambridge University Press, 1988).

23. Those who wish a detailed conspectus of scholarship on the medieval Middle East could begin with my *Islamic History: A Framework for Inquiry*, though it is

of course already out of date in certain areas. The state of the field in the mid-1960s is nicely captured in Claude Cahen, *Jean Sauvaget's Introduction to the History of the Muslim East: A Bibliographical Guide* (Berkeley: University of California Press, 1965), an extensively revised adaptation of a work first published in Paris in 1943. There is, so far as I know, nothing quite like either of these works for modern history, but Hourani, "Present State of Islamic and Middle Eastern Historiography," evaluates the field as it stood in 1974.

PART II

Colonialism and Nationalism

The Historiography of World War I and the Emergence of the Contemporary Middle East

CHARLES D. SMITH

World War I constitutes arguably the pivotal period in the history of the modern Middle East. The war caused the demise of the Ottoman Empire along with the collapse of the two other land-based empires whose fates intersected with the Turks: Russia and Austria-Hungary. New states were formed out of the lands still Ottoman in 1914: independent Turkey and the colonial mandate states of Iraq, Syria, Lebanon, and Palestine. The boundaries of these mandate states were drawn by the victors, England and France. In addition, new, tribal-based states began to emerge in the Arabian Peninsula. The war led to the collapse of empires, the initiation of processes of state formation, and the emergence of national consciousness as a primary basis of allegiance.

Decisions made by the victors during and after the war introduced tensions that have lasted to the present. The inclusion of the Balfour Declaration (1917) in the Palestine Mandate, promising Palestine as a national home (state) for the Jewish people, meant that the appearance of nationalism as an ideological force in the Middle East would be Jewish as well as Arab and Turkish. It also meant that Palestine's future was intended to contradict mandate expectations. Mandates stipulated that the inhabitants of a region would be prepared for self-government by the imperial state holding the mandate, a principle ignored for Palestine. Inclusion of the Balfour Declaration in the mandate meant that the Arab inhabitants, 90 percent of the population, would be denied self-government, which would be awarded to a Jewish population once it achieved majority status by immigration. This stipulation inaugurated the first major phase of the Palestinian-Israeli dilemma, leading in 1948 to the creation of the state of Israel, and the Arab-Israeli as well as Palestinian-Israeli conflicts that have lasted to the present. With respect to Syria and Lebanon, France carved modern-day Lebanon out of Syria in 1920 to create a stronger imperial base, but the new population mix set the stage for communal differences based on religious representation that still remain.

Much of the historiography of the period, particularly in English, has focused on the intentions of the imperial states that took over the Arab lands that were still Ottoman in 1914, especially with respect to Palestine. Historical writing on the subject published in the United States, less so in Britain, often remains an open defense of British imperialism intended to justify Zionist claims and condemn Arab arguments with clear implications for contemporary Palestinian-Israeli questions. This has been done, when necessary, by manipulation of sources, as shown below.

This approach to World War I and the Middle East violates scholarly standards but, nonetheless, finds publishers, among them university presses. Its defense of imperialism and scorn for non-Western actions and opinions justify charges of Middle Eastern "exceptionalism." Fields of Middle East history in general have often not reflected approaches and comparative criteria found in other areas of historical analysis. Including Arab as well as Turkish viewpoints, and the impact of the war on Arabs and Turks, should lead to new narratives, replacing that narrative that subjects historical processes to the political considerations held in imperial capitals.[1]

An excellent example of this exceptionalism is Bernard Lewis's *What Went Wrong: Western Impact and Middle Eastern Response.*[2] Lewis presents the contemporary Islamic world, notably the Arab Middle East, as seeking excuses to explain its technological backwardness and resentment of the West. Rather than defend imperialism, as do many scholars of World War I, Lewis dismisses the subject in one page in his conclusion. Anglo-French dominance "changed the face of the region" in Lewis's view, but it was "a consequence, not a cause, of the inner weakness of Middle Eastern *states* [my emphasis] and societies."[3] As a result, Middle East states now compare badly to former British Asian possessions such as India, Singapore, and Hong Kong—the latter two of which he compares to Aden.

Lewis's analogies are false and he reverses chronologies. There were no states, other than the Ottoman, in the region. The new mandate states were created by the British and French after the war, rather than existing beforehand as Lewis argues. Unconcerned with accuracy or with the scholarship on either imperialism or nationalism, Lewis likewise has no use for knowledgeable comparisons with other areas of the world. For example, Singapore and Hong Kong served as major commercial and banking centers for the British Empire where large, indigenous or minority commercial classes flourished under British protection (Hong Kong until 1997); Aden, now part of Yemen, was a supply port for the British navy, surrounded by a tribal hinterland.

Lewis seeks to exonerate Western imperialism from any role in creating the modern Middle East and to dismiss resentment of current American dominance. He wrote the book while advising the Bush administration, before the attacks on September 11, 2001, on its goals of regime change in the Middle East.[4]

I examine critically the historiography on World War I in light of these and other issues. First, what are the major questions that arise from consideration of the existing historiography with respect to the central Arab lands (excluding Egypt) of the Ottoman Empire, and then with respect to the Ottoman Empire itself? What differences, if any, emerge from considering French scholarship on particular matters as opposed to that in English, including sources consulted? What new trends in scholarship on World War I can we find that offer new modes of analysis for the period?

ANGLO-FRENCH IMPERIALISM, ZIONISM, ARAB NATIONALISM, AND THE ARAB LANDS OF THE OTTOMAN EMPIRE

The historiography on these various questions intersects in the discussion of European imperialism, especially British, during World War I and often amounts to a defense of British intentions in order to discredit Arab nationalist claims at the expense of Zionism. Linked to this effort in certain cases is the question of language and how descriptions of events and rival arguments can be used to assign blame rather than to explain developments in historical context. Historians' approaches to these matters vary widely, as does the quality of scholarship with respect to the accurate representation of sources as well as to the range of sources consulted.

Non-Arab Scholarship in English

For scholars of the Middle East and World War I, the book at the center of certain primary narratives—imperialism, Arab nationalism, and Zionism—is *The Arab Awakening* by George Antonius.[5] Antonius advanced four key arguments that have been disputed: (1) the Arab revolt of June 1916, led by the Sharif Husayn of Mecca, was the culmination of the development of an

Arab nationalist movement whose origins lay in the mid-nineteenth century; (2) the revolt was inspired by British promises of Arab independence after the war in Arab lands of the Ottoman Empire that included Palestine—these promises were embodied in the Husayn-McMahon Correspondence, which lasted from August 1915 to January 1916; (3) the Anglo-French Sykes-Picot Agreement of May 1916 knowingly violated these British promises to Sharif Husayn, as did the issuance of the Balfour Declaration of November 1917, promising a "national home" to the Jewish people in Palestine, intending to make Palestine a Jewish state; and (4) the British were duplicitous in their explanations of their practices and agreements to Sharif Husayn and others, notably during the visit of David Hogarth to Husayn in January 1918.

Antonius's arguments regarding the origins of Arab nationalism have long been discredited but still serve as a straw man on occasion, including efforts to impugn his motives for advancing such a thesis.[6] The second argument, regarding Palestine, has also been refuted in that Palestine was not explicitly included in the lands supposedly promised to Husayn by the British high commissioner in Cairo, Sir Henry McMahon. Nonetheless, the Arab revolt was the direct result of the Husayn-McMahon Correspondence, and Husayn's proposed frontiers for an Arab state in his first letter clearly included Palestine. Moreover, McMahon's carefully qualified promises to Husayn related directly to matters linked to the Sykes-Picot Agreement and to the Balfour Declaration.

Of special import has been the argument embodied in what has become known, from the title of an article by Elie Kedourie, as "The Chatham House Version." That version, propounded by British scholars and officials linked to the Foreign Office, argued that Britain had betrayed its trust to the Arabs by misleading them, deliberately or otherwise, with respect to their expectations of independence after the war.[7] Kedourie sought to refute that idea.

The literature in English on World War I pertaining to these issues, and particularly to the Husayn-McMahon Correspondence and the Sykes-Picot Agreement, has been dominated by the work of Elie Kedourie and Isaiah Friedman. Kedourie's impact has been greater for specialists in Middle East history; Friedman's arguments are listed with equal frequency by specialists in British, and occasionally French, diplomatic history.[8]

The focus of much of this work is Palestine, aimed at establishing proof of Arab acceptance of Zionist claims during the war. Friedman and Kedourie both argue that the Sharif Husayn of Mecca was told of British support for Zionism and, in Kedourie's words, "enthusiastically assented" to the news.

This claim is founded on their argument that Great Britain was consistently open in its dealing with Arab representatives and never withheld information as to its intentions or agreements with others. The conclusions to be drawn are that Arabs generally, personified in the Sharif Husayn of Mecca, agreed to Zionism at that time and therefore have no basis for challenging Israeli actions in the present.

Friedman and Kedourie both misrepresent sources in order to buttress their claims. Friedman, for example, inserts ellipses into a quotation of High Commissioner Henry McMahon's letter of October 24, 1915, to the Sharif Husayn in order to argue that the quotation referred to Palestine, which would be excluded from areas of Arab independence. The quotation in fact discussed areas west of "Damascus, Homs, Hama, and Aleppo," the words that were withheld and replaced by ellipses. Kedourie's statement that Husayn assented to the Zionist project was based on a quotation he used from a report by David Hogarth, who visited Husayn in Jidda in January 1918. There Hogarth assured Husayn that Palestinian Arabs' political rights were guaranteed by the Balfour Declaration. Hogarth deliberately misrepresented the declaration because Arab political rights were excluded from mention, as noted by Antonius. Kedourie attacked Antonius's analysis as "worthless" and defended Hogarth as merely "reiterating" the Balfour Declaration. It was on the basis of this "reiteration" that Kedourie claims that Husayn "enthusiastically assented" to the Balfour Declaration, based actually on the imparting of false information, but he goes further. While quoting Hogarth regarding Husayn's "assent," Kedourie omits the sentence immediately preceding the quote. There Hogarth acknowledged that Husayn would not accept a Jewish state in Palestine and that he had not informed Husayn that such a state was intended because he had not been instructed to do so by the Foreign Office. Friedman makes the same claims regarding Hogarth's honest presentation of the Balfour Declaration and Husayn's acceptance of it.[9]

The aim of this scholarship, to legitimize Zionism at the expense of Arab, especially Palestinian, national claims, is still current and popular, especially in the United States, as seen in the work of David Fromkin and Efraim Karsh.[10]

Fromkin paid homage to Kedourie in his preface and in general adhered to Kedourie's arguments.[11] Fromkin, without discussing Hogarth's visit to Sharif Husayn, followed Kedourie in arguing that the latter had been fully informed of Zionist ambitions in Palestine. He relied here on Prime Minister David Lloyd George, whom he also quotes approvingly, to the effect that the British could not discuss matters with the Palestinian Arabs because they fought with the Turks; this suits the imperial thesis of the British and French that they had a right to the lands controlled by their opponents and to dispose of them as they wished. Fromkin's charge, intended to discredit Palestinian claims, ignores the fact that Zionists also served the Turks. Moshe Sharett, first foreign minister and second prime minister of Israel, served as an Ottoman officer throughout the war.[12]

In addition Fromkin discredits Palestinian claims via discourse—the use of the language of omnipotence, "the form of language in which claims to validity are made"—rather than by analysis of treaties or promises.[13] Although he notes the conflicting promises made by Britain to various parties, he treats this sympathetically and analytically. In contrast, he refers to Sharif Husayn and his son Amir Faysal as "not keeping the faith" with the British when in contact with the Turks—a phrase never used when dealing with imperial promises to the Arabs or Lloyd George's duplicity in trying to renege on Britain's promise of Syria to France.

Fromkin's double standard for evaluating matters appears more explicitly, though couched in the language of discourse, when discussing Palestinian petitions to Winston Churchill in 1921. Seeking to rescind the Balfour Declaration, Fromkin compares Palestinian attitudes toward territorial claims to those of the British, the French, and the Zionists. He finds them lacking in "statesmanship" because, unlike the other three parties, the Palestinians refused to "take account of the needs and desires of [other] interested parties, including adversaries." This behavior, to Fromkin, was not "normal."

In contrast, the British and French were "normal" because they were willing to trade imperial possessions to avoid conflict. This was also "realistic," as was the Zionist willingness to compromise; they had acknowledged "Arab" rights in Syria. The Palestinians, on the other hand, refused to compromise, meaning they were unwilling to accept the Balfour Declaration and Zionist claims to Palestine and thus take account of their "needs and desires." At no point does Fromkin address the fact that for the Palestinians to be "statesmanlike" and "normal," they should willingly renounce their claim to their homeland and get nothing in return, unlike those to whom they were compared (Fromkin claims inaccurately that the Zionists offered autonomy to Palestinian Arabs in certain areas of Palestine). The British and French were trading the lands of others, not their own, and the Zionists were to get Palestine, having compromised with the Arabs, who got Syria.

This discourse, with its approving glance at imperialist practices, openly embraced the European right to use and manipulate non-European lands for imperial purposes. When Fromkin applauded Turkey's Mustafa Kemal as having a "European cast of mind," it was because he renounced his territorial claims to what his "neighbors" (i.e., Britain and France) were taking over in Syria, Lebanon, Palestine, and Iraq after the war. Fromkin's language privileges those with European "casts of mind" who willingly exchange or give up the land of others in order to get something in return, unlike the Palestinians, the native inhabitants, who would get nothing in return for giving up their homeland. And although the British certainly sought to avoid meeting commitments, as Fromkin documents, it is only Arabs who do not keep the faith, perhaps because they lack European casts of mind.

A less subtle approach, but one consistent with Fromkin's goals, is offered by Efraim and Inari Karsh in *Empires of the Sand*. Following Kedourie's argument in *England and the Middle East* (1956), the Karshes present European imperialism as benevolent, especially when compared with Middle Eastern imperialisms, notably that of the Ottomans but also including that of the Sharif Husayn of Mecca. Middle Eastern imperialists, whether Arab or Turk, were characterized by their greed and duplicity, traits not attributed to European imperialists. Middle Eastern greed ruined the chances for stability in the Middle East because these rulers drew in European imperialists, apparently innocents, and tried to manipulate them. Since Arab leaders were imperialists, this disqualified them from being nationalists, meaning that there was nothing that could constitute Arab nationalism. Therefore, the only "worthy national movement" was Zionism, which gained "international recognition" after the war, thereby legitimizing it at the expense of Arab claims.[14]

Efraim Karsh is known for his indictment of Israel's revisionist historians for "fabricating history," the title of his book that has been highly praised among mainstream Israeli scholars. He and his wife themselves fabricate history in *Empires of the Sand*, frequently misrepresenting the content of sources in order to support their own charges. Nonetheless, Harvard University Press has recently issued it in paperback. Similar misrepresentation of the events of World War I comes from Benny Morris, whom Karsh, ironically, vilifies as a revisionist scholar in his *Fabricating Israeli History*.[15]

These examples illustrate a school of historiography, predominantly but not exclusively Israeli, that has consistently presented the events of World War I surrounding the role of the Sharif Husayn, the Balfour Declaration, and the messages imparted by David Hogarth in such a way as to (1) implicate Arabs generally in an acceptance of Zionism at that time, and (2) accuse Arabs of bad faith as opposed to the sincerity of European imperialists. In the case of Efraim Karsh and Benny Morris, two historians who differ heatedly over other controversial issues of Israeli historiography—such as the 1948 war of independence and responsibility for the Palestinian refugee problem—present identical arguments with respect to the salient questions surrounding the Sharif Husayn and the Balfour Declaration in World War I. This has clear implications for positions taken, especially in the United States, with respect to Palestinian claims for the right to a state in the present.[16]

Linked to the above discussion is the notion of British integrity—that British officials always explained plans and agreements to the Arabs, and that the Sharif Husayn knew of agreements such as the Balfour Declaration and their implications. Kedourie first propounded this view in his *England and the Middle East*, and Friedman reiterated it in his *Question of Palestine*. Both lauded in particular the integrity of the British foreign secretary, Sir Edward Grey, who was deemed incapable of artifice or dissimulation.[17]

In his *Anglo-Arab Labyrinth* (1976), however, Kedourie paints a different and frequently contradictory picture. He is initially highly critical of Grey as one who paid little attention to detail and willingly accommodated conflicting or ambiguous positions that were intended to promise nothing, despite appearances to the contrary. On the other hand, Kedourie's determination to discredit the "Chatham House Version" of British dishonesty toward the Arabs leads him to contradict his own arguments in the same book. He attacked British officials for having "no intention of fulfilling promises to the Arabs," which, he argued, were phrased in terms that were "misleading and deceptive," but he still depicted Sharif Husayn as even more "disingenuous" than Henry McMahon because he believed what McMahon told him in the correspondence. Similarly, he could rail at the imprecision of the Sykes-Picot Agreement—that is, that it was compatible with the Husayn-McMahon Correspondence only because what had been said "was so vague and ambiguous that it was compatible with almost anything"— but then conclude the opposite: "the Sykes-Picot Agreement was worded precisely so as not to conflict—rather so as exactly to fit in with 'our pledges to the Arabs.'"[18] Ultimately then, the British were honest, and, even if they were not, Sharif Husayn was the responsible party because he was foolish enough to believe them.

This incoherence has affected later scholars who have wrestled with these questions, usually with Kedourie as their guide. Christopher Andrew and A. S. Kanya-Forstner, relying on Kedourie, explain that "neither Picot nor the British *deliberately* [my emphasis] set out to dupe the Sharif by concluding an agreement incompatible with assurances to him. But since neither expected that those assurances would ever have to be honored, it did not seem to matter that they were vague and ambiguous."[19] Similarly, Marian Kent alludes to Grey's "cynical [or] reluctant fatalism" that, for her, "is difficult to credit in a man of his personal integrity" when referring to the Husayn-McMahon Correspondence and the Sykes-Picot Agreement. But, because "no discrepancies were intended" between Husayn-McMahon and Sykes-Picot, there were in fact none, even though the latter agreement "was never intended by the Foreign Office to be anything other than a temporary solution to a difficult war-time situation."[20] This argument amounts to saying that even if the British were deliberately insincere in their assurances to Sharif Husayn, they were not deliberately seeking to dupe him. Similar contortions appear in other scholarship where Kedourie and Friedman are cited frequently with only the rare questioning of the account; as a result, older studies—notably the work of Elizabeth Monroe, Jukka Nevakivi, and Briton Cooper Busch—retain more veracity.[21]

In sum, with little else to rely on in English, Kedourie, Friedman, and their admirers dominate discussion of Anglo-Arab encounters during the war, especially in the United States. Friedman's *The Question of Palestine* was republished twice during the 1990s despite negative reviews calling attention to his misuse of sources.[22]

Arab Scholarship in English

As for scholarship on these subjects by Arab authors in English, no generalizations can be made. Abd al-Latif Tibawi's *Anglo-Arab Relations and the Question of Palestine* appeared a year after Kedourie's *Anglo-Arab Labyrinth* and could not have been consulted by Kedourie, though there is little doubt of their mutual enmity. Tibawi has mined the archives and has extensively documented his sources, Arabic as well as British, unlike Friedman, who does not know Arabic, and Kedourie, who had little use for such material. Where Kedourie sees British openness, Tibawi sees British perfidy and violation of agreements and promises. Where Kedourie sees Grey, and London generally, as misled by initiatives stemming from Cairo, Tibawi credits London with instigating approaches to Arabs. Tibawi is valuable because he does not argue against his sources, as does Kedourie. Where he goes wrong is in insisting that Palestine was clearly included in lands promised to Sharif Husayn by Henry McMahon in October 1915—a claim that cannot be sustained.[23]

Perhaps the most sophisticated consideration of these issues has been done by two other scholars of Arab origin, Zeine N. Zeine and Albert Hourani. Zeine argues that neither the British nor the French plotted to deceive the Arabs from the outset. Rather, as imperial powers, they focused on wartime aims, making promises to achieve immediate goals. Zeine's approach, with access only to published official documents, not the archives themselves, displays more balance than Kedourie's desperate, contradictory efforts to defend British honesty, an issue Zeine does not apparently believe worthy of any effort. Imperial objectives were paramount. Lesser countries and groups were pawns to be used in achieving those aims. What the latter believed was irrelevant to how Britain and France would deal with the import of such promises after the war—a view shared by Hourani.[24]

Finally, with respect to Arab scholars, there is the work of Sulayman Musa, most of whose prodigious output has not been translated from Arabic. Based in the Hashemite kingdom of Jordan, Musa dedicated himself to study the Hashemite role in World War I, notably Sharif Husayn's leadership of the Arab revolt and the creation of Jordan. Two of his books have been translated into English: *T. E. Lawrence: An Arab View* and *Cameos: Jordanian and Arab Nationalism. Cameos* contains an important chapter, "Arab Sources on Lawrence of Arabia: New Evidence," which calls attention to the papers of Amir Zayd, a son of Sharif Husayn, and the diaries of Rustem Haydar, Faysal's secretary at the peace conference. More significantly, Musa has published in Arabic a set of documents, often letters, that serve to question accounts based on the British archives. To give one example, British sources refer to one meeting between Amir Abdullah, another son of Husayn, and Lord Kitchener, high commissioner in Egypt, in spring 1914 when Abdullah sought British assurances of support if Sharif Husayn turned against his Ottoman overlords. Musa's documents, relying on Abdullah's letters to his father, mention several meetings in February and April 1914. These sources suggest more frequent discussions between British officials and Husayn's emissaries than appear in British accounts.[25]

French Scholarship

Recent French scholarship on this subject lacks the obsession with the contemporary political ramifications of the wartime promises and agreements found in the work of Kedourie, Friedman, and their adherents. French accounts can to a degree be classified as generational, those written between the two world wars, and those written since.

French works after World War I focused on the French claims to Syria and Lebanon, written either by Syrian/Lebanese protégés of the French arguing for French rights or by French strategists, military or civilian, who defended France's rights to the region and denounced British perfidy that strove to deny France its share of the spoils. An exception to these generalizations is the account of the French mission to the Hijaz during World War I by the head of that mission, Edouard Bremond, *Le Hedjaz dans la Guerre Mondiale*, still an important source for the period. It is not listed in the bibliographies of either Kedourie or Friedman despite the importance of events in the Hijaz for an interpretation of British policies of Sharif Husayn by a person on the scene.[26]

Two works that are typical of French accounts of their dealings with the British during the war are *Les Origines Orientales de la Guerre Mondiale* and *Le Partage de Proche-Orient*, by Jean Pichon. What characterizes these books is their total distrust of the British, based on the latter's imperial ambitions and presumed double-dealing before and during the war. To a degree, French accusations of British duplicity, regarding France's right to Syria under the Sykes-Picot Agreement, recall Arab accusations concerning promises of postwar independence.

Pichon's books are valuable. He provides the French viewpoint directly, along with much more information about Anglo-French meetings at the beginning of the war to discuss mutual interests in the Middle East than do either the British archives or books relying on them. For example, issues such as the Anglo-French blockade of the Mediterranean and Red Sea coastlines of the Arab lands, and exchanges that took place in March 1915 where France's ambitions for Syria were clearly stated, are not found in books relying on British documents.

In addition, Pichon mentions the famine that severely affected Syria and Lebanon, which Pichon blames on Jamal Pasha, governor of Syria and head of Ottoman forces there. Discussion of the famine has only recently become part of the scholarship in English on World War I, thanks initially to the work of Linda Schatkowski Schilcher, who, using the German archives, attributes some responsibility to the Anglo-French blockade itself.[27] Any doubts as to French interest in Syria and Lebanon can be dispelled by considering a bibliography of works in French on the two mandates for the years 1919–30; it contains 3,359 items.[28]

Recent French scholarship has varied somewhat in its approaches to the subject, but has been consistent in taking a detached view of the events of the war. Three contemporary works by Gerard D. Khoury, Henry Laurens, and Vincent Cloarec stand out.[29] Their tone is consistently analytical and lacks the partisanship masquerading as scholarship that one finds in many of the English-language works discussed above. Laurens has used the British as well as the relevant French archives; Khoury and Cloarec have not consulted British archival documents. On the other hand, none of the English-language sources mentioned above, except Andrew and Kanya-Forstner, consulted French archives, relying on British sources for their depiction of French positions. The availability now of the archives at Nantes in particular, with their consular reports from the Middle East, requires some reconsideration of this subject, in English, with respect to scholarship dating back a decade or more.[30]

Moreover, none of these studies relies on the work of Kedourie or Friedman with respect to Anglo-French policy toward the Arabs. Instead they turn to Jeremy Wilson's *Lawrence of Arabia: The Authorized Biography of T. E. Lawrence.* Wilson did extensive archival research in Britain and consulted the French Foreign Office archives at the Quai d'Orsay. He challenges Kedourie on several matters pertaining to British decision making with respect to the Arabs. Although not a full substitute for investigation of British archives, these French scholars have used him judiciously. Cloarec's *La France et la question de la Syrie* is now the best study of the subject and supercedes, while not totally displacing, Nevakivi's study published in 1969.[31]

ZIONISM AND THE DECISION TO ISSUE THE BALFOUR DECLARATION

Scholarship within this section differs from that previously analyzed in that its focus is the Zionist movement, its rivalries, and its achievement of the Balfour Declaration of November 2, 1917; other issues are peripheral rather than central to the discussion. Many of the important studies have appeared as articles rather than as monographs.

The key question for students of Zionism and the Balfour Declaration is whether the wartime Zionist leader in London, Chaim Weizmann, played the decisive role in persuading the British to issue the declaration, or whether the British decided to take the step themselves. Most of this scholarship has focused on Britain and Weizmann, using British and Zionist archives as well as the Weizmann Papers.[32] However, Laurens has called attention to the French role in encouraging British interest in late 1916, coinciding with the assumption of the prime ministership by David Lloyd George, an ardent Zionist, as was his foreign minister, Arthur Balfour. Of particular note is the role of Lucien Wolf as discussed in the excellent study by Mark Levene.[33]

With respect to the question of primary responsibility for the Balfour Declaration—Weizmann or the Lloyd George cabinet—the key point of reference for later studies has been the article by Mayir Verete, "The Balfour Declaration and Its Makers."[34] Verete downplayed Weizmann's contributions and stressed British eagerness to offer a declaration, a view backed by David Vital, who offers an unfavorable portrait of Weizmann.[35]

The stronger argument, particularly well made by Evyatar Friesel, is that Weizmann's role was crucial, particularly in maintaining ties to British policymakers before the Lloyd George cabinet took office, and then organizing the Zionist reply to the British overture.[36] The Balfour Declaration was part of a broader British wartime strategy, with Weizmann deserving credit for keeping British statesmen apprised of Zionist concerns and Zionism's supposed value to the war effort. A good summation of these issues can be found in Jehuda Reinharz's "The Balfour Declaration and Its Maker: A Reassessment," but Reinharz, relying on Verete, offers erroneous information regarding the Anglo-French agreements and promises to the Arabs.[37]

Of significance for the question of Zionism during World War I are studies of individuals or movements central to Zionism but somewhat peripheral to the Balfour Declaration, notably the work of Steven Zipperstein and Michael Berkowitz.[38]

THE OTTOMAN EMPIRE AND EUROPEAN IMPERIALISM ON THE EVE OF AND DURING WORLD WAR I

The two standard works in English on Ottoman policies just prior to and during the war were published more than thirty years ago by Feroz Ahmad and Ulrich Trumpener. Since then, a number of studies have appeared in English on British policies toward the Arab lands or Ottoman Turkey itself in the period just prior to World War I. These works have been straightforward, though valuable, diplomatic history with the rare study of British imperial goals—regarding oil or economic interests generally in the Middle East—that can compare with the studies in French noted below.[39] Other than Andrew and Kanya-Forstner's *The Climax of French Imperial Expansion*, the only significant studies in English on French diplomacy for this period are by William I. Shorrock and John Spagnolo.[40]

French scholarship has focused primarily on French economic interests in Turkey itself and the Levant, with major studies coming from Jacques

Thobie and his students. Thobie's first book, *Intérêts et impérialisme français dans l'Empire ottoman (1895–1914)*, has been followed by other important works branching into French imperialism in the Middle East or toward the entire eastern Mediterranean.[41] It is difficult to imagine Elie Kedourie or his followers titling a book on European imperialism in the Middle East, as does Thobie, *Ali and the Forty Thieves*.[42]

These works by Thobie are more substantial than the straightforward diplomatic histories of the period published in English, although Shorrock does note French economic interests. They lend themselves to an understanding of French and other European imperial interests in the empire, financial as well as political, on the eve of war. The only specific works on British imperialism and economic interests dealing with the Middle East concern Egypt in 1882. There are broader studies of recent vintage that include the Middle East within the entire panorama of what P. J. Cain has called *The Economic Foundations of British Overseas Expansion*. Cain and A. G. Hopkins have published a two-volume work of great importance that has triggered much debate, with its focus on "gentlemanly capitalism," namely, the interests of well-placed individuals to encourage imperial takeovers for personal economic benefit.[43] In addition, there is a rich French scholarship on the war and the sources to study it, including diplomatic correspondence, that has not been exploited by scholars in English.[44]

A welcome trend in Ottoman historiography is the study of late Ottoman history from within, according to Ottoman archives, rather than through the lens of the European imperial records. This scholarship, going well beyond the work of Ahmad and Trumpener, portrays the Ottoman system as a functioning government undertaking rational projects in the face of imperial threats and controls. Among these works are two studies on Ottoman finances and trade by Şevket Pamuk, and works on Ottoman administration, domestic policy, and actions during World War I by Selim Deringil, Eugene Rogan, and Hasan Kayali.[45]

Pamuk's first book complements the studies by Thobie, examining the Ottoman response to European capitalism and financial pressures down to the eve of World War I. It can be read with much profit by itself and in tandem with the several books by Donald Quataert on Ottoman society and economic development during the nineteenth century.[46] Pamuk's second book, the *Monetary History*, is a sweeping but intensive study of Ottoman monetary policies since the founding of the empire. Rather than be narrowly based, it examines Ottoman behavior within the framework of Eastern

Mediterranean Basin trade and economies, and concludes with a chapter on the Ottoman financing of its military effort during World War I.

Deringil examines Ottoman state efforts to legitimate itself domestically but in particular in Western imperial eyes in order to survive repeated threats to its existence in the decade prior to the war. His consideration of the well-thought-out, albeit futile, efforts undertaken by Ottoman officials stands in stark contrast to the gratuitously insulting portraiture bordering on racism (of Arabs as well as Turks) offered by the Karshes in *Empires of the Sand*.

Both Rogan and Kayali cover World War I, but from different vantage points. Kayali considers the war and the Arab negotiations with the British as well as the Turks. His account of Ottoman exchanges with the Sharif Husayn and Amir Faysal, relying on Ottoman sources, is valuable, but he occasionally relies on British sources whose accounts lack full clarification of events.[47] Rogan treats in more detail the impact of the war on what would become Transjordan, and Ottoman as well as local responses to the Arab revolt of 1916. Rogan and Kayali both note the impact of the famine on Syria and Lebanon, mentioned above, along with Rogan's treatment of food rationing and requisitioning in Jordan. Both attribute primary responsibility for the famine to the Anglo-French blockade of the Syrian-Lebanese coastline, in contrast to earlier accounts that placed the blame on the Ottoman commander, Jamal Pasha. The most recent discussion, which goes beyond Linda Schilcher's use of the German archives, is that of Elizabeth Thompson. Her findings confirm Schilcher's reporting that the Anglo-French blockade bore much responsibility and that "there is also evidence that the British and the French knowingly used the blockade as a weapon of war."[48]

The famine appears to have spread into Palestine by early 1917, affecting all sectors of the population. Palestinian Jews received special aid during the war from Jewish organizations, organized in the United States, whereas European, including Vatican, efforts to send food to Lebanon/Syria for Arab populations were blocked by the British.[49]

NATIONALISM

Scholarship on theories of nationalism, its origins and its constituent elements, has exploded in the past twenty years. Little of this literature has been exploited with respect to Middle Eastern nationalisms and World War I, or with respect to Arab nationalism generally. When investigated, the dominant paradigm has been that offered by Benedict Anderson in his *Imagined Communities*.[50]

Studies that pertain to the World War I period have focused on the origins of Arab nationalism set against a backdrop of loyalties to the Ottoman Empire and the transition from Ottoman to Arab identity. This shift has been hypothesized as linked to particular families and the possibility that the lack of opportunities for employment in the Ottoman bureaucracy on the eve of World War I encouraged younger sons in educated families to opt for Arabism, breaking with older siblings who had found work in Ottoman service. Here the key arguments can be found in the work of C. Ernest Dawn and the later two-volume study by Eliezer Tauber. Dawn's research, initially published in the late 1950s and 1960s, still demands attention, even though recent scholarship questions his findings on particulars.[51]

As for trends in Arab nationalism, the first scholar to challenge George Antonius's thesis of the nineteenth-century origins of the idea, noted above, was Zeine N. Zeine. In a different vein from his study of World War I, Zeine dismissed Antonius in order to argue that Islam brought with it true Arab nationalism, meaning a sense of identity originating in the seventh century that was never lost.[52] Zeine's pathbreaking but partisan work, clearly influenced by the Pan-Arab nationalist strands of the later 1950s and 1960s, has been superseded by a number of studies. Two edited volumes stand out: *Intellectual Life in the Arab East* and *The Origins of Arab Nationalism*. Both contain a series of articles on the nature of Arab nationalist tendencies prior to and during World War I, ranging throughout the Arab lands including the Hijaz, with the second volume offering broader assessments of the subject.[53]

The professional approach to the subject displayed by the authors in these books contrasts sharply with efforts by some scholars, notably Martin Kramer, to debase the subject of Arab nationalism by seeking to discredit the personalities of its advocates. His target has been George Antonius, whose views can be easily repudiated without the gratuitous resort to personal invective characteristic of those seeking to discredit Palestinian nationalism specifically, and Arab nationalism generally.[54] Kramer's eagerness to vilify Antonius bears out Rashid Khalidi's remark in his assessment of Islam and Arab nationalism that there is "a tendency to reduce ideology to the pettiest of personal motivations on the part of its formulators," thereby justifying "a tone of contempt for personal failings," which are then linked to the ideas of these individuals. Khalidi is referring to Elie Kedourie and Sylvia Haim, but his remarks can apply to Kramer as well.[55]

Theoretical works on Middle Eastern nationalism generally, let alone as applied to World War I, are few. However, two recent studies stand out: James Gelvin's on Syria and Rashid Khalidi's on Palestine.[56] Khalidi, focusing on the period just before and after World War I, investigates questions of Palestinian identity, suggesting the possibility of peoples having multiple strands of identity (loyalty) while possessing one dominant national consciousness; in short, the concept of identity itself can be questioned. Gelvin, addressing Syria immediately following the war, examines the attempt of the non-Syrian Arab leadership, led by Amir Faysal, the son of Sharif Husayn of Mecca, to impose a sense of nationalism and identity reflecting elite values on the Syrian population. This effort was resisted by most Syrians, led by men linked to urban factions relying on traditional bases of support.

Both books are imaginative and instructive, based on discussion of historical events as well as theoretical literature. Khalidi's study is more consistent in its application of theoretical criteria relevant to the events examined. Gelvin's brilliant examination of rival discourses and discursive fields, relying on Mikhail Bakhtin, is matched by his use of Charles Tilly's proposals regarding the roots of collective action and the limits of that action's effectiveness. He is less successful in his study of nationalism as such, postulating the idea of nationalism as a "cultural system" though the scholar to whom he attributes that view, Benedict Anderson, does not hold it. Gelvin's hypothesis of popular nationalism resisting both Faysal's rule and the French invasion of July 1920 ultimately proves invalid because, as he shows, no sustained collective action with an ideological base occurred. His evidence suggests that Tilly's theories of collective action are more applicable at the popular level, where fragmented collectivities inhibit expression of popular nationalism or a common sense of imagined community as conceived by Anderson.

IMPERIALISM AND/OR MULTIETHNIC EMPIRES

At the theoretical level, there are important studies of imperialism (listed in note 1), but until very recently there was nothing that addressed the Middle East specifically in a serious manner. This has now changed. The work that addresses World War I and the Middle East most directly is Aviel Roshwald's *Ethnic Nationalism and the Fall of Empires*. A comparable, edited, volume, though different in approach, is *After Empire: Multiethnic Societies and Nation-Building*. Perhaps the most ambitious work is Dominic Lieven's *Empire: The Russian Empire and Its Rivals*.[57]

Roshwald's investigation of ethnicity, nationalism, and the decline of multiethnic empires in comparative perspective opens new avenues of investigation for students of Middle East history for this period. Of particular note in *After Empire* are the broader, speculative essays, well summarized by the editors in their conclusion. Where the breakup of traditional empires led to the independence of its constituent "nations" that had remained more or less intact under imperial rule, there were inheritors ready to form states. The end of the Hapsburg Empire is the best example. However, where the end of empire led to new colonial states serving imperial ends, as in the central Arab lands, there was no direct inheritance with respect to ethnic identity or territorial boundaries, but state formation and frontiers designed by the imperial powers, in contrast to the inheritance experienced by Turkey as the legatee of the Ottoman state. Lieven is a student of tsarist Russia and of Soviet affairs. These topics dominate his book, but there are important chapters on the British, Ottoman, and Hapsburg empires, which Lieven draws on to suggest similarities or differences in experience.

Finally, there is the very useful book edited by Marian Kent, *The Great Powers and the End of the Ottoman Empire*. Though lacking in theory, the separate chapters provide much information for comparative purposes on the policies of all the combatants on the eve of and during the war.[58]

STATE FORMATION DURING AND IN THE AFTERMATH OF WORLD WAR I

The literature on state formation and the Middle East is extensive, but there is relatively little that pertains to events surrounding World War I, despite the fact that it was the collapse of the Ottoman Empire that would lead to the formation of new states in much of the Middle East. This can be explained by the fact that Anglo-French imperial control was imposed on the central Arab lands immediately after the war; it was only with the end of occupation after World War II that truly independent states began to emerge. Nonetheless, there is a body of work that should be consulted for theoretical insights even if it covers only peripherally the period 1914–18 and its aftermath.

The most significant study is by the late Nazih Ayubi, a tour de force that ranges back to the emergence of states after World War I but is rarely consulted by historians. Roger Owen's *State, Power, and Politics* has a good discussion of the colonial state along with a useful introduction to the scholarly literature.[59]

The literature that addresses specific examples of state formation focuses on Arabia. It can be divided into studies of the Hijaz as a separate entity, seeking to establish itself independent of Ottoman control, and studies that consider the rise of the Saud dynasty that would ultimately found the state of Saudi Arabia.

William Ochsenwald has addressed the question of nationalism in the Hijaz prior to World War I, ending with the arrival of the Sharif Husayn in Mecca in November 1908. A book that follows chronologically from Ochsenwald's is the recent study by Joshua Teitelbaum. Teitelbaum, drawing on the work of Joel Migdal, considers Sharif Husayn and his wartime government following the Arab revolt of 1916 as a "weak state."[60]

Concentrating on Husayn's ambitions, Teitelbaum notes but does not engage the controversies surrounding British promises in the Husayn-McMahon Correspondence. Though his theoretical approach is noteworthy, given the lack of previous efforts, his attempt to link Husayn's fall from power to his inability to form a strong state fails to adequately address the wartime circumstances and the simple fact that Husayn had no real state at all, but led a coalition of tribes whose loyalties were often contingent on British subsidies. As Teitelbaum notes, the British actually signed treaties, before or immediately after the war began, with Husayn's two major rivals, Ibn Saud and Ibn Rashid, but never with Husayn himself.

The problem lies in Teitelbaum's conflation of Husayn's "weak state" with a "failed chieftaincy," although the two concepts differ in scope. The state that did emerge from chieftaincy, as Teitelbaum observes, was that of the Saud, quite different from what Teitelbaum calls the "state within a state" that constituted the Hijazi sharifian government. Even though the Saud state structure was rudimentary, the Saud state acquired acknowledged boundaries, something Husayn never had; those he did claim were denied by Britain, whose subsidy was essential to Husayn's survival. A more theoretically consistent study is Joseph Kostiner's *The Making of Saudi Arabia* in which he traces the Saud transition from "chieftaincy" to "state," a process unavailable to Sharif Husayn. Husayn's experience appears to lie more within the realm of topics considered in the book edited by Philip S. Khoury and Joseph Kostiner, *Tribes and State Formation in the Middle East*. The essays in this study range far beyond World War I, but engage conceptual variables, such as the state and chieftancy, with greater consistency.[61]

In considering issues such as tribes and state formation, historians should not ignore anthropological contributions. Dale Eickelman has much to say about colonialism and colonial urban space, as well as nationalism, while Paul Dresch's study of Yemen, which includes the war, should be examined for the theme of tribes and government in comparative perspective, mentioned previously. It is noteworthy with respect to the literature on Saudi Arabia that some authors attribute to it the qualities of a state before the state ever existed.[62]

Other studies of state formation and national identity in the immediate aftermath of World War I exist, but without concern for theory. Malcolm B. Russell's *The First Modern Arab State* mines the imperial archives and is a useful discussion of Faysal's Syria, 1919–21; Gelvin relied on Russell for historical background. More wide-ranging is Mary C. Wilson's study of Transjordan, which engages the countervailing tendencies of British imperialism, Zionist influence, and Arab nationalist ambitions in a sophisticated manner.[63]

A more specific study of colonial state formation and French manipulation and interaction with local elites is Elizabeth Thompson's aforementioned *Colonial Citizens: Republican Rights, Paternal Privilege, and Gender in French Syria and Lebanon*, which can be read in concert with Philip Khoury's two studies of Syrian politics that span World War I and the mandate era. Thompson engages the questions of citizenry and paternal privilege more successfully than that of gender, but her work as a whole offers many insights while acknowledging a substantial body of scholarship that has been devoted to gender and nationalism in Egypt during the period before and after the war.[64]

CONCLUSION

As should be evident, the events of World War I serve as a touchstone for issues of great importance and debate even today. More significant for scholarship are the emerging trends that promise to open new vistas on the lives of peoples within the region, notably but not solely with respect to Ottoman policies before and during the war. This growing field of investigation, when linked to the literature now appearing on the nature of multiethnic empires and the reasons for their collapse during World War I, to give but one example, offers great hope for future scholarship pursued within the framework of comparative and theoretical investigation that the field has lacked until now.

NOTES

Because of the range of subjects, and limited space, I treat only the lands under Ottoman rule in 1914; this excludes Egypt. I also discuss works only in English and French, except for brief mention of the work of Sulayman Musa in Arabic.

1. See, e.g., Steven Fierman, "Africa in History: The End of Universal Narratives," in *After Colonialism: Imperial Histories and Postcolonial Displacements*, ed. Gyan Prakash (Princeton, NJ: Princeton University Press, 1995), 40–65, for the call to integrate Africa within broader historical contexts. For relevant theoretical works on colonialism and imperialism, see the contribution by Julia Clancy-Smith in this volume. Important overviews are Dane Kennedy, "Imperial History and Post-colonial Theory," *Journal of Imperial and Commonwealth History* 24, no. 3 (September 1996): 345–63; and Patrick Wolfe, "History and Imperialism: A Century of Theory, from Marx to Postcolonialism," *American Historical Review* 102, no. 2 (April 1997): 388–420. For India, see Bernard S. Cohn, *Colonialism and Its Forms of Knowledge: The British in India* (Princeton, NJ: Princeton University Press, 1996); and Richard M. Eaton, "(Re)Imag(in)ing Otherness: A Postmortem for the Postmodern in India," *Journal of World History* 11, no. 1 (Spring 2000): 57–78.

For the Middle East, including consideration of the question of exceptionalism, see Edmund Burke III, "Theorizing the Histories of Colonialism and Nationalism in the Arab Maghrib," *Arab Studies Quarterly* 20, no. 2 (Spring 1998): 5–19; Peter Gran, "Contending with Middle East Exceptionalism: A Foreword," *Arab Studies Journal* 6, no. 1 (Spring 1998): 6–9; and the essay by Asef Bayat, "Studying Middle Eastern Societies: Imperatives and Modalities of Thinking Comparatively," *Middle East Studies Association Bulletin* 35, no. 2 (Winter 2001): 151–58. An excellent essay on the need for applying theory to diplomatic history is that by Bruce Cumings, "'Revising Postmodernism,' or the Poverty of Theory in Diplomatic History," *Diplomatic History* 17, no. 4 (1993): 539–69. I will return to these questions in my conclusion.

2. Bernard Lewis, *What Went Wrong: Western Impact and Middle Eastern Response* (London: Oxford University Press, 2002).

3. Ibid., 153.

4. An excellent summary of Lewis's intellectual approach and political activity is by Caroline Finkel, "The Curiosity Test," *Times Literary Supplement*, January 7, 2005, 10, where she reviews Lewis's *From Babel to Dragoman: Interpreting the Middle East* (New York: Oxford University Press, 2004).

5. George Antonius, *The Arab Awakening: The Story of the Arab National Movement* (New York: Capricorn Books, 1965). Originally published in 1938.

6. Eliezer Tauber, *The Emergence of the Arab Movements* (London: Frank Cass, 1993), 1, accuses Antonius of labeling the Arab secret societies existing just prior to World War I as "Arab National Societies" for "propagandistic purposes," although he concedes that ignorance may have played a role. Tauber's book is the most detailed study of the nature of the movements, but his charge of propaganda reflects a school of Israeli historiography that seeks to impugn the motives of Arab historians of

nationalism, especially Antonius, to be discussed toward the end of this paper. See also C. Ernest Dawn's pathbreaking work published originally as articles and gathered together in *From Ottomanism to Arabism: Essays on the Origins of Arab Nationalism* (Urbana: University of Illinois Press, 1973).

7. Elie Kedourie, "The Chatham House Version," in *The Chatham House Version and Other Middle Eastern Studies*, 2nd ed., ed. Elie Kedourie (Hanover, NH: University Press of New England, 1984), 351–94.

8. The works by Friedman in question are his article "The McMahon-Hussein Correspondence and the Question of Palestine," *Journal of Contemporary History* 5, no. 2 (April 1970): 83–122, to which Arnold Toynbee, a doyen of Chatham House, responded, and his book *The Question of Palestine: British-Jewish-Arab Relations, 1914–1918* (London: Schocken Books, 1973; 2nd ed., Brunswick, NJ: Transaction Books, 1992). Toynbee's comments, questioning Friedman's arguments, and Friedman's reply, are in the *Journal of Contemporary History* 5, no. 4 (October 1970): 83–122.

Kedourie's works in question are *England and the Middle East: The Destruction of the Ottoman Empire, 1914–1921* (London: Bowes and Bowes, 1956; 2nd ed., Harvester Press, 1978); *In the Anglo-Arab Labyrinth: The McMahon Husayn Correspondence and Its Interpretations, 1914–1939* (Cambridge: Cambridge University Press, 1976; 2nd ed. 1996); and two articles, "Cairo and Khartoum on the Arab Question, 1915–1918" and "The Chatham House Version," both of which are included in the book of the same title, *The Chatham House Version* (full reference at n. 7 above), 13–32 and 351–94, respectively. Kedourie lacked access to British archival documents for his first book, but had such access for *Anglo-Arab Labyrinth*.

9. Kedourie makes this claim regarding the Sharif Husayn and the Balfour Declaration in "The Chatham House Version," 375, without evidence, and in *Anglo-Arab Labyrinth*, 190–91 and 283–84, referring to Antonius's interpretation as worthless on 284. Friedman argues likewise in "The McMahon-Hussein Correspondence," 196–97, and in his *The Question of Palestine*, 328–29. I have discussed these and other issues in much greater detail in my review essay of Friedman's *The Question of Palestine*: "The Invention of a Tradition: The Question of Arab Acceptance of the Zionist Right to Palestine during World War I," *Journal of Palestine Studies* 22, no. 2 (Winter 1993): 48–61.

10. David Fromkin, *A Peace to End All Peace: Creating the Modern Middle East, 1914–1922* (New York: Avon Books, 1989), which was nominated for the National Book Award; and Efraim Karsh and Inari Karsh, *Empires of the Sand: The Struggle for Mastery of the Middle East, 1798–1923* (Cambridge, MA: Harvard University Press, 1999).

11. Though Fromkin makes extensive use of private papers, he did not consult the F.O. 371 files, apparently relying on Kedourie, nor the F.O. 608 files on the peace conference. His overreliance on the Kitchener Papers, without consulting CAB 23

or CAB 24, leads to misleading conclusions regarding Lord Kitchener's role in decision making, just as does his decision to focus on Winston Churchill, who was out of office from early 1916 to the end of the war.

12. Tom Segev, *One Palestine Complete: Jews and Arabs under the British Mandate* (New York: Little, Brown, 2000), 16, discusses Zionists and the Ottomans. Fromkin never discusses Hogarth's visit to the Sharif Husayn in making his assertion, 297, that the latter had been fully informed of Zionist claims to Palestine; he presents Lloyd George's charge that the Palestinians fought with the Turks twice, on 297 and 401.

13. Manfred Frank, "On Foucault's Concept of Discourse," in *Michel Foucault, Philosopher*, trans. and ed. T. J. Armstrong (New York: Harvester, Wheatsheaf, 1992), 100, quoting Jürgen Habermas.

14. Karsh and Karsh, *Empires of the Sand*, 252, 258. The Karshes contradict themselves here. One of their major arguments is that Middle Eastern rulers, the local imperialists, were responsible for the nature of the settlements after the war, including the failure of the Arabs to win independence. However, when considering Zionism, it wins recognition because of the backing of external supporters, the European imperialists, not the failings or positive qualities of local rulers.

15. See my detailed review of *Empires of the Sand* in the *International Journal of Middle East Studies* 32, no. 4 (November 2000): 559–65. Karsh's attack on revisionist historians is in his *Fabricating Israeli History: The "New Historians"* (London: Frank Cass, 1997; 2nd ed., 1999). Morris's account is in his *Righteous Victims: A History of the Zionist-Arab Conflict, 1881–1999* (New York: Macmillan, 1999). The revisionist-nationalist controversy in Israeli historiography has to do with arguments over events surrounding Israeli independence in 1948, and Israeli responsibility, or lack of it, for the Arab refugee problem among other matters. The nationalist school, represented by Karsh, is highly defensive, justifying Israel's actions at the time and the official historiography that represents the period. The revisionists have been far more willing to investigate archives and challenge official versions.

16. This position is particularly clear with respect to Fromkin's comments on the Palestinians and the Karshes' manipulation of sources; Efraim Karsh contributes to journals that back rightist Israeli positions and challenge the Palestinian right to a state.

17. See Kedourie, *England and the Middle East*, 35–36; and Friedman, *Question of Palestine*, 109.

18. For McMahon and Sharif Husayn, see Kedourie, *Anglo-Arab Labyrinth*, 119–22. For the Sykes-Picot Agreement, compare ibid., 126 and 312.

19. Christopher Andrew and A. S. Kanya-Forstner, *The Climax of French Imperial Expansion, 1914–1921* (Stanford, CA: Stanford University Press, 1981), 91.

20. Marian Kent, "Asiatic Turkey, 1914–1916," in *British Foreign Policy under Sir Edward Grey*, ed. F. H. Hinsley (Cambridge: Cambridge University Press, 1977), 436–51. This entire volume is still of great importance for students of British diplomacy.

21. Elizabeth Monroe, *Britain's Moment in the Middle East, 1914–1956* (Baltimore: Johns Hopkins University Press, 1963); Jukka Navakivi, *Britain, France, and the Arab Middle East, 1914–1920* (London: Athlone Press, 1969); and two studies by Briton Cooper Busch: *Britain, India and the Arabs, 1914–1921* (Berkeley: University of California Press, 1971), and *From Mudros to Lausanne: Britain's Frontier in West Asia, 1918–1923* (Albany: State University of New York Press, 1976). The representative studies relying on Kedourie and Friedman listed below are concerned with British policy generally, not solely with the Middle East.

In addition to Andrew/Kanya-Forstner and Kent, see C. J. Lowe and M. L. Dockrill, *The Mirage of Power*, vol. 2, *British Foreign Policy, 1914–1922* (London: Routledge and Kegan Paul, 1972); David French, *British Strategy and War Aims, 1914–1916* (London: Allen and Unwin, 1986); French, *The Strategy of the Lloyd George Coalition, 1916–1918* (Oxford: Oxford University Press, 1995); David Stevenson, *The First World War and International Politics* (Oxford: Oxford University Press, 1988); Erik Goldstein, *Winning the Peace: British Diplomatic Strategy, Peace Planning, and the Paris Peace Conference, 1916–1920* (Oxford: Oxford University Press, 1991); and most recently John Fisher, *Curzon and British Imperialism in the Middle East* (Portland, OR: Frank Cass, 1999).

Among those who question this narrative, directly or indirectly, are David Stevenson, who challenges Kedourie's depiction of David Hogarth's explanation to Sharif Husayn of the Balfour Declaration (180 n. 2), and Michael L. Dockerill and J. Douglas Gould, *Peace without Promise: Britain and the Peace Conferences, 1919–1923* (London: Batsford, 1981).

22. For example, my critical review, "The Invention of a Tradition," cited in n. 9 above.

23. Abd al-Latif Tibawi, *Anglo-Arab Relations and the Question of Palestine* (London: Luzac, 1977). Tibawi explains why he did not list the work of Friedman and Kedourie, 514.

24. Zeine N. Zeine, *The Struggle for Arab Independence: Western Diplomacy and the Rise and Fall of Faisal's Kingdom in Syria* (Beirut: Khayats, 1960; 2nd ed., New York, 1977); and Albert Hourani, "*The Arab Awakening* Forty Years After," in *The Emergence of the Modern Middle East*, ed. Hourani (London: Macmillan, 1981), 193–215.

25. The primary sources edited by Musa in Arabic are *Al-Murasalat al-Tarikhiyya: Al-thawrah al-'Arabiyya al-kubra* (Historical Correspondences of the Great Arab Revolt), vol. 1, *1914–1918*; vol. 2, *1919*; vol. 3, *1920–1923* (Amman, 1973–78); and *Mudh-*

akkirat al-Amir Zayd: Al-harb fi al-Urdun, 1917–1918 (The Memoirs of Amir Zayd: The War in Jordan, 1917–1918) (Amman: Markaz al-Kutub al-Urduni, 1990). He also published numerous historical studies of the period, in Arabic. His book on T. E. Lawrence was published by Oxford University Press (1966). *Cameos: Jordan, Arab Nationalism, Sharif Husayn, King Abdullah, and T. E. Lawrence* was published by the Jordan Ministry of Culture (1997). British archives refer to Abdullah meeting Kitchener in February 1914. Ronald Storrs, in his memoir, *Orientations* (London: Nicholson and Watson, 1937), mentions a meeting in April only. Abdullah's letters from the period, published by Musa, mention meetings with Kitchener and Storrs in February and another with Storrs in April.

26. Edouard Bremond, *Le Hedjaz dans la Guerre Mondiale* (Paris: Payot, 1931). Fromkin lists Bremond in his bibliography.

27. Pichon's studies were published in Paris in 1937 and 1938, respectively. For Schilcher, see "The Famine of 1915–1918 in Greater Syria," in *Problems of the Modern Middle East in Historical Perspective: Essays in Honour of Albert Hourani*, ed. John Spagnolo (Oxford: Ithaca Press, 1992), 229–58.

28. *Eléments d'une bibliographie française de l'après-guerre pour les états sous mandats du Proche-Orient, 1919–1930*, Réunis par Philippe J. Bianquis (Beirut: American University of Beirut Press, 1934). Bianquis was a professor at the American University of Beirut. The bibliography ranged widely, including items on Turkey; Arabia and the pilgrimage; various religions, including Bahaism; and natural resources.

29. Gerard D. Khoury, *La France et l'Orient Arabe: Naissance du Liban moderne, 1914–1920* (Paris: Armand Colin, 1993); Henry Laurens, *La Question de Palestine*, vol. 1, *1799–1922: L'Invention de la terre sainte* (Paris: Fayard, 1999); and Vincent Cloarec, *La France et la question de Syrie, 1914–1922* (Paris: CNRS Editions, 1998).

30. As Laurens observes, *La Question de Palestine*, 675 n.11, Eliezer Tauber, in his *The Formation of Modern Syria and Iraq* (London: Frank Cass, 1995), used only Zionist and British documents and did not consult French sources for his discussion of Syria. See also the articles by Frank Brecher, "French Policy toward the Levant, 1914–1918," *Middle Eastern Studies* 29, no. 4 (1993): 641–63; and Dan Eldar, "French Policy toward Husayn, Sharif of Mecca," *Middle Eastern Studies* 26, no. 3 (1990): 329–50.

31. Jeremy Wilson, *Lawrence of Arabia: The Authorized Biography of T. E. Lawrence* (London: Heinemann, 1989).

32. For Weizmann, the essential source is the multivolume work *The Letters and Papers of Chaim Weizmann*, Series A, ed. Meyer Weisgall et al., vols. 1–3 (Oxford: Oxford University Press, 1968–72) and vols. 4–11 (Jerusalem: Israel Universities Press, 1973–77); and Series B., ed. Barnett Litvinoff, vol. 1, *1898–1931* (New Brunswick, NJ:

Transaction Books, 1983). See the ongoing biography by Jehuda Reinharz: *Chaim Weizmann: The Making of a Zionist Leader* (New York: Oxford University Press, 1985); and *Chaim Weizmann: The Making of a Statesman* (New York: Oxford University Press, 1993). The first volume brings the story to 1914; the second covers the period 1914–22.

33. Mark Levene, *War, Jews, and the New Europe: The Diplomacy of Lucien Wolfe* (New York: Oxford University Press, 1992).

34. Mayir Verete, "The Balfour Declaration and Its Makers," *Middle Eastern Studies* 6 (1970): 48–76; republished in Elie Kedourie and Sylvia G. Haim, eds., *Palestine and Israel in the 19th and 20th Centuries* (London: Frank Cass, 1982), 60–88.

35. David Vital, *Zionism: The Crucial Phase* (Oxford: Clarendon Press, 1987). This is the final volume of Vital's trilogy on Zionism. The other volumes are *The Origins of Zionism* (1975) and *Zionism: The Formative Years* (1982), also published by Clarendon Press.

36. Evyatar Friesel, "David Vital's Work on Zionism," *Studies in Zionism* 9, no. 2 (1988): 209–23; and Isaiah Friedman, "Zionist History Reconsidered," *Studies in Contemporary Jewry* 6 (1990): 309–14. Compare Friedman's harsh critique to Friesel's measured criticism.

37. Jehuda Reinharz, "The Balfour Declaration and Its Maker: A Reassessment," *Journal of Modern History* 64 (September 1992): 455–99. Reinharz repeats Verete's assertion, for which there is no substantiation, that McMahon suggested to Husayn that Palestine would be excluded from independent Arab lands after the war.

38. Steven Zipperstein, *Elusive Prophet: Ahad Haʿam and the Origins of Zionism* (Berkeley and Los Angeles: University of California Press, 1993), has excellent material on Weizmann and other Zionist notables in England during the war, and Weizmann's approaches to British statesmen. Michael Berkowitz, *Western Jewry and the Zionist Project, 1914–1933* (New York: Oxford University Press, 1997), provides information on financial matters pertaining to Zionism for the period. Other recent books pertinent to this subject are Michael Stanislawski, *Zionism and the Fin de Siècle: Cosmopolitanism and Nationalism from Nordau to Jabotinsky* (Berkeley and Los Angeles: University of California Press, 2001), and Paul J. Merkley, *The Politics of Christian Zionism: 1891–1948* (London: Frank Cass, 1998).

39. Feroz Ahmad, *The Young Turks: The Committee of Union and Progress in Turkish Politics, 1908–1914* (Oxford: Oxford University Press, 1969); and Ulrich Trumpener, *Germany and the Ottoman Empire, 1914–1918* (Princeton, NJ: Princeton University Press, 1968). Later studies include Rashid I. Khalidi, *British Policy toward Syria and Palestine, 1906–1914: A Study of the Antecedents of the Hussein-McMahon Correspondence, the Sykes-Picot Agreement, and the Balfour Declaration* (London: Ithaca Press, 1980); Joseph Heller, *British Policy toward the Ottoman Empire, 1908–*

1914 (London: Frank Cass, 1983); and Stuart Cohen, *British Policy in Mesopotamia, 1903–1914* (London: Ithaca Press, 1976). For the question of oil, see Marian Kent, *Oil and Empire: British Policy and Mesopotamian Oil, 1900–1920* (London: Macmillan, 1976).

40. William Shorrock, *French Imperialism in the Middle East: The Failure of Policy in Syria and Lebanon, 1900–1914* (Madison: University of Wisconsin Press, 1976); John P. Spagnolo, *France and Ottoman Lebanon, 1861–1914* (Oxford: Ithaca Press, 1977); and the articles by Brecher and Eldar cited in n. 30 above.

41. Jacques Thobie, *Intérêts et impérialisme français dans l'Empire ottoman (1895–1914)* (Paris: Publications de la Sorbonne, 1977).

42. Jacques Thobie, *Ali et les quarante voleurs: Impérialismes au Moyen-Orient de 1914 à nos jours* (Paris: Messidor, 1985). See also his *La France impériale (1880–1914)* (Paris: La Découverte, 1982); *La France et l'Est méditerranéen depuis 1850: Economie, Finances, Diplomatie* (Istanbul: Editions Isis, 1993); and his study of European control of the Ottoman debt and subsequent Turkish finances, *Phares Ottomans et emprunts turcs, 1904–1961* (Paris: Editions Richelieu, 1972).

43. P. J. Cain, *The Economic Foundations of British Overseas Expansion* (London: Macmillan, 1980); and Cain and A. G. Hopkins, *British Imperialism: Innovation and Expansion, 1688–1914* and *British Imperialism: Crisis and Deconstruction, 1914–1990* (London: Longman, 1993).

44. For example, Jean-Claude Allain, "Le Commandement unifié sur le front d'Orient: Théorie et practique en 1918," *Guerres mondiales et conflit contemporains* 42, no. 168 (1992): 37–50; Hâmit Batu and Jean-Louis Bacqué-Grammont, *L'Empire ottoman, la République de Turquie et la France* (Istanbul: Editions Isis, 1986); Jean-Jacques Becker and Stéphane Audoin-Rouzeau, eds., *Les Sociétés européennes et la guerre de 1914–1918: Actes du colloque organisé à Nanterre et à Amiens du 8 au 11 décembre 1988* (Nanterre: Publications de la Université de Nanterre, 1990); Antoine Hokayem and Marie Claude Bittar, *L'Histoire par les documents*, vol. 6, *L'Empire ottoman, les Arabes et les grandes puissances, 1914–1920* (Beirut: Editions universitaires du Liban, 1981); Antoine Hokayem, *Les Provinces arabes de l'Empire ottoman aux archives du ministere des Affaires étrangeres de France, 1793–1918* (Beirut: Editions universitaires du Liban, 1988); Adel Ismail, *Documents diplomatiques et consulaires relatifs à l'histoire du Liban et des pays du Proche-Orient du XVII siècle à nos jours*, 2 vols. (Beirut: Edition des oeuvres politiques et historiques, 1979); Nadine Picadou, *La Décennie qui ébranla le Moyen-Orient, 1914–1923* (Paris: Complexe Editions, 1992); Jacques Raphael Leygues, *Georges Leygues, 'le père de la Marine': Ses carnets secrets de 1914–1920* (Paris: France-Empire, 1983).

45. Şevket Pamuk, *The Ottoman Empire and European Capitalism, 1820–1913: Trade, Investment, and Production* (New York: Cambridge University Press, 1987),

and *A Monetary History of the Ottoman Empire* (New York: Cambridge University Press, 2000); Selim Deringil, *The Well-Protected Domains: Ideology and the Legitimation of Power in the Ottoman Empire, 1876–1909* (New York: Cambridge University Press, 1998); Eugene Rogan, *Frontiers of the State in the Late Ottoman Empire: Transjordan, 1850–1921* (New York: Cambridge University Press, 1999); and Hasan Kayali, *Arabs and Young Turks: Ottomanism, Arabism, and Islamism in the Late Ottoman Empire, 1908–1918* (Berkeley and Los Angeles: University of California Press, 1997).

46. See, in particular, Donald Quataert, *Social Disintegration and Popular Resistance in the Ottoman Empire, 1881–1908: Reactions to European Economic Penetration* (New York: New York University Press, 1983); *Workers, Peasants, and Economic Change in the Ottoman Empire, 1730–1914* (Istanbul: Isis Press, 1993); and the survey edited with Halil Inalcik, *An Economic and Social History of the Ottoman Empire, 1300–1914* (New York: Cambridge University Press, 1994).

47. Thus Kayali, *Arabs and Young Turks*, 202, states that Amir Faysal and the Turks negotiated anew in 1918 for a settlement even as Faysal's army collaborated with British forces in attacking Palestine and Syria. The suggestion is that Faysal was double-dealing. Kayali does not check the original source, T. E. Lawrence, who states that Faysal conducted these exchanges with the full knowledge of Lawrence and the British in order to ascertain Turkish intentions.

48. Elizabeth Thompson, *Colonial Citizens: Republican Rights, Paternal Privilege, and Gender in French Syria and Lebanon* (New York: Columbia University Press, 1999), 21–22, and 15–27, for broader discussion, using the British and French archives. Schilcher's article, "The Famine of 1915–1918 in Greater Syria," is fully cited in n. 27 above. An estimated five hundred thousand died.

49. When war broke out, American Jewish organizations decided to take over relief functions heretofore provided by European groups. Aid was distributed through the American consul in Jerusalem, Mr. Glazebrook. Once America entered the war, the Turks prohibited continuance of American-sponsored aid even though the United States did not declare war on Turkey. The Joint Distribution Committee then chose a Dutch national, Mr. Hoofien, to distribute financial assistance, which he did, from summer 1917, through the help of the Spanish consul, Count de Ballobar, who also figures prominently in the early chapters of Tom Segev's *One Palestine Complete*. See S. Hoofien, *Report of Mr. S. Hoofien to the Joint Distribution Committee of the American Funds for Jewish War Sufferers* (New York: Arno Press, 1977); and the report of an apparent rival organization, the American Jewish Committee, *The Jews in the Eastern War Zone* (New York, 1916), microform. Segev claims that Palestinians supposedly ate the bodies of their children, whereas his source refers to rumors of such events in Lebanon, accurately noted by Elizabeth Thompson in *Colonial Citizens*.

50. Benedict Anderson, *Imagined Communities: Reflections on the Origins and Spread of Nationalism* (New York: Verso, 1983; 2nd ed., 1991). For discussion of Anderson's applicability to Middle East nationalisms, see Israel Gershoni and James Jankowski, *Redefining the Egyptian Nation, 1930–1945* (Cambridge: Cambridge University Press, 1995), and the exchanges fostered by this writer's review essay of that book: Charles D. Smith, "Imagined Identities, Imagined Nationalisms: Print Culture and Egyptian Nationalism in Light of Recent Scholarship," *International Journal of Middle East Studies* 29 (1997): 607–22; the Gershoni-Jankowski reply, "Print Culture, Social Change, and the Process of Redefining Imagined Communities in Egypt," 81–94, and my surrejoinder, "'Cultural Constructs' and Other Fantasies: Imagined Narratives in *Imagined Communities*," 95–102, *International Journal of Middle East Studies*, vol. 31 (1999). See also the important collection of essays in Israel Gershoni and James Jankowski, eds., *Rethinking Nationalism in the Arab Middle East* (New York: Columbia University Press, 1997), and my review in the *International History Review* 21, no. 2 (June 1999): 513–15.

51. C. Ernest Dawn, *From Ottomanism to Arabism* (Urbana: University of Illinois Press, 1973); and the two-volume study by Eliezer Tauber, *The Emergence of the Arab Movements* and *The Arab Movements in World War I* (London: Frank Cass, 1993).

52. Zeine N. Zeine, *Arab-Turkish Relations and the Emergence of Arab Nationalism* (Beirut: Khayats, 1958).

53. Marwan R. Buheiry, ed., *Intellectual Life in the Arab East* (Beirut: American University of Beirut Press, 1981); and Rashid Khalidi, Lisa Anderson, Muhammad Muslih, and Reeva S. Simon, eds., *The Origins of Arab Nationalism* (New York: Columbia University Press, 1991).

54. Martin Kramer, "Ambition's Discontent: The Demise of George Antonius," in *The Great Powers in the Middle East, 1919–1939*, ed. Uriel Dann (New York: Holmes and Meier, 1988), 405–16. See also Kramer's assault on Antonius in his review of Derek Hopwood, ed., *Studies in Arab History: The Antonius Lectures, 1978–1987* (New York: St. Martin's Press, 1990), in *Middle Eastern Studies* 28, no. 3 (July 1992): 592–95; and a similar tone in Eliezer Tauber "The Role of Lieutenant Muhammad Sharif al-Faruqi: New Light on Anglo-Arab Relations during World War I," *Asian and African Studies* 24 (1990): 17–50. Contrast these arguments in tone and substance with the critical but professional assessments of Antonius by Albert Hourani in his essay "*The Arab Awakening* Forty Years After" (cited in n. 24, above), and by William Cleveland, "The Arab Nationalism of George Antonius Reconsidered," in Gershoni and Jankowski, *Rethinking Nationalism in the Arab Middle East*, 65–86.

55. Rashid Khalidi, "Arab Nationalism: Historical Problems in the Literature," *American Historical Review* 96, no. 5 (December 1991): 1370.

56. James Gelvin, *Divided Loyalties: Nationalism and Mass Politics in Syria at the Close of Empire* (Berkeley and Los Angeles: University of California Press, 1998); and Rashid Khalidi, *Palestinian Identity: The Construction of Modern National Consciousness* (New York: Columbia University Press, 1997). The first to investigate Arab nationalism in theoretical perspective was Bassam Tibi, *Arab Nationalism: A Critical Inquiry*, ed. and trans. Marion Farouk Sluglett and Peter Sluglett (New York: Macmillan, 1981; 2nd ed., 1990).

57. Aviel Roshwald, *Ethnic Nationalism and the Fall of Empires: Central Europe, Russia and the Middle East, 1914–1923* (New York: Routledge, 2001); Karen Barkey and Mark von Hagen, eds., *After Empire: Multiethnic Societies and Nation-Building; The Soviet Union and the Russian, Ottoman, and Habsburg Empires* (Boulder, CO: Westview Press, 1997); Dominic Lieven, *Empire: The Russian Empire and Its Rivals* (New Haven, CT: Yale University Press, 2000). For Barkey and von Hagen, *After Empire*, see, in particular, Charles Tilly, "How Empires End," 1–11; E. J. Hobsbawm, "The End of Empires," 12–16; and Alexander J. Motyl, "Thinking about Empire," 19–29. For material more directly relevant to World War I and the Ottomans, see Lieven's article, "Dilemmas of Empire, 1850–1918: Power, Territory, Identity," *Journal of Contemporary History* 34, no. 2 (1999): 163–200.

58. Marian Kent, ed., *The Great Powers and the End of the Ottoman Empire* (London: Frank Cass, 1996).

59. Nazih Ayubi, *Over-Stating the Arab State: Politics and Society in the Middle East* (New York: I. B. Tauris, 1995); Roger Owen, *State, Power, and Politics in the Making of the Modern Middle East* (London: Routledge, 1992; 2nd ed., 2000).

60. William Ochsenwald, *Religion, Society and the State in Arabia: The Hijaz under Ottoman Control, 1840–1908* (Columbus: Ohio State University Press, 1984). See also his article, "Arab Nationalism in the Hijaz," in Khalidi et al., *Origins of Arab Nationalism*, 189–203. Joshua Teitelbaum, *The Rise and Fall of the Hashemite Kingdom of Arabia* (New York: Hurst and Co., 2001); Joel Migdal, *Strong Societies and Weak States: State-Society Relations and Capabilities in the Third World* (Princeton, NJ: Princeton University Press, 1988).

61. Joseph Kostiner, *The Making of Saudi Arabia, 1916–1936: From Chieftaincy to Monarchical State* (New York: Oxford University Press, 1993); Philip S. Khoury and Joseph Kostiner, eds., *Tribes and State Formation in the Middle East* (Berkeley and Los Angeles: University of California Press, 1990). Still, the fact that Teitelbaum's study calls attention to these issues is an important conceptual advance over Randall Baker's descriptive but still valuable *King Husain and the Kingdom of the Hejaz* (New York: Oleander Press, 1979), which does engage the controversies of Britain's promises to Sharif Husayn.

62. Dale Eickelman, *The Middle East and Central Asia: An Anthropological Approach* (Upper Saddle River, NJ: Prentice Hall, 1981; 3rd ed., 1998); Paul Dresch, *Tribes, Government and History in Yemen* (Oxford: Oxford University Press, 1989), covers Arabia during the war. Confusion on statehood can be found in Jacob Goldberg's title, *The Foreign Policy of Saudi Arabia: The Formative Years, 1902–1918* (Cambridge, MA: Harvard University Press, 1986), which attributes qualities to a state not yet in existence. John Habib's title, *Ibn Saud's Warriors of Islam: The Ikhwan of Najd and Their Role in the Creation of the Saudi Kingdom, 1910–1930* (Leiden: E. J. Brill, 1978), more accurately depicts the course of events, as does the title of an unpublished PhD dissertation listed by Teitelbaum, Ronald Coleman, "Revolt in Arabia: Conflict and Coalition in a Tribal Political System" (Columbia University, 1976).

63. Malcolm B. Russell, *The First Modern Arab State: Syria under Faysal, 1918–1920* (Minneapolis: Biblioteca Islamica, 1985); Mary C. Wilson, *King Abdallah, Britain, and the Making of Jordan* (Cambridge: Cambridge University Press 1987).

64. Philip S. Khoury, *Urban Notables and Arab Nationalism: The Politics of Damascus, 1880–1920* (New York: Cambridge University Press, 1983), covers the period in question, but see also his *Syria and the French Mandate: The Politics of Arab Nationalism, 1920–1945* (Princeton, NJ: Princeton University Press, 1987). The work that most specifically addresses the question of gender and nation with respect to World War I (and World War II also) is Margot Badran, *Feminists, Islam, and Nation: Gender and the Making of Modern Egypt* (Princeton, NJ: Princeton University Press, 1995).

3

Twentieth-Century Historians
and Historiography of the Middle East

Women, Gender, and Empire

JULIA CLANCY-SMITH

In contrast to Great Britain or the Dutch East Indies, the construction of French Algeria was as much the forging of a gaze—or spectrum of gazes fixed upon Muslim women—as the assembling of coercive mechanisms for knowing and controlling . . . While elements of this existed in other European empires, nowhere was the colonized Muslim woman manipulated to this degree for the political purposes of settler communities.

The proliferation of colonial and gender studies in the humanities and social sciences during the past decade invites critical reflection on how these fields have transformed—or could potentially transform—the historiographies of the modern Middle East and North Africa. As scholars armed with novel methodologies, questions, and theoretical perspectives scrutinize anew the histories of European empires, older interpretations have proven unsatisfactory. Classic notions of unidirectional and univalent *mère-patrie*–colony relations—the center-periphery model—have been decentered. Colonial encounters—political, economic, cultural, and ideological—now appear as multidirectional, if uneven, exchanges between colonies and metropoles as well as among various colonial possessions worldwide. One major change is that historians now pose cultural questions about the most basic elements of imperialism. This has resulted in the realization that empire and nation-state were part of the same historical process and that this process was deeply gendered. Another conse-

quence of the cultural approach to imperialism is that scholars now work
on all three sides of the colonial equation—the colonizer, the colonized, and
the hybrid arrangements continually secreted by *la situation coloniale*—
which has moved previously marginalized peoples and relationships to the
foreground.[1] This conceptual repositioning owes much to newer fields not
solely concerned with empire, such as world history and women and gender theory. In addition, literary theory and its unruly offshoots, postcolonial theory and cultural studies, have also significantly advanced our
understanding of certain aspects of imperialism. However, as some historians have observed, these two fields often suffer from a theoretical "embar-
rass de richesse" and a corresponding penury of evidence, context, and thus
historicizing.[2]

For the Middle East and North Africa until very recently, most writing
on European interventions from 1798 to decolonization fell into the genres
of either diplomatic history whose subjects were "great white men" or nationalist history with its "heroic founding fathers."[3] Imperial and nationalist histories were seen as distinct; but in fact they hail from the same forces,
traditions, and worldviews. Excised from these interrelated narratives were
the losers, women, marginal folk, failed movements of protest, religious or
ethnic minorities, and the hundreds of thousands of Mediterranean migrants
who settled the Maghreb and Egypt from 1830 on and either preceded formal European rule or followed in its wake. Some of the conceptual shortcomings in the historiography of imperialism in the Middle East and North
Africa can be detected in the scholarship for other world regions during the
age of empire.

This essay does three things: First, it briefly surveys traditional or conventional scholarship on imperialism in general, and the Middle East in
particular. Second, it then discusses work produced from about 1978 on,
but with occasional side-long glances at other historiographies, especially
research on British India and the French Empire in Indochina. It employs
1978 as a moment of rupture associated with the publication of *Orientalism* but argues that Edward Said's work was part of a larger intellectual sea
change. Indeed that same year proved critical for women and gender studies on the Middle East since Nikki Keddie and Lois Beck published their
edited volume, *Women in the Muslim World*.[4] Third, it considers how gender analysis and women's history has effected paradigm shifts in older understandings of the region's colonial moment with regard to Egypt, and above
all, the Maghreb.

THE HISTORIOGRAPHY OF IMPERIALISM
PAST AND PRESENT: AN OVERVIEW

We seem to have conquered and peopled half of the world
In a fit of absence of mind. —SIR JOHN SEELEY,
The Expansion of England (1883)

It used to be that scholars of empire closely resembled the object of inquiry. Empire was imagined as a global "great game" whose players were almost exclusively European men from elite backgrounds—the Cromers, Lyauteys, and Ferrys of overseas expansion. The official agendas, secret strategies, and backroom deals worked out in European capitals were seen as the motive force behind this expansion. However, empire building, cloaked at it was in the mantle of the civilizing mission, meant different things to different national elites and colonial lobbies in the nineteenth and twentieth centuries. The three "Cs" of the mission— civilization, commerce, and Christianity—frequently interacted in unpredictable ways with equally unpredictable consequences. Generally the drive for empire triggered multilayered historical processes whereby changes internal to Europe became entangled with the establishment of colonies. Civilizing the natives in Asia and Africa replicated programs in the metropoles aimed at socially "backward" or culturally unassimilated European populations, such as the Bretons, the Irish, and others, or the "dangerous" working classes born of industrialization. While all European powers manipulated the civilizing mission to justify subjugating peoples worldwide, French universalism meant that France alone had a special duty to civilize its colonial subjects. In contrast Great Britain never envisioned transforming imperial subjects into Englishmen and women, although British policies in overseas territories were shot through with contradictions and inconsistencies as was true of other imperial powers. Finally, imperial exploitation was camouflaged not only in the idealism of civilization but also in a maternalist or parental discourse of the "mother-country." Maternal imperialism transformed subject populations into dependent children at best. Algerian soldiers who enrolled in the French army were told that "if you serve France like your mother, she will treat you like her son." The Dutch Empire's "Ethical Policy," expounded in the late nineteenth century for Indonesia, represented an unabashed expression of parental imperialism. Although it was primarily a political project, the civilizing mission's social and cultural expressions meant that documentation on colonized women increased dramatically.[5] Nevertheless the data thus assembled were rarely incorporated into imperial historical narratives—with the exception of colonial crises, such as the debates around suttee in India, which were deployed as evidence of the beneficence of imperial rule.

The traditional imperial narrative was based on narrow readings of mainly archival diplomatic sources, such as written decrees, treaties, military reports, and the policy proposals of statesmen. When scholars used oral data, they privileged the statements of ministers, civil servants, colonial lobbies, or bankers and pashas. African and Asian collaborators or half-hearted participants in empire were virtually ignored; the colonized were just that— "the colonized" or "the natives," an anonymous mass. Historians from this generation were just as imperial in their approach to the past as the soldiers, administrators, and adventurers who gloried in the fact that by 1914 roughly four-fifths of the world's inhabited surface was controlled in one way or another by the Great Powers.[6] As Dane Kennedy observed recently: "The historiography of British imperialism has long been coloured by the political and methodological conservatism of its practitioners. Arising as it did from the imperial metropole in the late nineteenth century, it originally served as an ideological adjunct to empire."[7] Dissenters there were, however, even during imperialism's high-water mark in the late nineteenth century. For example, the Boer War aroused a critique of Britain's imperial ambitions, mainly from the Left, and culminated in J. A. Hobson's 1902 *Imperialism: A Study*.[8] The point is that neither pro-imperial forces nor the opposition spoke with one voice. Moreover, current scholars of the history of imperialism must admit that those who expounded whatever variant of the civilizing mission generally believed in that mission—the rhetoric was not just "smoke and mirrors" but invariably translated a deeply felt worldview. This weltanschauung did not necessarily end with decolonization; scholars, such as J. B. Kelly, professed everlasting faith in the Pax Britannica long after British troops left the Middle East and explained the demise of empire as due to "a general infirmity of will" on the part of European powers.[9]

Orientalism, the academic, artistic, and aesthetic handmaiden to empire, was not without its critics. As some British thinkers were questioning the logic or desirability of colonies, France experienced what Edmund Burke III has characterized as "the first crisis of Orientalism" between 1890 and 1914. Burke detects a transient moment when European conceptualizations of Islam and Muslims, tied to larger currents of science and knowledge, might have produced a counterdiscourse challenging mainstream academic Orientalist thought. The impetus for this opening came from careful, on-site ethnographic research among the Maghreb's peoples "in which Muslims appeared as the subjects as well as objects of study," an approach that questioned the legitimacy of certain key concepts and categories purporting to "explain" Islamic societies.[10] The Great War ended this critical juncture and its possibilities; the old paradigm was reimposed until the decades of independence in the 1950s and 1960s. The colonial and colonized history of the Maghreb reached its fullest expression during the lavish, self-congratulatory 1930 centenary of the Algerian conquest, which churned out a huge corpus of ostensibly objective and scientific materials, including *Histoire et historiens de l'Algérie*. Authored by colonial writers, the volume portrayed the centuries prior to 1830 as "siècles obscurs," marked by ineluctable decline that was stemmed only by "des tentatives malheureuses faites par les États chrétiens pour venir á bout des corsaires d'outre-mer Méditeraneén ou pour les rendre moins nuisibles."[11]

After World War II, powerful critiques arose, significantly from outside the discipline of history, for example, in the work of the sociologist and Africanist, Georges Balandier, or from researchers then on the margins of the French academy. The most noteworthy for North Africa is Jacques Berque, whose 1955 ethnography of the Seksawa of the High Atlas paradoxically questioned the colonial vulgate while simultaneously being a product of Berque's position as a colonial officer in Morocco.[12] Also in the 1950s and 1960s, powerful literary exposés of the excesses of empire were penned by North African writers, such as Albert Memmi, Mouloud Feraoun, and Frantz Fanon.[13]

In the years after decolonization, historians trained largely in sub-Saharan Africa, such as Ronald Robinson, John Gallagher, and Terence Ranger, among others, radically questioned the assumptions of colonial historiography.[14] More than three decades ago, Robinson offered a provocative theory of indigenous collaboration to account for the transition from informal to formal empire. In the long term, Robinson contributed to theories of agency on the part of the colonized, previously portrayed as simply overawed or overwhelmed by European technological, military, and moral might. Absent from most conventional narratives until the 1960s were the colonized unless they fell into the category of traditional (male) rebels, religious dissidents, or nationalist agitators, such as 'Abd al-Qadir, 'Abd al-Krim, or Sa'ad Zaghloul. Also ignored were socially marginal European settlers residing in culturally promiscuous expatriate communities scattered across Asia and Africa. Often characterized as "poor whites," these "Europeans" and "not-quite-Europeans" sometimes took native partners, producing offspring termed "mixed bloods" or "half-breeds." Not infrequently, expatriates functioned as the principal social and cultural intermediaries between colonial officials and subject peoples, a relationship that was occulted in the earlier literature. Subjecting India Office records from the eighteenth and nineteenth centuries to new scrutiny, William Dalrymple discovered that marriages between East India officials and South Asian women were more numerous than previously believed and many Anglo-Indian children were sent back to England for education. As racism grew in intensity after the middle of the nineteenth century, later generations in the United Kingdom expunged South Asian wives and children from family records and thus from memory.[15]

From the 1970s on, scholars turned to anticolonial protest, examining movements of resistance from the viewpoint of African and Asian actors, thereby restoring voice and agency to those previously portrayed as a monolithic entity. This approach revealed that imperial policies and practices were formulated not only in Paris or London but also in Delhi, Cairo, and Algiers as well as along the ragged, shifting frontiers of expansion in villages, oases, and mountain strongholds. The significance of complex, semi-concealed negotiations between European administrators, travelers, and military men on the spot and local elites, chiefs, or peasant elders also came to light. In short, colonial encounters spawned a broad spectrum of political behaviors, from various forms of resistance and nonresistance to complicity or accommodation.[16] Along these lines, scholars such as Michael Adas, Edmund Burke III, Ross E. Dunn, James C. Scott, and Peter von Sivers connected movements of anticolonial protest to changing world market forces, thereby initiating debates about the political economy of collective action.[17] Coming from a slightly different analytical position, Eric Hobsbawm and Terence Ranger posited in the early 1980s that traditions—including colonial durbars and most of the ceremonial trappings of empire—were not rooted in some distant past but rather were continually invented and reinvented. It was also realized that initial European interventions constituted less of a rupture than a continuity in the arrangements of power; on the other hand, colonial history did not begin with the advent of the white men, armies, or imperial bureaucrats in Asia or Africa. While these newer approaches endowed colonial subjects with much needed agency, some scholarship tended to treat "the Europeans" or "the French" as undifferentiated categories, which duplicated earlier portrayals of colonized peoples. Not coincidentally, that same year, Benedict Anderson published the first edition of his provocative *Imagined Communities*.[18]

Reconsiderations of imperialism were influenced by the emergence of the world history movement in the 1980s, which advanced new paradigms and narrative structures. World history subverts Western civilization periodizations that construct causation and meaning in humankind's past principally through the "European tunnel of time" and the "coloniser's model of the world." Also challenged is the nationalists' scheme of history that curiously reproduces, in many respects, the very colonial historiography it aimed to dismantle. "Among the methodologies in the world history armature is comparative history as well as approaches that de-centre historical master narratives in order to transcend arbitrarily 'bounded' units of analysis, such as nation-states and civilisations, or oppositional, mutually exclusive binaries."[19] In addition to world history, women's history, gender studies, and the debates over Said's *Orientalism* were part of a much broader rethinking of the relationship between power, discourse, and epistemology. Indeed one could trace the critique of Orientalism back to the 1963 article by the Egyptian historian Anouar Abdel-Malek, titled "The End of Orientalism," as well as to the seminal works of Michel Foucault dating from the 1960s.[20]

Related to these intellectual trends and political shifts, subaltern studies emerged in the early 1980s, partially in response to the crises experienced by the Indian state.[21] Composed mainly of historians, this movement launched a powerful critique of conventional scholarship on the British Empire with its almost exclusive absorption with elites. Its goal was to recuperate and thus valorize the contributions made by ordinary people or subaltern social groups to the defeat of the colonial state and birth of the nation-state. Leading subaltern scholars, such as Ranajit Guha, further generalized the notion that colonialism, as one form or manifestation of power, created categories of knowledge and ways of knowing that were open to contestation.[22] While subaltern studies infused research on the colonial era with a new intellectual energy, the increasing tilt toward opaque textual analysis—the consequence of thin historical evidence—tended paradoxically to obscure the subaltern subject. Moreover, as Geraldine Forbes noted recently regarding the place of women and gender analysis in the movement's program: "Although they have paid some attention to women, the uncovering of women's subalternity has not been their forte."[23] Finally, another legitimate critique is that some of the subaltern scholarship ironically rendered the British in South Asia far more powerful than even "traditional" imperial history had claimed. Nevertheless, until the late 1980s, colonial India remained the theoretical model informing discussions of imperialism and colonialism worldwide and across time, despite the fact that the Raj in many

respects was unique historically speaking. The focus on South Asia as a privileged site for theorizing on empire deflected attention from other areas
under direct or indirect British rule—Egypt and Palestine or Iran/Persia—
which offered important opportunities for broad generalizing generated by
comparative historical analysis. A final critical element to consider are the
widely varying institutional and/or academic arrangements for studying
colonial history within metropole educational establishments, for example,
the existence, or absence, of university chairs devoted to imperial studies
or the intellectual climate in research centers, such as the Écoles des hautes
études en sciences sociales, Paris (particularly its "sixième section"), that
either favored—or devalued—such colonial research at specific junctures
in time.

The imperial past has become more crowded and contentious as scholars
in cultural studies, film and media studies, and postcolonial studies ran-
sack the texts, images, and artifacts left behind by modern European imperialisms. While historians have not entirely been edged aside, they have been
forced to acknowledge work from other disciplines. Hitherto unexamined
social groups from the colonial past—poor white laborers, servants, native
converts, children, and women of all social conditions—have emerged as
legitimate objects of inquiry, although often their stories are more difficult
to reclaim. As part of the recovery process, scholars now mine unorthodox
sources: manuals for colonial housewives, juvenile adventure novels set in
Asia and Africa, tourist advertising, photography, colonial cinema, world's
fairs, and urbanization projects.[24]

At the same time, reappraisal of the older colonial archive has yielded
additional historical sources—in some cases, relatively abundant—for
socially marginalized or subaltern peoples overlooked in past scholarship.
More flexible and creative definitions of what constitutes historical evidence,
combined with wide-ranging scholarly conversations on the nature of texts
and their reading, have considerably expanded the fund of imperial records.
Documentation extracted from new sources, or from older materials subjected to novel interpretive methods, has questioned every chapter of the
classic imperial narrative about indomitable European men in foreign
lands.[25] Recent work demonstrates that colonial societies were hybrid communities deeply divided by local political quarrels, sharp class antagonisms,
and competing cultural claims. Simple dyadic models of a monolithic, hegemonic Europe imposing mastery over supine colonial victims no longer
suffice. Recent work on migratory communities in the nineteenth-century
Mediterranean world has raised the question of who and what was "Euro-

pean" and argued that even this hitherto unproblematized category must be subjected to critical scrutiny.[26] In short a new multidisciplinary lens trained on imperialism has profoundly altered thinking.[27]

As important, recent scholarship inspired by Said, but going beyond his original formulation, has launched a lively debate on how exactly Orientalist texts and images were received by Middle Eastern readers, viewers, and consumers. Zeynep Çelik's study of photographic albums and architecture from the late Ottoman Empire has uncovered wide-ranging "strategies of speaking back" as Middle Eastern people responded to European cultural and visual forms imposed from without. Carter V. Findley's analysis of a late nineteenth-century Ottoman writer and traveler, Ahmed Midhat, made us aware of "Occidentalism"—the process through which a "Western Other" was created by Turkish and other observers.[28]

One principal vector behind the current scholarly dash toward European empires has been gender analysis, although more has been done to date in the genre of women's history than in gender history—an important distinction. As stated above, the field of modern imperial history was virtually moribund not too long ago; its practitioners constituted a small club of mainly male scholars. Women, whether European or non-European, were rarely seen as worthy of scholarly notice and empire was regarded as immune to gender analysis. The one exception was the pernicious argument that the influx of female settlers in overseas colonies from the middle of the nineteenth century on heightened social distance between colonized and colonizer, thereby fueling racism and eventually nationalist opposition. Taking on this myth, feminist historians began posing questions about how women—European, Asian, and African—experienced imperialism, thereby reinvigorating the entire field. They began by contesting the notion that the colonies were "no place for a white woman" and because of this, their transgressive presence made women responsible for the loss of empire. The 1992 collection of essays edited by Nupur Chaudhuri and Margaret Strobel, *Western Women and Imperialism: Complicity and Resistance*, proved pivotal for the fields of both colonial and gender history. Strobel and Chaudhuri argued against casting European women in simplistic roles, as either heroic opponents of or complicit agents in worldwide imperialism.[29] Subsequently scholars of identity construction concerned with intersections of race, class, and gender began to see colonial societies as a new frontier for research. For the moment, scholarship on the British Empire—especially on the Raj—tends to set the research agenda on gender thanks to first-rate studies by Antoinette Burton, Geraldine Forbes, Barbara Metcalf,

Barbara Ramusack, Mrinalini Sinha, Gayatri Spivak, and, most recently, Elizabeth Buettner and Philippa Levine. Mention must also be made of the important work of Ann Stoler on sexual and racial boundaries in Southeast Asia.[30] Until recently, however, we knew much more about Western women's myriad activities as memsahibs, settlers, travelers, missionaries, or teachers than about colonial female subjects who were often wrongly portrayed as mute, powerless, and oppressed.

Comparatively speaking, in the annals of scholarship on modern European imperialism in the Middle East and North Africa, there is nothing comparable to the massive, multivolume, multitiered *New Cambridge History of India*; nor has there been a movement similar to subaltern studies.[31] Since previous generations of Middle Eastern historians had assumed that race was not a fully operative analytical category for understanding Middle Eastern/North African/Islamic societies, theorizing on race and empire has been somewhat limited, although this is currently changing as a result of cutting-edge research, such as Eve M. Troutt Powell's study of race and slavery in Sudan.[32] For the Maghreb, little work on women and empire exists to date—with several important exceptions discussed below. Key issues such as sexuality and miscegenation studied by Owen White, colonial masculinity, or intersections between European feminists, feminist organizations, and North African women remain unexplored, although scholars of the British Empire have long investigated these issues.[33] However, for Egypt, and more recently Syria and Lebanon, the corpus of scholarship is currently expanding.

A final observation regarding "old time" historians of the Middle East steeped in the ethos of the traditionalist school is in order. Surprisingly, one of the first scholars to point out that European writings on colonized women—the term *gender*, of course, did not yet exist—served to legitimate subjugation was Malcolm Yapp. In the 1962 volume *Historians of the Middle East*, Yapp surveyed "Two British Historians of Persia"—Sir John Malcolm and Sir Percy Sykes.[34] Malcolm's *History of Persia* was published in 1815; Sykes's two-volume work, *A History of Persia*, appeared in 1930. More than forty years ago, Yapp critiqued Malcolm's reliance on sexuality in accounting for Islam's "lack of progress," which was due to the degraded position of women, particularly the practices of polygamy and seclusion. Sexual indulgence in Eastern harems produced political enervation that insinuated itself in all organs of society and state: "The Muslim is a despot in the house; therefore he is a despot in Government."[35] Yapp also analyzed Sykes's obsession with virility and effeminacy as key forces in history; indeed the collapse of Muslim empires was the consequence of effeminacy, associated with sexual profligacy and, of course, the harem. In any case, Yapp's realization that European male fixation on Muslim women, sexuality, and gender undergirded imperial discourse on subject populations is worthy of note.

At the risk of simplification, research on colonialism/imperialism in North Africa tended to follow a different trajectory than work for the Middle East. The reasons for this are straightforward. Large portions of the Middle East were never subject to outright domination, while the Maghreb was the first to fall under direct rule in 1830 (Algeria) and again in 1881 (Tunisia). True, Egypt was occupied by the British in 1882; yet the exact nature of the political relationship was deliberately left unspecified until 1914. This, coupled with the precocious emergence of the Egyptian nationalist movement, has discouraged theorizing from the Anglo-Egyptian case to other parts of the region or to different imperial sites. Because it was incorporated into the French Empire so early, the Maghreb has wrongly been regarded as distinct from the eastern Arab world. The intellectual ghettoization of the Maghreb was based on the faulty assumption that French colonialism in western North Africa was inherently different from French imperial practices elsewhere, for example, in Greater Syria after World War I, and above all, from British-ruled Egypt. North African history in general has been imagined as a poor affine at best of Middle Eastern history, receiving only perfunctory attention when the "Easterners" went west or when Maghrebis journeyed east.

The somewhat marginalized status of scholarship on the Maghreb vis-à-vis the Middle East has impeded broad comparative analysis, with the exception of work by Edmund Burke III, F. Robert Hunter, and Kenneth J. Perkins.[36] However, Timothy Mitchell in *Colonising Egypt* (1988) integrated comparative material from French Algeria into his important study of "the power to colonise."[37] Mitchell aimed not to write a history of British imperialism per se but rather to understand how a new order insinuated itself into Egyptian political culture during the nineteenth century. His contribution was to demonstrate how modalities of ordering and knowing preceded British control, and his use of both a theoretical and a comparative methodology brought scholarly recognition from outside the field. Along similar lines, both Robert Ilbert's 1996 two-volume study of Alexandria and Michael J. Reimer's *Colonial Bridgehead* scrutinized foreign settlement in Alexandria and Egyptian responses, thus providing a prehistory of how subsistence and other kinds of migration to one of the Mediterranean's most dynamic migratory frontiers unwittingly aided—and undermined—competing imperial designs on the port-city.[38]

Another group of scholars has spent decades reconstructing the political economy of imperialism in the Middle East. Jacques Marseilles, Jacques Thobie, Robert Tignor, Roger Owen, David Landes, and, most recently, Samir Saul have recalculated the balance sheets of imperial ventures in the Ottoman Empire and Egypt. Although France exerted considerable cultural clout in Egypt, it was assumed that Great Britain held most of the political and therefore financial cards. Building on previous work by economic historians, Saul's massive study demonstrates otherwise: "Until 1914, indeed until 1956, French economic interests in Egypt were greater than those of the occupying power."[39] A 1902 inquiry by the Quai d'Orsay of France's global investments revealed that Egypt came in sixth in importance, putting Egypt in the same league with Russia, the Austro-Hungarian Empire, Spain, and Turkey for French investment capital. Saul's work questions a major assumption of scholarship devoted to the connection between imperialism and capitalism—that the internationalization of capital and its extensive implantation in a dependent country necessarily resulted in colonial hegemony. In the chronicles of modern European imperialism, the ménage á trois involving Egypt, France, and Great Britain represents a most curious episode calling for more research into intersections between cultural influence and financial dominance. The impact of this school of imperial historiography on the French Empire in North Africa is clearly seen in Hubert Bonin's 2004 monograph, which is a comparative history of the Crédit Foncier in Algeria and Tunisia between 1880 and 1997.[40]

France's cultural weight in Egypt has been considered from other angles by Donald M. Reid in numerous articles and a recent monograph, *Whose Pharaohs?*[41] Reid's work clearly aims to dismantle the binary of "Western imperialism versus Egyptian nationalism" by uncovering spaces where alternative arrangements—neither nation nor empire—operated. Reid also produced an important earlier study of Cairo University that viewed British and French imperialism through the lens of the hotly contested issues of education and national identity. In a similar vein, Amira Sonbol traces the professionalization of medicine during the precolonial and colonial periods. Here once again imperialism, in and of itself, did not constitute—not that it should—the primary object of scholarly scrutiny.[42] A lot of very fine historical work on Egypt has concentrated on the pre-1882 era. Studies by Kenneth Cuno, Juan Cole, and Khaled Fahmy, to name but a few, have grappled with the complex issues subsumed under the notion of modernities.[43]

The year 1985 saw the publication of Judith E. Tucker's landmark *Women in Nineteenth-Century Egypt*, which played a role similar to Keddie and Beck's *Women in the Muslim World* in validating women's history. Together with scholarship on women and gender in Iran, the work for modern Egypt is characterized by theoretical and methodological sophistication.[44] Because of the nature of the sources, most work on women, and increasingly on gender, tends to be woven into research nationalism and nationalist discourse. Taking a slightly different tack, Marilyn Booth's *May Her Likes Be Multiplied* does not deny the centrality of nationalist projects; she, however, does complicate nationalism's multiple meanings for individual women through her analysis of a rich vein of female-authored work.[45] Most work on women/gender, while squarely situated in the colonial era, is not about imperialism per se since the point of departure is Egyptian state and society—and not the colonial order or the Europeans. This may explain why the substantial corpus of first-rate works on Egypt was not accorded the place it merits either in macro-level theorizing on empire or in comparative studies of modern European imperialisms.[46] Two very recent studies—Lisa Pollard's *Nurturing the Nation* and Mona Russell's *Creating the New Egyptian Woman*—are emblematic of a new phase in historiography since they deal with women and gender in the precolonial and colonial periods. Moreover, both works employ interpretive approaches that are somewhat novel for the field. Pollard uses the family to probe issues of identity, politics, and representation; Russell tackles the politics of consumerism and gendering of urban consumption.[47] Finally, studies such as these will assure that fields other than that of the Middle East may increasingly take note of scholarly production devoted to women, gender, and imperialism.

The Maghreb and French North Africa

As stated above, scholarly investment in the British Empire never waned, although students of empire were peripheral to the larger field of British history until the reawakened interest in things colonial. In contrast, studies of the French Empire, particularly of colonial North Africa, experienced a period of intellectual lassitude on both sides of the Atlantic during the late 1970s and 1980s—with some exceptions. The disinterest of French scholars in their own colonial past left in place large syntheses of colonial history, particularly of Algeria, by historians, such as Charles-André Julien and Charles-Robert Ageron, but discouraged monographic studies into new questions raised in other fields of historical or social science writing.[48] Panels or papers on French colonialism in North Africa at annual American Historical Association or Middle East Studies Association meetings were rare and inevitably devoted to Algeria; frequently the panelists exceeded in number the members of the audience. Scholarly disengagement from colonial North Africa coincided with the spectacular expansion of women/gender history in North America and the English-speaking world—on which more momentarily. Until the recent upsurge in colonial studies on an international scale, non-French scholars tended to carry the flag of colonial history, although this is now rapidly changing.[49]

Neglect of France's empire was based on the larger assumption that, relative to the British Empire, the French public was apathetic about imperialism during the second wave of empire building from about 1830 on. From this flowed the erroneous notion that, while France claimed extensive imperial real estate worldwide, overseas involvements did not transform, alter, or even shape the course of national history. Until a decade or so ago, scholars seemed to accept Jules Ferry's quip, made during the 1889 Paris exhibition: "All that interests the French about the Empire is the belly dance." The explanation offered for alleged indifference was the failure of colonial lobbies, such as the *Ligue Coloniale*, to entice business, government, and the public to participate in—indeed to imagine—the French Empire. More important, perhaps, French historians of France were hardly disposed to reach outside the nation-state paradigm in constructing national histories. Historians of modern France remained safely within the borders of the nation-state, while scholars in the French Colonial Historical Society went their own separate way, mainly following fur trappers around Canada. Those studying the colonized in diverse parts of *la plus grande France* were considered too exotic to have much to say about the metropole or even about Europeans residing in North Africa (or anywhere else in the French Empire). This division of labor resulted in three parallel historical narratives that, more often than not, failed to engage in scholarly conversation. Events across the Mediterranean were only woven into France's national history when extraordinary upheavals, like the Algerian War, brought colonial crises home. This was especially true for textbook syntheses that have long been resistant to including colonialism or the colonies—much less the colonized—into master narratives. Thus, histories that were intimately, and often tragically, intertwined remained largely segregated.

The most provocative work on colonial history by French scholars from the mid-1950s on was by sociologists who transgressed disciplinary and institutional boundaries, notably Jacques Berque and Fanny Colonna. In *Insti-*

tuteurs algériens, 1883–1939, published more than twenty-five years ago, Colonna made two critical conceptual advances.[50] First, she proved the theory of the "double bind" (first developed by Gregory Bateson) by using colonial schooling for Algerian youth as a case study. Second, she pointed out not only the similarities but also the actual intersections between Third Republic attempts to civilize rural or ethnically different regions of France and similar efforts aimed at Arab or Berber Muslims. Only recently have historians realized the importance of these points of convergence in metropole-colony political, social, and cultural policies and practices.

In North America as opposed to France, scholars of North African history were frequently marginalized in their discipline largely because of the Maghreb's liminal position. Not quite African, not quite Arab, not quite European or Mediterranean—the Maghreb historically occupied "a space between the essentialisms evoked by each."[51] Scholars trained principally in North African Muslim societies focused on Arabs or Berbers, while relegating all others—including, until very recently, indigenous Jews—to monolithic and largely residual categories, such as "the settlers" or "the Europeans." An exception was Daniel J. Schroeter's *Merchants of Essaouira* (1988), which analyzed shifting interactions among Jewish merchants (*tujjar al-sultan*), ordinary Moroccan Jews, the makhzan, and Europe.[52] Along these lines, Allan Christelow's *Muslim Law Courts* (1985) posed fundamental questions about colonial law and culture by employing a comparative methodology.[53] His study brought to light a number of colonial debates revolving around native women—age of marriage, Muslim female orphans, the "sleeping baby controversy"—that still await monographic treatment. Once again the Maghreb's marginal status in scholarship at the time—relative to Middle Eastern and other histories—meant that avenues of research critical to the field and to related fields were not pursued. Recently, historians of the French Empire have returned to the question of legal systems in colonial regimes worldwide; for example, Isabelle Merle's work on New Caledonia's *code de l'indigénat* shows that the oppressive system of extra-penal law developed in Algeria to control "the natives" served as a model for law codes elsewhere in the French empire.[54] This renewed interest in the legal armature of domination signals a turn away from studies of representation, discourse, and rhetoric that exist in overabundance. The realization that Algeria became the template for imperial policies and legislation throughout la plus grande France could have come only through sustained comparative analysis—an approach that begs for more widespread, systematic adoption by historians. Another area that needs scholarly attention is the history of various kinds of pop-

ulation displacements to, and from, the Maghreb, especially the nineteenth-
century migratory streams from the Mediterranean.

Most historians of French North Africa—of whatever nationality, training, or background—have slighted the troublesome European settlers. An
exception was Emanuel Sivan's work on popular colonial culture in Algeria, some of it published in the late 1970s.[55] Aside from Pierre Nora, Sivan
was one of the first to see the cultural and political hybridities of pied-noir
society. However, a full monographic treatment had to wait until David Prochaska's 1990 *Making Algeria French*, which dissected colonial cultures and
identities in novel fashion by employing new kinds of historical evidence,
such as picture postcards, and a comparative methodology.[56] Scholarly aversion to studying the lives of European settlers established permanently in
the Maghreb, who numbered more than one million by the 1950s, may seem
curious today, yet can be explained by the politics of decolonization. The
ideological commitments of French historians from the earlier colonial school,
Julien and Ageron, played a determining role in the way they wrote history.
These scholars, whose sympathy for indigenous North African societies deeply
marked their work, viewed the Europeans as illegitimate occupiers and thus
marginalized the *colons* in historical narratives. Of the nearly twelve hundred pages in the two-volume *Histoire de l'Algérie*, less than 10 percent of
the text discusses the settlers. Moreover, the fact that ex-colonials in today's
France form the constituency for the *Front National* rendered close scrutiny
of their historic origins distasteful for French scholars of the Left until
recently, although this is no longer the case. In the Maghreb, the institutional politics of national universities often rendered North African historians reluctant to devote research to the Mediterranean folk who had peopled
the Maghreb so abundantly but departed en masse in the 1950s and 1960s.
At the present time, however, scholarly indifference has given way to active
interest as a new generation of younger historians at the University of Tunis,
such as Dalenda and Abdelhamid Larguèche and Habib Kazdaghli, reject
the notion of investigating the colonial past solely through the lens of nationalism. French historians, such as Anne-Marie Planel and Odile Moreau,
working closely with North African colleagues, have reconfigured fundamental questions about the Maghreb's connections with Europe and the
Ottoman Empire, thereby overturning long-standing myths—for example,
regarding Moroccan isolationism in the nineteenth century. Others have
treated previously taboo topics, such as conversions to Christianity by Muslim Kabyles.[57]

The year 1993 saw two key publications. Fanny Colonna's edited volume

Etre Marginal au Maghreb and Edmund Burke III's *Struggle and Survival*, both of which recovered the stories of individuals excised from the historical record and wrote ordinary people into narratives of the past. Another major contribution of Burke's collection is that it reconnected North African and Middle Eastern histories by means of individual lives. Eugene Rogan's edited volume, *Outside In: On the Margins of the Modern Middle East* (2002) responded to Burke's challenge to reclaim the histories of marginalized people and processes, although the collection does not deal with colonialism and imperialism per se.[58] Another current trend is that historians now freely borrow theoretical approaches from other fields and disciplines. When applied to North African history, theories of difference (or identity) have deepened understanding of the force of ethnic categories in colonial politics, which Patricia Lorcin's 1995 examination of the Kabyle myth so compellingly argued.[59] Much of the most innovative work on the French Empire outside of the Middle East and North Africa—Canada, West Africa, and Indochina—is by scholars, like Lorcin, Alice L. Conklin, or Eric Jennings, who are trained as French historians first and foremost.[60] And an increasing number of Italian researchers are presently studying the Italian Empire in the Mediterranean and East Africa and frequently frame their inquiries around gender theory, for example, Giulia Barrera's research on sex and citizenship in Eritrea.[61]

Women and Gender in Colonial North Africa and Syria

To return to our initial query: how have women and gender theories altered our understanding of imperialism in the Middle East and North Africa? In general the histories of Egypt, the Levant, and the late Ottoman Empire are under revision as scholars formulate questions primarily around this rapidly expanding body of theory.[62] Building on previous work by Philip Khoury and James Gelvin, Elizabeth Thompson's *Colonial Citizens* (2000) offered a model of what historical work devoted to *both* gender and colonialism can accomplish.[63] Despite the shifts in knowledge referred to above, relatively little historical work on women/gender has appeared for colonial North Africa, which is paradoxical since sources in French and Arabic are abundant.[64] One of the first inquiries into colonial prostitution was published in 1853, Edouard Adolphe Duchesne's *De la prostitution dans la ville d'Alger depuis la conquête*, which had been virtually ignored until recently.[65] Scholars from the generation of Jacques Berque and Jean-Paul Charnay did not completely ignore the "woman question," and ethnographers, such as Germaine Tillion, published on women from the 1960s on and even much earlier.[66] Malek Alloula's *The Colonial Harem* (1986) applied male gaze theory to salacious picture postcards of Algerian women (and men) produced at the fin de siècle. This work awakened scholars to the close fit between exploitation, images, and representations of colonized women's sexuality, although it did not adequately historicize the visual evidence in terms of production as well as consumption or reception. Thus the appearance of Christelle Taraud's *La prostitution coloniale: Algérie, Tunisie, Maroc (1830–1962)* in 2003 represented a landmark in historical research.[67]

Compared to the British Empire, the tardy emergence of women/gender history for colonial North Africa can be partially explained by the fact that the French academy only belatedly recognized gender analysis. This is curious since Simone de Beauvoir's 1949 *The Second Sex* exerted a tremendous impact on feminist writers in the second wave of feminism.[68] The disinterest in women's history in France in turn influenced historians from the Maghreb, who still follow French intellectual trends more than others. As noted above, North African scholars did not begin to explore the lives of the hundreds of thousands of Europeans who called the Maghreb home until very recently. Integrating the settlers into a larger examination of French rule would inevitably have raised women and gender issues, demonstrating that *la situation coloniale* was cultural as much as political in dynamic. One critical set of questions revolves around social theories of space originally developed by Henri Lefebvre. Historians of class and identities in modern Europe have come to appreciate the highly gendered nature of urban space and how different social, religious, or cultural groups interpret and use different kinds of space. In addition, art, and especially architectural, historians, such as Zeynep Çelik, Nabila Oulebsir, and Gwendolyn Wright, have forced us to see colonial politics at work in urban design, sanitary regulations, and public housing projects; indeed Çelik's emphasis on the built environment has reinvigorated the field of colonial history and studies.[69] Finally, landscapes and their representations—which were almost invariably feminized after the imposition of European rule—have been fundamental to the colonial project worldwide since imperial conquests and mapping or cartography worked hand in hand.

The continued hegemony of nationalist history and historiography in postcolonial North Africa may also account for inattention to women/gender. Research on, and in, the three North African states enclosed these multiple histories within a male-centered and -dominated nation-state narrative opposing colonizer and colonized, rulers and ruled. Yet the significance of women to all phases of the nationalist movements was apparent. By 1900 Muslim women were deployed as symbols of the nation oppressed by foreign rule in the Maghreb and Egypt. However, these were often representations of women as various nationalists groups wanted to see them and did not necessarily translate the experiences of women per se. In the interwar period, a Tunisian nationalist, Sulayman al-Jadhi, observed: "Nationhood is a secret guarded by woman" who remains "the ultimate foundation of our social edifice."[70] Al-Jadhi's remarks protested a public address made by the resident general's wife, Mme. Lucien Saint, to Muslim women in Tunis, an event interpreted as an exercise in "moral domination." Al-Jadhi's outrage at social mixing between French and Tunisian Muslim women suggests that these relationships were important enough to condemn. Nevertheless, to date few historians have pursued the multiple questions that this incident raises for colonial Tunisia.[71]

Previous generations of North African historians have, for the most part, resolutely focused on male ideologues or leaders, such as ʿAllal al-Fasi in Morocco, the FLN (National Liberation Front) elite, ʿAbd al-ʿAziz al-Thaʿalbi, or the Neo-Destur and Habib Bourguiba. One of Bourguiba's claims immediately following independence was that he had liberated the nation from France and women from the oppression of both tradition and colonialism through access to modern education and far-reaching legal changes in personal status. This wrongly implied that Tunisian (or North African) women entered public life only in the post–World War II era and that girls schooling was insignificant until then as well. It is undeniable that nationalist movements empowered women by creating new identities and legitimating social roles and activities, including learning and the production of knowledge, as well as generating new historical sources. Yet these same movements also subverted emancipation by subordinating women's needs to those of the nation. More important, subtle shifts as well as sea changes in nationalist ideology, aims, and strategies are best reflected in shifts in positions on women and gender relations—a methodology that has not yet been employed for colonial North Africa, although Mounira Charrad has used it compellingly for the independent period.[72]

Moreover, women and gender analysis expose fundamental differences between colonialism as lived in the three North African states; for example, huge contrasts emerge between Algeria and Tunisia when considering the eroticized body of the Algerian woman, for whom, it was argued, formal education was pointless, and the Tunisian female mind, which was judged capable of modern learning by liberal Protectorate officials in 1900. Here a critical difference comes to light in male versus female experiences under European colonial rule. The classroom and school yard represented one of the few spaces where colonized women encountered the colonial regime in sustained fashion. Being highly contested sites, schools, education, and learning in the colonial context frequently served as nodal points of inter-section for global reform programs—for social movements communities, and their local bearers—which invariably focused on women by the end of the nineteenth century. Despite the obvious importance of schooling to the evolution of North Africa since 1830, few histories of female education exist; we know little about how colonial regimes dealt with children and youth, above all girls—in other words, *la situation coloniale* as seen from the school-room remains a largely blank page. On a broader level, it is often assumed that women experienced colonialism in the ways similar to colonized men and, therefore, that female education followed the same trajectory as boys schooling—only later in time. However, an experiment in colonial school-ing for girls in Tunis proves otherwise.[73]

Finally, by using gender theory and methodology for reconceptualizing France's North African empire, notions of core and periphery are displaced. Some French feminists employed the condition of North African Muslim women to argue for domestic reforms in France in the realm of female legal and voting rights. This strategy was used by the radical suffragist Hubertine Auclert (1848–1914), founder of "Droits des Femmes" and a self-appointed advocate for Muslim Arab women in *L'Algérie Française*. Auclert deployed the degraded social, legal, and moral condition of Algerian Muslim women to agitate for the enfranchisement of women in France as well as for fun-damental changes in French colonial praxis in Algeria. Thus, we see a com-plex layering of colonial and national campaigns that attest to the existence of circular flows of opinions, doctrines, and advocacies between colony and metropole—and back again.

CONCLUSIONS

Despite the fact that France was second only to Great Britain in terms of Asian and African real estate holdings and the number of peoples subject to France's imperial embrace, most theoretical and empirical scholarship on colonial history has revolved around the British Empire, especially in India. Moreover, the historiography of French imperialism has to a great extent been "colonized" by the approaches and methodologies of British imperial studies, especially those devoted to India and South Asia. And if the newer approaches discussed above have opened new debates, often they lack the explanatory weight to deal with historical process in the complicated and contradictory encounters so facilely termed "colonial." As I have argued elsewhere, the agents of modern European empire are frequently essentialized in the same way that the "natives" were in the older historiography.[74] And the totalizing nature and impact of Western hegemony worldwide is curiously reaffirmed by scholars claiming to dismantle that hegemony.

What needs to be realized is that dominant projects have always historically called forth subordinate projects and counterprojects, as Geoffrey Oddie and others have shown. In his 1997 article, Pier M. Larson observed that "Neo-Foucauldian studies of imperial discourse have underestimated the intellectual resilience of 'colonized minds.'" Larson's argument, well taken, is that peoples under European imperial regimes systematically filtered colonial discourses of power and subordination, "fitting them into local systems of knowledge."[75] An additional argument needs to be made, however: that European men and women, residing permanently in the Maghreb as administrators, teachers, wives of colonial farmers, or traders, also engaged, rearranged, and filtered the multiple, and frequently contradictory, discourses produced by colonialism. Some of the Europeans calling North Africa home encountered the colonized on a daily basis and in intimate ways—and not only in situations of unambiguous power asymmetry. Indeed the mutually exclusive and oppositional binaries informing the notion of "colonizer" and "colonized" demand redefinition. This is not to deny the objectifying gaze of Europeans or the power wielded by colonial officials, lobbies, banks, and armies. Yet the colonial divide could be fuzzy or permeable; in many instances the traffic was two-way—although the degree of permeability and the density and meaning of reciprocal exchanges depended heavily on how "the woman question" was articulated. What needs further analysis are the processes through which the "colonizers" or "the Europeans" responded to—even absorbed—local cultures, customs, or knowledge, all of them gendered, and how that shaped the historical terrain we understand to be "colonial."

Finally the nationalist narrative and tunnel of time has until now dominated most thinking on, and historical writing devoted to, imperialism in the Middle East and North Africa. While the Maghreb potentially offers a rich site for understanding colonialism as a three-cornered and multitiered process, the Maghreb's marginalized position relative to Middle Eastern history has discouraged comparative collaborations or intellectual cross-fertilization. In short the power of comparative history has yet to be exploited fully by historians revisiting colonialisms of the modern Middle East and North Africa. Nevertheless, a substantial shift is under way on both sides of the Mediterranean and the Atlantic. For the Maghreb, this is particularly in evidence, once again, among Tunisian historians whose concerted efforts to integrate the history of minorities, specifically North African Jews, women, and former colonials, into a transnational and national—but not nationalist—narrative constitutes a historiographical sea change.[76]

NOTES

Epigraph. Julia Clancy-Smith, "European Empires, Colonialism, and Sources of Knowledge about Women & Islamic Cultures, c. 1700–1900," in *Encyclopedia of Women & Islamic Cultures,* ed. Suad Joseph (Leiden: E. J. Brill, 2003), 1:12.

1. Georges Balandier was among the first scholars to both critique and theorize about colonialism as the Algerian war drew to a close; see his "La situation coloniale, approche théorique," *Cahiers Internationaux de Sociologie* 11 (1951): 44–79. Alice L. Conklin, *A Mission to Civilize: The Republican Idea of Empire in France and West Africa, 1895–1930* (Stanford, CA: Stanford University Press, 1997); and Daniel J. Sherman, "The Arts and Sciences of Colonialism," *French Historical Studies* 23, no. 4 (Fall 2000): 707–29.

2. Recent overviews of colonial historiography, past and present, include Edmund Burke III, "Theorizing the Histories of Colonialism and Nationalism in the Arab Maghrib," *Arab Studies Quarterly* 20, no. 2 (Spring 1998): 5–19; Dane Kennedy, "Imperial History and Post-colonial Theory," *Journal of Imperial and Commonwealth History* 24, no. 3 (September 1996): 345–63; and Richard M. Eaton, "(Re)imag(in)ing Otherness: A Postmortem for the Postmodern in India," *Journal of World History* 11, no. 1 (Spring 2000): 57–78. See also Edmund Burke III and David Prochaska, eds., *Historicizing Orientalism: From Postcolonial Theory to World History* (Lincoln: University of Nebraska Press, 2006).

3. For examples, see Pierre Espérandieu, *Lyautey et le protectorat* (Paris: Éditions R. Pichon et R. Durand-Auzias, 1947); Sir Auckland Colvin, *The Making of Modern Egypt* (London: Seeley and Co., 1906); and the Earl of Cromer, *Modern Egypt* (London: Macmillan, 1908).

4. Lois Beck and Nikki R. Keddie, eds., *Women in the Muslim World* (Cambridge, MA: Harvard University Press, 1978).

5. Julia Clancy-Smith, "Colonialism: 18th to Early 20th Century," in *Encyclopedia of Women & Islamic Cultures,* Vol. 1 (Leiden: E. J. Brill, 2003), 100–115.

6. Julia Clancy-Smith and Frances Gouda, eds., "Introduction," in *Domesticating the Empire: Race, Gender, and Family Life in French and Dutch Colonialism* (Charlottesville: University Press of Virginia, 1998), 1–20.

7. Kennedy, "Imperial History," 345.

8. Peter Cain, *The Empire and Its Critics, 1899–1939: Classics of Imperialism*, 8 vols. (London: Routledge, 1998).

9. J. B. Kelly, *Arabia and the Gulf* (New York: Basic Books, 1980), vii.

10. Edmund Burke III, "The First Crisis of Orientalism, 1890–1914," in *Connaissances du Maghreb: Sciences Sociales et Colonisation*, ed. Jean-Claude Vatin (Paris: CNRS, 1984), 213–26; quote from 221.

11. Anonymous, *Histoire et historiens de l'Algérie*, Collection du Centenaire de l'Algérie (Paris: Librarie Félix Alcan, 1931), 1.

12. Jacques Berque, *Structures sociales du haut-atlas*, 2nd ed., with Paul Pascon, *Retour aux Seksawa* (Paris: Presses Universitaires de Frances, 1978); see also François Pouillon, ed., "Enquêtes dans la bibliographie de Jacques Berque. Parcours d'histoire sociale," special issue, *Revue des mondes musulmans et de la Méditerraneé*, nos. 83–84 (1998).

13. Albert Memmi, *La statue de sel* (Paris: Gallimard, 1966), first published in 1955; Memmi, *Portrait du colonisé précédé du portrait du colonisateur* (Paris: Editions Buchet/Chastel, 1957); Mouloud Feraoun, *Journal, 1955–1962* (Paris: Éditions du Seuil, 1962); and Frantz Fanon, *Les Damnés de la terre* (Paris: Maspero, 1961). Fanon, of course, was not a North African.

14. Ronald Robinson, John Gallagher, and Alice Denny, *Africa and the Victorians: The Official Mind of Imperialism* (London: Macmillan, 1961); and above all, Ronald Robinson, "Non-European Foundations of European Imperialism: Sketch for a Theory of Collaboration," in *Studies in the Theory of Imperialism*, ed. R. Owen and B. Sutcliffe (London: Longman, 1972), 117–42.

15. William Dalrymple, *The White Mughals: Love and Betrayal in Eighteenth Century India* (New York: HarperCollins, 2003).

16. For examples, Alf Andrew Heggoy, "Looking Back: The Military and Colonial Policies in French Algeria," *Muslim World* 73 (January 1983): 57–66; and C. M. Andrew and A. S. Kanya-Forstner, "Centre and Periphery in the Making of the Second French Colonial Empire, 1815–1920," *Journal of Imperial and Commonwealth History* 16, no. 3 (1988): 9–34.

17. Michael Adas, *Prophets of Rebellion: Millennarian Protest Movements against the European Colonial Order* (Chapel Hill: University of North Carolina Press, 1979); Edmund Burke III, *Prelude to Protectorate in Morocco: Precolonial Protest and Resistance* (Chicago: University of Chicago Press, 1976); Burke, ed., *Global Crises and Social Movements: Artisans, Peasants, Populists, and the World Economy* (Boulder, CO: West-

view Press, 1988); Ross E. Dunn, *Resistance in the Desert: Moroccan Responses to French Imperialism, 1881–1912* (Madison: University of Wisconsin Press, 1977); James C. Scott, *The Moral Economy of the Peasant: Rebellion and Subsistence in Southeast Asia* (New Haven, CT: Yale University Press, 1976); Peter von Sivers, "Insurrection and Accommodation: Indigenous Leadership in Eastern Algeria, 1840–1900," *International Journal of Middle East Studies* 6, no. 3 (1975): 259–75; and Julia Clancy-Smith, "Saints, Mahdis, and Arms: Religion and Resistance in 19th-Century North Africa," in *Islam, Politics, and Social Movements*, ed. Edmund Burke III and Ira M. Lapidus (Berkeley and Los Angeles: University of California Press, 1988), 60–80.

18. Eric J. Hobsbawm and Terence Ranger, eds., *The Invention of Tradition* (Cambridge: Cambridge University Press, 1983); and Benedict Anderson, *Imagined Communities: Reflections on the Origin and Spread of Nationalism* (London: Verso, 1983). It is important to note that the most important work on modern European colonialism in the Ranger and Hobsbawm volume came from African and Indian histories. Anderson was trained in Asian, specifically Indonesian, history and politics.

19. Julia Clancy-Smith, ed., introduction to *North Africa, Islam, and the Mediterranean World from the Almoravids to the Algerian War* (London: Frank Cass, 2001), 1–2. On World History, see Edmund Burke III, "Marshall G. S. Hodgson and the Hemispheric Interregional Approach to World History," *Journal of World History* 6, no. 2 (Fall 1995): 237–50; for a critique of Eurocentric scholarship and geographical diffusionist thought, see J. M. Blaut, *The Colonizer's Model of the World: Geographical Diffusionism and Eurocentric History* (New York: Guilford 1993).

20. Burke, "The First Crisis," 213; Michel Foucault, *Histoire de la folie* (Paris: Plon, 1961).

21. See the "AHR Forum" devoted to subaltern studies in *American Historical Review* 99, no. 5 (December 1994): 1475–1545.

22. Ranajit Guha, "On Some Aspects of the Historiography of Colonial India," in *Subaltern Studies*, vol. 1, *Writing on South Asian History and Society*, ed. Ranajit Guha (New Delhi: Oxford University Press, 1982), cited in Firdous Azim, "Postcolonial Theory," in *The Cambridge History of Literary Criticism*, vol. 9, *Twentieth-Century Historical, Philosophical and Psychological Perspectives*, ed. Christa Knellwolf and Christopher Norris (Cambridge: Cambridge University Press, 2001), 239–40.

23. For recent critiques of subaltern studies, see the articles by Eaton and Kennedy in note 3 above. Geraldine Forbes, *Women in Modern India*, pt. 4, vol. 2 of *The New Cambridge History of India* (Cambridge: Cambridge University Press, 1996), 3. Partha Chatterjee, *The Nation and Its Fragments: Colonial and Postcolonial Histories* (Princeton, NJ: Princeton University Press, 1993), did consecrate several chapters to women and the nation.

24. Zeynep Çelik was among the first to study world's fairs in *Displaying the*

Orient: Architecture of Islam at Nineteenth-Century World's Fairs (Berkeley and Los Angeles: University of California Press, 1992).

25. An example of a new source for Egyptian history is found in John David Ragan, "Jehan D'Ivray," in *Egyptian Encounters*, ed. Jason Thompson, *Cairo Papers in Social Science* 23, no. 3 (Fall 2000): 24–42, which discusses the library of the Jesuit Collège de la Sainte Famille in Cairo, housing a rich, but underconsulted, collection of travel accounts, many by women.

26. Julia Clancy-Smith, "Marginality and Migration: Europe's Social Outcasts in Pre-colonial Tunisia, 1830–81," in *Outside In: On the Margins of the Modern Middle East*, ed. Eugene Rogan (London: I. B. Tauris, 2002), 149–82.

27. This is the argument in Julia Clancy-Smith, *Rebel and Saint: Muslim Notables, Populist Protest, Colonial Encounters (Algeria and Tunisia, 1800–1904)* (Berkeley and Los Angeles: University of California Press, 1994).

28. Zeynep Çelik, "Speaking Back to Orientalist Discourse," *Orientalism's Interlocutors: Painting, Architecture, Photography*, ed. Jill Beaulieu and Mary Roberts (Durham, NC: Duke University, 2003), 19–41; and Carter V. Findlay, "An Ottoman Occidentalist in Europe: Ahmed Midhat Meets Madame Gülner," *American Historical Review* 103, no. 1 (February 1998): 15–49.

29. A few examples of work that triggered interest in women, gender, and empire are Nupur Chaudhuri and Margaret Strobel, eds., *Western Women and Imperialism: Complicity and Resistance* (Bloomington: Indiana University Press, 1992); Cheryl Johnson-Odim and Margaret Strobel, eds., *Expanding the Boundaries of Women's History: Essays on Women in the Third World* (Bloomington: Indiana University Press, 1992); Frances Gouda, *Dutch Culture Overseas: Colonial Practices in the Netherlands Indies, 1900–1942* (Amsterdam: Amsterdam University Press, 1995); Clare Midgley, ed., *Gender and Imperialism* (Manchester: University of Manchester Press, 1998); and Ruth Roach Pierson and Nupur Chaudhuri, eds. *Nation, Empire, Colony: Historicizing Gender and Race* (Bloomington: Indiana University Press, 1998).

30. Mrinalini Sinha, *Colonial Masculinity: The 'Manly Englishman' and the 'Effeminate Bengali' in the Late Nineteenth Century* (Manchester: Manchester University Press, 1995); Antoinette Burton, *Burdens of History: British Feminists, Indian Women, and Imperial Culture, 1865–1915* (Chapel Hill: University of North Carolina Press, 1994); Burton, *At the Heart of the Empire: Indians and the Colonial Encounter in Late-Victorian Britain* (Berkeley and Los Angeles: University of California Press, 1998); Forbes, *Women in Modern India*; and Anne McClintock, *Imperial Leather: Race, Gender and Sexuality in the Colonial Context* (London: Routledge, 1995). Among her numerous works, Ann Laura Stoler, "Sexual Affronts and Racial Frontiers: European Identities and the Cultural Politics of Exclusion in Colonial Southeast Asia," in *Tensions of Empire: Colonial Cultures in a Bourgeois World*, ed. Frederick

Cooper and Ann Laura Stoler (Berkeley and Los Angeles: University of California Press, 1997), 198–237; Ann Laura Stoler, *Carnal Knowledge and Imperial Power* (Berkeley and Los Angeles: University of California Press, 2002); Elizabeth Buettner, *Empire Families: Britons and Late Imperial India* (Oxford: Oxford University Press, 2004); and Philippa Levine, ed., *Gender and Empire* (Oxford: Oxford University Press, 2004).

31. For example, Thomas R. Metcalf, *Ideologies of the Raj*, pt. 3, vol. 4 of *The New Cambridge History of India* (Cambridge: Cambridge University Press, 1994).

32. Eve M. Troutt Powell, *A Different Shade of Colonialism: Egypt, Great Britain, and the Mastery of the Sudan* (Berkeley and Los Angeles: University of California Press, 2003).

33. Owen White, *Children of the French Empire: Miscegenation and Colonial Society in French West Africa, 1895–1960* (Oxford: Oxford University Press, 1999); Susan G. Miller, "Gender and the Poetics of Emancipation: *The Alliance Israélite Universelle* in Northern Morocco, 1890–1912," in *Mission Civilisatrice, Coloniale, Culturelle: France, the French and the Arabs*, ed. L. Carl Brown and Matthew Gordon (Beirut: AUB Press, 1996), 229–52; and Julia Clancy-Smith, "The Colonial Gaze" in Brown and Gordon, *Mission Civilisatrice, Coloniale, Culturelle*, 201–28.

34. M. E. Yapp, "Two British Historians of Persia," in *Historians of the Middle East*, ed. Bernard Lewis and P. M. Holt (Oxford: Oxford University Press, 1962), 343–56.

35. Ibid., 349–50.

36. Edmund Burke III, "A Comparative View of French Native Policy in Morocco and Syria, 1912–1925," *Middle Eastern Studies* 9 (May 1973): 175–86; and Kenneth J. Perkins, *Port Sudan: The Evolution of a Colonial City* (Boulder, CO: Westview Press, 1993).

37. Timothy Mitchell, *Colonising Egypt* (Berkeley and Los Angeles: University of California Press, 1988), ix.

38. Robert Ilbert, *Alexandrie, 1830–1930: Histoire d'une communauté citadine*, 2 vols. (Le Caire: Institut Français d'archéologie orientale, 1996); and Michael J. Reimer, *Colonial Bridgehead: Government and Society in Alexandria, 1807–1882* (Cairo: American University in Cairo Press, 1997).

39. Samir Saul, *La France et l'Égypte de 1882 à 1914: Intérêts économiques et implications politiques* (Paris: Comité pour L'Histoire Économique et Financière de la France, 1997), vx.

40. Hubert Bonin, *Un Outre-Mer Bancaire Méditerranéen: Histoire du Crédit Foncier d'Algérie et de Tunisie (1880–1997)* (Paris: Publications de la Société Française d'Histoire d'Outre-Mer, 2004).

41. Donald M. Reid, *Whose Pharaohs? Archaeology, Museums, and Egyptian*

National Identity from Napoleon to World War I (Berkeley and Los Angeles: University of California Press, 2002); and Reid, *Cairo University and the Making of Modern Egypt* (Cambridge: Cambridge University Press, 1990).

42. Amira el-Azhary Sonbol, *The Creation of a Medical Profession in Egypt, 1800–1922* (New York: Syracuse University Press, 1991), in addition to her numerous other studies.

43. Kenneth M. Cuno, *The Pasha's Peasants: Land, Society, and Economy in Lower Egypt, 1740–1858* (Cambridge: Cambridge University Press, 1992); Juan Cole, *Colonialism and Revolution in the Middle East* (Princeton, NJ: Princeton University Press, 1993); Khaled Fahmy, *All the Pasha's Men: Mehmed Ali, His Army and the Founding of Modern Egypt* (Cambridge: Cambridge University Press, 1997); and Fahmy, "Women, Medicine, and Power in Nineteenth-Century Egypt," in *Remaking Women: Feminism and Modernity in the Middle East*, ed. Lila Abu-Lughod (Princeton, NJ: Princeton University Press, 1998), 35–72.

44. Judith E. Tucker, *Women in Nineteenth-Century Egypt* (Cambridge: Cambridge University Press, 1985). The subsequent literature is too vast to cite here; Nikki R. Keddie's "Women in the Limelight: Some Recent Books on Middle Eastern Women's History," *International Journal of Middle East Studies* 34 (2002): 553–73, is an excellent survey.

45. Marilyn Booth, *May Her Likes Be Multiplied: Biography and Gender Politics in Egypt* (Berkeley and Los Angeles: University of California Press, 2002).

46. For example, see the work by Israel Gershoni and James P. Jankowski, *Redefining the Egyptian Nation, 1930–1945* (Cambridge: Cambridge University Press, 1995).

47. See Lisa Pollard, *Nurturing the Nation: The Family Politics of Modernizing, Colonizing, and Liberating Egypt, 1805–1923* (Berkeley and Los Angeles: University of California Press, 2005); Pollard, "The Family Politics of Colonizing and Liberating Egypt, 1882–1919," *Social Politics* 7 (Spring 2000): 47–79, inspired by Lynn Hunt's work on the French Revolution; and Mona Russell, *Creating the New Egyptian Woman: Consumerism, Education, and National Identity, 1863–1922* (New York: Palgrave Macmillan, 2004).

48. Charles-André Julien, *Histoire de l'Algérie contemporaine*, vol. 1, *1830–1871* (Paris: Presses Universitaires de France, 1964); and Charles-Robert Ageron, *Histoire de l'Algérie contemporaine*, vol. 2, *1871–1954* (Paris: Presses Universitaires de France, 1979).

49. A discussion of these issues is found in Julia Clancy-Smith and Alice L. Conklin, "Introduction," in "Writing French Colonial Histories," special issue, *French Historical Studies* 27, no. 3 (Summer 2004): 497–505; see also the review article by Isabelle Grangaud and Christelle Taraud in "Forum des livres: histoire," *L'Annuaire de l'Afrique du Nord* 29 (2000–2001): 585–612, which surveys studies by French

scholars or scholars in French institutions on "le fait colonial." Numerous dissertations are currently under way in French and European universities devoted to the French Empire worldwide.

50. Jacques Berque's work is too extensive to cite here; see the special issue, "Enquêtes dans la bibliographie de Jacques Berque"; and Fanny Colonna, *Instituteurs algériens, 1883–1939* (Paris: Presses de la fondation nationale des sciences politiques, 1975). See also Guy Pervillé, *Les étudiants algériens de l'université française, 1880–1962* (Paris: CNRS, 1984); and Alf Andrew Heggoy, "Colonial Education in Algeria: Assimilation and Reaction," in *Education and the Colonial Experience*, ed. Philip G. Altbach and Gail P. Kelly, 2nd rev. ed. (New York: Advent Books, 1991), 97–116.

51. Burke, "Theorizing," 5.

52. Daniel J. Schroeter, *Merchants of Essaouira: Urban Society and Imperialism in Southwestern Morocco, 1844–1886* (Cambridge: Cambridge University Press, 1988); and Schroeter, *The Sultan's Jews: Morocco and the Sephardi World* (Stanford, CA: Stanford University Press, 2002).

53. Allan Christelow, *Muslim Law Courts and the French Colonial State in Algeria* (Princeton, NJ: Princeton University Press, 1985).

54. Isabelle Merle, *Expériences coloniales: La Nouvelle Calédonie (1853–1920)* (Paris: Belin, 1995).

55. Emanuel Sivan, "Colonialism and Popular Culture in Algeria," *Journal of Contemporary History* 14 (1979): 21–53.

56. David Prochaska, *Making Algeria French: Colonialism in Bône, 1870–1920* (Cambridge: Cambridge University Press, 1990), as well as his numerous articles.

57. Dalenda Larguèche and Abdelhamid Larguèche, *Marginales en terre d'Islam* (Tunis: Centre de Publication Universitaire, 1992). Anne-Marie Planel has brilliantly reconstructed the microhistories of expatriate European, particularly French, communities in precolonial North Africa in "De La Nation à la Colonie: La Communauté Française de Tunisie au XIXème siècle d'aprés les archives civiles et notariées du consulat général de France à Tunis," 3 vols. (Doctorat d'état, Ecole des Hautes Etudes en Sciences Sociales, Paris, 2000). Odile Moreau, "Les ressources scientifiques de l'Occident au service de la modernisation de l'armée Ottomane (fin XIXe début XXe siècle)," *Revue des mondes musulmans et de la Méditerranée* 101–2 (2003): 51–67; and Karima Direche-Slimani, *Chrétiens de Kabylie, 1873–1954: Une action missionaire dans l'Algérie coloniale* (Paris: Editions Bouchene, 2004).

58. Edmund Burke III, *Struggle and Survival in the Modern Middle East* (Berkeley and Los Angeles: University of California Press, 1993); and Fanny Colonna and Zakya Daoud, eds., *Etre Marginal au Maghreb* (Paris: Edisud, 1993).

59. Patricia Lorcin, *Imperial Identities: Stereotyping, Prejudice and Race in Colonial Algeria* (London: I. B. Tauris, 1995); see also Julia Clancy-Smith, "Algeria as *mère-*

patrie: Algerian 'Expatriates' in Tunisia, 1850–1914" in *Identity, Memory and Nostalgia: France and Algeria, 1800–2000*, ed. Patricia Lorcin (New York: Syracuse University Press, 2006).

60. Eric Jennings, "From Indochine to Indochic: The Lang Bian/Dalat Palace Hotel and French Colonial Leisure, Power, and Culture," *Modern Asian Studies* 37, no. 1 (February 2003): 159–94.

61. Giulia Barrera, "Sex, Citizenship and the State: The Construction of the Public and Private Spheres in Colonial Eritrea," in *Gender, Family and Sexuality: The Private Sphere in Italy, 1860–1945*, ed. Perry Willson (London: Palgrave, 2004), 157–72. On Italian scholarship in women and gender history, see Julia Clancy-Smith, "Women's History: Where We Are" [in Italian], *Genesis* (Roma), vol. 11, no. 2 (2003).

62. Julia Clancy-Smith, "The Shaykh and His Daughter: Coping in Colonial Algeria," in Burke, *Struggle and Survival*, 145–63; Clancy-Smith, "The House of Zainab: Female Authority and Saintly Succession in Colonial Algeria," in *Women in Middle Eastern History: Shifting Boundaries in Sex and Gender*, ed. Nikki R. Keddie and Beth Baron (New Haven, CT: Yale University Press, 1992), 254–74; and Clancy-Smith, "The 'Passionate Nomad' Reconsidered: A European Woman in *L'Algérie Française*," in Chaudhuri and Strobel, *Western Women and Imperialism*, 61–78.

63. Elizabeth Thompson, *Colonial Citizens: Republican Rights, Paternal Privilege, and Gender in French Syria and Lebanon* (New York: Columbia University Press, 2000).

64. To date, Tunisian historians at the faculty of La Manouba campus, Université de Tunis I, have produced the most comprehensive historical studies in North African women's history. However, much of it addresses either the precolonial era, mainly the late Ottoman/Husaynid periods, or the late colonial and nationalist eras, with scant attention to colonialism per se; Dalenda Larguèche, ed., *Histoire des femmes au Maghreb: Culture matérielle et vie quotidienne* (Tunis: Centre de Publication Universitaire, 2000). The women's oral history project, undertaken by the Centre de Recherche, de Documentation et d'Information sur la Femme in Tunis, represents an important effort at recuperation; see Habib Kazdaghli, ed., *Nisa' wa dhakira/ Mémoire de femmes: Tunisiennes dans la vie publique, 1920–1960* (Tunis: Edition Média Com, 1993).

65. Edouard Adolphe Duchesne, *De la prostitution dans la ville d'Alger depuis la conquête* (Paris: J. B. Baillière, 1853); a discussion of Duchesne's study is found in Julia Clancy-Smith, "Islam, Gender, and the Identities in the Making of French Algeria, 1830–1962," in Clancy-Smith and Gouda, *Domesticating the Empire*, 154–74.

66. Jacques Berque, *Le Maghrib entre deux guerres* (Paris: Editions du Seuil, 1962); Jean-Paul Charnay, *La Vie Musulmane en Algérie d'après la jurisprudence de la première moitié du XXe siècle* (Paris: Presses Universitaires de France, 1965); and

Germaine Tillion, *Le harem et les cousins* (Paris: Seuil, 1966), among her many other works.

67. Malek Alloula, *The Colonial Harem*, trans. Myrna Godzich and Wlad Godzich (Manchester: Manchester University Press, 1986); and Christelle Taraud, *La prostitution coloniale: Algérie, Tunisie, Maroc (1830–1962)* (Paris: Payot, 2003).

68. Christa Knellwolf, "The History of Feminist Criticism," in *The Cambridge History of Literary Criticism*, vol. 9, *Twentieth Century Historical, Philosophical and Psychological Perspectives*, 193–205.

69. Henri Lefebvre, *The Production of Space*, trans. Donald Nicolson-Smith (Oxford: Blackwell, 1991); Gwendolyn Wright, *The Politics of Design in French Colonial Urbanism* (Chicago: University of Chicago Press, 1991); Zeynep Çelik, *Urban Forms and Colonial Confrontations: Algiers Under French Rule* (Berkeley and Los Angeles: University of California Press, 1997); Nabila Oulebsir, *Les usages du patrimoine: Monuments, musées et politique colonial en Algérie, 1830–1930* (Paris: Maison des Sciences de l'homme, 2004); and Jean-Louis Cohen, Nabila Oulebsir, Youcef Kanoun, and Dominique Delaunay, *Alger: Paysage urbain et architectures, 1800–2000* (Paris: Imprimeur, 2003). See also Abdelhamid Larguèche, "The City and the Sea: Evolving Forms of Mediterranean Cosmopolitanism in Tunis, c. 1700–1881," in *North Africa, Islam and the Mediterranean World from the Almoravids to the Algerian War*, ed. Julia Clancy-Smith (London: Frank Cass, 2001); Clancy-Smith, "Gender in the City: the Medina of Tunis, 1850–1881," in *Africa's Urban Past*, ed. David Anderson and Richard Rathbone (Oxford: Currey, 2000), 189–204; and Clancy-Smith, "The Peopling of Algiers: Exoticism, Erasures, and Absence, c. 1830–1900," in *Les murs d'Alger/The Walls of Algiers*, ed. Zeynep Çelik (Los Angeles: Getty Research Institute Press, 2006), in which I argue that immigration to Algiers after 1830 poses visual and textual problems revolving around presence and absence. While indigenous Algerians, above all women, came to be depicted amply in image and text, the growing Mediterranean presence composed mainly of subsistence migrants was signaled by a striking visual absence.

70. Sulayman al-Jadhi, *Al-fawa'id al-jamma* [Abundant Moral Lessons] (Tunis, ca. 1930).

71. On the porous nature of social boundaries in colonial Tunisia, see Julia Clancy-Smith, "Educating the Muslim Woman in Colonial North Africa," in *Essays in Middle Eastern History in Honor of Nikki Keddie*, ed. Beth Baron and Rudi Matthe (Los Angeles: Mazda, 2000), 99–118.

72. Mounira M. Charrad, *States and Women's Rights: The Making of Postcolonial Tunisia, Algeria, and Morocco* (Berkeley and Los Angeles: University of California Press, 2001).

73. Julia Clancy-Smith, "L'École Rue du Pacha à Tunis: L'Education de la femme

arabe et 'la plus grande France' (1900–1914)," in *Clio: Histoire, Femmes et Société* 12 (Decembre 2000): 33–55.

74. Julia Clancy-Smith, "Women, Gender and Migration along a Mediterranean Frontier: Pre-colonial Tunisia, c. 1815–c. 1870," *Gender and History*, vol. 17, no. 1 (April 2005): 62–92; and œ Clancy-Smith, "The Maghrib and the Mediterranean World in the 19th Century," in *The Maghrib in Question*, ed. Kenneth J. Perkins and Michel Le Gall (Austin: University of Texas Press, 1997), 222–49.

75. Geoffrey A. Oddie, "'Orientalism' and British Protestant Missionary Constructions of India in the Nineteenth Century," *South Asia* 17, no. 2 (1994): 27–42; and Pier M. Larson, "'Capacities and Modes of Thinking': Intellectual Engagements and Subaltern Hegemony in the Early History of Malagasy Christianity," *American Historical Review* 102, no. 4 (October 1997): 969–1002; quotes from 969–70.

76. *Histoire Communautaire, Histoire Plurielle: La Communauté juive de Tunisie*, Actes du colloque de Tunis organisé les 25–26–27 Février à la Faculté de la Manouba (Tunis: Centre de Publication Universitaire, 1999).

4

Reading Genocide

Turkish Historiography on the Armenian Deportations and Massacres of 1915

FATMA MÜGE GÖÇEK

The current analyses of the formation and reproduction of the category of the "other" based on gender and race theories, as well as studies on prejudice grounded in critical theory, provide significant theoretical insights into the study of the Armenian relocations and deaths in 1915. To demonstrate this, the present essay first undertakes a sociological reading of Turkish historiography on the Armenian relocations and massacres of 1915. It then reviews Turkish historiography on the topic both chronologically and by contextualizing the existing literature in the tension between past and contemporary political circumstances. I argue that the narratives of the Armenian massacres can be analyzed within three categories: the Ottoman investigative narrative, the Republican defensive narrative, and the postnationalist critical narrative. The article concludes by suggesting a new periodization of Turkish history to encourage Turkish recognition of the Armenian tragedy that occurred in the Ottoman Empire in 1915.

THE SOCIAL CONSTRUCTION OF KNOWLEDGE AND THE SCHOLAR'S STANDPOINT

Gender theory derives from the main premise that the personal is political and, therefore, has to be included in the study of the political that predominates the public sphere. Failure to do so undermines gender analysis because women's experiences in particular are often related to the personal sphere, beyond the purview of scholarly analysis, and the public sphere in turn becomes dominated by research that privileges men's experiences. These

nequal power relations, which affect the knowledge constructed in the public sphere to the detriment of women, can be eradicated only by tracing their
roots through analysis of the private sphere. Only then will gender cease to
be "the other" in scholarly analysis.

Yet such a move necessitates a reexamination of the scholars who create
and reproduce knowledge in the scientific community. These scholars need
to be aware, and critical, of how and why they formulate their research questions, and how these formulations, in turn, affect their results. Dorothy Smith,
in her seminal work on the subject, states that unequal power relations in
the construction of public knowledge are also hidden in the "standpoint"
of scholars, who often employ scientific objectivity to distance themselves
from their subject matter and use the pronoun "we" to obfuscate the privileges their public position entails. It is further conjectured that these embedded privileges and power relations are revealed only when scholars explicitly
discuss their own standpoints, disclosing the assumptions they make about
their scholarship and their interpretations of subject matter.[1]

Smith's theoretical perspective, together with that of Patricia Hill Collins,
is based on the critical approach to knowledge developed by the Frankfurt School. This school gained prominence after World War II, with the
explicit intent to understand the Holocaust. The early works of scholars of
this school, such as Theodore Adorno and Max Horkheimer, discussed the
formation of the authoritarian personality that obeyed Nazi orders to
destroy Jews en masse. How was it possible, they asked, to get humans to
obey orders for human destruction in the twentieth century, an age of scientific and human progress, in the heartlands of Europe, which claimed to
spearhead the enlightened Western civilization? It is in seeking an answer
to this question that they identified a dark side of science and the modern
state, namely, that science and the state have power, authority, and legitimacy in the contemporary world. They contended that racist theories that
relegated the Jews to a subhuman category were not adequately questioned
and criticized because of the assumed objectivity and value-neutrality of
science—the implications embedded in these racist theories were thus overlooked and legitimated in the name of science. The modern state was likewise presumed to have acted for the progress of all its citizens and in turn
employed science in doing so—in this instance as well, the interests of the
nation-state, or, specifically, the ideological agendas of the political leaders, were not adequately problematized.[2]

After the Frankfurt School revealed the value-ladenness of scientific
knowledge, and the employment of science to legitimate particular human

interests to the detriment of humanity, it proposed instead a vigilant "critical" approach that questioned all knowledge presented as "scientific facts."
Works by scholars such as Jürgen Habermas further developed this approach
as they revealed the human interests hidden in the construction of public
knowledge; they argued in turn that a truly democratic society where everyone participated on equal terms could be possible only if the privileged
position some assumed over others, through their access to knowledge legitimated by science, could be overcome.[3]

Smith and Collins employed the critical approach to reveal and surmount
the effect of unequal gender and race relations in shaping contemporary
social-scientific discussions of women's position in society. They did so in
order to legitimize women's own standpoint, which was often banished to
the private sphere and marginalized as being personal, subjective, and therefore unscientific. Smith and Collins argued that a gender-neutral analysis
of society could be undertaken only if the personal and the subjective standpoints of women were introduced into social-scientific research, so as to
bear as much weight in the subsequent explanation of human action as existing public knowledge legitimated by scientific practice. This epistemological intervention led them to reveal their own standpoint as scholars and
demonstrate how it had shaped their analyses, and it is in this context that
their insights are used here.[4]

I reveal my particular standpoint as a scholar in approaching the study
of the tragedy that befell the Armenians in the Ottoman Empire in the late
nineteenth and early twentieth centuries. Likewise, the discussion of Turkish historiography presented below brings in vantage points of the scholars who work on this topic. As is evident to all of them, what happened to
the Armenians toward the end of the Ottoman Empire is highly politicized.
Even the way my colleague Ronald Grigor Suny and I initially apportioned
the review of the literature on the topic into "Armenian" and "Turkish" historiographies itself shows a divide; this seemingly simple heuristic divide
privileges some sources and knowledge over others.[5] Notably, linguistic
barriers prevented each of us from using, in my case, Armenian, and in his,
Turkish, sources. Even though we both had access to works in the current
scientific lingua franca, I consciously restricted myself to those works in
English that reflected the Turkish discourse, and this strategy, by definition,
precluded almost, if not all, the works by Armenian scholars.

The Armenian tragedy is a subject I knowingly avoided for a long time,
in both my academic career and personal life, because of its highly politicized nature. The limitations of the official Turkish view are painfully obvi-

ous in the many unofficial social sanctions in contemporary Turkish society that prevent Turkish-Armenian citizens and other minorities from participating in society on equal terms with Turkish Muslims. Likewise, the limitations of the dominant Armenian view of the Armenian diaspora have been manifest at panels of the Middle Eastern Studies Association over the past twenty years; many scholars there either stated openly or seemed to imply that there was an inherently violent, destructive streak in all Turks, regardless of time and space, that had caused the tragedies at the beginning of the twentieth century and, by implication, would bring about their occurrence even today unless constant and vigilant guard was kept.

I approach the analysis of Turkish historiography on the Armenian deaths and population transfers of 1915 informed by my previous research on the Ottoman Empire. Because of my scholarly interest in the causes of Turkey's contemporary problems, I began my studies in historical sociology and by examining Ottoman population transfers (*sürgün*) between the fourteenth and seventeenth centuries.[6] Two important insights emerged from that study: first, it was impossible to claim in the contemporary context who was a real Turk, since there had been so much intermixing of populations; second, from the advent of their state and throughout its history, the Ottomans frequently and efficiently transferred populations. The Ottoman state undertook these transfers to rejuvenate (the Ottoman term is *şenlendirmek*) newly conquered territories. It was in this context that the Turcoman nomads of Anatolia were transferred to the Balkans, and later villagers and artisans were moved from the Balkans and Egypt to Constantinople. This type of transfer also increased Ottoman state control over the territories from which these groups had been moved. Punitive transfers of religious groups, errant governors and their households, and non-Muslim minorities who happened to reside along Ottoman campaign routes—and, therefore, posed a threat to the security and provisioning of the Ottoman army—occurred regularly.

My subsequent work focused on the very understudied eighteenth-century Ottoman Empire to identify the structural origins of its eventual demise, tracing the nineteenth-century transformation of the Ottoman state from the eighteenth century, and narrating the Ottoman demise not through Western sources alone but also through Ottoman sources, and especially through the abundant archival material. It was the Ottoman inheritance registers that afforded a clear view of the process of Ottoman Westernization throughout the eighteenth century in general and the use of Western goods by Ottoman rulers and subjects in particular. These registers also included the inheritance registers of Ottoman minorities, namely, *dhimmi*s, who registered their legacies in the Islamic courts alongside those of Muslims. These records revealed that the most significant social group in adopting Western goods, ideas, and institutions was not, as I had originally hypothesized, rulers but, rather, the subjects of the empire, a social group including Ottoman minorities, which I termed the Ottoman "bourgeoisie."[7]

Yet why had this social group not been able to transform, Westernize, and modernize the Ottoman Empire? Unlike the western European bourgeoisie, who spearheaded such a transformation in Europe, the Ottoman bourgeoisie had been bifurcated along religious lines, a divide the empire had not been able to overcome in spite of its many, initially well-intentioned, attempts. Religious minorities, principally Ottoman Greeks, Jews, and Armenians, attained significant administrative positions, but this did not occur at all levels. While these minorities were indeed recruited into newly established Western-style educational institutions, non-Muslim graduates of these schools, who staffed most of the mid-level administrative positions throughout the empire, were not promoted at the same rate as Muslims, because they were socially disadvantaged and perceived to be untrustworthy. It was the inability of the Ottoman state to overcome the "social disadvantage" deeply embedded in the religious divide that formed the foundation stone of the empire leading, I argued, both to its demise and to the eventual tragic elimination of the non-Muslim Ottoman bourgeoisie. Even though religious minorities were indeed given political and economic privileges in the Ottoman Empire, they led separate social lives because non-Muslims could not marry into, form families with, or inherit from Muslims; they were thus unable to form the significant social networks that would have enabled them to participate fully in the Ottoman social system. The same minorities were also forbidden to bear arms (until the twentieth century) and had to pay a special poll tax (*cizye*) to compensate the state for the protection it offered them. Sumptuary laws required them to wear special clothes, publicly separating them from the Muslims. Even though they had access to the Islamic courts, in addition to their own communal courts, the Islamic legal system based on religious law (*şeriat*) did not recognize them as equal to Muslims and thereby disadvantaged them legally.

The emergent Ottoman social system was thus based on and legitimized by Islam. Minorities were permitted to participate in society in a limited fashion, according to terms set by the ruling Muslim group. For many centuries while the rest of the world was engaged in religious wars to destroy one another, this system was an enlightened one, yet one based on a premise of social inequality that reproduced itself to ossify over time. This inequality was accepted as "natural" because there were no known alternatives until the eighteenth century. The social transformation in that century, set in motion especially by the French Revolution, radically redefined the relationship between people and society through a social contract that identified the "rights of man" spiritually in relation to God and politically in relation to a particular state.

The social impact of this transformation on the Ottoman Empire led both Muslims and minorities to reevaluate their positions within Ottoman society. Muslims focused more on the challenge of sharing the political power concentrated in the sultan and were less interested in questioning their dominant social position as Muslims within the society at large, a position they had long accepted as a natural one. They also assumed that their political aspirations did not significantly differ from those of the non-Muslims of the empire. The Ottoman minorities, who had historically accepted their location in Ottoman society for the lack of a better, politically viable option, became increasingly aware of their unequal standing and started to search for ways to alleviate this inequality. I have argued that the demise of the empire occurred because of the inability of the Ottoman state to overcome the initial religious divide that, through time, generated clear social and political separations in Ottoman society. In the process of demise, the non-Muslim bourgeoisie was dissolved mostly through direct or indirect pressure, even force of the state, while the Ottoman Muslim bourgeoisie formed under state protection at the expense, and often based on the resources, of its non-Muslim counterpart. Eventually this Ottoman Muslim bourgeoisie was transformed into the national Turkish bourgeoisie, with state support that continues until today.

Subsequent research comparing Greek, Armenian, Arab, and Turkish nationalisms during the demise of the empire clarified the reasons for the success of some nationalisms and the failure of others. In the case of Armenian nationalism, the precedent of the Greek success in 1832 sharpened the resistance of the Ottoman state to the demands of the Armenians; the Ottoman defeat in the subsequent Balkan Wars (1911–13) further radicalized this resistance. At the same time, the Ottoman elites who manned the state were also transformed, becoming dominated by "Young Turk" officers and, later, members of the Committee of Union and Progress (CUP), who were educated in Western-style schools and formed an allegiance not to the sultan but to the Ottoman state, a state increasingly defined as "Turkish." The emergent Turkish nationalism supported by the Ottoman state precluded the aims of Armenian nationalism in Anatolia.[8]

Finally, more recent work on gender, race theory, and nationalism has continuously alerted me to the power inequalities that developed in social analysis. These inequalities do not reveal themselves with respect only to the topic under study, but traverse multiple levels that range from the stand-point of the researcher, and the construction of the research question, to the sources employed in its analysis, the assumptions made in the inter-pretation of findings, and the effect of contemporary concerns on this interpretation.

THE HIDDEN SOCIAL ASSUMPTIONS IN THE USE OF TERMINOLOGY

Informed once again by critical theory, postmodern theory in general and specifically postcolonial theory identify how a particular body of knowl-edge, in their cases particular social, often written, texts, contain embed-ded power relations. In analyzing such texts, scholars who employ these frameworks engage in a critical reading with the intent to identify the hid-den assumptions of unequal power relations. Gayatri Spivak and Ranajit Guha, Partha Chatterjee, and others have applied these insights in analyz-ing British colonial documents in India, thus forming the school of "sub-altern studies," named after the work of Antonio Gramsci. Their works engage the research question of why India has not been able to overcome British hegemony, even after the elimination of colonial rule and the estab-lishment of an Indian nation-state. The roots of domination, they argue, extend deep into language and meaning structures that have been implanted in Indian society. In order to overcome the existing epistemological hege-mony, they suggest scholarly analyses of both the past and the present in terms of these roots.[9]

When the terminology employed in the debates on the Armenian tragedies is analyzed within this framework, the conflict over the meanings embedded in the debates becomes clear. My work addresses "Turkish" his-toriography on the subject. Take, for example, the use of the terms *genocide* and *massacre*. If I had approached the subject matter from the viewpoint of the official Turkish thesis, I would have needed to indicate that I objected to the acceptance of the genocidal nature of the massacres by employing the term *genocide* in quotations, or by using the term *population transfers*. By doing so, I would have thus clearly signaled my political stand on the

topic. I think this example not only demonstrates how the choice of particular terms announces a scholar's standpoint, but it also indicates how highly
this subfield is politicized.

What does this political divide between "Turkish" and "Armenian" historiography comprise? From the perspective of my focus on Turkish historiography, the more appropriate question to ask is who speaks for "the
Turks," who defines what comprised "the Armenian experience" in the Ottoman Empire during the late nineteenth and early twentieth centuries, and
who controls its interpretation. Most often, these questions immediately
evoke the predominant Republican narrative, one promoted and sustained
by the modern Turkish nation-state and its various institutions. This
narrative considers the Turkish state and Turkish society to be one and
the same—a consideration many Armenian scholars also accept without
question—and thereby assumes that it speaks on behalf of all Turks. The
researchers who work within this narrative are a special group, often including current or former state officials who consider themselves loyal citizens
of the Turkish nation-state and who, as true citizens, justify, document, and
prove the official state interpretation of events concerning the Ottoman
Armenians before, during, and since 1915.

As I indicated above, the main assumption behind their stand is that the
official view of the state is one and the same with that of the nation. Therefore, their scholarship does not evaluate historical documentation in an
attempt to question what happened, but instead focuses on proving, through
historical documents, that what the official state narrative claims happened
is indeed what happened. Their use of historical material is selective and
skewed, since it favors and highlights only those sources that are in agreement with the official interpretation while overlooking and thus silencing
those that are not. While a graduate student, I received a letter from one
Turkish ministry inviting me to undertake research in the Ottoman archives
"to challenge the Armenian claims and prove instead the Turkish thesis." I
of course threw away the letter, because it did not fall within the ethical framework of what I define as "scientific" scholarship, that is, the formulation of
a research question, rather than a predetermined answer, before engaging
in archival work, and the interpretation of findings not in accordance with
a predetermined framework but, rather, within the most extensive theoretical
and empirical context possible.

Scholarship in Turkey and at Turkish state universities is supposed to
operate according to these same scientific principles, that is, scholarly independence in the formulation, analysis, and discussion of research on social

topics. Yet the fact that most scholars in state universities are by definition state employees often leads to sanctions against them by the state if their views and interpretations contradict those of the official state narrative on the topic. In some cases scholars have even been dismissed from their posts. This situation makes scholarly analysis of social topics extremely difficult in Turkey. There are many scholars at Turkish universities who, as a consequence of their own research, disagree with the official narrative regarding what happened to the Armenians and ridicule the official state view in private, yet they are unable to express these views in public. This situation clearly demonstrates the strength of the Turkish nation-state, which is able to coax all its citizens into supporting tacitly an imagined interpretation of the Armenian issue; nationalism enforced by the state prevails on citizens not to challenge publicly the state contention as to what happened. Those few who disagree, often outside of the state-university system, run the risk of being called traitors to the nation and have to bear both insinuations about their mixed blood and tainted character, and implications that they are in the pay of one foreign country or another. Their arguments are therefore often dismissed, not on the grounds of scholarship but of character.

To counter these destructive boundaries of Turkish nationalism, which preclude scholarly analysis, it is imperative to focus on and help further to develop the alternate narrative burgeoning outside the boundaries controlled by the Turkish nation-state. It is no accident that most of the representatives of the alternate narrative are faculty members either at one of the new private universities in Turkey, which are to a certain degree beyond state control, or at universities outside Turkey. It is to be hoped that this alternate narrative will, in time, challenge and bring down the walls erected by the official state narrative. In the meantime, it is a necessary, but not sufficient, undertaking to promote the emergence of true scholarship on the Armenian issue.

True scholarship on the events of 1915 will emerge only when separate historiographies no longer exist, when scholars shed their identities as members of a particular nation-state, who unquestioningly support the master state narrative, and instead conduct research first and foremost as scholars. This does not mean, of course, that scholars by definition engage in objective, value-free research. Yet, they can move closer to this ideal, if, as race and gender theories recommend, they articulate their personal standpoints on the issue. These theories also stress that there can be meaningful change only when scholars with a painful personal connection to the issue are joined by others unconnected to it, whose work can therefore not be delegitimized as easily by political powers. An entirely new approach to the topic becomes possible when scholars who approach the issue as a matter of human principle join those who specialize in the topic because of their life experiences.

Let me now describe the rather unconventional approach I take, in accordance with the parameters outlined above. Here, Turkish historiography on the Armenian tragedy does not comprise only those who explicitly claim ownership of the "Turkish" position, that is, those who expound the official thesis of the Turkish Republic. Instead, it includes a multiplicity of works that pertain to the period before the emergence of the Turkish Republic, as well as other "unofficial" studies that concern the periods during and after the emergence of the same republic. The historiography therefore divides into pre-Republican (cum Ottoman), Republican, and postnationalist phases. Even though the works discussed often relate directly to the Armenian deaths in 1915, they also include others that touch on the subject only indirectly. Some of the works describing the pre-Republican period were actually published by the Republic in defense of its thesis; some in the postnationalist period contain literary work. I would argue that even though these works do not specifically focus on the events of 1915, they nevertheless provide significant clues about how and why the official narrative on 1915 emerged. In the analysis of all these works, I methodologically approach the standard Turkish texts and archival sources on the Armenian genocide within a critical framework. This is done in order to discover new meanings through not only what is said but also what is not; I introduce new texts to comment on either what is said or what should have been said instead. Such critical reading amplifies the silences, assumptions, and particular interpretations contained in the master narrative; it also opens up new space for the other, Ottoman and postnationalist, narratives.

Turkish historiography on the Armenians can be viewed within three historical periods, each with its own distinct narrative. The first, the *Ottoman Investigative Narrative*, is based on contemporaneous accounts pertaining to the Ottoman Armenians and the Armenian deaths of 1915, published either by the Turkish state or by opposing political groups. The second is the *Republican Defensive Narrative*, which emerges from works written with the intent to justify, document, and prove the nationalist master narrative of the Turkish state. It explicitly denies the allegation that an Armenian genocide occurred in 1915 and is often published or kept in circulation by the Turkish state. The third, the *Postnationalist Critical Narrative*, is found in works that are directly or indirectly critical of the nationalist master narrative but that do not, in most cases, focus specifically on the Armenian deaths of 1915. Their concern is much more with the silences in contemporary Turkish society pertaining to Turkish history and, related to this, Turkish society's ethnic composition. I think that reading genocide within this framework can create a new space for a different Turkish interpretation of the Armenian deaths of 1915.

THE OTTOMAN INVESTIGATIVE NARRATIVE ON READING GENOCIDE

My reading of the works written during the Ottoman period on the Armenian relocations and deaths reveals two characteristics that distinguish the Ottoman investigative narrative from the others. First, since all of these works were written around the time of the events of 1915, they do not question the occurrence of the Armenian "massacres" (*genocide* was not a term then employed), but focus instead on asking what happened and why. Later, as the temporal distance between the events of 1915 and the scholarship increased, the events become distant memories; consequently, the narratives of both the Republican and postnationalist periods focus not on the events themselves but, rather, on the meanings these events acquired.[10]

Second, the Ottoman investigative narrative reveals a very strong tension between two worldviews. Some of the authors maintain a more traditional Ottoman imperial view and regard the existing structure of empire as just and the position of the Armenian subjects within it reformable; they also blame the events on both the Armenian subjects and the Muslim officials who deviated from Ottoman norms under pressure from European powers. Other authors, however, display a more "protonational" state view and perceive the existing structure of the empire as inadequate and the position of the Armenian subjects within it problematic; while they are not quite clear about what to do about these inadequacies and problems, they give priority to the preservation of the state and its Muslims over all other concerns.

The central tension in the Ottoman investigative narrative regarding the Armenian deaths and massacres in 1915 is over the attribution of responsibility for the crimes. Not only did the Ottoman state acknowledge what happened, but it also published the proceedings of the military tribunal that tried some of the perpetrators. Yet the memoirs of Ottoman officials reveal that the tendency to shrink from responsibility for the crimes against the Armenians increased with the surge of protonationalist sentiments. The tension over responsibility mounted especially after World War I, with the defeat of the Ottoman Empire; the Treaty of Sèvres, signed between the Allied powers and the empire, put forward the Armenian tragedy as a reason not only to take away Ottoman lands where there were significant minorities but also to establish the conditions for an Armenian homeland. Works on the subsequent transition from the Ottoman Empire to the Turkish state illustrate how responsibility for the crimes gradually shifted from the perpetrators to the victims. Significant in this shift is the strong connection between the CUP, which justified the Armenian tragedy as an unfortunate consequence of its attempts to protect the Ottoman state, and the nationalist movement, which gradually adopted this Unionist stand as its own.

This connection between Ottoman and Turkish rule has never been extensively documented and studied because Republican rhetoric has dismissed, and still dismisses, any connection to the CUP, which was responsible for losing the empire. Yet the works I analyzed in this category clearly demonstrate the strength of the connection between the Republic and the CUP in terms of transfer of wealth, ideology, and manpower. Some of the accused perpetrators of the Armenian massacres escaped to Anatolia to evade Allied attempts to bring them to justice; those perpetrators who evaded Allied investigation, as well as silent participants in the massacres, simply stayed put and threw in their fortunes with the burgeoning nationalist movement. Once the oppositional struggle in Anatolia commenced and assumed the form of an independence movement that would eventually triumph in establishing the Turkish nation-state, the former perpetrators, some of whom occupied significant positions in the nationalist struggle and became patriotic citizens of the new state, could no longer be accused, because there was no political entity left to accuse them: the Allied powers had retreated, the reigning sultan had been deposed, and the empire was now defunct.

The new nation-state and its leader, Mustafa Kemal, could not take a stand against the former perpetrators, who became comrades in the struggle, because they were needed to sustain the new nation-state. Aware that he needed to have his country recognized by the Western powers, who still took issue with what happened during the Unionist leadership, and anxious to take credit for the establishment of a nation-state that was actually built with resources provided by the CUP, Mustafa Kemal took a public stand against the Unionists, denied his Unionist credentials, liquidated those Unionists who challenged his authority, and claimed his passage to Anatolia on May 19, 1919, was the starting point of the War of Independence that eventually led to the establishment of the Turkish nation-state, with the Treaty of Lausanne.

The treaties of Sèvres and Lausanne form important landmarks in the discussion of the Armenian deaths and massacres of 1915, because the first acknowledges and the second rejects them. Accusations about the Armenian massacres encouraged the inclusion in the Treaty of Sèvres of provisions for an Armenian homeland in Anatolia. While, for Armenians, the treaty promised them a political entity, a country, they could call their own, Muslim Turks viewed it as a death sentence guaranteeing their disappearance as a political entity. Armenians in Anatolia and the diaspora struggled and cooperated with the Allied powers to attain their promised homeland, and they tried to bring to justice those who had perpetrated the massacres. The Muslims of Anatolia, who now defined themselves with the new, formerly radical identity that had not been embraced by the Ottomans, because of its exclusion and limited scope, namely, that of "a Turk," fought against the Allied powers and the Armenians who were allied with them.

The Turkish War of Independence, fought between the Muslim Turks and the Armenians, ended with the victory of the Muslim Turks. Yet this victory was predicated on the atrocious injustices the Unionists had committed against the Armenians in Anatolia in the name of a protonational ideal. First, they had physically removed the Armenians from their homeland and eventually settled in their stead the Turkish Muslim refugees fleeing the Balkans and Russia, thereby irreversibly altering the population composition of Anatolia. Second, they decimated the Armenian population through the massacres, and traumatized and dispersed them in a manner that made it extremely difficult for Armenians to reunite as a coherent political entity. And finally, the Unionists capitalized on the property and goods left behind by dead or relocated Armenians, using these resources to help mobilize and finance an army and populace in support of the nationalist cause.

After the Unionist victory in the subsequent War of Independence, they began to justify their actions against the Armenians as a tragic but necessary move for the preservation of the Turkish state. Contrary to the terms of the Treaty of Sèvres, which had promised a homeland to the Armenians and political death to the Ottomans, the Treaty of Lausanne, signed by the nationalist Turks, guaranteed the Turks a state and homeland at the expense of the homeland and state that had been promised to the Armenians by the Allied powers in the Treaty of Sèvres. The immediate interests of the Allied powers took precedence over their support of the Armenian homeland, and Armenian strength to establish a presence in Anatolia and to claim their homeland was exhausted. In contrast to the Treaty of Sèvres, the Lausanne treaty brought the Armenians political death.

Thus the treaties of Sèvres and Lausanne offered contradictory solutions for the Armenians and the Turks, and this also comes through in the subsequent narratives the two sides have formulated. The discussion of the Treaty of Sèvres psychologically unnerved the Turkish nation-state and brought back memories of the insecurity and the impending doom of destruction felt before and during the War of Independence. The Treaty of Lausanne, however, became, for Turks, one of birth, celebration, and rejoicing; it recalled the pride and glory they felt as they went to the Europe that had shamed them with its frequent political interventions leading to the ultimate shame—for the first time in their six-century-long history—occupation of the central lands of their empire, where they had long considered themselves to be the dominant people. When the Turks signed the Treaty of Lausanne as victors, they claimed for themselves the national homeland they had imagined had been theirs from the beginning of time.

Yet the Armenians had exactly the opposite experience. The contemplation of the Treaty of Sèvres kindled in the Armenians hope and joy, bringing back memories of when they had almost had a homeland of their own in the lands they had lived on from time immemorial. It took them back to a time when they had flourished financially and intellectually, had reared a new Armenian generation educated with the European ideals of freedom and liberty, and were on the brink of establishing a homeland where they aspired to create a new, advanced civilized nation-state that would have brought back their proud ancient civilization, the cradle of Christianity. The Treaty of Lausanne had the opposite effect on the Armenians, however, as it reminded them of the final destruction of the dreams of that magical homeland where they hoped to bring out the best in their culture and civilization and build for their sons and daughters the society they had so long envisioned. Yet the possibility of such a homeland was categorically denied by the Turks, who not only established a nation-state, such as the Armenians had so long yearned for, but did so in their stead, at their expense, with wealth that was confiscated from them, and with the energy sapped out of the lives of their own children, who were not able to flourish in their dreamed-of homeland, but were instead massacred as they hopelessly marched in columns not toward the rebirth of their nation but, instead, to their deaths.

Both of these narratives contain great sorrow, for they have both been constructed at the expense of those who lost their lives and saw their dreams destroyed. Many scholars have noted how Western imperialism aggravated this suffering on both sides. Yet I would argue that then, as now, the role of

another social actor—nationalism—needs to be emphasized in contextualizing past and present Turkish and Armenian narratives. Nationalism
polarized the Armenians and the Turks and caused them each to challenge
the other's existence. It was also nationalism that instilled in each the idea
of a primordial right to create a homeland filled with compatriots in pursuit of the same dreams, and it was nationalism that decreed that these goals
could be exclusively theirs, accomplished at the expense and exclusion of
the other.

It is morally unproductive to discuss who suffered more, because using
the degree of human suffering to establish rights only increases the tendency
to cause suffering. Yet it is worth noting in this instance that nationalism
caused considerably more physical, social, and psychological suffering to
Armenians than Turks, since the members of the CUP, who espoused an
imagined community of Turks, had the support of state mechanisms to realize their goals and had no qualms about employing them fully against the
Armenians, who, ironically and tragically, were the subjects of the same state.

Let us now turn to the question of why it has been so difficult to sustain
scholarly analyses of the tragic events of 1915. The context of the transition
from the political form of an empire to that of a nation-state has caused
this difficulty, because the scholars who undertake the analysis have themselves been born and raised in nation-states, an experience that colors their
standpoints. If one acknowledges this epistemological limitation and
approaches the period critically, however, it is possible to identify two concurrent narratives: one was formulated by former Ottomans who continued to interpret events that took place around them within the framework
of the empire; the other was formulated by select groups, like some CUP
members, as a new exclusionary nationalist framework. Authors from the
second narrative forcefully shaped the events around them, using every available means in order to create their envisioned homeland. Their vision also
gave them a new sense of empowerment and entitlement, preyed on the
deeply felt, general resentment for non-Muslims, and enabled them to follow their vision with a comparable degree of passion.

From the standpoint of the present, I think it is unfortunate that the latter, nationalist vision prevailed. While both the Armenians and the Muslims
of the Ottoman Empire had "peacefully coexisted" in an imperial system that
did not treat them equally, this inequality had been part and parcel of their
social system for so long that even those groups in the empire that periodi-
cally challenged this inequality did so within the boundaries of the imperial
framework. It was only after the Enlightenment, and the French Revolution

it helped spark, that an alternate vision of society, based on nationalism and an alternative political structure, the nation-state, was introduced. The Ottoman Empire became one of the many testing grounds around the world of both a nationalist vision and the political structure this vision attempted to create. The experiment itself created a very strong sense of empowerment and entitlement to transform everything at all costs to realize what was such a promising and liberating alternative vision and the political structure it entailed. At the time, it appeared almost natural to exclude, remove, or destroy those who did not fit the vision. The world had to fight and suffer through two global wars to appreciate fully the destructiveness embedded in this new way of thinking about the world. Ultimately, the two concurrent narratives of the supporters of empire and the advocates of nation were reconciled, and together they produced the Republican narrative.

The emergence of a Turkish "nation-state" on the ashes of the Ottoman Empire precluded the discussion of any claims about the land the Turks had now identified as their homeland; it was no accident that Mustafa Kemal said, and the Turks constantly reiterated, that there was not "a handspan of the soil of their motherland" (*bir karış vatan toprağı*) to be relinquished. What Mustafa Kemal had forcefully articulated was shared by many who had no qualms about the directive, as taught to all Turkish schoolchildren: "Fight for the motherland until the last drop of our blood" (*Kanımızın son damlasına kadar*). People's willingness to annihilate themselves for a vision demonstrates both the ideological strength of nationalism and its incredibly destructive power. Since the people wishing to destroy themselves have no intention of taking that chance alone, they call on their compatriots to join them in the effort and to define a common target to destroy, a clearly specified group, which differs from them according to a definition they have composed as patriots.

This nationalist tone dominates the Republican defensive narrative I next discuss. Yet I want to draw attention to a significant historical occurrence that colored this narrative: the Armenian deaths and massacres in 1915 were followed by the Russian and Allied occupation of the central lands of the Ottoman Empire, directly and also with the help of the Greeks. During these occupations, the Armenian revolutionary committees, now joined by those polarized by the tragic turn of events against their people, sided with the occupying forces, took up arms, and in some places perpetrated atrocities against the Muslim Turkish populace that were similar to those that the Armenians had suffered.[11] The Turkish massacres of 1917, especially those in eastern Anatolia, became central to the defense of the Republican

narrative. Hence, Turkish nationalism was further articulated as a consequence of these massacres by Armenians, as well as the massacres committed by the Greeks who occupied western Anatolia, with the support of
the Allied forces, until they were forced to retreat by the nationalist forces
of the Turkish Independence Movement.

The other defensive element on which the Republican narrative capitalized was provided by the ASALA (Armenian Secret Army for the Liberation of Armenia) murders of Turkish diplomats throughout the world in
the late 1970s and early 1980s, an ill-fated attempt to draw attention to the
Armenian genocide. When combined with Turkish nationalist rhetoric, the
murders polarized Turkish public opinion, not only against ASALA and
Armenian claims but, unfairly, against all Armenians. The Turkish diplomats served as representatives of the Turkish Republic. They had no connection to the Armenian deaths of 1915 other than the fact that they were
citizens of the Turkish nation-state founded on what could have been the
Armenian homeland, and their murders demonstrate the harmful effect
nationalism has had on the Armenians. The murders presented Republican Turkey with the opportunity to include in its narrative, again a nationalist move, a claim to avenge the deaths; thus, they strengthened the
Republican resolve to resist Armenian claims and further radicalized the
Turkish official stand on the issue, to a total denial of the Armenian massacres of 1915.

REPUBLICAN DEFENSIVE NARRATIVE ON READING GENOCIDE

The master Republican nationalist narrative on the Armenian deaths of
1915 traces the origins of the tragedy to the intervention of Western powers in the affairs of the empire and justifies the Armenian relocations and
subsequent massacres as responses to subversive acts of the Armenian committee members. This narrative does not recognize, on one hand, the significance of the preexisting structural divide in Ottoman society among
social groups, and the naturalized Muslim superiority this divide entailed,
and, on the other hand, the fact that Turkish nationalism was one of many
nationalisms that emerged during this period, with claims no more just than
those of the others, even though it was the one that happened to triumph
over them, at their expense.[12]

This nonrecognition engendered by Turkish nationalism, which sought
the preservation of the Turkish state at all costs, has led the Republican state
to assign all moral responsibility for the Armenian deaths and massacres to

anyone but the Ottoman Turkish perpetrators. As a consequence of this non-recognition, the Armenian victims themselves, tragically and ironically, have emerged in the Republican narrative, alongside the guilty Western powers, as the main perpetrators of the crimes. Any feeble attempt to assign blame to the Turkish perpetrators is immediately dismissed in the Republican narrative with the defense that what happened was a tragic but necessary act for the preservation of the "state."

No significant studies on the Armenian deaths and massacres appear until the two works by Esat Uras and Y. G. Çark in 1953.[13] Their publication was accompanied by declarations of loyalty to the Turkish nation-state at every opportunity. Then, from 1953, there is a gap in the scholarship until 1976.[14] The scholarship that has appeared since 1976 is clearly dominated by Turkish nationalism, from the start, which constantly not only demands that its authors pledge their allegiance to the Turkish nation-state as citizens but also requires them to preserve Turkish state interests in their works, even at the cost of critical scholarship. These two significant gaps in the scholarship on the Armenian deaths and massacres of 1915 warrant further examination.

Why were there no works on this important social and moral issue of the Armenian deaths and massacres of 1915 during the first thirty years of the Turkish Republic? This long silence regarding an event so crucial and central to the period immediately succeeding it might be due to several factors. First, it is reasonable to assume that the trauma and devastation endured by Ottoman subjects during the war afterward created a climate in which people were more eager to "forget" the immediate past than to question it. Further, the close link between the Armenian deaths and the Unionist leadership that funded and staffed the War of Independence led the leaders of the Turkish nation-state to employ a nationalist Republican rhetoric to silence discussion of the Armenian issue.[15]

Moreover, by 1926, Mustafa Kemal had effectively eliminated the Unionist leadership he regarded as a potential threat to his rule; only those who declared and proved their personal loyalty to the person of Mustafa Kemal by taking positions against their former friends were able to survive. Some Unionists who were considered dangerous to Mustafa Kemal's rule were executed following the 1926 trials of those who attempted to assassinate him; based on shoddy evidence, and with the help of those Unionists who had declared their personal allegiance to him, Kemal was able to eliminate all those who criticized the ruling regime in Turkey. Others chose exile in order to survive and did not feel safe returning to Turkey until after Mustafa Kemal's death in 1938, while those who did remain in Turkey risked their lives to do so and survived so long as they withdrew from political life and strictly maintained their silence. The fact that the young Turkish Republic underwent a series of traumatic social reforms during the era of Mustafa Kemal's single-party rule also precluded such discussions. Finally, the subsequent promulgation of the laws of treason against the Turkish state and Kemal rendered any counterinterpretation of the official version subversive.

The same political framework dominated the rule of Mustafa Kemal's successor and close friend, İsmet İnönü (1938–50); even though some of Kemal's opponents were able to return to Turkey after his death, they did so while maintaining their silence and censoring their views in tacit support of the existing political rule. During this period, Turkey was also coming to terms with the trauma of World War II. Further, both the Kemal and İnönü periods were marked by strong Turkish nationalism that informally defined citizenship in terms of religion and ethnicity. Muslim-Turkish citizens, like their Muslim-Ottoman predecessors, were dominant. All other social groups were co-opted, disregarded, or silenced by methods ranging from censorship to population exchanges.

Turkey made the transition to a multiparty system in 1946. Censorship restrictions were initially eased after the sweeping electoral victory of the Democratic Party in the elections held in 1950. This transition may have encouraged some members of Kemal and İnönü's Republican People's Party (RPP), such as Uras, who retired from active politics, to find time to write. Many former Unionists, such as Rauf Orbay, began to publish their memoirs during this period. The choice taken by authors Uras and Çark to write about the Armenians may also have resulted from concerns about the increasing visibility and strength of populist and Islamic elements since the rise to power of the Democratic Party; these concerns were realized in the incidents of September 6–7, 1955, during which minorities, particularly Greeks, were attacked and killed.

Why was there a gap in the scholarship between 1953 and 1976? Quite likely it resulted from the 1960 purge of the Democratic Party from power by the Turkish military and the ensuing reintroduction of censorship and state control over scholarship and the knowledge it produced. Yet, this state of affairs changed once again in the 1970s as a result of the assassination of Turkish diplomats by the radical Armenian group ASALA in an attempt to draw international attention to the Armenian genocide. The defensive Republican narrative became even more radicalized during this period, drawing selectively on Ottoman documents and the two early

Republican works of scholarship, and it has remained the hegemonic narrative until today.[16]

I have criticized this defensive Republican narrative for its inherent Turkish nationalism, which, I argue, makes critical scholarship impossible. The nationalist cloak over this narrative creates shortcomings: the use of archival material is highly selective, and nationalist scholars almost unanimously overlook other source material that contradicts the narrative, such as the investigation records of the Ottoman military tribunals and contemporaneous accounts in Ottoman newspapers documenting the deaths and massacres of 1915. These scholars also assume that pre-nineteenth-century Ottoman communal relations were peaceful and just, until the intervention of Western powers subverted the Ottoman Armenians. Yet, these communal relations naturalized Muslim dominance over the minorities, and the nationalist rhetoric reflects only the Muslim view of these relations. Even though Western powers did have a destructive effect on Ottoman communal relations, one must recognize yet again the equally, if not more destructive force, of nationalism.

The French Revolution and the social transformations it envisioned altered the expectations of all social groups in the Ottoman Empire. The frustrations of Ottoman Muslims created the social group of the Young Turks and their Muslim followers, who assumed power in 1908 and ultimately carried out the massacres of 1915. In turn, the frustrations of Ottoman minorities first generated demands for reform; when these failed, and Ottoman-Muslim aggression against them increased, minority members took up arms and revolted. While both Ottoman Muslims and minorities nurtured nationalist visions, any realization of their visions ultimately implied the decimation and destruction of the other.

Since Muslims as a group had the support of the Ottoman state and the advantage of a social structure that protected their privileged position, they eventually triumphed over the minorities. Their triumph was couched in the ideology of nationalism, which condoned all actions carried out in the name of the imagined community and the nation-state. This nationalist ideology enabled nationalists in the Ottoman state to justify the Armenian massacres on behalf of the imagined community of Turks, and it inspired them to join the Turkish independence movement to actualize the imagined community. In turn, the emergent Turkish nation-state rejected its Ottoman past and the massacres in which its leaders had been implicated. Republican scholars who engaged in research into the Armenian deaths and massacres of 1915 institutionalized Turkish nationalism. As a consequence, they

could identify in their research the subversion of only two "others" of Turkish nationalism, namely, the Western powers and the Ottoman minorities,
while failing to see that their own actions had been no less destructive. As
a result, they denied the massacres and argued that they themselves had been
victims. Only within the current postnationalist era has a more critical and
self-reflective reading of Turkish historiography, which places the blame
equally on all social groups, including Turks, become possible. I next focus
on how a postnationalist critical narrative of the events of 1915 has started
to emerge in contemporary Turkey.

POSTNATIONALIST CRITICAL NARRATIVE
ON READING GENOCIDE

The most significant factors uniting the works in this category are that none
is written to defend a particular thesis and that none is supported in its publication to any extent by the Turkish state. Additionally, these works are not
colored by the nationalism that pervades the Republican narrative but instead
take a postnationalist stand. As such, they are knowledge products of the
emerging civil society in Turkey. They fall into three broad groups: those
written specifically on the Armenian issue; those penned on various other
dimensions of Turkish history but that, indirectly, illuminate and contex-
tualize the Armenian deaths and massacres of 1915 within Turkish history
at large; and literary works, mostly novels by Turkish-Armenian writers,
which have recently begun to be translated into Turkish.[17]

The most significant dimension of the postnationalist critical narrative
emerging in Turkey is its willingness to recognize Turkish society not as an
imagined community of nationalist Turkish compatriots but, rather as a
cultural mosaic that comprises many diverse social groups, including Kurds,
Alevis, and the much-atrophied minorities—Armenians, Greeks, and Jews.
Turkish society at large is involved in an exploration of these social groups
through their literature and their historical narratives, and some societal
segments have started to engage in more critical self-reflection. Islamists have
begun to challenge the dominant, secular nationalist writing of history with
the publication of many memoirs that highlight the agency of religion in
Turkish history. Liberal Turkish intellectuals have taken on the task of critical self-reflection about what comprises and ought to comprise Turkish identity. These groups are willing to move beyond the narrow boundaries of the
nationalist cloak, which blames others for everything that happened. Some
are also ready to recognize how Turkish nationalism caused Armenians pain

and suffering. If these burgeoning groups transform themselves into a movement organized around the recognition of human rights, and if they are
able to overcome the resistance of nationalist elements embedded in society and especially in the military, the Armenians deaths and massacres in
1915 may come to be widely recognized in contemporary Turkey.

CONCLUSION

Why is Turkey, like other countries, still not fully able to make the transition from a nationalist phase to a postnationalist one? In this context, Turkey
faces one major obstacle, the periodization of nationalism in contemporary Turkey. It is extremely significant that current Turkish nationalist rhetoric identifies the passage of Mustafa Kemal to Anatolia on May 19, 1919, as
the starting point of the nationalist struggle that culminated in the establishment of the Turkish nation-state. This periodization dismisses the significance of prior historical events and interprets the nationalist movement
as a spontaneous development predicated solely on the agency of a single
person, Mustafa Kemal.

The discussion and recognition of the Armenian deaths and massacres
of 1915 in particular, and the demystification of nationalism as it continues
to cloak contemporary Turkey in general, will be possible only if an alternate periodization is applied. The emergence of Turkish nationalism as a
significant historical force needs to be traced to 1839, when the Ottoman
Empire officially recognized the need to undertake political and social
reforms. These "reforms" triggered the first stage of Turkish nationalism,
initiated by the 1839 reform, and then continued with the subsequent 1856
and 1879 reforms, which all mark unsuccessful attempts by the Ottoman
Empire to incorporate its minorities into the empire on equal terms.

The suppression of the counterrevolution by the Action Army on April
25, 1909, signals the beginning of the second, "protonationalist" stage, when
military officials assumed control of the emerging political structure in the
name of the state and the nation. The January 1913 coup d'état formed the
high point of Turkish protonationalism, and the November 1, 1918, escape
of Unionist leaders to Germany its demise. It was during this pernicious
period of protonationalism that the Armenian deaths and massacres
occurred.

The third stage, "official nationalism," emerged on May 15, 1919, when
many groups throughout the central lands of the empire started to mobilize the arms, military personnel, and financial capital prepared by the CUP

leadership throughout Anatolia. This third stage reached its high point not with the signing of the Treaty of Lausanne or the establishment of the Turkish Republic but, rather, with the Greek-Turkish population exchange of 1923–24, the final mass movement of populations to realize the imagined Turkish Muslim community. This peak of nationalism sustained itself until 1983, although weathering repeated attempts to sever the connection between the military, which has assumed the guardianship of Turkish nationalism, and the transforming political structure. These attempts include the establishment of the Progressive Republican Party in 1924 and the foundation in 1946 of the Democratic Party. Both parties were ultimately crushed by the military. The demise of the third stage of "official nationalism" began with the establishment of political organizations within civil society, organizations that, at least initially, have withstood the state-cum-military-centered nationalism. The 1983 creation of the Motherland Party under the leadership of Turgut Özal, the 1995 emergence of the New Democracy movement, and the 2001 formation of the liberal Islamist party represent such developments.

According to this alternative periodization, Turkey is now at a turning point; as the third stage of "official nationalism" comes to an end, the first sparks of the fourth stage of "postnationalism" are in the making by a new generation that has come of age not during the foundation of the republic but, rather, in a period when the republic is being contested. This new generation will have to determine what to make of these postnationalist sparks. If the connection between the military and the political system is severed, and if the Turkish Republic is integrated into the European Union, this may mark the beginning of the fourth, postnationalist stage in Turkey. It remains to be seen how such developments might affect the official Turkish position on the Armenian deaths in 1915.

NOTES

1. Dorothy Smith, *The Conceptual Practices of Power: A Feminist Sociology of Knowledge* (Boston: Northeastern Press, 1990).

2. Patricia Hill Collins, *Black Feminist Thought: Knowledge, Consciousness, and the Politics of Empowerment* (Boston: Unwin and Hyman, 1990); Rolf Wiggerhaus, ed., *The Frankfurt School: Its History, Theories, and Political Significance* (Cambridge: Polity Press, 1994); Theodore Adorno, ed., *The Authoritarian Personality* (New York: Harper, 1950); Max Horkheimer, *Critique of Instrumental Reason* (New York: Seabury Press, 1974).

3. Jürgen Habermas, *Knowledge and Human Interests* (Boston: Beacon Press, 1971).

4. Smith, *Conceptual Practices of Power*; Collins, *Black Feminist Thought*.

5. Ronald Grigor Suny, *Looking toward Ararat: Armenia in Modern History* (Bloomington: Indiana University Press, 1993).

6. Fatma Müge Göçek, "Ottoman *Sürgün* (Population Transfer) Policy: 14th–17th Centuries" (master's thesis, Bosporus University, 1981).

7. These registers are located in the archives of the prime minister of Turkey, the Topkapı Palace, and the Office of Islamic Religious Opinion (İstanbul Müftü-lüğü). See Fatma Müge Göçek, *Rise of the Bourgeoisie, Demise of Empire: Ottoman Westernization and Social Change* (New York: Oxford University Press, 1996). This book evolved from my PhD thesis, where I first became aware of the significance of the *dhimmi*s in the Ottoman Empire in general, and in the process of Ottoman Westernization in particular, through the work of my mentor Bernard Lewis, *The Muslim Discovery of Europe* (New York: W. W. Norton, 1982).

8. Fatma Müge Göçek, ed., *Social Constructions of Nationalism in the Middle East* (Albany: State University of New York Press, 2002).

9. Ranajit Guha, and Gayatri Spivak, *Selected Subaltern Studies* (New York: Oxford University Press, 1988); Partha Chatterjee, *The Nation and Its Fragments: Colonial and Post-colonial Histories* (Princeton, NJ: Princeton University Press, 1993); Antonio Gramsci, *Letters from Prison*, 2 vols. (New York: Columbia University Press, 1994).

10. Among the works that constitute this narrative are the memoirs of Kamil Said and Talat Pashas, Mehmed Asaf and Dr. Reşid, the Ottoman Military Tribunal Records of 1919–20, the collections of Ottoman documents published by the Turkish state, and the official reports on the Armenian massacres by Hüseyin Nazım Pasha and the National Congress of Turkey. Let me note there that I do not have space to review individually each of the works within this narrative. However, they include the following works: *8 Mart Sene 335 Tarihinde İrade-i Seniye-i Hazret-i Padişahiye İktiran Eden Kararname ile Müteşekkil Divan-ı Harb-i Örfi Muhakematı Zabıt Ceridesi* (Turkish Military Tribunal Records, 1919–20); Anonymous [Esat Uras?], *Ermeni Komitelerinin A'mal ve Hareket-i İhtilaliyesi* [The Actions and Revolutionary Movements of the Armenian Committees], ed. Erdoğan Cengiz (1916; Ankara: Başbakanlık, 1983); Mehmed Asaf, *1909 Adana Ermeni Olayları ve Anılarım* [1909 Adana Armenian Incidents and My Memoirs] (Ankara: TTK, 1982); Başbakanlık Devlet Arşivleri Genel Müdürlüğü, *Osmanlı Belgelerinde Ermeniler (1915–1920)* [Armenians in Ottoman Documents] (Ankara: BDAGM, 1994); Gül Çağalı-Güven, *Kamil Paşa ve Said Paşanın Anıları: Polemikler* [Memoirs of Kamil Pasha and Sait Pasha: The Polemics] (Istanbul: Arba, 1991); Hüseyin Nazım Paşa, *Ermeni Olayları Tarihi* [History of the Armenian Incidents], 2 vols. (Ankara: Başbakanlık, 1994);

Mehmet Kasım, *Talat Paşa'nın Anıları* [Memoirs of Talat Pasha] (Istanbul: Say, 1986); Ahmet Mehmedefendioğlu, *Sürgünden İntihara: Dr. Reşid Bey'in Hatıraları* [From Deportation to Suicide: Memoirs of Dr. Reşid Bey] (Izmir, 1982); National Congress of Turkey, *The Turco-Armenian Question: The Turkish Point of View* (Constantinople: Societe Anonyme de Papeterie et d'Imprimerie, 1919); Prime Ministry Directorate General of Press and Information, *Documents,* 2 vols. (Ankara: Başbakanlık, 1989); Sadrazam Sait Paşa, *Anılar* [Memoirs of Grand Vezir Sait Pasha] (Istanbul: Hür, 1977).

11. İsmet Parmaksızoğlu, *Ermeni Komitelerinin İhtilal Hareketleri ve Besledikleri Emeller* [The Ambitions and Revolutionary Movements of the Armenian Committees] (Ankara: DSI, 1981).

12. This narrative is established in works such as Türkkaya Ataöv, *The Armenians in the Late Ottoman Period* (Ankara: TTK for the Grand National Assembly of Turkey, 2001); Ataöv, *The "Armenian Question": Conflict, Trauma and Objectivity* (Ankara: SAM, 1997); Kamuran Gürün, *Ermeni Dosyası* [The Armenian Dossier] (Ankara: TTK, 1983); Mim Kemal Öke, *Ermeni Sorunu 1914–1923* [The Armenian Question] (Ankara: TTK, 1991); Salahi Sonyel, *The Great War and the Tragedy of Anatolia (Turks and Armenians in the Maelstrom of Major Powers)* (Ankara: TTK, 2000); Sonyel, *Minorities and the Destruction of the Ottoman Empire* (Ankara: TTK, 1993); Bilal Şimşir, *Lozan Telgrafları: Türk Diplomatik Belgelerinde Lozan Barış Konferansı* [The Lausanne Telegraphs: Lausanne Peace Conference through Turkish Diplomatic Documents] (Ankara: TTK; 1990); Şimşir, *The Deportees of Malta and the Armenian Question* (Ankara: TTK, 1984); Şimşir, *British Documents on the Ottoman Armenians (1856–1880)* (Ankara: TTK, 1983); Şimşir, *The Genesis of the Armenian Question* (Ankara: TTK, 1983); Şimşir, *British Documents on the Ottoman Armenians (1880–1890)* (Ankara: TTK, 1983); and Esat Uras, *Tarihte Ermeniler ve Ermeni Meselesi* [Armenians in History and the Armenian Question] (Istanbul: Belge, 1953). The narrative is also found in other works: Nuri Adıyeke, "Islahat Fermanı Öncesinde Osmanlı İmparatorluğunda Millet Sistemi ve Gayrımüslimlerin Yaşantılarına Dair" [Concerning the Millet System and the Lives of Non-Muslims in the Ottoman Empire before the Reform Edict of 1856], in *Osmanlıdan Günümüze Ermeni Sorunu* [The Armenian Question from the Ottomans to Our Time], ed. Hasan Celal Güzel (Ankara: Yeni Türkiye, 2000), 183–92; Anadolu Basın Birliği, *Katliam Efsanesi* [The Massacre Myth] (Ankara: ABB, 1987); Ataöv, *Armenians in the Late Ottoman Period*; Ataöv, *Armenian Question*; Atatürk Üniversitesi Yirminci Yıl Armağanı, *Ermeniler Hakkında Makaleler Derlemeler* [Articles and Selections on the Armenians] (Ankara: Kalite, 1978); Cemil Birsel, *Lozan* [Lausanne], 2 vols. (Istanbul: Sosyal, 1933); Y. G. Çark, *Türk Devleti Hizmetinde Ermeniler (1453–1953)* [Armenians in the Service of the Turkish State] (Istanbul: Yeni Matbaa, 1953); Hüseyin Çelik, *Gören-*

lerin Gözüyle Van'da Ermeni Mezalimi [Armenian Atrocities in Van through Eye-witness Accounts] (Ankara: THK, 1995); Neşide Kerem Demir, *Bir Şehid Anasına Ta-rihin Söyledikleri: Türkiye'nin Ermeni Meselesi* [What History Told a Martyr's Mother: The Armenian Question in Turkey] (Ankara: Hülbe, 1976); Dokuz Eylül Üniversitesi Rektörlüğü, *Türk Tarihinde Ermeniler Sempozyumu* [Symposium on the Armenians in Turkish History] (Manisa: Şafak, 1983); Bilal Eryılmaz, *Osmanlı Devletinde Gayrımüslim Teb'anın Yönetimi* [The Administration of the Non-Muslims in the Ottoman State] (Istanbul: Risale, 1990); Erol Göka, "'Ermeni Sorunu'nun (Gözden Kaçan) Psikolojik Boyutu" [(The Overlooked) Psychological Dimension of the "Armenian Question"], *Ermeni Araştırmaları* [Armenian Studies] 1, no. 1 (2001): 128–36; Gürün, *Ermeni Dosyası*; Güzel, *Osmanlıdan Günümüze Ermeni Sorunu*; Jamanak, *Facts from the Turkish Armenians/Realites Exprimees Par Les Armenien Turcs/Türk Ermenilerinden Gerçekler* (Istanbul: Jamanak, 1980); Kinyas Kartal, *Van'dan Erivan'a Hatıralarım* [My Memoirs from Van to Erivan] (Ankara: ABB, 1987); Cevdet Küçük, *Osmanlı Diplomasisinde Ermeni Meselesinin Ortayaı Çıkışı (1878–1897)* [The Emer-gence of the Armenian Question in Ottoman Diplomacy] (Istanbul: İstanbul Üniver-sitesi, Edebiyat Fakültesi, 1984); Şinasi Orel and Süreyya Yuca, *Ermenilerce Talat Paşa'ya Atfedilen Telgrafların Gerçek Yüzü* [The Truth about the Telegrams Attributed by the Armenians to Talat Pasha] (Ankara: TTK, 1983); Öke, *Ermeni Sorunu*; Gürsoy Sol-maz, *Yaşayanların Dilinden Erzurum-Sarıkamış-Kars'ta Ermeni Zulmü* [Armenian Cruelties in Erzurum, Sarıkamış, and Kars from Eyewitness Accounts] (Van: YYÜ, 1995); Sonyel, *Great War and the Tragedy of Anatolia*; Sonyel, *Minorities and the Destruction of the Ottoman Empire*; Azmi Süslü, *Ermeniler ve 1915 Tehcir Olayı* [Armenians and the Population Transfer Incident] (Ankara: Sistem, 1990); Musa Şaş-maz, "Ermeniler Hakkındaki Reformların Uygulanması (1895–1987)" [The Applica-tion of the Reforms concerning the Armenians], in Güzel, *Osmanlıdan Günümüze Ermeni Sorunu*, 93–104; Şimşir, *Lozan Telgrafları*; Şimşir, *Deportees of Malta*; Şimşir, *British Documents (1856–1880)*; Şimşir, *Genesis of the Armenian Question*; Şimşir, *British Documents (1880–1890)*; Uras, *Tarihte Ermeniler*; Süleyman Yeşilyurt, *Atatürk, İnönü, Menderes, Gürsel Dönemlerinin Ermeni Yahudi, Rum Asıllı Milletvekilleri* [Parliamen-tary Deputies of Armenian, Jewish, and Greek Origin during the Atatürk, İnönü, Menderes, and Gürsel Eras] (Ankara: Zine, 1995).

13. Uras, *Tarihte Ermeniler*; Çark, *Türk Devleti Hizmetinde Ermeniler*.

14. Demir, *Bir Şehid Anasına Tarihin Söyledikleri*.

15. Erik Jan Zürcher, *Turkey: A Modern History* (London: I. B. Tauris, 2001); and Zürcher, *Milli Mücadelede İttihatçılık* [The Unionist Factor] (Istanbul: Bağlam, 1987), 101–9.

16. Çark, *Türk Devleti Hizmetinde Ermeniler*; Uras, *Tarihte Ermeniler*.

17. Among works in this category are those by Taner Akçam and Taner Timur,

which focus specifically on the atrocities committed against the Armenians in 1915, and others such as those by Şükrü Hanioğlu, which deal with different subject matter but produce very significant insights into the events of 1915. Taner Akçam, *İnsan Hakları ve Ermeni Sorunu* [Human Rights and the Armenian Problem] (Istanbul: İmge, 1999); Taner Timur, *Türkler ve Ermeniler: 1915 ve Sonrası* [Turks and Armenians: 1915 and Its Aftermath] (Ankara: Imge, 2000); and Şükrü Hanioğlu, *Preparation for a Revolution: The Young Turks, 1902–1908* (New York: Oxford University Press, 2001); Hanioğlu, *Young Turks in Opposition* (New York: Oxford University Press, 1995). Also included in this category are works that produce worlds of meaning pertaining to the events, namely, literary works by Muslim Turks such as İsmail Arıkan and Armenians such as Hagop Mintzuri. İsmail Arıkan, *Mahallemizdeki Ermeniler* [Armenians in Our Neighborhood] (Istanbul: İletişim, 2001); and Hagop Mintzuri, *Atina, Tuzun Var mı?* [Athena, Do You Have Some Salt?] (Istanbul: Aras, 2000). Other works within this narrative include Akşam, *İnsan Hakları ve Ermeni Sorunu*; Arıkan, *Mahallemizdeki Ermeniler*; Fuat Dündar, *İttihat ve Terakki'nin Müslümanları İskan Politikası (1913–1918)* [The Muslim Settlement Policy of the Union and Progress Party] (Istanbul: İletişim, 2001); Hanioğlu, *Preparation for a Revolution*; Hanioğlu, *Young Turks*; Osman Selim Kocahanoğlu, *İttihat-Terakki'nin Sorgulanması ve Yargılanması: Meclis-i Mebusan Zabıtları* [The Interrogation and Trial of the Union and Progress Party: Proceedings of the Ottoman Assembly] (Istanbul: Temel, 1998); Mintzuri, *Atina*; Hüdavendigar Onur, *Ermeni Portreleri: Milet-i [sic] Sadıkadan Hayk'ın Çocuklarına* [Armenian Portraits: From the Loyal Community to the Children of Hayk] (Istanbul: Burak, 1999); Antan Özer, *Yaşamı Beklerken* [Awaiting Life] (Istanbul: Aras, 1997); Yervant Sırmakeşliyan, *Balıkçı Sevdası* [Passion of Fishermen] (Istanbul: Aras, 2000); Timur, *Türkler ve Ermeniler*; Pars Tuğlacı, *Ermeni Edebiyatından Seçkiler* [Selections from Armenian Literature] (Istanbul: Cem, 1982); Türk Tarih Vakfı, *75 yılda Tebaa'dan Yurttaş'a Doğru* [From Subject to Citizen in 75 years] (Istanbul: Tarih Vakfı Yayınları, 1999); and Krikor Zohrab, *Hayat, Olduğu Gibi* [Life, as It Is] (Ankara: Ayraç, 2000).

PART III

Narratives of Crisis

5

The Theory of Crisis and the Crisis in a Theory

Intellectual History in Twentieth-Century Middle Eastern Studies

ISRAEL GERSHONI

ntellectual history as a subdiscipline of Middle Eastern studies was not in vogue in the last decades of the twentieth century. In fact, the study of the history of ideas and concepts produced by intellectual elites has for a long time been out of the forefront of the historical discipline. From the time that more materialistic, structural, and quantitative modes of history became dominant in the profession in the 1960s and 1970s, and later with the profound changes that occurred in history studies and gave rise from the late 1970s to "new social history," followed by "the cultural turn," which led to "the new cultural history," intellectual history has been relegated to the sidelines of professional interest. Even during the 1980s when cultural history—which stresses text, representation, meaning, and narrative—became hegemonic and took shape "as an upstart critique of the established social, economic and demographic histories,"[1] intellectual history remained peripheral in Middle Eastern studies. In the general study of history, intellectual history took on new life in the 1980s and 1990s, after a temporary crisis in the 1970s, and it was redefined as a new intellectual history after the linguistic turn.[2] New methods and approaches, the fertile influences of poststructuralist culturalism, "the return of literature" and the "invasion" of literary criticism into the study of history, Hayden White's narrativism, the radical contextualism of the Cambridge school espoused by Quentin Skinner, J. G. A. Pocock, and John Dunn, and, more recently, the study of collective memory, have given new momentum to "old" history and reshaped it into a more attractive, forward-looking discipline.[3]

In Middle Eastern studies, however, similar changes have not taken place, and intellectual history has not been rescued from its diminished status.

Apparently in our profession, the flight from any type of elitist history, certainly from the history of ideas produced by intellectual luminaries; the continued avid interest in "history from below," both socioeconomic and sociocultural; the ongoing emphasis on political history and the history of political economy, world systems, and dependency theory; the reception and emulation of postmodernist and postcolonial paradigms and their application to the study of nonelitist groups; the growth of women's studies and the history of gender—have all combined to impede the recovery of intellectual history. What Murray G. Murphey stated at the end of the 1970s in regard to intellectual history in general continued to characterize the dominant mood in Middle Eastern studies in the 1980s and 1990s: "Students no longer see intellectual history as the place 'where the action is,' and the profession seems to concur that the 'cutting edge' of historical scholarship lies elsewhere" (in "the history of the inarticulate and the oppressed," what we today call the "subaltern").[4]

Significantly, Edward Said's *Orientalism* (1978), which used the method of the history of ideas (generally European), or discourse analysis, had a paralyzing effect on Middle Eastern intellectual history.[5] After *Orientalism*, Middle Eastern intellectual history was subsequently identified as a subdiscipline that applied distinctly Orientalist methods, and it continues to be viewed as obsolete, a history where confirmed Orientalism finds one of its most characteristic expressions. With a good deal of justification, the history of ideas and intellectual history have been perceived as a direct continuation of the overtextualism and philological hermeneutics that marked classical Oriental studies, against which *Orientalism* brilliantly inveighed.

In the first half of the twentieth century, however, intellectual ecology and the historiographical fashion were entirely different. In the 1930s and 1940s, the history of ideas and intellectual history were on the rise. After World War II, intellectual history reached new heights and in the 1950s, as Robert Darnton so aptly put it, was "the queen of the historical sciences"— a fashionable history highly regarded by the historians' guild.[6] The effect of these developments on Middle Eastern studies was obvious. In this early period, some of the most respected Orientalists studying Islam and the societies and cultures of the Arab Middle East were intellectual historians or historians of ideas. The paradigm common to these Orientalist scholars was that inner understanding of "Islamic" or "Arab" ideas would not only provide the key to understanding the meaning and ideational quality of ideas but, moreover, that these ideas contained the secret to comprehending Arab-Islamic reality as a whole—patterns of social behavior, economic institutions, systems of political control, and cultural symbols and icons. The idea and the thinker provided the sites for methodical study, and it was assumed that only from them was it possible to glean knowledge about the historical evolution of Muslim cultures and societies. Orientalist intellectual historians thus focused their efforts on reading and presenting Islamic clusters of thought or belief systems that, they posited, were autonomous, coherent, and essential entities.

Given the overall correspondence in this early period between the popularity of the history of ideas in the historical profession and its broad acceptance in the study of modern Islam, it is all the more surprising that those engaged in this subdiscipline, that is, Orientalist scholars, did not refer to these links and influences. The Orientalist scholars developed their approach to the history of "Islamic ideas" without reference to methods, theories, and insights then taking shape in professional schools of intellectual history and the history of ideas in Europe and America. It is sufficient to note that some of the intellectual historians of the era who made the greatest contributions to shaping the subdiscipline—Carl L. Becker in the 1930s, Arthur O. Lovejoy and the *Journal of the History of Ideas* under his editorship in the 1940s, Isaiah Berlin and John Higham in the 1950s and 1960s—are not cited in any of the hundreds of works produced by these Orientalists.[7] Apparently, one reason for the severance of the study of Middle Eastern ideas from the history of ideas as studied in Europe and America was the essentialist efforts by Orientalists to prove the cultural uniqueness of the "Islamic worldview" and its detachment and even alienation from Western ("Judeo-Christian" or modern-scientific) worldviews.

The purpose of this essay is to take a critical look at several of the characteristics that marked the development of the writing of Middle Eastern intellectual history in the twentieth century. In this limited framework it is, of course, impossible to cover the broad scope of the historiography of intellectuals and intellectual histories of Middle Eastern societies and cultures. I have chosen to address only one chapter, in my view a central one, that engaged a considerable portion of this historiography and its narrators. By speaking of one central chapter, I refer to the large number of intellectual studies that focused on the historical development of an intellectual school of thought commonly known as the "modernist school," which was justifiably thought to have enormous impact on the way the intellectual, ideological, literary, and artistic contours of the modern Arab print culture were shaped. The founding father of this school was Muhammad 'Abduh, who was active and wrote at the end of the nineteenth century. At the beginning of the twentieth century, his immediate disciples, Qasim Amin and, more notably, Ahmad Lutfi al-Sayyid and the journal he edited, *al-Jarida*, imbued this school with modern European methods of thought. They brought about a radical reformist shift and introduced a secular, liberal, humanistic, and feminist discourse, accompanied by the promotion of Egyptian territorial nationalist ideas. This school served as a training ground for the community of discourse of the generation of intellectuals that reached maturity in the decade following the 1919 revolution. Led by talented luminaries in the fields of social thought, literature, journalism, and the arts, such as Taha Husayn, Muhammad Husayn Haykal, 'Abbas Mahmud al-'Aqqad, 'Ali 'Abd al-Raziq, Ibrahim 'Abd al-Qadir al-Mazini, Mansur Fahmi, Ahmad Amin, Salama Musa, and the somewhat younger Tawfiq al-Hakim, it was this new intellectual generation that gave the modernist school its full ideological historical expression. Beginning in the 1920s and for several decades, members of this modernist community of discourse controlled the centers of power in the field of print culture production. They manipulated the major production and dissemination agencies of the print media— newspapers, magazines, books, and other texts—and turned them into hegemonic forces in the cultural, literary, and artistic arenas.

Western Orientalist scholarship, which, as I mentioned, included the most respected intellectual historians and scholars of the history of ideas, developed what I define as a "theory" or "narrative" of "intellectual crisis" as a conceptual framework for a description and explanation of the historical evolution of this prominent intellectual cohort. According to the theory, the 1918–33 period marked the most productive and creative years for the modernist intellectuals. They succeeded in producing a clear, Westernized, modernist, secular, and liberal message, and in imparting it to broad readerships in Egypt and the larger Arabic print world. Moreover, they laid the intellectual foundations for a modern scientific culture based on freedom of expression, cultural pluralism, rationalist thought, and scientific and critical literary methods.

According to the crisis narrative, however, from the mid-1930s, and more so during the 1940s and 1950s, the modernist school faced a crisis that led it into cultural disarray and ideological confusion, and brought it to an impasse. The majority of its members retreated from their previous modernist and progressive positions and instead began to concentrate their intellectual efforts on writing *Islamiyyat*: popular Islamic literature about early Islamic society and the Islamic heroes of the seventh century, the Prophet Muhammad chief among them. The narrative of crisis placed the major historical responsibility for what it defined as this "failure" on the modernist intellectuals. For the authors of the narrative, not only were intellectuals' efforts to return to early Islam and to revive it as a contemporaneous, normative cultural system unsuccessful in offering a sound alternative to modern Western culture, but they had also embroiled the modernist school in an intellectual crisis that undermined the self-confidence of its members, destroyed the ideal of a progressive society and scientific culture, and led the modernists down a dead-end road.

INVENTING THE NARRATIVE OF CRISIS: GIBB AND HIS ORIENTALIST LEGACY

In the first half of the twentieth century, and especially from the 1920s through the early 1960s, Hamilton A. R. Gibb played a key role in shaping modern Islamic and Middle Eastern studies in the West. His formative influence was evident in nearly every scholarly work, and his imprint on the works of scholars in the 1940s and 1950s is clearly visible. Gibb took an interest in subjects far beyond the history of ideas, but his systematic treatment of the evolution of "Islamic" ideas and patterns of thought held a central position in all of his work. In this essay, I relate to Gibb as an Orientalist intellectual historian who invested great effort in an analysis of the systems of thought, attitudes, concepts, and worldviews produced by "Islamic" intellectual elites. Significantly, though, throughout the span of his academic career Gibb wrote intellectual history with marked indifference toward contemporary theoretical, methodological, and practical developments in Western intellectual history.

Gibb began his academic career in the 1920s, and some of the more prominent of his early works considered the processes by which ideas were then taking shape in the Islamic world.[8] One of his best-known studies from this period was "Studies in Contemporary Arabic Literature," published as a series of four articles in the Bulletin of the School of Oriental Studies of the London Institute between 1928 and 1933. This comprehensive study was a pioneering attempt to depict the major intellectual and literary trends and schools that had developed in Egypt and Greater Syria of the modern era, from the nineteenth century to the 1920s.[9] As Albert Hourani justifiably noted, Gibb's studies of contemporary Arabic literature "were the first attempt by a scholar trained in the European tradition of literary study to apply critical standards to the new writing in Arabic."[10] The third part of this study formed the cornerstone of Gibb's discussion. "Egyptian Mod-

ernists," published in 1929, was an initial, broad look at what Gibb defined
as "the rise of a distinctive Egyptian school of writers, which, from small
beginnings in the years immediately preceding the war, gathered strength
in the interval, and emerged into sudden prominence on the resumption
of literary activities."[11] Gibb showed that this intellectual avant-garde,
whose "training ground" prior to World War I was *al-Jarida*, led by Ahmad
Lutfi al-Sayyid, followed by more modest preparatory activity during the
war years, entered the field of print culture after the war and dominated it
in the 1920s. Gibb was the first to define this group as a "well-defined literary movement" in modern Arab culture, "one school" with common and
"distinctive aims" and "shared characteristics." Specifically, Gibb focused
on describing the intellectual development of Muhammad Husayn Haykal,
Taha Husayn, Mahmud 'Azmi, Ahmad Dayf, Mustafa 'Abd al-Raziq, 'Abbas
Mahmud al-'Aqqad, Ibrahim 'Abd al-Qadir al-Mazini, and Salama Musa.[12]

Gibb had high hopes for these intellectuals as a distinctive community
of modernist discourse. In his estimation, these talented young writers were
rising to new heights of intellectual sophistication and bringing about a revolution in Arabic literature. The members of the "Egyptian school," he stated,
"are striving to give greater depth and range to modern Arabic writing, and
to rescue it from the fluent superficiality to which a literature based on journalism is particularly liable." Above all, Gibb's third article was filled with
great confidence in the ability of "Egyptian modernists" to rapidly engender
the modernization of Arabic literature. Intellectual or literary modernization meant for him the rapid secularization and Westernization of Arabic print culture and the creation of an Arabic literature, patterned after
models of European literature, that would internalize modern artistic and
literary genres and adopt methods of literary criticism and rationalistic,
scientific techniques of text analysis. Gibb draws our attention to several of
the modernist intellectuals' more influential projects, such as Haykal's idea
to create an Egyptian national literature based on a particularist, neopharaonic national identity, or Taha Husayn's radical polemic, *Fi al-Shi'r al-Jahili*
(On Pre-Islamic Poetry, 1926), which applied Cartesian criteria to a critical examination of Arabic *jahili* poetry and undermined traditional orthodox Islamic precepts. Gibb also expressed his conviction that the educated
Egyptian public would support the intellectuals' modernist agenda; as
proof, he pointed out that their circle of readers was rapidly expanding. He
concluded the article with lavish praise for the great accomplishments of
Egyptian modernists, asserted that they had "brought into Arabic literature
new values and ideals," and placed it in a position to make a "distinctive

contribution of Arabs and Egyptians to modern civilization." This new literature, he continued, was being imparted by the creative elite, "with increasing success and a strong assurance of ultimate victory," to broad sectors of society; its goal, he wrote, was to "convert and educate the people."[13]

Charles C. Adams's *Islam and Modernism in Egypt* was a further development of Gibb's themes as well as a sort of initial canonization of them. His book was published in 1933, the year that the final article in Gibb's series came out, and Adams noted Gibb's direct influence on his work. Adams extended and deepened the "story" of the intellectual history of modern Egypt, covering the period from the last quarter of the nineteenth century to the early 1930s. His method, an adaptation of Gibb's approach, was to present the intellectual biographies and works of the pioneers of Egyptian modernism. He presented Muhammad 'Abduh as the founding father of the Islamic reformism that would pave the way for the development of Islamic modernism and the patterns of thought of the secular, liberal, Westernizing, nationalist schools that would advocate social reforms. He noted the contributions of Qasim Amin and of Ahmad Lutfi al-Sayyid and *al-Jarida* in fostering 'Abduh's rationalist and reformist legacy. More relevant to the current discussion, Adams concluded his description of this intellectual evolution with the emergence of what he viewed as an assertive and dynamic intellectual generation of young Egyptian modernists, "who are displaying a marked literary activity of a progressive, in some cases extremely liberal, tendency." Among the younger Egyptian modernists, Adams counted Muhammad Husayn Haykal and *al-Siyasa*, 'Abbas Mahmud al-'Aqqad, Ibrahim 'Abd al-Qadir al-Mazini, Mansur Fahmi, Mustafa 'Abd al-Raziq, 'Ali 'Abd al-Raziq, and Taha Husayn. For him, their intellectual products were the ideological culmination of Egyptian modernism, which had originated with "'Abduh's doctrines."[14]

About twenty years after the publication of "Studies in Contemporary Arabic Literature," Gibb published his *Modern Trends in Islam* (1947).[15] Based on his 1945 lectures at the University of Chicago, the book was a turning point in the now-mature Gibb's Orientalist work, and it had enormous influence on the development of Islamic and Middle Eastern studies in the 1950s, 1960s, and beyond. R. P. Mitchell, for example, in his classic work on the Muslim Brothers (published in 1969, more than two decades after Gibb's work), wrote that *Modern Trends in Islam* was "the first and yet most important [work] of all" on modern Islam.[16] *Modern Trends in Islam* was important mainly for Gibb's attempt to sketch, for the first time, a complete map of the various modern Islamic schools and trends and to describe the intellectuals' ideas and frames of mind as they grappled with modern reality. He identified, organized, and cataloged the "currents of religious thought among Muslims of the present day," introduced hierarchical order into them, defined their ideological essence, and examined whether these thoughts were adaptable to the modern era.

Although recounting the biographies of the fathers of Islamic modernism, such as Jamal al-Din al-Afghani, Muhammad 'Abduh, and Rashid Rida (for which Gibb relied on Adams), and drawing historical comparisons between Islamic modernist concepts and medieval Islamic ideas, in the main Gibb's work was a textualist analysis of ideological situations in the modern era. Gibb exhibited scant sensitivity for the specific changes occurring in the ideas of Islamic modernism or their historical dynamism, the results of their encounters with changing political and social realities, or political and social explanations of the changes that took place in the texts and their producers over time. Gibb examined "modern trends" through an analysis of "unit-ideas": "the religious tension in Islam," "the principles of modernism," "modernist religion," "law and society," and the like. His approach was strikingly different, however, from Lovejoy's history of ideas, which was then at the height of its popularity. Lovejoy dealt with the transformation of ideas or clusters of thought along the time axis and their casting off of one form and taking on another according to changing environments and new contexts.[17] Thus, if Lovejoy could be considered a geologist or archaeologist of ideas, Gibb, then, was a morphologist or geographer of them.

The major importance of Gibb's book for our purposes is the change in attitude it presented toward the modernist movement. Gibb now harshly and often vehemently criticized modernist trends and ideas. It is also noteworthy that his discussion of modernism and modernist religion was not restricted to Egyptian modernists; Gibb also brought into his discussion Islamic modernist schools in other parts of the Arab Middle East, and in North Africa and Asia. In his general discussion, Gibb refrained from naming the Egyptian modernists or dealing with their individual activities and writings (although one can find occasional mention of Taha Husayn, 'Ali 'Abd al-Raziq, and Muhammad Husayn Haykal), but they are present, nonetheless. Gibb's aggressive criticism was leveled first and foremost against the *Islamiyyat* literature. Gibb regarded the intellectual effort "to return to early Islam" and the intellectuals' admiration of the personality of the Prophet as a cult of sterile apologetics that represented a disappointing retreat from the modernist, Western-oriented paradigm based on commitment to secular, scientific, rationalist, and liberal principles.[18] Gibb was "shocked" by the modernists' "apologetic" methods of argumentation. Their attempt to rely on the assumptions of "Western liberalism" and "to interpret Islam in terms of liberal humanitarian ideas and values" seemed to him groundless. The modernists had a "Romantic outlook" that resulted in irrationalism, emotionalism, populism, and arbitrary subjectivity.[19] They had renounced textual criticism and analytical methods of empirical historical thinking, and this, similar to the case of European Romanticists, "opened the way to the rejection of objective standards in all fields of thought." Gibb, who thought of himself as a neoclassicist—an advocate of the values of the Enlightenment, objectivity, rationality, and historical empiricism—revealed a flagrant intolerance toward what he viewed as an expression of the romantic, demonic, and destructive forces that resulted from "exalting the imagination against reason."[20]

In Gibb's analysis, the intellectual retreat from the principles of the Enlightenment also caused severe damage to the tradition of orthodox Islam as it had been experienced and practiced by generations of Muslim believers. The intellectuals had undermined the foundations of canonical Islam by adopting the "Protestant principle" of "the right of free examination of the sources and the application of modern thought to their interpretation." They denied the classical Islamic principles of interpretation (*fiqh*, *tafsir*, *hadith*) and broke the chain (*silsila*) of authority stretching from earlier jurists, teachers, and witnesses, sweeping aside "the old classical science of tradition with its careful controls" and replacing it with "purely subjective appreciation." In doing so, they proved "their disregard of all objective standards of investigation and of historical truth," which, Gibb pointed out, were also part of their Islamic legacy. Moreover, they were severely undermining Islam's ability and that of broad communities of believers to defend themselves against the tyranny of internal rulers as well as against external threats. As Hourani had so adeptly done, Gibb accused the modernist intellectuals of "trahison des clercs," writing that they had "exploited religious feeling for political ends."[21]

Gibb, it should be emphasized, made his readers aware that the modernists were acting and writing under the immense pressures of modern life: they were defending Islam against Western slander and stereotyping; they had repulsed an attack by a Christian missionary on the Islamic faith and Muhammad; they had challenged "petrified orthodox Islamic thought"; and their Islamic modernist writings were becoming increasingly popular within broad publics of educated middle classes whose faith in Islam had been weakened and who, through *Islamiyyat* literature, were once again relating to

Islam as a modern culture and an authentic collective identity.[22] But none of these extenuating circumstances dulled the edge of Gibb's trenchant criticism. He mercilessly lashed out at the modernists, describing them as "theologically null"; "that intellectual confusion with which the whole modernist movement is burdened"; "the intellectual confusions and the paralyzing romanticism which cloud the minds of the modernists of today"; "the superficiality of its historical method"; "in their historical outlook there is no external control to restrain the exuberance of the romantic imagination"—these are but a few examples of Gibb's critical rage.[23] Thus, the creative modernism of the 1920s had deteriorated into destructive romanticism by the 1940s. "By this, too, we can realize more clearly the profound disservice done to Islam by the modernists. So far from guiding Muslim thought into this creative channel, they have fastened on it still more firmly the shackles of the romantic imagination and encouraged it to interpret history in terms of the capricious impulses of the moment."[24]

What led Gibb, in the late 1940s, to hurl this venomous criticism against modernism and to express such profound disillusionment with the Egyptian modernists, who, in the 1920s, had embodied for him the great promise of the creation of a modern culture in Egypt and throughout the Arab world? Gibb, interestingly, made no serious attempt to explain either the historical changes that occurred in the Middle East and Egypt in the 1930s and 1940s or the reasons for the change in his own attitude toward Islamic and Egyptian modernism. In the 1940s, Gibb began to emphasize in his writing the anti-Western mood that he believed was spreading throughout educated Arab publics. In his view, Arab nationalism, to which he devoted increasing attention, was a clear reflection of this anti-Western trend. Although Gibb himself expressed qualified support for the ideal of Arab unity (albeit warning against the "irrational," "intolerant," and "destructive" potentials it embodied) and often criticized the patterns of British imperialistic rule, he still found it difficult to accept growing Arab criticism of Western culture as an imperialistic foreign culture.[25] Beyond his disappointment with the intellectual luminaries, Gibb was also discouraged by the failure of the broad "westernized classes" to transmit the modernist message to the masses, who remained alienated from and hostile toward Western culture. To his dismay, Gibb found that this anti-Westernism often included criticism of him, other Orientalists, and Oriental studies itself, which had all come to be seen as by-products of an imperialistic mentality. Whatever the reasons for this change, however, the result was that in *Mod-*

ern Trends in Islam Gibb laid the foundation for the theory of crisis and the narrative of the intellectuals' "moral bankruptcy."[26]

CANONIZING THE NARRATIVE:
VON GRUNEBAUM, W. C. SMITH, AND SAFRAN

Gustave E. von Grunebaum's work on "the culture" of "modern Islam," published in the second half of the 1940s, the 1950s, and the early 1960s, constituted an elaboration on some of the central themes of Gibb's crisis narrative and a kind of preliminary canonization of them. Von Grunebaum was engrossed in a systematic study of what he defined as "Islamic culture" and a perusal of the ideas, basic premises, approaches, and concepts that comprise it. While Gibb can be regarded as a historian of ideas, von Grunebaum was a sociologist and an anthropologist of ideas and, in a certain sense, also a sociologist of religion and culture.

In von Grunebaum's work, historical time and intellectual changes carried little weight. The general intellectual history of the 1940s and 1950s hardly influenced him. Nonetheless, one cannot help being impressed by the profusion and diversity of the philosophical, psychological, sociological, and anthropological theories and insights that shaped his research methods and that he introduced into the field. The symbolic cultural approaches of Ernest Cassirer, the phenomenology of Edmond Husserl (von Grunebaum learned from him that "there is no world, only a world-view" and that the study of culture is the study of worldviews and the collective self-views of those who belong to the culture and experience it), and later, the structuralism of Claude Lévi-Strauss, greatly influenced his treatment of "Islamic culture" in its encounter with "Western culture." Following them, von Grunebaum defined culture as "a 'closed' system of questions and answers concerning the universe and man's behavior in it which has been accepted as authoritative by a human society."[27] "Culture," he assumed, was an essentialist, coherent, and homogeneous system. In order to interpret it, the scholar needed first to identify and isolate its self-view and self-image, based on the "value judgment" of the individuals and groups living in it. The "cultural self" and a knowledge of it were believed to be the key to true internal understanding of a culture. For von Grunebaum, culture was manufactured by elites. Hence, he studied it through an analysis of the cultural discourse of elites and the selective texts written by "intellectual leaders." Lovejoy's unit-ideas were defined and analyzed by von Grunebaum in synchronic space, as static entities. He aspired to study the structures, frames of mind, forms of representation, and above all, the collective self-images of Islamic culture. Despite the distinctiveness of von Grunebaum's approach, Gibb exerted an enormous influence on him.[28]

Between 1947 and 1950, von Grunebaum wrote his extended essay "Attempts at Self-Interpretation in Contemporary Islam." He attempted to present "the attitude of the Muslim intelligentsia toward its own background and toward the West" through a selective but, in his view, representative examination of "the work of a number of outstanding literary figures." The essay is actually a general, horizontal (ahistorical) analysis of several representative texts of "intellectual leaders"—al-Afghani, 'Abduh, and Rida are discussed somewhat briefly, and Gibb's "Egyptian modernists"—Haykal, Taha Husayn, and 'Ali 'Abd al-Raziq—are presented in more depth. Von Grunebaum also included the important Indian thinkers Sayyid Ameer 'Ali, Muhmmad Iqbal, and the Syrian historian Kurd 'Ali in his discussion.[29] For him, these thinkers represented the "self-interpretation" and "self-view" of contemporary Islam. It also seems that von Grunebaum represented through them no less his own self-image as a Western-oriented scholar, who sees it as "his duty to interpret Islam from the point of view of the Westerner deeply steeped in his own civilization at its best."[30]

Muhammad Husayn Haykal's intellectual identity, for example, is presented solely on the basis of his *Hayat Muhammad* (The Life of Muhammad, 1935). Von Grunebaum expressed his admiration for Haykal's "courageous" willingness to cope with the most "sacred" and sensitive core of his cultural legacy and to reinterpret and reconstruct it. He viewed him as a representative of "progressive conservatism" who "proposes to set forth the life of Muhammad on purely modern and Western lines." In von Grunebaum's view, however, Haykal's attempt was rife with contradictions, raised essential problems, and revealed "the limitations of his [Haykal's] insight into the basic features of Islamic civilization." The Western reader trying to understand Haykal's text, he stated, will sense "a feeling of awkwardness, of a certain provincialism," particularly when Haykal presumes to explain Muhammad's ascension to heaven in terms of modern psychology. In his view, Haykal's entire project was a failure: "It is, unfortunately, undeniable that this bold, though arbitrary, construction of Western and Islamic civilizations fails to offer any explicit observations as to the inner workings of either the Western or the Eastern mind."[31]

Taha Husayn's book, *Mustaqbal al-Thaqafa fi Misr* (The Future of Culture in Egypt, 1938), is also analyzed at length. As we might expect, von

Grunebaum looks favorably on Taha Husayn's Western orientation and Husayn's claims that "in the modern age Egypt has taken Europe for her model in all aspects of the material life. Her spiritual '*aql*, too, is purely European, appearances notwithstanding." Like Gibb, he regarded Taha Husayn as "her [Egypt's] most philosophical and most aggressive educational reformer and probably the leading scholar-littérateur of the Arab world." Also like Gibb, he considered only one work by Husayn, the one that supposedly represented his "self-interpretation" of "contemporary Islam" (despite the fact that Husayn's interest was clearly contemporary Egypt).[32] The explicitly Western-oriented position taken in *The Future of Culture in Egypt* was a source of hope for von Grunebaum that his expectation—that "modern Islam" would learn how to assimilate the principles and method of Western modernity—might be realized. It was with optimism that von Grunebaum wrote at the end of the 1940s that the intellectual elites might be capable of creating a humanistic model of man "that may, as in the Western Renaissance five centuries ago, release dormant resources of creative energy. [For] it is the revaluation of man that has at all times presaged a cultural renewal."[33]

In the 1950s and the early 1960s, however, von Grunebaum's view of the ability of the intellectual leaders to modernize and Westernize their Islamic societies became far more skeptical. In his opinion, their writings reflected a crisis in the self-image and self-view of Islamic culture. In his 1959 essay, "The Intellectual Problem of Westernization in the Self-View of the Arab World," von Grunebaum again selectively and noncontextually analyzed texts of modernist thinkers and writers. Although texts by Egyptian intellectuals were again prominent, by this time Taha Husayn's *The Future of Culture in Egypt* was under strong attack from the hegemonic, Pan-Arab nationalist forces. As a result of the influence of Jamal 'Abd al-Nasir and radical Arab nationalism, the modernist and Egyptianist views expressed in Husayn's book were now represented by von Grunebaum as the worldview of a diminishing minority.[34]

Von Grunebaum's most important and most representative essay of the period was "Self-Image and Approach to History." In this study, his criticism of the failure of the intellectuals was much harsher and more blatant. The *Islamiyyat* writings of Haykal, Taha Husayn, and 'Abbas Mahmud al-'Aqqad in the 1930s and 1940s provided the basis of his discussion, and von Grunebaum further developed Gibb's conclusion that the intellectuals failed to understand correctly the history of their own culture because they did not internalize the Western, objective, scientific, empirical approach to historical research and historical knowledge. Their historical writings revealed a lack of commitment to basing "historical truths" on empirical evidence; the intellectuals were unwilling to record real events if they exposed weaknesses and flaws in Islamic culture or shattered accepted myths. He saw *Islamiyyat* literature as a Gordian knot that tied the Islamic self-image together with the intellectuals' approach to history. The intellectuals, in his opinion, suffered from gross presentism directed at recruiting the past to serve aims of the present, an apologetic maneuver to defend Islam.[35]

It is probably no coincidence that Taha Husayn and his Islamic writings became the focus of von Grunebaum's criticism. Husayn's historical trilogy, *'Ala Hamish al-Sira* (On the Margin of the Life of the Prophet), published in the 1930s and early 1940s, was, for von Grunebaum, an example of the weakness he found inherent in Islamic historiography: it was mobilized solely for the purpose of reasserting the cultural self-image and serving it. Von Grunebaum criticized Taha Husayn for his uncritical praise of the *Sahaba* and their lives, and for his rejection of critical testimonies by classical Muslim historians who found in the *Sahaba*'s "lofty example" serious flaws. "Nor does he [Taha Husayn] hesitate," von Grunebaum added, "to utilize anachronistic traditions where they suit his purpose." Von Grunebaum severely criticized Taha Husayn's use of legends and tales from the life of the Prophet with "the goal of recreating ancient history as an inspiration for the contemporaries." Husayn's attempt to revive "tales of the past" and to narrate them for his readers as relevant modern stories "represent the other elements that have shaped and limited Taha Husayn's presentation of historical events. Fact-finding as such is not among them."[36]

Here, we can see that von Grunebaum was indeed Gibb's most faithful follower. Like Gibb, von Grunebaum concluded that Egyptian intellectuals remystified arbitrarily chosen heroes, stories, and events to enhance the existing Islamic self-image. Consequently, in von Grunebaum's reworked narrative of crisis from the early 1960s even Taha Husayn, the man who symbolized the great hope of "radical modernism," had bowed to the overriding need to serve the "Islamic self-image." He himself had put in place the obstacles that impeded his culture from developing the "Western man's" brand of "humanistic historicism," and, therefore, he also reflected his culture's failure to understand itself "as it truly is," and then to modernize and progress.[37]

In the late 1950s and in the 1960s, Wilfred Cantwell Smith's *Islam in Modern History* made a significant impact on Middle Eastern studies. Following Gibb and von Grunebaum, the scholar of religions and the history of religious ideas remapped the trends, schools, clusters of thought, and worldviews developing in the modern Islamic world. The influence of Gibb's *Modern Trends in Islam* is particularly evident in Smith's work. Methodologically, Smith reproduced some of Gibb's and von Grunebaum's conceptual frameworks and research methods. He analyzed ideological structures and systems of thought synchronically, based on the assumption that ideas have an autonomous status beyond the contexts in which they are created. "Ideas," he wrote, "ever bear marks of the environment in which they are born, and are understood in ways related to the environment in which they are interpreted, yet have a life and power of their own. This is supremely true of religious ideas, whose persistence and persuasiveness far outstretch in space and time the original milieu to which they are, as it were, naturally correlated."[38] Smith studied the development of Islamic ideas in the modern era based on key unit-ideas: the Muslims' sense of the essence of Islamic history and how it should be, "and their [growing] awareness, on the other hand, of what their actual history is today observably."[39] He, too, concluded that the growing discrepancy between the ideal—the historical promise of a life of grandeur, power, and supremacy—and the bitter, humiliating, and inferior reality had given rise to a grievous cultural crisis. Since "the Arabs" saw themselves as the founders of Islam and its most intimately faithful followers, their modern reality was one of ongoing crisis: "The crisis of the Arabs is acute. And within it, the crisis of Islam is acute."[40]

After a brief survey of the pioneers who reformulated "Islamic thought in recent history," first among them Jamal al-Din al-Afghani, Smith examined "liberalism" or, more specifically, "Islamic liberalism," which, in his view, had had a strong impact on Muslim cultures and societies throughout the first half of the twentieth century. Smith explained that he used the term *liberalism* "in a deliberately broad sense," on the assumption that it is expressed in diverse forms and voices. As was soon realized, his "liberalism" was in fact "modernism" with an accentuated Western orientation. Taha Husayn, Haykal, al-ʿAqqad, and al-Hakim remained the typical representatives of "Islamic liberalism." Smith devoted a brief, superficial discussion to the Islamic writings of these four writers, concentrating mainly on their portraits of the Prophet. Time, space, and place are indiscriminately jumbled together. Smith, for example, draws no distinction between the "Egyptian liberalism," or "radical modernism," of the 1920s and that of the 1930s. And although he discusses the writings of liberal intellectuals in Egypt that were produced in the 1930s and 1940s, he does so within the context of a broader discussion of composers of "Islamic liberal literature." He states that the intellectual effort to create "an indigenous Islamic formulation" by linking the Prophet and early Islam to modernist and liberal ideas was "impressive," merited appreciation, and was, "it would seem, a creative synthesis." "Yet this ideology," he added, "has in fact proven neither contagious and inspiring, nor even sustained. It was admirable, and was admired. But it was not cogent. And if one examines it more closely, one discovers that this is after all not really Islamic liberalism."[41]

Smith reasoned that for the intellectuals, who internalized their liberal (modernist) principles from external, European sources, this project may have been "satisfying." But for the broad readership, "the [liberal] movement has not served to instigate a creative reform, nor to nourish the integrity of committed loyalties."[42] Another source of intellectual weakness was "the endeavor to prove, to oneself or others, that Islam is sound." The use of apologetics as a basis for a modernist representation of Islam "has diverted the attention of contemporary Islamic thinkers from their central task— the central task of all thinkers: to pursue truth and to solve problems." In Smith's narrative, the blame falls entirely on the intellectuals and their failure to demonstrate integrity, resoluteness, and courage: "A lack of integrity always leads to disintegration; and any failure of intellectual integrity in a society raises the threat of disastrous intellectual disintegration." In a bold dramatization of Gibb's "trahison des clercs," Smith delivered his verdict: "The Muslim world, including its intelligentsia, has hardly recognized what a responsible, crucial role its intellectual class plays in the present crisis; and how far the future of Islam and of the Muslim community depends on the ability of the intellectual to face, understand, analyse, and solve the new issues that confront them."[43]

When Smith does specifically discuss "the Arabs," casting Egypt in the leading role, he states that "apologetics is the ideological expression of the reaction against attack," and "the modern Arab is first and foremost a person defending himself and his society against onslaught [by the West]."[44] Following Gibb and von Grunebaum, Smith, with patronizing authority, criticized the Arabs' approach to history. "The Arab writing of history has been functioning, then, less as a genuine inquiry than as a psychological defense."[45] Smith accepted Gibb's position that the modernists were irresponsibly and unrestrainedly swept up in "paralyzing romanticism" that prevented them from adopting "objective historiography."[46] This apologetic modernism suffered, in his view, from a twofold failure: it failed to reinforce modernity, and it had failed to reach the masses of believers. The "essential tragedy" of "Muslim modernism," as expressed, for example, in Farid

Wajdi's writing, was that "it has lost touch with the heart of faith."[47] The modernist intellectuals lacked not only "intellectual honesty," "integrity," and "self-critical humility" but also "effective faith." Their defensive writing was self-defeating. Its aim was to console and sooth without offering a challenging agenda for constructive action that would lead to genuine reform. Thus, Smith concluded, the intellectuals had betrayed themselves, their readers, and their society.[48]

It was through Nadav Safran, however, in *Egypt in Search of Political Community*, that the crisis narrative received its fullest conceptual and historical canonization. Published in 1961, the book was written in Gibb's and Smith's shadows, and Safran acknowledges Gibb in his book. Again, one finds no mention of the influence of the methods of intellectual history that were then prominent in the historical discipline. Nonetheless, *Egypt in Search of Political Community* is patently a history of ideas that traces the dynamics of "belief systems" and presents and analyzes them within the framework of the key political and social developments of modern Egypt. Safran's endeavor to clarify the "intimate connection between material realities— economic, social and political conditions—and modes of thought, ideas, norms, and values," although at times too general and not rigorous enough, is the raison d'être of his historical analysis of the weight of ideas in society and politics.[49] Although adopting a different approach, Safran's work provided full theoretical and historical legitimation of the theory of the intellectual crisis.

It is through Safran's lengthy discussion of intellectual developments during the interwar period that his reaffirmation of the crisis narrative is most apparent. After briefly discussing, in the third part of his work, "the triumph of the liberal nationalist movement" in Egypt after the 1919 national revolution and explaining the historical background for its victory, Safran devotes the entire fourth part of his work to "The Progress and Decline of Liberal Nationalism." The sharp dichotomy between the 1920s—described by Safran as "the Progressive Phase"—and "the Crisis of Orientation," "the Crisis of Liberal Nationalism," and the inception of the "Reactionary Phase" when, in the 1930s and 1940s, the intellectuals withdrew from their modernist positions, is substantiated in a systematic, assertive manner. Safran's discussion of the progressive phase, from 1919 to 1933 approximately, is clearly an expansion of Gibb's treatment of the intellectual modernist literature of the period. Safran analyzed the progressive body of thought as a collective intellectual project led by "the liberal intellectuals." He also focused his analysis on the writings of al-Raziq, Husayn, al-'Aqqad, Haykal, al-Mazini, al-Hakim, and Ahmad Amin. For Safran, the three polemic, orthodoxy-challenging books—'Abd al-Raziq's *Al-Islam wa-Usul al-Hukm* (1925), Taha Husayn's *Fi al-Shi'r al-Jahili* (1926), and al-Hakim's novel *'Awdat al-Ruh* (1933)—are the key expressions of the progressive intellectual discourse of the era.[50]

Safran analyzed major themes common to these progressive, liberal intellectuals: separation of religion and state; elimination of orthodox Islamic domination of culture and politics; rationalistic, empirical, and critical approaches to Islamic and Egyptian history; and the effort to establish a distinctive local Egyptian national identity by reviving the heritage of the ancient pharaonic civilization and forming the nation-state through democratic, liberal, constitutional government. Safran explains the progressive phase in the specific historical context of 1919–24 Egypt, a time when, in his view, radical modernist trends were reinforced and, moreover, perceived by the intellectuals as furthering their progressive cultural agenda.[51]

The progressive age, in any event, was short-lived. In its course, several inherent weaknesses were already apparent in the intellectuals' mode of thinking and Safran in particular doubted their commitment to adhere firmly to their radical modernism.[52] He tells us that these weaknesses were fully exposed in the 1930s, leading to a profound intellectual metamorphosis. Safran described and explained the crisis of orientation as an internal crisis within the modernist community of discourse. The starting point of the crisis was what he viewed as Taha Husayn's rapid withdrawal from his modernist, rationalist position, from his belief that "reason should prevail,"[53] as it was expressed in his *Fi al-Shi'r al-Jahili*. Safran had expected Taha Husayn to lead a revolution that would replace the value system based on revealed truth "with a world view, more applicable to a new reality, that would be based on a conception of truth as something that is ascertained by the human faculties." But under "tremendous pressure" from traditionalist circles and Islamic orthodoxy, who strongly opposed the provocative theses of *Fi al-Shi'r al-Jahili*, "Taha was compelled to retract this position and he hastily adopted a new one which placed no limits on what might validly be accepted on faith." Husayn, whom Gibb had once defined as "the most radical modernist," now wrote that every individual has "'two distinct personalities, one a rational personality and the other a sentient personality.'" Further proof for Safran was to be found in the fact that when Husayn republished his book, he changed the title to *Fi al-Adab al-Jahili* (On Pre-Islamic Literature, 1927) and deleted the polemic sections in order to appease Islamic opposition. In Safran's view, Taha Husayn's capitulation gave legitimacy to

"emotional truth," to the equation of revelation with reason, and to an intolerable "dualism" that removed rational restrictions on "nonrational truth"
and "thereby opened the door to intellectual anarchy . . . which destroyed
the chief basis of the common ideological endeavor of the Liberal leaders."[54]

For Safran, with the publication of the first volume of 'Ala Hamish al-
Sira in 1933, Husayn had become the prophet of the crisis of orientation.
His defense of early Islamic figures and heroes, the legitimation he gave to
the stories and legends that surrounded the birth and life of the Prophet,
his statements that "reason is not everything" and that people need an imaginary, emotional dimension in their lives, and his sycophancy toward inarticulate readerships—"the fallacies of the new position"—provided for
Safran "a concrete illustration of its [this position's] perils."[55]

Haykal's publication of Hayat Muhammad early in 1935 was, as Safran
saw it, a "logical continuation" of the apologetic trend aimed at recovering
and rehabilitating early Islam and presenting its modernity and relevance
to the present generation. In composing his biography of the Prophet, Haykal
attempted to establish harmony between revelation and reason by arguing
that "the Tradition and the Qur'an were rational according to the modern
scientific method." For Haykal, supernatural phenomena that occurred in
the life of the Prophet, such as his ascendance to heaven or his contract with
angels, could be rationally explained and scientifically ascertained. Safran
regarded this position as "the distortion of the thinking process that is
entailed in apologetics" that "subordinate reason to the teachings of an uncritically accepted belief." Thus, Haykal "weakened one of the foundations [i.e.,
rationalism] on which the intellectual leaders' endeavor had rested."[56]

In 1937, Haykal published Fi Manzil al-Wahy (At the Site of Revelation)
as a kind of sequel to Hayat Muhammad. In it, Haykal wrote that the foundations of modern Western civilization—science and rationalism—had
failed to bring happiness to humankind. Europe, like all of humanity, was
in need of the superior spiritual sources of the East and Islam to redeem
itself from the wretched state into which it had fallen by the late 1930s. Safran
held that this openly anti-Western stance not only further damaged the principle of "reason" (as the first guiding principle of the "humanist liberal-
national outlook") but also seriously undermined "the second guiding
principle by its denigration of Western culture, and thus denied subsequent
intellectual activity any common center of gravity."[57]

Toward the end of the 1930s and during the 1940s and early 1950s, the
crisis of orientation, Safran tells us, produced the reactionary phase. Taha
Husayn completed his trilogy 'Ala Hamish al-Sira; Tawfiq al-Hakim com-

posed his large-scale play *Muhammad*; Haykal published his monumental series of the biographies of *al-Khulafa' al-Rashidun*; al-'Aqqad published his *'Abqariyyat* series; and other intellectual leaders, in particular Ahmad Amin, also concentrated on writing about early Islamic society and culture. According to Safran, the intellectuals inundated the cultural field with pseudohistorical Islamic literature, a popular literature that was no more than a passionate defense of seventh-century Islam and an attack on the "defects" of materialist Western culture. By "subordinating reason to faith" the liberal intellectual leaders had lost their singular identity and "joined the Islamic Reformists ['Abduh and Rida], and even the orthodoxy." But Safran, following Gibb, stressed that "whereas, to the orthodox, faith was really a way of perceiving the truth, and its content was a practical guide to life, to the 'repentant' Liberal Nationalists [intellectuals] faith only remained as a limitation on the intellect, and the interpretation of its content a means of vain intellectual aggrandizement."[58]

How did Safran explain this serious crisis? Although he purported to explain changes in systems of belief and ideology in terms of structural changes in the economy, society, and politics, the contexualism to which he explicitly committed himself in the introduction to his book is almost absent. The Islamic literature that led to the crisis and represented it is neither located nor examined in the specific historical contexts in which it was written. One relatively broad chapter, "The Historical Crisis of Liberal Nationalism," describes what he regards as a crisis in the material structures of Egyptian society between 1922 and 1952: in the operation of the economy, the social structures, "the political and social failure of the liberal democratic regime," and "the failure of public education." But this contextualist discussion is broad and generalized and does not adequately explain why specific texts were written by specific intellectuals at specific times and places.[59]

As the faithful disciple of Gibb and Smith, Safran's verdict could only be severe and uncompromising. The liberal intellectuals were morally bankrupt, guilty of trahison des clercs. They were caught up in a "general emotional glorification of a vague Islam, and an aggressive attitude toward its antithesis, the West"; they had channeled their efforts to a cult of sterile idealization of Islamic heroes and norms, without being aware of the catastrophic consequences for them and their society;[60] they had lost control and allowed themselves to plunge into "intellectual disorientation" and "ideological confusion." As a result, they "surrendered their previous guide and bearing—rationalism and a Western cultural orientation—without being able to produce viable Muslim-inspired alternatives." The intellectuals, Safran wrote, had thus paved the way for the extreme reactionary era that emerged in Egypt after World War II, in which "the whole ideological sphere was dominated by a romantic, vague, inconsistent and aggressive Muslim orientation."[61] In this atmosphere, the absolute victory of "the ideology and mentality of Mahdism" (another term Safran borrowed from Gibb) as expressed in the militant Islamic fundamentalism of the Muslim Brothers, was, to Safran's thinking, assured.[62]

The impact of the "intellectual crisis" paradigm on Middle Eastern studies in general and on Egyptian intellectual history in particular was enormous. It offered at one and the same time a powerful interpretation of the "failure of the liberal experiment," the "demise of parliamentarianism," or the "failure of Westernized modernism" in the era of the "ancien régime" (the first half of the twentieth century), on the one hand, and the rise of authoritarian military regimes, revolutionary Arab nationalism, and radical political Islam in the second half of the century, on the other. Bernard Lewis, in an attempt to explain "the revolt of Islam," posited that ʿAli ʿAbd al-Raziq had failed "to separate religion from politics" in the 1920s because of the "entrenched opposition of Al-Azhar." In Lewis's estimation, "The beginnings of a more active and general concern with religion can already be seen in the thirties, in the wave of popular literary works extolling Muhammad and the early heroes of Islam." For Lewis, this wave was a clear indication of a retreat from a framework of communal identity and a culture based on "Western liberalism" and a return to one based on Islam. Further confirmation of this retreat was reflected by the vast popularity of Haykal's *Hayat Muhammad* and Taha Husayn's "romantic works" about "the lives of the Prophet and the caliphs" (*ʿAla Hamish al-Sira*).[63]

P. J. Vatikiotis's understanding of the reality of Egypt and other countries in the Arab Middle East between 1930 and 1950 was aptly reflected in his "The Failure of Liberalism and the Reaction against Europe." His assessment was that the modernist attack on Islamic tradition in the 1920s "turned out to be a short-lived affair." By the 1930s, the leading modernists—Taha Husayn, Haykal, and al-ʿAqqad—"were already in hasty retreat" from secular liberalism and their embracement of European culture. "Their reverential studies of the early fathers of the Islamic Community smacked of frantic and solicitous apologia for their earlier rationalist-secular attacks upon the religion and its cultural heritage. A romantic proclivity for an epic quality of Islam now became a major characteristic of their writings." For Vatikiotis, this "regressive" literature was a clear-cut expression of the abandon-

ment of the "liberal values of Western civilization as an ideological foundation for a modern Egypt." Like Gibb and Safran, he viewed this intellectual metamorphosis as dangerous and reactionary. First, it had instilled in
the general public an emotional religious sentiment and a sense of "the
supremacy of their religion." Second, it "strengthened the position of the
new radical conservative movements" such as the Muslim Brothers and
Young Egypt, who regarded "a return to Islam" as the panacea for Egypt's
economic, social, and political ills. And third, it eroded the conceptual and
practical legitimacy of the constitutional parliamentary government.[64]

Afaf Lutfi al-Sayyid-Marsot presented a more complex approach. She
accepted several of the conclusions of the scholars who had deconstructed
the narrative of crisis and stressed that the intellectuals had remained committed to modernist and liberal principles. In her view, though, the 1930s
presented "a period of despondency and a general feeling of failure." She
viewed Haykal's attempt in the 1930s to assert that "reason would itself
become the basis of religious belief" as a new position that "ran diametri-
cally opposite to [Taha] Husain's [claim] that religion and reason operate
on different spheres." In her estimation, Haykal's change was part of a larger,
new tendency among liberal intellectuals to adopt Islam as an "indigenous
ideology," a trend, she concluded, that would be very difficult to anchor in
"the liberal humanist tradition" that the disciples of Ahmad Lutfi al-Sayyid
strove to foster and transmit to their society. Rather, she viewed the turn
to Islam as a sterile attempt to search for "salvation" in the far distant past of
the Islamic community, a trend that indirectly served the populist Islam
of the Muslim Brothers.[65]

In the 1990s, Selma Botman's discussion of the intellectual and cultural
developments of "Egypt from independence to revolution" was another
reproduction of the crisis narrative. It would be hard to argue that by this
time she was unaware of the critique of Safran, according to which Taha
Husayn's "religious books" were an attempt to reformulate Islam "in new
ways that were more appropriate to the modern Egyptian consciousness."
Nonetheless, she corroborated Safran's approach and, like him, espoused
the view that Taha Husayn's writings about Islam were "a complete retreat
from his adherence to rationalism." Her criticism of Haykal, though, was
more severe. She stated that in his writings on the Prophet and al-Khulafa'
al-Rashidun, "Haykal essentially abandoned his commitment to the liberal values inherent in Western civilization and instead stressed the intellectual and ethical content of early Islam." He asserted, she wrote, that
reason and science were "insufficient for the happiness of man." He

"attacked the West, rejected much of European culture, and apologetically offered Islam as the best answer to modern problems."[66] Indeed, Botman provides us with solid proof of the resilience and endurance of the narrative of crisis. At the end of the twentieth century, more than fifty years after it was invented, it still served as a "practical narrative" for writing the history of the modern Middle East in general and the intellectual history of modern Egypt in particular.

DECONSTRUCTING THE NARRATIVE OF CRISIS: COLOMBE, CACHIA, HOURANI, AND SMITH

Since the early 1950s, a more convenient historical perspective has developed for a scholarly evaluation of the collective endeavor of the Egyptian intellectuals. *L'Évolution de l'Égypte* (1951) may be regarded as the first of these histories. Marcel Colombe was not only an intellectual historian; his book also deals with social, institutional, and political developments. Nevertheless, the intellectual part of his work, "L'Évolution des idées de 1924–1944," forms a central part of his book.[67] Although he made some use of Gibb's studies of modernist intellectuals of the 1920s, *Modern Trends in Islam* is only a footnote to his work, and no traces of von Grunebaum's work are to be found. Colombe presented the major themes of the *Islamiyyat* literature produced by Taha Husayn, Haykal, and al-'Aqqad in the 1930s and 1940s. He was not uncritical of some of the modernist intellectuals' themes, but he did not regard their approach as a "retreat" or a "crisis." In his opinion, the intellectuals did not intend to write serious historical or theological works, and therefore it was a mistake to use the scholarly criteria of history and theology to judge the "new genre" of Islamic literature. Colombe perceived two clearly defined goals in this literature. First, its writers hoped to offer their readership relevant, modernized images of the founders of Islam. Second, they wanted to create an imaginative, epic literature that would please and entertain the average modern reader by means of anecdotes and legends, largely fictional and imagined, from the days of the Prophet and the first orthodox caliphs. Colombe emphasized the wide popularity and impressive success of these Islamic works throughout the Arab world. He concluded that the intellectuals had proved that they could appeal to the new, young readerships that, because of the profound sociopolitical changes that had occurred in Egypt and in the Middle East during the 1930s, were capturing a key place in the literate cultural arena.[68]

Pierre Cachia's study of Taha Husayn (1956) was the first complete intellectual biography in English of a leading Egyptian modernist intellectual. Cachia justifiably regarded Husayn as the most important and most influential of the modernist intellectuals; in this respect he continued the tradition begun by Gibb, and he thanked him warmly in his acknowledgments. This, however, is the only expression of Gibb's influence to be found in the work. Being a literary critic Cachia used an altogether different approach from Gibb, and suggested new interpretations of Taha Husayn's life and thought. Cachia detected no significant reversal in Husayn's cultural orientations over the course of the first half of the century; for him, the intellectual's commitment to modernism and the "Egyptian literary renaissance," and his courage and the provocative manner in which he promoted Westernized modernism, remained basically firm. This seems to explain Cachia's choice to locate Husayn's Islamic writings, *'Ala Hamish al-Sira* in particular, in a chapter dealing with "story-telling." His emphasis on the fictional literary character of this work is significant. Cachia in effect deconstructed the attempt to classify the book as a scholarly, historical work expressing empirical truths. He stressed that *'Ala Hamish al-Sira* was "not a novel or a unified tale, but a collection of narratives connected in one way or another with the life of Muhammad." He surmised that Taha Husayn had devoted himself to writing mythological, imaginary, engaging, and "delightful legends" to charm and entertain; *'Ala Hamish al-Sira* was "in fact the most impious of Taha Husayn's books."[69]

Albert Hourani's work *Arabic Thought in the Liberal Age, 1798–1939* made an even more significant contribution to the deconstruction of the "narrative of crisis."[70] First published in 1962, it has been recognized as a classic on the intellectual evolution of the modern Arab Middle East. Hourani's later insightful comments about his own work, together with an illuminating article by Donald M. Reid and important observations made by Roger Owen, Gaby Piterberg, and Derek Hopwood have contributed much to our understanding of the background to Hourani's book and its subsequent vast influence on Middle Eastern historiography in general and the intellectual history of the region in particular.[71] In 1981, in the introduction to *The Emergence of the Modern Middle East*, Hourani wrote that "I now consider it [*Arabic Thought in the Liberal Age*] to have been an extended footnote to Gibb's *Modern Trends in Islam*."[72] Like Gibb, Adams, and other intellectual historians who preceded him, Hourani also attributed great importance to 'Abduh and his "disciples"; the "school" led by Qasim Amin and by Lutfi al-Sayyid and *al-Jarida*; and Rashid Rida.[73] Moreover, in the same fashion as Gibb, Hourani too believed that "liberal thought" had reached the peak of its mature expression with Taha Husayn, who "can be regarded as the last great representative of a line of thought, the writer who has given the final statement of the system of ideas which underlay social thought and political action in the Arab countries for three generations." Hourani devoted an entire chapter specifically to this great Egyptian thinker, and a large section of it to a thorough analysis of *The Future of Culture in Egypt* (1938).[74]

One should not, however, be misled by the similarity between Gibb's and Hourani's arguments nor the credit Hourani so generously awarded Gibb in his works. *Arabic Thought in the Liberal Age* was a far cry from *Modern Trends in Islam*. In it, Hourani applied a research method and conceptual framework for organizing ideas and their producers, and the way ideas were presented and understood, that were distinctively different from Gibb's. Hourani, one could say, introduced time to Middle Eastern intellectual history, through his chronological framework of historical development. He demonstrated great sensitivity for shifts in the flow of ideas and for changes in the historical rhythm of intellectual dynamics. His interest was "in taking an idea, showing how it grew, was linked with others within a system, answered certain questions and gave rise to others."[75]

Hourani may disappoint in that he does not directly engage in dialogue with or otherwise relate to the European and American schools of intellectual history that were flourishing at the time. The most important influences on his decision to specialize in intellectual history, as he identified them, were his philosophy studies at Oxford and his interest in the history of philosophical ideas and philosophers. Hourani belonged to the "generation of those for whom the study of philosophy was essentially the study of its history."[76] Hegel and Hegelian idealism, what Owen later defined as "Oxford Hegelianism," had a special influence on the young Hourani, as did R. G. Collingwood in *The Idea of History*.[77] Hourani was captivated by the possibility of tackling clusters of unit-ideas in a given historical period—their initial formation by diverse thinkers and schools of thought, their development through various stages, and their changing contexts. Although he recognized in each of these intellectual forces distinctive biographical, social, political, and cultural characteristics, for him they all belonged to one ideological movement and therefore shared common intellectual dilemmas and posed similar questions, even though the solutions they offered were varied and sometimes contested one another. In consideration of Hourani's methodological approach, it seems best to locate *Arabic Thought in the Liberal Age* within the developing tradition of the his-

tory of ideas that originated with Arthur O. Lovejoy. A historian of philosophical ideas, Lovejoy proposed, already in the 1940s, a well-defined
agenda for "the study of the history of ideas."[78]

The method Hourani applied in *Arabic Thought in the Liberal Age* extri-
cated it from the Orientalist, textualist, and static fetters that had characterized the works of many of his predecessors. Hourani, nevertheless,
shared with them a general paradigm of the history of ideas—the basic
assumption "that ideas can largely determine the direction of social and political change, that popularizing intellectuals play central roles in their societies."[79] John Higham, whose method was similar to the one adopted by
Hourani, succinctly expressed this when he stated that "for the intellectual
historian, not culture, politics, society or art, but states of mind make up
the foreground of interest and the focus of curiosity. . . . He should feel the
appeal of an idea, and weigh critically its tenability. In that sense, he is an
amateur philosopher."[80]

The concept of studying an "age," as Hourani did, came directly from
intellectual histories of the 1940s, 1950s, and 1960s. "The Age of Enlightenment," "The Age of Reason," "The Age of Reform," and "The Age of Revolution" are typical titles of works from these years produced by intellectual
historians. In 1961, Higham put forth the opinion that "the largest distinctive aim of the intellectual historian, therefore, is to describe and explain
the spirit of an age."[81] Hourani, for his part, defined the period from 1830
to approximately 1939 as a distinctive age. Although not assuming that an
age implied a single, homogeneous, unifying framework of thought, he
nonetheless attempted to identify unit-ideas that were common to the
schools and the individual thinkers of this particular age. It was, in his view,
the "liberal age" or, as he later qualified it, an age of modernity (or modernism) characterized by "those movements of Arabic thought which accepted
the dominant ideas of modern Europe."[82] Specifically, Hourani identified
unit-ideas and "the movement of thought" in the modes by which Arab intellectuals reacted to the growing influence of Western culture and its ideas:
how they understood European modernity, how and to what extent they
assimilated it, and how they attempted to change and reconstruct indigenous cultural traditions so as to incorporate Western principles, concepts,
and terminology and carry out their agendas for social, cultural, and political change. One could characterize Hourani's method as an analysis of the
modernist (for him, liberal) discourse that evolved within the Arab Middle Eastern intellectual community in a defined age.[83]

The community of discourse that provided Hourani's "unit" of research was rather broad. It contained dozens of thinkers and writers. In retrospect, Hourani was critical of his selective choice of "a small number of thinkers" whom he had considered "individual representatives." He suspected that his selection was somewhat arbitrary, and he problematized his earlier assumption that the modernist discourse and its producers were the hegemonic force in the cultural field. He admitted that he had excluded traditionalist and conservative voices from his "representative" selection and expressed doubt as to whether the voices he had neglected were any less central than the ones he had presented.[84] But Hourani tended to exaggerate in his retrospective self-criticism. The truth is that in *Arabic Thought in the Liberal Age* he made important breakthroughs both in defining the intellectual community and in formulating a method by which to study it. His community of discourse was a conglomerate of several trends, schools, and individuals. It gave expression to the hegemonic voices of the discourse, but also to peripheral and suppressed ones. It combined "founding fathers" with "disciples-students." In contrast to Gibb, von Grunebaum, and Smith, Hourani did not include Islamic thinkers and schools that existed outside the world of the Arabic print culture. And unlike Safran, Hourani included in his broad Arabic community writers, thinkers, and journalists of Greater Syria as well as Egypt, including a number of Christians. Although Hourani would later categorize most of the intellectuals in his study as "derivative thinkers of the second or third rank of importance,"[85] the truth is that he presented methodical descriptions of about thirty luminary intellectuals in his book (fifteen of them were discussed in depth, and individual chapters were devoted to al-Afghani, 'Abduh, Rida, Shibli Shumayyil, Farah Antun, and Taha Husayn) and also discussed, though more briefly, about twenty second-tier intellectuals, in addition to a number of third-tier publicists. As for conservative, or "fundamentalist," voices, he included Shaykh Muhammad Bakhit and Hasan al-Banna, among others.[86] By any criterion, it presented a decidedly representative community of this specific cultural landscape and, more largely, of the entire course of the liberal age.

Arabic Thought in the Liberal Age successfully merged a discussion of individual intellectuals with climates of opinion, schools of thought, ideological movements, and generational developments. In all, Hourani considered four "generations" of producers and thinkers. The first generation (1830–70) belonged to bureaucratic intellectuals. The second (1870–1900) was marked by Islamic modernism, and its major task was to "reinterpret Islam so as to make it compatible with living in the modern world." The third generation (1900–1939), intellectually mature, included two diverse trends: first, Rida and his Islamic reformism, which led, in Hourani's words, "to a kind of Muslim fundamentalism," such as that typified by the Muslim Brothers; and, second, Lutfi al-Sayyid and his Lebanese Christian contemporaries and, following them, Egyptian Muslim liberal thinkers who "held that life in society should be regulated by secular norms, of individual welfare . . . a line of thought . . . [that] reached its logical end in the work of Taha Husayn."[87] The fourth generation (1939–60) was that of revolutionary Arab socialist nationalism, represented most notably by Jamal 'Abd al-Nasir.[88]

Hourani's focus on the historical dynamics of ideas allowed him to attribute them more concretely to the social and political contexts in which they were created and that they addressed. His discussion of the biographical—family, social, and political—backgrounds of the producers of ideas was pioneering. Moreover, Hourani was adept at recovering the intellectuals' motivations and intentions for saying what they said and writing what they wrote—in Hourani's words, what "may have led them to think about certain matters in a certain way."[89] But Hourani's contextualism was limited. He concentrated on the contexts in which ideas were born and the reasons for their emergence at specific times and places; he gave much less attention to an examination of the contexts of transmission and reception of ideas—the patterns of social or political consumption. Hourani later questioned the wisdom of this, noting that "I had said little in the book about the connection between the movements of thoughts . . . and the movements of social and political change with which they were connected."[90] Although Hourani was able to clarify the link between thought and family and social origin—noting, for example, the connection between 'Abduh's and Lutfi al-Sayyid's intellectual formations and their "village families'" 'umda backgrounds—he was not, however, able to assess concretely the precise influences of the intellectuals' thought on shaping public opinion, determining political action, or engendering social change.[91] Hourani would later acknowledge this shortcoming as "a failure . . . to go beyond individual thinkers, and try systematically to see how far their ideas expressed those of any substantial element in the societies to which they belonged, or how far they had an influence upon them."[92]

Above all, *Arabic Thought in the Liberal Age* was a product of a liberal humanist. Hourani abandoned the patronizing, moralistic, and essentialist Orientalist tradition of judging texts and their producers according to the most stringent criteria of Western "humanism" and "liberalism," an ahistorical, ideal-type kind of test that very few intellectuals in the West would have successfully passed. Since Hourani, nevertheless, was influenced by theories of modernization and the vestiges of Orientalism, his work is not entirely free of modernist expectations. But these never brought him to the point of rendering verdicts, assigning blame, or making value judgments that seemingly had one purpose, whether explicitly stated or not—to ensnare ideas and their creators into a "crisis" or "failure," "intellectual confusion," or "paralyzing romanticism." As a "successful scholarly middleman in explaining the Middle East to the West," it appears that Hourani understood, far better than others of his generation, the role of the scholar of Middle Eastern ideas in an age of decolonization.[93]

Hourani did not relate directly to the topic of the "crisis of the intellectuals." Nevertheless, his views on it are clear in his book. First, the liberal age (or, according to Safran, the progressive phase) continued, in Hourani's view, well into the 1930s and was brought to further philosophical and programmatic heights by Taha Husayn at the end of the decade. As additional proof of the stable, continuous existence of reformist modernism throughout this period among the intellectual elite, Hourani presented contemporary texts by Salama Musa and Hafiz 'Afifi that leveled rationalist and Fabian social criticism at Egyptian society and offered an alternative, liberal, reformist agenda for structural change. Second, Hourani did not discern the profound differences between early and later radical modernism and its challenge to the foundations of Islamic orthodoxy; for him, al-Raziq's writing of the 1920s was not significantly different from Taha Husayn's in the late 1930s. Third, and most important, Hourani forcefully rejected the claim that Taha Husayn's (and, similarly, Haykal's and al-'Aqqad's) Islamic writings of the 1930s and 1940s, in particular 'Ala Hamish al-Sira, reflected a change in his stance vis-à-vis Islam, a retreat from rationalist and humanist principles, or submission to sterile apologetics. He accepted Cachia's argument that "Husayn's religious books must therefore be seen as attempts to re-tell the story of Islam in ways which will appeal to the modern Egyptian consciousness." Husayn was interested in reshaping the story of the life of the Prophet and the first caliphs so as to stress specifically their role as harbingers of "social justice" and "a reign of worldly justice," and, more generally, he aimed to create a new symbolic world from early Islamic sources "in order to make an appeal to minds formed by western education."[94]

In Middle Eastern studies in the 1960s and 1970s, *Arabic Thought in the Liberal Age* was a source of inspiration for a whole array of new intellectual histories, in particular intellectual biographies.[95] For our purpose, it is important to note that Hourani inspired a new revisionist approach to the issue of the crisis of the intellectuals, which brought about a reevaluation of the role of intellectuals in modernization processes in Egypt and other Arab societies and cultures.

Kenneth Cragg suggested a constructive and rationalist reading of the Islamic writings of Taha Husayn, Haykal, al-'Aqqad, and Ahmad Amin. He argued that their liberal modernist worldview in the 1920s did not significantly change during the 1930s and 1940s. Cragg opined that 'Ala Hamish al-Sira should not be judged according to the academic criteria of "historical scholarship" and that to view it as an apologetic text would be incorrect. Taha Husayn's aim, he wrote, was "to renew the ancient 'hagiography' of Islam for the contemporary reader by retelling it in a fresh idiom and freeing it from an archaic or forbidding guise." And, in Cragg's view, Husayn successfully realized this goal. For Cragg, Haykal's Hayat Muhammad was a further example of the intellectual effort to establish a relevant, modern image of the Prophet. Haykal had attempted to free the "Life of Muhammad" from the dogmatic shackles of the traditional Sira and to reshape it using an empirical, rationalist method. While Cragg was more reserved about Haykal's success in accomplishing the task he had set for himself, he concluded that, "judged in the light of its own modest plea to have made only a beginning, Hayat Muhammad, with its fervour and candour, is a notable waymark." As in his estimations of Husayn and Haykal, Cragg also viewed Ahmad Amin's writings as an attempt to renew Islam and to bridge the world of faith and the modern, rational world.[96]

In the 1970s, Majid Khadduri suggested a different interpretation of the development of intellectual life in monarchical Egypt. In his view, the centrality of "free thought and secularism" in the Egyptian cultural field until 1952 had been expressed in diverse ways, including the "radical secularism" of 'Ali 'Abd al-Raziq in the 1920s, the frontal attack of Isma'il Mazhar and the al-'Usur group on religion and tradition at the end of that decade, the Fabian socialism of Salama Musa between the two world wars, the "legal secularism" of 'Abd al-Razzaq al-Sanhuri in the 1930s and 1940s, the "Islamic reformation" of Mustafa 'Abd al-Raziq and Khalid Muhammad Khalid in the 1940s and 1950s, and the assertive, Westernized modernism of Taha Husayn throughout the period.[97] Salama Musa's socialist modernism (ignored by Safran) was Khadduri's test case. Later examinations of this intellectual's career by Lutfi al-Sayyid-Marsot and, in a more complete fashion, by Vernon Egger showed that an important part of Musa's radical modernist agenda—which included pharaonism, Westernism, positivism, scientism, national socialism, and humanist liberalism—was formed in the 1930s.[98]

Mustafa Badawi, using literary criticism methods, praised the artistic achievements of Tawfiq al-Hakim's *Muhammad* and Taha Husayn's *'Ala Hamish al-Sira*. He regarded Hakim's innovative attempt "to use the life of the Prophet as a theme for a play" as a "significant new departure." Husayn's imaginative stories and spiritual richness were "the most original work of Islamic prose literature produced by this [intellectual] generation." For Badawi, Husayn was a committed modernist who "underlines the need for modern Arab writers to rework themes of their early literary heritage, since this is one way of keeping it alive." Examining also Islamic texts by Haykal, al-'Aqqad, and Mahmud Taymur, Badawi did not view *Islamiyyat* literature as an "intellectual retreat" or an "intellectual crisis." He viewed it as an expression of the ability of intellectual luminaries to create new literary genres, and, through them, it "attains heights of lyrical utterance of great poetic beauty indeed."[99]

Antonie Wessels, in his comprehensive study of *Hayat Muhammad*, offered a complex explanation for what he perceived as a need felt by the modernist intellectuals of Egypt to write about the Prophet Muhammad and early Muslim society. Dealing with the Islamic writings of Taha Husayn, al-Hakim, Amin, al-'Aqqad, and, of course, Haykal, he enumerated three specific reasons for the collective motivation to focus on Islam. First, he reasserted the argument that "religious literature," or "literature of religious inspiration," was intended for readerships that sought new, updated images of the Prophet and the first great caliphs. Second, he argued that in the 1930s, Islam as a historical heritage and a cultural identity became a vital element in Egyptian life and that the intellectuals thus sought a way to incorporate it as a formative component of the national imagination. Third, the Christian missionary attack on Muhammad's image, together with the distortion of his image by Orientalists, had, he put forth, created "a desire to defend Muhammad against these attacks." Accordingly, Wessels viewed Haykal's *Hayat Muhammad* as an attempt "to use the Western method in order to offer an answer to the orientalists and to give new heart to the young who had come under the influence of the West and become detached from traditional Islamic culture."[100]

Yet it was Charles D. Smith, in his comprehensive work on Muhammad Husayn Haykal, who carried out the most systematic deconstruction of the crisis narrative. Smith explicitly challenged the Orientalist conceptual frameworks and theories of modernization of Gibb, von Grunebaum, and Safran and persuasively showed that their severe judgment of the intellectuals' behavior was victim to their exaggerated (nonhistorical) expectations that the intellectuals would Westernize their societies and transplant a "humanist" Western culture into them, one that originated in "Greece's classical cultural legacy." More significant, in my view, is the fact that Smith introduced the "social turn" into the study of Middle Eastern intellectual history. Under the influence of the social history of ideas, and specifically inspired by sociologists of ideas and intellectuals such as Edward Shils, S. N. Eisenstadt, Joyce Appleby, Mary Douglas, and J. P. Nettl, Smith initiated a rigorous social and political contextualist reading of the texts of Haykal and other intellectuals.[101] He argued that the social context of the intellectual production and the changes taking place in it, factors given little consideration by his predecessors, were vital for understanding the birth and growth of ideas and essential for recovering authorial intent, and for understanding how ideas circulated and the ways they were transmitted to various levels of the society and culture.

It is thus unfortunate that Smith, also, did not explicitly and consciously appropriate methods and insights offered by contemporary European and American intellectual history. It is particularly regrettable that he did not apply Quentin Skinner's rigorous contextualist method, which suggested procedures to recover a writer's intention, from which one could then decode the intended meaning embodied in the text by situating it in its specific sociolinguistic context.[102] Nonetheless, Smith's accomplishment is impressive. He skillfully balanced the internal, textualist approach he used to examine Haykal's ideas and the external, contextualist approach he applied to understand them better. Highly sensitive to the historical-developmental dimension of Haykal's worldview, he examined the intimate interactions between the changes in his writings and those occurring in the social, political, and cultural landscapes in which he worked and to which he reacted.

Smith's contributions to Middle Eastern intellectual history were threefold. First, he demonstrated the connections between Haykal's social origins and his views and positions. Second, he recovered additional dimensions of the intellectual thought of the 1920s. Third, and most important, he located the Islamic texts of the 1930s and 1940s in their sociopolitical contexts, and thus he was able to deconstruct the crisis of orientation narrative.

In the first part of his work, Smith attempted to recover the social context of Haykal's youth, when his modernist worldview took shape. Smith portrayed Haykal's background and his origins in the landowning family of a village 'umda. He refined the notion of "formative context" that molded the young Haykal, carried him through his life, and played a continuous role in shaping and reshaping his worldview.[103] It was within this context, Smith noted, that Haykal (following 'Abduh, Q. Amin and Lutfi al-Sayyid) developed his defined elitist self-image and a clear idea of his aim and destiny as a modernist intellectual in society. Smith argued that Haykal, in line with his elitism, had believed that only a select group of intellectuals who had received a diverse, universal education and had internalized European principles of reason, science, progress, and freedom would be capable of leading their society to modernity and transforming their culture into a progressive, scientific one. Smith identified in Haykal's formative self-image a distinctively conservative element. Haykal had attempted to grant the avant-garde intellectual elite authority to lead Egyptian society to modernity in a way that would not subject Egypt to social upheavals or cultural traumas. Further, he had attempted to prevent the masses, especially the illiterate lower classes, from participating in the determination of the processes of modernization. Smith stated that Haykal viewed the masses as being guided by ignorance, irrational impulses, and religiosity, and, therefore, he deemed it necessary that they be excluded from the circle that decided on society's ideological and political transition from its traditional order to a modern nation-state. This guiding circle was to be the exclusive domain of the leading enlightened elite. In Haykal's opinion, Smith wrote, the masses had to bow to authority, "to be led unquestioningly and 'unawares' into the future," to a progressive society and the coming "scientific phase."[104]

During the decade after the 1919 national revolution, Haykal concentrated on an attempt to realize the formative vision of a modern, progressive Egypt. Smith relates to Haykal's deep commitment to secular modernism, rational and empirical positivism, particularist neopharaonic Egyptian nationalism, the construction of an Egyptian "national culture and literature," the neutralization of the influence of Islam and official Islamic orthodoxy on social and cultural life, and the separation of religion and state.[105] Smith placed Haykal's 1920s body of thought in the immediate political context in which it was constructed; specifically, he established the connection between his modernist message and his activity in the Liberal Constitutionalist Party. Haykal became the chief ideologue of the party and served as the editor of both al-Siyasa, its daily organ, and al-Siyasa al-Usbu'iyya, its cultural weekly. For Haykal, the Liberal party provided an ideal political framework for realizing his elitist self-image—its social base was the landowning elite, and its agenda was progressive modernism anchored in Western-oriented conservative liberalism.[106]

In the late 1920s, though, and more so in the early 1930s, in light of the severe economic, social, and political crises that affected Egypt, the political survival of the Liberal Constitutionalists and Haykal became doubtful.

The party suffered chronic political defeats and came to be overshadowed by the popularity of the Wafd, its main rival. Haykal, Smith relates, realized that his disregard of religion, faith, and Islam in an arena in which Islam was becoming a conventional political weapon might cause the further marginalization of his party or even bring it to political ruin. Additionally, changes in the economy, society, and culture also forced him to question his methodological framework for presenting and transmitting his reformist message. Thus, Smith surmised, he searched for new, more effective methods to impart his modernist strategy to the changing scene; he had realized it was necessary to use a formula that, on the one hand, was consistent with changes in the sociopolitical environment and, on the other, would preserve his formative vision of controlled and restrained modernization that would preserve the social order and protect intellectuals' individualism and freedom of thought.[107]

Smith traced Haykal's intellectual development incrementally and precisely from 1924 to 1933, a path Smith defined as "The Road to Islam." He demonstrated that this development was gradual, occurring in measured stages, and that Haykal himself was quite aware of the changes in position he made. They were, Smith opined, calculated choices and not due to the pressures of a crisis of orientation or to dramatic shifts or loss of control; nor were they a retreat from his modernist liberal program. His development occurred as he abandoned his dogmatic materialist positivism, replacing it with a Bergsonian approach aimed at merging science and faith, the rational and the spiritual.[108]

For Smith, what was important in Haykal's shift were his motives and intentions and the discursive means he adopted for expressing them. Smith characterized the shift as both tactical and instrumental, "a readjustment of terminology which reflected the intensification of religious involvement in the political arena in the [early] 1930s and the Liberal Constitutionalists' attempt to use it for their own purposes." Haykal concluded that if he were to continue appealing to the elite "without regard for mass opinions," he and his modernist message faced the danger of becoming sterile and irrelevant in the new sociopolitical environment of the 1930s. Responding to the growing pressures of the politics of religion and the emerging power of the masses in culture and politics, he thus strove to employ a popular, "religious form of discourse" between intellectuals and broader sectors of society. In this popular discourse, Smith wrote, the modernist message was packaged as "Eastern spirituality" so that it would appeal to and be accepted by the newly literate masses. For him, then, Haykal's shift to "Easternism" was merely tactical. Haykal's original agenda remained almost completely intact while "maintaining the distance between elite and mass which he believed would safeguard his freedom and freedom of thought in general."[109]

Smith also investigated Taha Husayn's 1920s radical modernist position and he showed that it likewise underwent no significant change over the decade, rejecting Safran's claim that by the end of the 1920s Husayn had become the harbinger of the crisis of orientation. Smith argued that Husayn was not, in fact, deterred by venomous attacks from official orthodox Islamic circles on his book *Fi al-Shiʿr al-Jahili* (1926). Other than paying lip service to these circles by making a few deletions in the renamed version of the book, *Fi al-Adab al-Jahili* (1927), Husayn did not retreat from his modernist rationalist position. Moreover, Husayn was, Smith noted, more aware than Haykal that the intellectuals needed to relate to the Islamic heritage, adapt it to modern needs, and disseminate it to a broader audience. As a result, already by the mid-1920s he had developed a model of addressing two distinct readerships. Alongside his elitist writing for educated, modernist communities of readers (*Fi al-Shiʿr al-Jahili* was such a text), he also established a channel of communication with the masses, through a type of popular writing designed to appeal to broad audiences (e.g., *Qadat al-Fikr* [The Leaders of Thought, 1925]). This model was meant to meet the needs of both the intellectual elite—and prompt it to carry out social reform and produce a modern scientific culture for Egypt—and the literate masses—by enabling them to take part in the developing culture while being both guided and controlled by the intellectuals.[110]

In Smith's revisionist narrative, Taha Husayn continued to adhere to this strategy in the 1930s. He published, for example, *Min Baʿid* (From Afar, 1935) and *Mustaqbal al-Thaqafa fi Misr* (1938), two radical modernist statements intended for consumption by the educated elite, and *ʿAla Hamish al-Sira* for mass consumption, the intention of which was not only to entertain and please broad audiences but also "to educate the masses, rather than the elite, in terms understandable to them."[111] Armed with this strategy, Husayn, Smith showed, continued to promote modernist scientific culture, even in the age defined by Safran as a crisis of orientation.

Returning to Haykal, Smith wrote that in the 1930s he had adopted Husayn's model of double discourse and manipulated it for his own intellectual and political ends. Thus, Haykal's decision early in 1932 to start writing *Hayat Muhammad* was not a sudden, unexpected move that reflected a dramatic crisis; nor was it a direct continuation of Husayn's *ʿAla Hamish al-Sira*. Smith clearly showed that Haykal began to write his biography of the Prophet before Husayn started *'Ala Hamish al-Sira* and, further, that in relation to *Islamiyyat* literature it was Haykal who influenced Taha Husayn, and not the other way around. Smith located *Hayat Muhammad* in the context of Egypt in the early 1930s and thus was able to delineate more accurately Haykal's intentions and motives for producing it. Smith's contextualism is at its best in this part of his discussion. He viewed *Hayat Muhammad* first and foremost as a product of the new political and social environments that took shape in Egypt and Haykal's efforts to react to them. The major influencing factors that Smith pointed to were the dictatorial regime of Isma'il Sidqi (which Haykal and the Liberal Constitutionalists were militantly opposed to); the growing power of Islam as a political force and the Liberals' adoption of it as a defensive weapon against attacks from rivals who used religious rhetoric; attacks by Christian missionaries on the image of the Prophet Muhammad; the rise of radical nationalist and Islamicist forces, particularly among youth; and the need felt by Haykal and his party to reformulate their modernist message urgently in order to reach and gain the support of broader audiences and, thus, to survive politically and intellectually. Haykal's move to Islamic writing was, in Smith's interpretation, a shift (not a crisis), a planned reorientation intended to reassert and reinforce the "progressive modernist orientation" of the intellectuals.[112]

In Smith's narrative *Hayat Muhammad* represented Haykal's desire to produce a modern image of the Prophet to counter attacks by Christian missionaries on his image, the distorted images of him produced by Orientalists, and the reactionary, traditional images of the Prophet created by the official Islamic establishment, the al-Azhar *'ulama*.[113] Haykal, Smith observes, stressed that his study of the Prophet was "scientific research conducted with a modern Western [scientific] method," with the sole intention of finding historical truth through scientific and empirical tools.[114] Smith persuasively showed that *Hayat Muhammad* cannot be construed as a total retreat on Haykal's part from the scientific, rationalist, and humanist tenets of modern Western culture that he supported in the 1920s.[115] For Smith, the work was an "attack on Muslim conservatism," and it consciously presented rationalist and humanist values by demonstrating their existence in the Prophet's life. Haykal rationalized and humanized revealed truths to adapt them to a modern secular society and placed reason at the center while rejecting the supposed supernatural miraculousness of the Prophet's divine revelations. "Far from questioning scientific norms," Smith wrote, "Haykal validated them through the rationalization of Islam."[116] He strove, Smith put forth, to prove that early Islam was completely dissimilar from the "stagnated" images of orthodox Islam produced by reactionary *ulama*, and in this way he challenged the *ulama*'s authority to determine the essence of Islam. His aim, Smith showed, was to create a modern Islamic culture in which the modernist and secular intellectuals would have the authority to determine the status of Islam in society and culture.[117]

Haykal wrote *Fi Manzil al-Wahy* as a sequel to *Hayat Muhammad*. In this later book, there was no expression of a deepening crisis of orientation. Documenting the religious and spiritual experience of his pilgrimage to the holy places, Haykal again attempted to reformulate the modernist message in an Islamic framework, to appeal to the popular, literate public. Haykal, Smith argued, was convinced that the broad strata of society, "the masses" (in contrast to the educated elite, who were capable of absorbing the modernist message, including both its material and ideological aspects), were capable of assimilating the materialist life of the West, its technology and industrial products, but were incapable of absorbing its "spiritual life." He felt, Smith surmised, that the "spiritual source" for his society needed to be rooted in its Islamic heritage—"an indigenous ideology was necessary because of the role of mass opinion." Haykal had concluded that it was the duty of the intellectuals to produce such an authentic ideology. Heavily influenced by Henri Bergson, Haykal now regarded early Islam as the source of spiritual life, the basis for "spiritual culture," and the framework of collective identity that would provide happiness and consolation to Muslims and non-Muslims alike. But Haykal, like Bergson, still assumed that people attained faith and spirituality through reason and the scientific method.

In the 1940s, Haykal became increasingly aware that Egypt's ability to march toward modernity was being endangered by the rise of a mass culture manipulated by militant mass movements such as the Muslim Brothers. He stepped up his efforts to provide a modernist Islamic framework that would serve as an alternative both to rising populist Islam and to traditional orthodox Islam. His strategy was to restrain the radical revolutionary potentials he saw latent in the masses and to safeguard the progress of the modernization project run and controlled by the enlightened intellectuals. The result was his additional works on *al-Khulafa' al-Rashidun*. 'Abbas Mahmud al-'Aqqad, following in the footsteps of Haykal, composed his monumental *'Abqariyyat* series, and Taha Husayn authored additional books that historically or fictionally narrated tales about Islamic religious heroes.[118] However, Smith argued that by the end of the 1930s and during the 1940s Haykal was becoming aware of the limitations of his strategy to produce concrete political, social, and cultural results. Despite the great popularity of his books and the enthusiastic public reception of their themes, Smith argues that the public did not really understand "his real intentions" to reaffirm, through the instrumental use of an Islamic framework, the essence of Western secular methods and ideas. These intentions "seem to have been known only to his fellow intellectuals." Thus, Haykal had, in effect, unwittingly "contributed to the very resurgence of religious assertiveness he had hoped to restrain without corresponding recognition of [the] need for the changes he had called for."[119] Instead of changing mass public opinion "and reserving his own intellectual freedom, Haykal, in addressing himself to the masses, was himself led 'unaware' to a point where he was circumscribed with respect to his writings because of his political aims."[120] As Smith viewed it, "this was the true crisis of the Egyptian intellectuals."[121]

As Smith demonstrated, Haykal, particularly in his fictionalized prose, expressed growing feelings of despair, alienation, pessimism, and isolation. In this low-key medium, he admitted that he had failed to gain mass support for his elitist, formative vision through a modernist Islamic strategy. Haykal "now thought that his ideals were inapplicable to Egypt because of the triumph of the lower classes." Thus, even though thoroughly deconstructing the narrative of crisis, Smith nevertheless pointed to a (different type of) crisis, more internal and reflexive. It had beset Haykal and other intellectuals of his generation on the eve of the July 1952 revolution. Smith did not, however, charge the intellectuals with failure or blame them for this crisis; he depicted the requiem world of "Haykal's disillusionments" and his bitter feeling of self-defeat with sensitivity and empathy. For Smith, it was not intellectual betrayal but, rather, a tragedy of the intellectual blues.[122]

CONCLUSION—BEYOND THE "CRISIS": FURTHER COUNTERNARRATIVES

The deconstruction of the crisis narrative has encouraged further research on this intellectual topic. Since the early 1980s, new revisionist narratives have been developed. Through a new reading of some major texts of the intellectuals and through their rigorous contextualization in the sociopolitical environments in which they were produced, the new narratives share an effort to undermine further "the crisis theory." In this later stage, the application of methods and conceptual frameworks taken from contemporary general intellectual history is more evident. In what follows, I briefly present some of the major new narrativist elements, findings, and arguments.

First, the polar opposition between a severe "crisis of orientation"

(Safran's approach) on the one hand, and a tactical and instrumentalist intellectual shift, in which the crisis is represented as a later inner awareness by
the intellectuals that they failed to realize their modernist project (Smith's
narrative), on the other, present extreme interpretative alternatives. Although
mutually exclusive, both approaches are captive of what can be defined as
the dogma of the "crisis of intellectuals." Nevertheless, these two dichotomous options do not exhaust the possibilities embodied in the processes of
the intellectual evolution nor the full range of explanations for the transformation that occurred within it. A non-crisis-oriented reading of intellectual history shows that the intellectuals' shift to Islamic subjects in the
1930s and 1940s was a genuine and substantial process that cannot be reduced
to "a device . . . to achieve their [the intellectuals'] previous goals by different
means."[123] The principal aim of the *Islamiyyat* literature was to lay an intellectual foundation for a "common culture" shared by intellectual elites and
the growing, educated, urban middle classes (*effendiyya*), who, from the 1930s
on, became a major consumer-power in the print culture market. It was a
calculated and well-planned reorientation led by the intellectuals and, in
many ways, controlled by them as well. Exploiting the existing reservoir of
Islamic symbols, icons, and themes, sometimes reinventing them, they reconstructed an entire repertoire of Arab-Islamic cultural traditions. They sec-
ularized and modernized them and relocated their meanings within the
modern reality. This process of reconstruction, or reinvention, of Islamic
cultural "traditions" involved not only their revival and presentation in ide-
alistic and triumphal guises but also their defense, sometimes apologetically.

Beyond this, the intellectual shift also reflected a strategic change in the
intellectuals' approach to the critical question of how, and by what methods, they could modernize their society under the growing pressures of mass
society and the continued British colonial presence. In the 1930s, with an
increase in literacy rates, the introduction of mass politics, the radicalization of the *effendiyya* classes, and the growing alienation from colonial rule
that involved the denunciation of the elements and symbols of the "foreign," "imperialist," Western civilization, the intellectuals adopted a different agenda of cultural assimilation. It promoted a modernist strategy that
attempted to borrow selectively elements of European culture, especially
scientific and technological products, but also the ideas of humanism and
rationalism, and incorporate them into local (Islamic-Arab-Egyptian) cultural traditions. The goal was to fashion an indigenous common culture that
would be open to broad (and ever-increasing [i.e., a larger reading public])
subaltern sectors of the literate society. The intellectuals, who developed a

new social sensitivity, saw this strategic change as an effective way of continuing to assimilate Western *moderna* while simultaneously transmitting a clear, indigenous modernist message to the changing society.[124]

Second, the intellectual shift must be narrated and explained not only from the vantage point of authorial intent but also through the readers and readership of the intellectual production. Working from the assumption that the author is not the exclusive authority for determining a text's meaning, we must consider autonomous reader responses, "the act of reading," in order to weigh a text's concrete historical impact on the cultural field. It is important to determine how texts are interpreted and reproduced by readers, and what specific intentions and meanings they give them. A focus on the community of readers of *Islamiyyat* literature, therefore, is indispensable. An initial study of this readership seems to reinforce the argument that "the shift of the intellectuals to Islamic subjects" (Smith's phrasing) was indeed essential and strategic. For the majority of reading publics, the intellectual change was neither a crisis of orientation nor a shift in tactics and terminology alone; it was a constructive cultural reorientation, an authentic effort on the part of the intellectuals to produce a modern, Islamic culture that spoke to the average culture consumer. The overwhelming enthusiastic reception of *Islamiyyat* literature by larger reading publics shows that the intellectuals did succeed in producing cultural artifacts that penetrated the larger strata of literate society and, in large measure, did meet readers' cultural expectations.[125]

Third, the attempt by Middle Eastern intellectual historians to identify "a collective mind" and to demonstrate that the intellectual community of discourse behaved as a unified body with similar ideas and motivations, and was therefore collectively "responsible" for the same "successes" and "failures," is misleading. A recent sociological theory, which argues that intellectual thought and activity occur in group- and network-coalitions "by the experience of interaction rituals," seems reductionist.[126] Hourani's suspicion, that through a focus on the history of thought of various intellectual schools, "there is a risk . . . of imposing an artificial unity on their [intellectuals'] thought . . . to do so may blur the differences between individual thinkers," was correct.[127] Even Randall Collins admits that "intellectual life is first of all conflict and disagreement."[128] A close examination of the "collective biography" of the intellectuals shows that although they shared a common historical experience, substantial differences in thought and modes of action existed among them. Actually, it is more accurate to speak of a variety of distinct intellectual biographies; the common element among them was the general (and loose) framework provided by their shared site of time

and place. Thus, for instance, while Haykal's or al-'Aqqad's intellectual shift
to Islam was of a more fundamental nature, for Taha Husayn and al-Hakim
it was less profound. Salama Musa, 'Ali 'Abd al-Raziq, Ahmad Amin, and,
in a different fashion, Ibrahim 'Abd al-Qadir al-Mazini represented, each
in his own way, different intellectual trajectories. If we are to judge by the
rich corpus of autobiographical memoirs produced by individual intellectuals, it seems that the argument regarding the heterogeneity and the
différence of life is reinforced. Beyond this, in contrast to other, fragmented
texts that intellectuals produced (Smith emphasizes fiction), their memoirs
do not leave us with an impression of "crisis," "failure," or "despair." The
intellectuals narrated their lives and recorded their experiences as those who
envisioned themselves as "founders" creating a new world for themselves
and Egyptian and other Arab consumers of the print culture.[129]

Fourth, the counternarratives have tended, as did the narrative of crisis
itself, to create an intellectual canon based on the selected works of six to
eight intellectual luminaries ("representatives" or "intellectual leaders"). However, it is easy to show that such a selection of intellectual gurus is reductionist. True, it includes important intellectuals, but by the same token, it
has ignored others who were no less influential or visible. Thus, for example, some of the more modernist liberal voices of the era, such as Isma'il
Mazhar, Mahmud 'Azmi, Husayn Fawzi, Muhammad 'Abdallah 'Inan, and
Mirrit Butrus Ghali have not been included in the canon.[130] Mustafa Sadiq
al-Rafi'i, located in the more conservative, Islamic camp, is also absent. In
the Arab Islamic modernist discourse, the voices of Ahmad Hasan al-Zayyat,
Zaki Mubarak, and 'Abd al-Wahhab 'Azzam have been ignored.[131] Women's
voices cannot be found at all in this intellectual canon. Especially notable
absences are Nabawiya Musa and Labiba Ahmad, who represented influential nationalist Islamic voices and views.[132] None of the works by these
intellectuals represented crisis, or a shift in thinking from the 1920s to the
1940s. This selective sample seems sufficient to demonstrate that the commonly held historiographical canon is far from exhaustive and is in fact
unrepresentative of the intellectual field of cultural production. A more comprehensive and nuanced historical treatment is needed to reconsider the
question of what a canon should include and eventually to redefine the
canon, so as to reflect more accurately the intellectual evolution and its role
in shaping and reshaping the cultural field.

Fifth, the focus on *Islamiyyat* literature as a major key to understanding
the nature of the intellectual evolution has been reductionist and, in many
senses, misleading. It has ignored a whole cluster of intellectual fields of dis-

course created not only by the "luminary" intellectual community but also by "second-tier" intellectual communities, who played an equally important role in shaping the print culture and in the overall evolution of intellectual life. An examination of these "peripheral" other fields of discourse clearly demonstrates that the major argument of the narrative of crisis is false. A few examples should provide sufficient evidence to demonstrate this. In the 1930s and early 1940s, a huge intellectual effort was devoted, particularly in Egypt, to the advancement of a liberal and democratic intellectual discourse that challenged the Nazi and fascist forms of totalitarianism. This antifascist discourse was led by luminary modernist intellectuals, but hundreds of other voices—secondary intellectuals and contributors to dailies, journals, and magazines—also took part. This coalition of intellectuals viewed Nazism and fascism as authoritarian, imperialist, and racist and rejected them, presenting an alternative, liberalist, humanist, and anticolonialist position.[133] The promulgation of the New Egyptian Civil Code of 1949, the brilliant work of the jurist 'Abd al-Razzaq al-Sanhuri, was a significant achievement for liberal and secular modernism. This progressive civil code promoted "social justice" and "a new social order" to be based on the preservation of constitutional, parliamentary government. The civil code also intended to secure individual and group civil liberties, and further, it attempted to create "contractual justice" between the elite and other strata of society. The code's enactment clearly demonstrates that not only had the liberal tradition not disappeared from the intellectual scene, its impact on politics and society remained substantial.[134] In Egypt and the Arab Middle East in the 1930s, and more so in the 1940s and 1950s, new, left-wing socialist trends and movements emerged and were consolidated. These forces constructed a program that can best be defined as liberal, democratic, and socialist reformism. They were led by intellectuals who strove to mold a modern social order that would be both socialist and secular, democratic and progressive. It posed a conceptual and practical alternative, not only to the "old liberalism"—which for the intellectuals was too elitist, a device to secure the class interests of the landowning elite and other ruling elites—but also to authoritarian communism, military dictatorships, and a variety of fundamentalist or theocratic Islamicist movements and organizations. It is important to recognize that these socialist, democratic voices adhered to radical modernism. The modernist ethos, "the quest for modernity," and the "modernist discourse" provided for them a common ground.[135]

Thus, the theory of intellectual crisis can be seen as another relic of an outmoded, Orientalist paradigm. Terms such as *crisis, disorientation, anarchy, chaos, reactionary phase, retreat, bankruptcy,* and *betrayal* were invented to create an explosive dramatization of a false and ahistorical crisis story. It is not the intellectuals who sinned through emotional "paralyzing romanticism," as Gibb so confidently accused them; rather, it was Gibb and his Orientalist followers who sinned, through their emotional and imaginative, yet patronizing Orientalist romanticism, which was based on false expectations that modern Middle Eastern intellectuals would be "like us," scholarly, Western, rational, and humanist. In this Orientalist scheme, the most pressing task for the intellectual was, as Haykal had critically phrased it at an earlier juncture, to "Westernize the East" (*taghrib al-Sharq*).[136] However, the intellectuals could not (and did not) disappoint their culture and society. Relative to their time and place, they played a significant role in the formation of the print culture and the shaping of its contours as both an elite and a popular Arab-Egyptian culture. Of course, it would be a gross exaggeration to assume that this culture and society were constructed and evolved during the twentieth century thanks only to the works of the intellectuals and their artistic and literary texts. There were many obstacles and failures that impeded the way. However, it is inconceivable to see the forms, genres, themes, and the very language developed by the modern culture in Egypt and the Arab Middle East during the past century without recognizing the tremendous intellectual contribution of Taha Husayn, Muhammad Husayn Haykal, ʿAbbas Mahmud al-ʿAqqad, Tawfiq al-Hakim, Ahmad Amin, Ibrahim ʿAbd al-Qadir al-Mazini, Salama Musa, and hundreds of other intellectuals and writers—predecessors, peers, and followers.

NOTES

1. Richard Biernacki, "Method and Metaphor after the New Cultural History," in *Beyond the Cultural Turn*, ed. Victoria E. Bonnell and Lynn Hunt (Berkeley and Los Angeles: University of California Press, 1999), 62.

2. See, e.g., John E. Toews, "Intellectual History after the Linguistic Turn: The Autonomy of Meaning and the Irreducibility of Experience," *American Historical Review* 92 (October 1987): 879–907. For the "contemporary crisis in intellectual history studies" in the 1970s, see, e.g., Felix Gilbert, "Intellectual History: Its Aims and Methods," *Daedalus* 50 (1971): 80–97; Gene Wise, "The Contemporary Crisis in Intellectual History Studies," *Clio* 5 (1975): 55–69; Paul K. Conkin, "Intellectual History: Past, Present and Future," in *The Future of History*, ed. Charles F. Delzell (Nashville, TN: Vanderbilt University Press, 1977), 111–33.

3. For the new methods and approaches suggested by intellectual history since the late 1960s, see, e.g., John Dunn, "The Identity of the History of Ideas," *Philosophy* 43 (1968): 85–104; Quentin Skinner, "Meaning and Understanding in the History of Ideas," *History and Theory* 8 (1969): 3–53; J. G. A. Pocock, *Politics, Language and Time: Essays on Political Thought and History* (London: Methuen, 1972); Hayden White, *Metahistory: The Historical Imagination in Nineteenth-Century Europe* (Baltimore: Johns Hopkins University Press, 1973); John Higham and Paul K. Conkin, eds., *New Directions in American Intellectual History* (Baltimore: Johns Hopkins University Press, 1979); William J. Bouwsma, "Intellectual History in the 1980s: From History of Ideas to History of Meaning," *Journal of Interdisciplinary History* 12 (1981): 279–91; Dominick LaCapra and Steven L. Kaplan, eds., *Modern European Intellectual History: Reappraisals and New Perspectives* (Ithaca, NY: Cornell University Press, 1982); Dominick LaCapra, *Rethinking Intellectual History: Texts, Contexts, Language* (Ithaca, NY: Cornell University Press, 1983); LaCapra, *History and Criticism* (Ithaca, NY: Cornell University Press, 1985); David A. Hollinger, *In the American Province: Studies in the History and Historiography of Ideas* (Bloomington: Indiana University Press, 1985); Toews, "Intellectual History after the Linguistic Turn"; Donald R. Kelley, "Horizons of Intellectual History: Retrospect, Circumspect, Prospect," *Journal of the History of Ideas* 48 (1987): 143–69; James Tully, ed., *Meaning and Context: Quentin Skinner and His Critics* (Cambridge: Polity Press, 1988); David Harlan, "Intellectual History and the Return of Literature," *AHR* Forum, *American Historical Review* 94 (1989): 581–609; David A. Hollinger, "The Return of the Prodigal: The Persistence of Historical Knowing," *AHR* Forum, *American Historical Review* 94 (1989): 610–21; Donald R. Kelley, "What Is Happening to the History of Ideas?" *Journal of the History of Ideas* 51 (1990): 3–25; the articles by Susan A. Crane, Alon Confino, and Daniel James in the *AHR* Forum on "History and Memory," *American Historical Review* 102 (1997): 1372–1412. For more recent developments, see, e.g., the editorial in *Modern Intellectual History* 1, no. 1 (April 2004): 1–2; Lloyd Kramer, "Intellectual History and Philosophy," *Modern Intellectual History* 1, no. 1 (April 2004): 81–95; Dominick LaCapra, "Tropisms of Intellectual History," *Rethinking History* 8, no. 4 (2004): 499–529; and Allan Megill, "Intellectual History and History," *Rethinking History* 8, no. 4 (2004): 549–57.

4. Murray G. Murphey, "The Place of Beliefs in Modern Culture," in Higham and Conkin, *New Directions in American Intellectual History*, 151.

5. Edward W. Said, *Orientalism* (London: Routledge and Kegan Paul, 1978).

6. Robert Darnton, "Intellectual and Cultural History," in *The Past before Us: Contemporary Historical Writing in the United States*, ed. Michael Kammen (Ithaca, NY: Cornell University Press, 1980), 327–54.

7. For major stages in the theoretical and methodological development of the

"history of ideas" and "intellectual history" from the 1930s to the 1980s, see, e.g., Carl L. Becker, *The Heavenly City of the Eighteenth-Century Philosophers* (New Haven, CT: Yale University Press, 1932); Arthur O. Lovejoy, *The Great Chain of Being: A Study of the History of an Idea* (Cambridge, MA: Harvard University Press, 1936); Lovejoy, "Reflections on the History of Ideas," *Journal of the History of Ideas* 1 (1940): 3–23; Isaiah Berlin, "Political Ideas in the Twentieth Century," *Foreign Affairs* 28 (1950): 351–85; John Higham, "The Rise of American Intellectual History," *American Historical Review* 56 (1951): 453–71; Higham, "Intellectual History and Its Neighbors," *Journal of the History of Ideas* 15 (1954): 339–47; John C. Greene, "Objectives and Methods in Intellectual History," *Mississippi Valley Historical Review* 44 (1957): 58–74; John Higham, "American Intellectual History: A Critical Appraisal," *American Quarterly* 13 (1961): 219–33; Rush Welter, "The History of Ideas in America: An Essay in Redefinition," *Journal of American History* 51 (1965): 599–614; Maurice Mandelbaum, "The History of Ideas, Intellectual History, and the History of Philosophy," *History and Theory* 64–65 (1965): 33–66; George Boas, *The History of Ideas: An Introduction* (New York: Scribner, 1969); Philip P. Wiener, ed., *Dictionary of the History of Ideas: Studies of Selected Pivotal Ideas*, 4 vols. (New York: Charles Scribner's Sons, 1973); Isaiah Berlin, *Against the Current: Essays in the History of Ideas* (London: Hogarth Press, 1979); Carl E. Schorske, *Fin-de-Siècle Vienna: Politics and Culture* (New York: Vintage Books, 1980); Daniel J. Wilson, "Lovejoy's *The Great Chain of Being*, after Fifty Years," *Journal of the History of Ideas* 48 (1987): 187–206.

8. Albert Hourani, "H. A. R. Gibb: The Vocation of an Orientalist," in *Europe and the Middle East* (London: Macmillan, 1980), 107–10.

9. See H. A. R. Gibb, "Studies in Contemporary Arabic Literature," pt. 1, "The Nineteenth Century," in the *Bulletin of the School of Oriental Studies* 4 (1928): 745–60; pt. 2, "Manfaluti and the 'New Style,'" vol. 5 (1929): 311–22; and pt. 4, "The Egyptian Novel," vol. 7 (1933): 1–22, republished in Hamilton A. R. Gibb, *Studies on the Civilization of Islam*, ed. Stanford J. Shaw and William R. Polk (Princeton, NJ: Princeton University Press, 1962), 245–319.

10. Hourani, "H. A. R. Gibb," 109. For an overview of Gibb's approach to modern Islam, see also Zachary Lockman, *Contending Visions of the Middle East: The History and Politics of Orientalism* (Cambridge: Cambridge University Press, 2004), 103–11.

11. H. A. R. Gibb, "Studies in Contemporary Arabic Literature," pt. 3: "Egyptian Modernists," *Bulletin of the School of Oriental Studies* 5 (1929): 445–66, republished in Gibb, *Studies on the Civilization of Islam*, 268–86; quotation from 269.

12. Gibb, *Studies on the Civilization of Islam*, 269–86.

13. Ibid., 270–86.

14. Charles C. Adams, *Islam and Modernism in Egypt* (London: Oxford University Press, 1933), preface, 1–3, 18–268.

15. H. A. R. Gibb, *Modern Trends in Islam* (Chicago: University of Chicago Press, 1947).

16. Richard P. Mitchell, *The Society of the Muslim Brothers* (London: Oxford University Press, 1969), viii, n. 2.

17. Compare Gibb's *Modern Trends* with Lovejoy's *Great Chain of Being*.

18. Gibb, *Modern Trends*, 39–86.

19. Ibid., 63–105.

20. Ibid., 108.

21. Ibid., 57–58, 76–77; Hourani, "Gibb," 126–27.

22. Gibb, *Modern Trends*, 121–29.

23. Ibid., 77, 100, 105, 106–8.

24. Ibid., 127.

25. See, e.g., H. A. R. Gibb, "The Future for Arab Unity," in *The Near East: Problems and Prospects*, ed. Philip W. Ireland (Chicago: University of Chicago Press, 1942), 67–99; Gibb, "Toward Arab Unity," *Foreign Affairs* 24 (1945): 119–29.

26. H. A. R. Gibb, "The Reaction in the Middle East against Western Culture," in Gibb, *Studies on the Civilization of Islam*, 320–35. This article was originally published in 1951 (in French). See also Gibb's earlier essay, "Middle Eastern Perplexities," *International Affairs* 20 (1944): 458–72.

27. G. E. von Grunebaum, "The Problem of Cultural Influence," in *Modern Islam: The Search for Cultural Identity* (1962; New York: Random House, 1964), 19. For von Grunebaum's intellectual background, see also Franz Rosenthal, "In Memoriam: Gustave E. von Grunebaum, 1909–1972," *International Journal of Middle East Studies* 4 (1973): 355–58; and David Waines, "Cultural Anthropology and Islam: The Contribution of G. E. von Grunebaum," *Review of Middle East Studies* (London) 2 (1976): 113–23.

28. See, e.g., G. E. von Grunebaum, *Islam: Essays in the Nature and Growth of a Cultural Tradition*, 2nd ed. (1955; London: Routledge and Kegan Paul, 1961), 185. See also von Grunebaum, *Modern Islam*, 71–75.

29. G. E. von Grunebaum, "Attempts at Self-Interpretation in Contemporary Islam," in von Grunebaum, *Islam*, 185–236. This article was originally published in two parts (in 1947 and 1950).

30. Rosenthal, "In Memoriam," 356.

31. Von Grunebaum, *Islam*, 196–98.

32. Ibid., 208–16.

33. Ibid., 231; see also 226–31.

34. G. E. von Grunebaum, "The Intellectual Problem of Westernization in the Self-View of the Arab World," in von Grunebaum, *Modern Islam*, 172–243, and see, in particular, 194–207. This article first appeared in 1959 (in German).

35. G. E. von Grunebaum, "Self-Image and Approach to History," in *Historians of the Middle East,* ed., Bernard Lewis and P. M. Holt (London: Oxford University Press, 1962), 460–78, and, more generally, 457–83; this article was republished in von Grunebaum, *Modern Islam,* 129–71.

36. Von Grunebaum, "Self-Image," 460–62, 475–77; quotations from 461, 477.

37. Ibid., 472–83. See also von Grunebaum, *Modern Islam,* 135–71.

38. Wilfred Cantwell Smith, *Islam in Modern History* (Princeton, NJ: Princeton University Press, 1957), viii, 27, and, more generally, 93–296. Smith writes that "all of us working in this field find, as R. Mitchell has indicated, that the more closely we study the modern Islamic world, the more we find ourselves simply 'writing footnotes on Professor Gibb's survey [i.e., *Modern Trends in Islam*]'" (121 n. 32).

39. Smith, *Islam in Modern History,* 27–28, and, more generally, 3–40.

40. Ibid., 160.

41. Ibid., 58–60, 62–63, and, see also 47–73.

42. Ibid., 63; see also 64–92.

43. Ibid., 85, 87.

44. Ibid., 115, 113; more generally, see 93–115.

45. Ibid., 120; more generally, see 115–20.

46. Ibid., 120–22, and 151 n. 179.

47. Ibid., 148, and 122–52.

48. Ibid., 115–22; quotations from 87, 152.

49. Nadav Safran, *Egypt in Search of Political Community: An Analysis of the Intellectual and Political Evolution of Egypt, 1804–1952* (Cambridge, MA: Harvard University Press, 1961), preface, 1–4, and 267 n. 3.

50. Ibid., 101–21, 125–228.

51. Ibid., 126–64.

52. Ibid., 143–64.

53. Ibid., 165–66; quotation from 166.

54. Ibid., 155, 165–67, 180.

55. Ibid., 168.

56. Ibid., 169, 170–72.

57. Ibid., 173–75; quotation from 174.

58. Ibid., 209–28, 247–52; quotation from 250.

59. Ibid., 181–228.

60. Ibid., 210.

61. Ibid., 140.

62. Ibid., 231–44.

63. Bernard Lewis, *The Middle East and the West* (London: Weidenfeld and Nicolson, 1964), 108–9.

64. P. J. Vatikiotis, *The Modern History of Egypt* (London: Weidenfeld and Nicolson, 1969), 292–312, 315–42, in particular 323–24. For different approaches to the intellectual evolution using the "crisis" or "retreat" narratives, see Baber Johansen, *Muhammad Husain Haikal: Europa und der Orient im Weltbild eines Ägyptischen Liberalen* (Beirut: In Kommission bei F. Steiner Verlag, Wiesbaden, 1967), 61–250; and David Semah, *Four Egyptian Literary Critics* (Leiden: Brill, 1974), 96–100.

65. Afaf Lutfi al-Sayyid-Marsot, *Egypt's Liberal Experiment, 1922–1936* (Berkeley: University of California Press, 1977), 217–51, in particular 229–31.

66. Selma Botman, *Egypt from Independence to Revolution, 1919–1952* (Syracuse, NY: Syracuse University Press, 1991), 140, 142–43, and, more generally, 136–47.

67. Marcel Colombe, *L'Évolution de l'Égypte, 1924–1950* (Paris: G. P. Maisonneuve, 1951), 121–221.

68. Ibid., 139–59, in particular 146–58.

69. Pierre Cachia, *Tâhâ Husayn: His Place in the Egyptian Literary Renaissance* (London: Luzac and Company, Ltd., 1956), v–vi, 3–37, 58, 192, 197–98. For a broader perspective, see also 77–225.

70. Albert Hourani, *Arabic Thought in the Liberal Age, 1798–1939* (London; Oxford University Press, 1962). See, in particular, the Cambridge University Press edition, 1983, esp. iv–x.

71. Donald M. Reid, "Arabic Thought in the Liberal Age Twenty Years After," *International Journal of Middle East Studies* 14 (1982): 541–57; Roger Owen, obituary for Albert Hourani, *St. Antony's College Record* (Oxford, 1993), 101–4; Gaby Piterberg, "Albert Hourani and Orientalism," in *Middle Eastern Politics and Ideas: A History from Within*, ed. Moshe Ma'oz and Ilan Pappé (London: Tauris Academic Studies, 1997), 75–88; Roger Owen, "Albert Hourani the Historian," in Ma'oz and Pappé, *Middle Eastern Politics and Ideas*, 7–19; Derek Hopwood, "Albert Hourani: Islam, Christianity and Orientalism," *British Journal of Middle Eastern Studies* 30, no. 2 (November 2003): 127–36. See also Abdulaziz A. al-Sudairi, *A Vision of the Middle East: An Intellectual Biography of Albert Hourani* (Oxford: Center for Lebanese Studies, 1999).

72. Albert Hourani, *The Emergence of the Modern Middle East* (London: Macmillan Press, in association with St. Antony's College, Oxford, 1981), xiv.

73. Albert Hourani, *Arabic Thought in the Liberal Age, 1798–1939*, Oxford paperback ed. (London: Oxford University Press, 1970), 103–244.

74. Ibid., 324–40; quotation from 326.

75. Hourani, *Emergence*, xiv.

76. Ibid.

77. Owen, obituary for Albert Hourani, 101; Owen, "Hourani," 7–19, and, particularly, 12–13; see also R. G. Collingwood, *The Idea of History* (Oxford: Oxford University Press, 1946).

78. See, e.g., by Arthur O. Lovejoy: "Introduction: The Study of the History of Ideas," in his *Great Chain of Being*, 3–23; and Lovejoy, "Reflections." In his "Patterns of the Past," in *Paths to the Middle East: Ten Scholars Look Back*, ed. Thomas Naff (Albany: State University of New York Press, 1993), chap. 2, particularly 41–42, which appears to be his last autobiographical account, Hourani mentioned Edmond Wilson's *To the Finland Station* (London: M. Secker and Warburg, 1941), as a work "which had a deep impact on me" (he had read the book in the early 1940s).

79. Reid, "Arabic Thought," 547.

80. Higham, "American Intellectual History," as republished in *American Studies: Essays on Theory and Method*, ed. Robert Merideth (Columbus, OH: C. E. Merrill Publishing Co., 1968), 220.

81. Higham, "American Intellectual History," 220, 231.

82. Hourani, *Arabic Thought*, 1970 ed., viii.

83. Ibid., Cambridge ed., 1983, iv–x.

84. Ibid., iv–vi.

85. Ibid., v, vii.

86. Ibid., 1970 ed., vii–viii, 189–92, 193, 360.

87. Ibid., 1983 ed., vi–vii; Reid, "Arabic Thought," 547–49.

88. Hourani, *Arabic Thought*, 1983 ed., vii; 1970 ed., 341–73.

89. Ibid., 1983 ed., v.

90. Hourani, *Emergence*, xvi; Hourani, *Arabic Thought*, 1970 ed., viii.

91. Hourani, *Arabic Thought*, 1970 ed., 130, 171.

92. Albert Hourani, "How Should We Write the History of the Middle East?" *International Journal of Middle East Studies* 23 (1991): 134.

93. Reid, "Arabic Thought," 541–47, 550–54.

94. Hourani, *Arabic Thought*, 1970 ed., 324–40, in particular 333–35; see also 183–92.

95. Reid, "Arabic Thought," 549–50, and, more generally, 541–57.

96. Kenneth Cragg, *Counsels in Contemporary Islam* (Edinburgh: Edinburgh University Press, 1965), 89–100, in particular 89–95, and, more generally, 67–109. See also Cragg's review of al-ʿAqqad's Islamic writings, 95–96. For slightly different approaches, see Louis Awad, "Cultural and Intellectual Developments in Egypt since 1952," in *Egypt since the Revolution*, ed. P. J. Vatikiotis (London: Allen and Unwin, 1968), 149–55; and Jacques Berque, *Egypt: Imperialism and Revolution* (London: Faber and Faber, 1972), 505–6, 514–16.

97. Majid Khadduri, *Political Trends in the Arab World: The Role of Ideas and Ideals in Politics* (Baltimore: Johns Hopkins University Press, 1970), 89–128, 212–52, 258–59.

98. Ibid., 89–97, 100–101; Lutfi al-Sayyid-Marsot, *Egypt's Liberal Experiment*,

237–43; Vernon Egger, *A Fabian in Egypt: Salamah Musa and the Rise of the Professional Classes in Egypt, 1909–1939* (Lanham, MD: University Press of America, 1986).

99. M. M. Badawi, "Islam in Modern Egyptian Literature," *Journal of Arabic Literature* 2 (1971): 154–77; republished in M. M. Badawi, *Modern Arabic Literature and the West* (London: Ithaca Press, 1985), 44–65, in particular 57–60.

100. Antonie Wessels, *A Modern Arabic Biography of Muhammad: A Critical Study of Muhammad Husayn Haykal's Hayāt Muhammad* (Leiden: Brill, 1972), 1–19, 32–48, 248, and more generally, 194–248.

101. Charles D. Smith, "The 'Crisis of Orientation': The Shift of Egyptian Intellectuals to Islamic Subjects in the 1930s," *International Journal of Middle East Studies* 4 (1973): 382–410; Smith, *Islam and the Search for Social Order in Modern Egypt: A Biography of Muhammad Husayn Haykal* (Albany: State University of New York Press, 1983), 3–7; and Smith, "The Intellectual and Modernization: Definitions and Reconsiderations: The Egyptian Experience," *Comparative Studies in Society and History* 22 (1980): 513–33.

102. See, in particular, Skinner's classic, "Meaning and Understanding in the History of Ideas."

103. Smith, *Islam and the Search*, 9–60.

104. Ibid, 33–60; Smith, "Crisis of Orientation," 392.

105. Smith, *Islam and the Search*, 61–87.

106. Ibid., 61–108.

107. Ibid., 89–108.

108. Ibid.

109. Ibid., 106–8, quotations from 107–8; and, more generally, see 95–108.

110. Ibid., 90–96; Smith, "Crisis of Orientation," 393–98.

111. Smith, "Crisis of Orientation," 398–99, 407–9; Smith, *Islam and the Search*, 94, 150–53, quotation from 94.

112. Ibid., 109–16.

113. Ibid., 113–15.

114. Ibid., 114–15; Muhammad Husayn Haykal, *Hayat Muhammad*, 2nd ed. (Cairo: Matba'at Misr, 1935), 37.

115. Smith, *Islam and the Search*, 113–30; Smith, "Crisis of Orientation," 401–3.

116. Smith, *Islam and the Search*, 115, 125, and, more generally, 117–25.

117. Ibid., 113–19, 129–30.

118. Smith, "Crisis of Orientation," 405–7; Smith, *Islam and the Search*, 131–57, 184–85.

119. Smith, *Islam and the Search*, 145.

120. Smith, "Crisis of Orientation," 407.

121. Smith, *Islam and the Search*, 145.

122. Ibid., 153–57, 178, 174–80; Smith, "Crisis of Orientation," 409–10.

123. Smith, "Crisis of Orientation," 384.

124. I have attempted to emphasize this line of approach in my study of the subject. See, e.g., I. Gershoni, "Reconstructing Tradition: Islam, Modernity, and National Identity in Egyptian Intellectual Discourse, 1930–1952," *Tel Aviver Jahrbuch für Deutsche Geschichte* 30 (2001–2): 155–211; see also Ruth Roded, "Gendered Domesticity in the Life of the Prophet: Tawfiq al-Hakim's Muhammad," *Journal of Semitic Studies* 47 (2002): 67–95.

125. See, e.g., I. Gershoni, "The Reader—'Another Production': The Reception of Haykal's Biography of Muhammad and the Shift of Egyptian Intellectuals to Islamic Subjects in the 1930s," *Poetics Today* 15, no. 2 (1994): 241–77.

126. See Randall Collins, *The Sociology of Philosophies: A Global Theory of Intellectual Change* (Cambridge, MA: Belknap Press / Harvard University Press, 1998), 19–53; quotation from 23.

127. Albert Hourani, *Arabic Thought*, 1983 ed., v.

128. Collins, *Sociology of Philosophies*, 1.

129. See, e.g., Taha Husayn, *Al-Ayyam*, vol. 1 (Cairo: Matbaʿat Amin ʿAbd al-Rahman, 1929), vol. 2 (Cairo: Dar al-Maʿarif, 1940), and vol. 3 (Cairo: Dar al-Maʿarif, 1973); Tawfiq al-Hakim, *Zahrat al-ʿUmr* (Cairo: Maktabat al-Adab, 1943); al-Hakim, *Sijn al-ʿUmr* (Cairo: Maktabat al-Adab, 1965); al-Hakim, *Wathaʾiq fi Tariq ʿAwdat al-Waʿy* (Cairo: Dar al-Shuruq, 1975); Salama Musa, *Tarbiyat Salama Musa* (Cairo: Salama Musa liʾl-Nashr waʾl-tawziʿ / Muassasat al-Khanaji, 1947; rev. 2nd ed., 1958); Ahmad Amin, *Hayati* (Cairo: Matbaʿat Lajnat al-Taʾlif, 1950; rev. 2nd ed., 1952); ʿAbbas Mahmud al-ʿAqqad, *Ana* (Cairo: Dar al-Hilal, 1964); and Muhammad Husayn Haykal, *Mudhakkirat fi al-Siyasa al-Misriyya*, 3 vols. (Cairo: Maktabat al-Nahda al-Misriyya / Dar al-Maʿarif, 1951, 1953, 1977).

130. See I. Gershoni and J. Jankowski, *Egypt, Islam, and the Arabs: The Search for Egyptian Nationhood, 1900–1930* (New York: Oxford University Press, 1986); and I. Gershoni, *The Emergence of Pan-Arabism in Egypt* (Tel Aviv: Shiloah Center for Middle Eastern and Arabic Studies, 1981).

131. See Giora Eliraz, "The Cultural and Social World View of Mustafa Sadiq al-Rafiʿi" [in Hebrew], *Hamizrah Hehadash* 27 (1978): 203–24; and Eliraz, "Egyptian Intellectuals in the Face of Tradition and Change, 1919–1939" [in Hebrew] (PhD diss., Hebrew University, Jerusalem, 1980).

132. See Muhammad Abu al-Isʿad, *Nabawiya Musa wa-Dawruha fi al-Hayat al-Misriyya, 1886–1951* (Cairo: al-Hayʾa al-ʿAmma liʾl-Kitab, 1994); Beth Baron, *Egypt as a Woman: Nationalism, Gender, and Politics* (Berkeley and Los Angeles: University of California Press, 2005).

133. See I. Gershoni, "Egyptian Liberalism in an Age of 'Crisis of Orientation':

Risala's Reaction to Fascism and Nazism, 1933–1939," *International Journal of Middle East Studies* 31 (1999): 551–76; and Gershoni, *Light in the Shade: Egypt and Fascism, 1922–1937* [in Hebrew] (Tel Aviv: Am Oved, 1999).

134. For more recent scholarly treatment of this intellectual development, see Guy Bechor, "'To Hold the Hand of the Weak': The Emergence of Contractual Justice in the Egyptian Civil Law," *Islamic Law and Society* 8 (2001): 179–200; Amr Shalakany, "Between Identity and Redistribution: Sanhuri, Genealogy and the Will to Islamise," in ibid., 201–44.

135. See, e.g., Egger, *Fabian*, 169–234; Joel Beinin and Zachary Lockman, *Workers on the Nile: Nationalism, Communism, Islam, and the Egyptian Working Class, 1882–1954*, (Princeton, NJ: Princeton University Press, 1987), 310–62, 395–447; Selma Botman, *The Rise of Egyptian Communism, 1939–1970* (Syracuse, NY: Syracuse University Press, 1988); Joel Beinin, *Was the Red Flag Flying There? Marxist Politics and the Arab-Israeli Conflict in Egypt and Israel, 1948–1965* (Berkeley and Los Angeles: University of California Press, 1990), 55–65, 84–101, 103–17, 144–59; Rami Ginat, *Egypt's Incomplete Revolution: Lutfi al-Khuli and Nasser's Socialism in the 1960s* (London: Frank Cass, 1997), 49–68; and, in particular, Roel Meijer, *The Quest for Modernity: Secular Liberal and Left-Wing Political Thought in Egypt, 1945–1958* (London: Routledge Curzon, 2002).

136. Muhammad Husayn Haykal, "Thawrat al-Adab: Min Haykal ila Taha," *al-Risala*, June 15, 1933, 41.

6

The Historiography of Crisis
in the Egyptian Political Economy

ELLIS GOLDBERG

W riting the political economy of twentieth-century Egypt has remained largely faithful to the path blazed by Charles Issawi in 1947 when he published *Egypt: An Economic and Social Analysis*. The periodization he established, which divides Egypt's history into a post-Napoleonic era (1798–1882), a period of British occupation (1882–1922), and a monarchical era, is still widely accepted and has since been extended as the monarchy was replaced in 1952 by a republic whose basic institutions, established by Gamal Abdel Nasser, have persisted into the twenty-first century.

The challenges to and revisions of Issawi's 1947 arguments appear to have been affected mainly by the discourses and experiences of the military government that came to power in 1952. Arguments about whether Egypt after Napoleon was Arab in character or remained Ottoman frequently reject arguments of the early 1950s that attribute to Mehmet Ali the role of creator of an Egyptian state for an Egyptian people. There is one major, paradoxical difference between our understanding of the Egyptian economy today and Issawi's understanding of it in the first half of the twentieth century. Where Issawi saw difficult but soluble problems, we now see crisis; where Issawi saw truly critical problems, we now affect to see nothing amiss. In this essay I focus on two aspects of the transformation of Issawi's theory of a liberal political economy into the now-dominant paradigm: an ecological crisis that never happened and the disappearance of child labor as an issue in the study of the Egyptian political economy. This, I believe, is the result of viewing Egypt through the lens of anticolonial discourse, with the unconscious and unintended consequence that many of the conventional judgments of colonial apologists have been adopted.

The well-defined and widely accepted narrative of the political economy of Egypt has neither been seriously challenged nor been seriously questioned since it was first elaborated in the late 1940s by Issawi. Several elements compose the basis of this narrative. First, the British occupation effected the complete integration of Egypt into the global economy as an exporter of cotton around 1900. Second, the forced specialization of Egypt as a commodity exporter created an economy that was structurally imbalanced. Third, the liberal political institutions of the day were a facade that sheltered a corrupt and brutal ruling class headed by a royal family without any links to local society. The fourth basis of this narrative posits that Egypt's political economy was wracked by a prolonged structural crisis due to the weak social, economic, and political institutions of the Old Regime, and this was resolved only after the coup of a group of young army officers in 1952.

Although elements of this narrative may be found in studies before 1952 on Egypt, it was only after 1952 that the narrative appeared as a coherent story, and only after that were its elements routinely linked to a narrative of crisis. Egyptian perceptions before 1952 of what constituted a crisis, and of the links between economic structures and crisis, were markedly different from their perceptions post-1952. In effect, a narrative designed to legitimate a military coup has been uncritically accepted as though it were self-evidently rooted in objective facts of Egypt's political, economic, and social life. In the process, and in line with the needs of the military government that came to power in 1952, Egyptians have by and large been written out of the picture as agents before 1952.

Although some of the elements of this narrative have been challenged, it has not been subjected to direct critique, nor have some of the important claims about colonial crisis been confronted. The two most important elements of the narrative that have been subjected to criticism are the concepts (1) of comprador capitalism and (2) of political stasis verging on prolonged crisis after the 1948 Palestine war.

That a crisis occurred in Egyptian agriculture in the second decade of the twentieth century is one of the most important building blocks of contemporary understanding of Egypt's political economy during the imperial era. That the crisis had its source in imperial tampering with the ecology is widely accepted by liberal economists and radical historians alike. The evidence for such a crisis, let alone an explanation of its causes, is remarkably slender: a series of numbers without context and a handful of accounts in published memoirs of British officials. Nevertheless, since the early 1970s the idea of an agricultural crisis in the early twentieth century has been uncritically accepted and reproduced by successive authors. Each retelling of the tale increases its authority, but its repetition has not strengthened its empirical foundation; it is simply not true.

In this essay I briefly demonstrate why there was not a crisis and then consider the discursive traditions, both historiographical and official, in which crisis played so prominent a role. Exploring the historiography of the crisis allows us to place the history of the Egyptian political economy on sounder footing and to understand the importance of the concept of crisis in contemporary academic writing about Egypt specifically and the third world more generally. Whether Egypt experienced more crises in the twentieth century than other countries, I cannot say, but its historiographical tradition is certainly replete with warnings of crisis.

There are two basic ways of thinking about crisis: structural embeddedness and exogenous occurrence. During the twentieth century the notion of a structurally embedded crisis in political economy was probably most strongly associated with Marxism. According to this view, economic forces naturally move society and social classes toward irreconcilable conflict. Other structural explanations of crisis exist and are found, for example, in the literature on game theory, where a payoff structure induces agents to inefficient, noncooperative interaction. The concept of exogenous shock, on the other hand, suggests that a structured system exists in equilibrium but can be unexpectedly transformed by external events such as climate change or the invention of a new technique of production.

The standard account regarding Egypt, one that can probably be generalized to many other parts of the imperial world in the early twentieth century, is a picture of ecological and political crises in a global capitalist system. The imposition of capitalist institutions under colonial rule led to a structural crisis:

> After the First World War, the moral, economic, and political crisis of Anglo-French colonialism created an environment conducive to a new political order in Egypt. The nationalist movement was an effect of urban middle strata educated in modern, western-style schools—the *effendiyya*—and circles of large landowners simultaneously articulating and responding to collective anti-colonialist sentiment and action. . . . A central element of the political economy of the 1892–1924 era was a multifaceted rural ecological crisis. After expanding rapidly in the 1890s, crop yields and cultivated areas reach a plateau, as agriculture attained the economic limits of the environment, deployed technology, and the social relations of production. . . . Consequently, agricultural

yields declined by about 15 percent from 1900 to 1920 and recovered only in 1930.[1]

The causal relations seem clear: the area under cultivation and average yields per unit of area in Egypt expanded in the 1890s but then declined after 1900 and continued to decline until 1920. In some unspecified way, environmental constraints, limited technological innovation, and the structure of property rights combined to cause this decline, which was reversed only after 1930. A decline of 15 percent in yield must have affected rural incomes significantly unless, of course, prices increased equally significantly. It is certainly plausible that a 15 percent decline in incomes (applied to a world in which prices were constant) would have caused economic distress of crisis proportions that, combined with weakened institutions in Britain and France, led to the emergence of a new political culture—a nationalist movement—among rural and urban elites.

We might begin by asking just how much the landed elite perceived the period as one of social or economic structural crisis. My own reading of the writing they produced suggests no sense of structural crisis. Most of the institutions and people prominently involved in Egyptian politics were already in place by 1912 and continued to play crucial (and often the same) roles until the mid-1930s. World War I presented a profound challenge to the established order in Egypt, and there were some profound conflicts over policy-making during the war years. No perception of structural crisis existed, but the war was perceived as an exogenous shock, and Egyptian landowners, like English textile-mill owners, were slow to perceive how the war transformed the structure of global markets.

Of course, the historiographical discourse of crisis in Egypt written since the 1970s is not founded primarily on elite perceptions of the period and certainly not on the idea of exogenous shock.[2] It is, as the excerpt above indicates, founded on a claim of structural crisis backed up by hard evidence: a steep decline in yields that lasted for two decades. If anything, the absence of a discussion of crisis among Egyptian elites during the period might be adduced to show how removed they were from the concerns of their own society.

First, I show briefly here (and deal with far more extensively in *Trade, Reputation, and Child Labor*) that there is no evidence pointing to a crisis, and what appears to be a decline in natural productivity was due to a calculated shift in the composition of the Egyptian cotton crop.[3] What the literature describes as an ecological crisis is really an example of what in statistics is known as the ecological fallacy. The claim about ecological crisis employs highly aggregated quantitative data. As is well known, the existence of a correlation at the aggregate level does not imply that similar relationships are obtained at individual or causal levels.

Second, describing a crisis and locating a causal explanation for it in government policies invariably suggests the need for desirable, corrective structural reform. The discourse of crisis has frequently been deployed or invoked in support of one strand of a debate over policy rather than as an easily perceived empirical fact of Egyptian life. As it turns out arguments about agricultural crisis in Egypt were frequently connected to arguments about government expenditures, and especially government expenditures for construction, one of the most important industries controlled by Egyptian entrepreneurs.[4]

Observers noted the decline in yields during the first two decades of the twentieth century, and they noted changes in the cropped area. There were lively discussions about policy, but there was no sense of profound crisis. Well-understood ecological problems that existed before 1900, and that continue to exist today, became the basis for a plausible narrative of ecological crisis and thereby replaced a contemporaneous narrative that understood declining cotton yields as the straightforward outcome of choices about which varieties of cotton to grow. The decline in aggregate yields that resulted from a change in cropping decisions—and that is now regarded as a crisis—was long ago understood to be a statistical mirage.[5]

BRITISH DEMAND: COLONIAL POWER, LABOR, AND PALEOTECHNOLOGY

The extension of global markets to subsistence peasant communities in the late nineteenth century was viewed in the twentieth primarily as structurally catastrophic,[6] and the case of Egypt is no exception.[7] Crisis and disruption were seen as arising from the demand for raw materials by the metropolis, the supply of cheap manufactured goods in return, and the consequent transformation of an entire culture.[8]

Britain, according to a variant of this view common among nationalists in Egypt, was not only the dominant colonial power, it was the most advanced industrial economy in the world. A typical description of British power would note that in the 1890s Britain was the country with the most cotton spindles, the most mechanical looms, the largest workforce, and the most capital invested in textile production. Liverpool was the center of a

global market in fiber, and textiles were England's most important industrial product and its largest export.[9] Britain was also the world's dominant
naval power and had used its warships to project force around the world,
including bombarding Alexandria in 1882. It is thus no wonder that powerful England easily subordinated Egyptian interests to its own and exploited
the Nile Valley to provide the Lancashire mills with raw cotton.

Correct as each item is, as a whole the impression is misleading. The
description of Great Britain as a strategic actor is confused with the effect
of its demand for raw materials. Growing cotton in Egypt to supply English
demand was a strategy designed to return a premium to growers realized
in a global market, and it was predicated on a limited but real understanding of English economic vulnerability. Around 1900, Egyptians began to specialize in the production of uniform bales of extra-long-staple cotton. This
had effects that were generally understood at the time but have slipped out
of the historical literature. The most important effect was that plants that
produced finer cotton generally had lower yields and thus were profitable
only if the quality premium was sufficiently high.[10]

SCIENCE IN THE SERVICE OF QUALITY:
VICTORIAN BIOTECHNOLOGY

The scientific study of agriculture dates from the late nineteenth century,
and through the state the Egyptian elite rapidly acquired powerful technology
for improving the quality of Egyptian cotton. Much has been written about
water supply and drainage.[11] To understand why it appeared there was an
ecological crisis it is necessary to review the arguments about irrigation and
then to look briefly at the varieties of cotton produced in Egypt as a result
of early biotechnological advances.

Water supply is a capital-intensive, necessary undertaking, and it seems
self-evident that agriculture in a desert can exist only with irrigation.[12] Irrigation is preferable to rainfall when strict regulation of water is necessary
to ensure optimum growth of plants. Fertile deserts are locations where
large-scale investments in irrigation can be made to pay by growing high-
quality crops (such as cotton, melons, or strawberries) that prosper when
watering is stringently controlled. Providing large capital investment is often
less difficult than resolving conflicts over the apportionment of social costs,
benefits, and risks from agricultural production in rural society.

A disastrous flood in 1909 dramatically decreased the yield of that year's
crop. This exogenous shock was widely understood to be a result of the ran-

dom variation in Nile flood levels over long periods of time, and not a structural problem. As a consequence, however, Lawrence Balls discovered that cotton yields declined when the plants received too much water. His conclusion that plant survival (and consequently yield) was adversely affected by insufficient drainage and overwatering was increasingly accepted as the appropriate technical explanation for the secular declines in yield.[13] Balls's research was both more limited and broader than successive accounts have suggested. He showed that damage to the crop was caused mainly by random variations in the height of the annual flood and that this could be alleviated by drainage in appropriate (low-lying) areas. Balls certainly showed that too much water caused cotton yields to decline; he did not show (and logically could not have shown) that all declines in yields were caused by too high a water table.

In fact, Balls's research was methodologically innovative. He recognized that peasants constantly made difficult decisions, trading off the costs of physical effort and monetary investment for income. Balls came to appreciate what we now call the evolutionary economics equilibrium (rather than rational choice) inherent in peasant learning. One crucial innovation that Balls—whose work is central to understanding the Egyptian investment in innovation—made in his early study of cotton yields was to shift the focus of research away from the abstract measurement of plant growth to that of peasant agency. In his own words, he decided to study "the number of plants per square metre, or any other unit area, as the basis of computation, instead of taking the individual plant . . . to obtain curves showing the time distribution of yield . . . it results that the greatest yield per area for the first few weeks is given by the spacing which contained most plants per area."[14] Balls became sensitive to the relationship between costs and cropping decisions.[15] He investigated areal yields so that he could focus on peasant decisions. His conclusion that peasants tended to maximize yield per unit of area[16] suggests that if areal yields declined the cause might lie in peasant responses to the market as much as to ecological constraints.

Large- and small-scale Egyptian farmers adopted new technologies with remarkable alacrity. The extra-long-staple cotton called Sakellaridis, or Sakel, whose seed was supplied commercially, was one such technology. It is instructive to compare the curve for the acceptance of this variety of cotton from its introduction in 1911 with the curve for the acceptance of hybrid corn in the United States.[17] Seven years after the introduction of Sakellaridis in Egypt, it was grown on about 70 percent of the cropping area. Comparing this to the adoption of new hybrids by farmers in the American

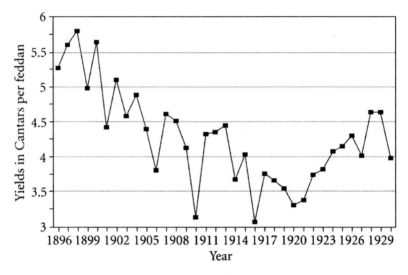

FIG. 1. Aggregate yields 1896–1930

Midwest, as presented in the classic studies of demand-driven technologi-cal innovation by Zvi Griliches, or to the rate that new strains of cotton were adopted on the highly capitalized farms of central California in the 1940s, one can see that Egyptian farmers adopted Sakellaridis more rapidly.[18] The relatively small area of the Nile Valley of course makes this rapid diffusion more comprehensible. One can also see that peasant farmers' poverty and illiteracy evidently did not negatively affect the rate of adoption of this new cotton strain. Sakel was not uniformly profitable for all growers, but the widespread adoption and relative uniformity of the crop due to the regu-latory undertakings of the state rapidly made it a recognizable type.[19]

Aggregate yields declined in step with the introduction of the new strain of extra-long-staple fiber and were due to the rapid response of a highly commercialized agricultural society to demand, via the adoption of a tech-nical innovation. More concretely, the rate at which the proportion of the cropping area devoted to Sakellaridis increased and declined accounts directly for most of the variation in aggregate yields between 1910 and 1930.

Figure 1 presents the story of aggregate-yield declines of Egyptian cot-ton from 1896 to 1930. The curve of the numbers is obvious. This is the most basic evidence, initially presented before World War II and later employed to adduce an argument of crisis.[20] What must be clear from the discussion above, however, is that the concept of "aggregate yield" hides the mix of cotton types that constituted the Egyptian cotton crop. For analytical pur-

TABLE 1. Average varietal yield

Name	Cantars/feddan	Ginned ratl/cantar	Start	End
Ashmuni	5–8	108–112	1860	
Hamuli		110		
Abyad			1864	1890
Gallini		85–88	1867	1890
Hariri		65–69		
Bamia	7–8	100–107	1873	?
Mit Afifi		107–110	1885	1927
Zafiri			1893	
Abbasi	4	106	1892	1913
Joannavitch	4	108	1890	1923
Voltos	6–7	110	1910	?
Nubari	4.5	108	1909	1923
Asili	4.5	113		
Britannia	4.3	110	1914	
Sakel	3.25	98–100	1911	1942
Zagoura		110–114	1917	

poses the aggregate "crop" for the 1900–1930 period must be divided into at least three subcrops: Mit Afifi, Ashmuni, and Sakellaridis. As table 1 shows, Mit Afifi and Ashmuni yielded between 5 and 8 cantars per feddan, while Sakel yielded on average about 3.25 cantars per feddan.[21] Decisions to grow Sakel rather than the other two crops (especially Mit Afifi in Lower Egypt) depended on the size of anticipated (quality) premium. On average one can expect a premium of about 50 percent to induce a shift from a higher-yielding crop to a lower-yielding one. This is what occurred around the time of World War I. Thus, Sakel accounted for less than 7 percent of the area planted with cotton in 1911, but by 1921 it comprised 75 percent of this area. By 1926 it had declined to about 50 percent of the area.

As shown in table 2 the aggregate "Egyptian crop" was a complex combination of subtypes. Between 1911 and 1924 it was increasingly dominated by one subtype that yielded nearly 25 percent less than the others.[22] Clearly, if 50 percent of the area of the cotton crop was switched over to a variety yielding 25 percent less fiber, then the aggregate national yield must have decreased by at least 12.5 percent, which approximates the figure Joel Beinin has proposed as the ecological-crisis effect. Visual inspection of the two

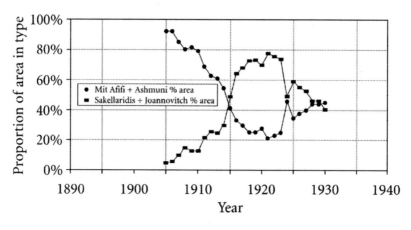

FIG. 2. Cotton types

curves presented in figure 2 suggests that the decline in yields after 1910, the year in which Sakel was first grown commercially, is roughly the inverse of the spread of this strain. The visual impression is sustained by a quantitative analysis: nearly 80 percent of the variation in aggregate yields in that decade is explained by the proportion of the cropping area devoted to Sakel. Confirmation that the decrease in aggregate yield is explained by the switch from long to extra-long-staple cotton is gained by looking at the yields of Mit Afifi and Ashmuni. Nearly 50 percent of the variation in aggregate yields between 1905 and 1930 is explained by the proportion of the total cropping area of these slightly shorter-staple but higher-yielding varieties. This single variable (acreage by type) goes a long way in explaining an extremely complex biological process.

The price differentials of different varieties of Egyptian cotton are shown in table 3. They reflect what was needed to encourage the shift in crops. Before 1917 these figures do not relate to Sakellaridis but, rather, refer to the difference between the contract grades known as "Fully Good Fair," for Ashmuni cotton (and after 1917, also for Sakellaridis) and American Middling. The reason for the late appearance of Sakellaridis, of course, is that it was just becoming an important component of the crop in the 1910s. American Middling was medium staple, Ashmuni long staple, and Sakellaridis was extra-long-staple. Just as the shift to Sakellaridis is statistically correlated with declining yields, so too both price and the premium for Egyptian cotton were statistically correlated negatively with aggregate yield: -0.53 and -0.4, respectively. In other words, higher prices for cotton tended to be linked to lower

TABLE 2. Types and areas of Egyptian cotton

Year	Total area	Mit Afifi area	Ashmuni area	Joannovitch area	Sakel area	% Mit Afifi	% MA +Ash	% Sakel	Aggregate yield
896									5.27
897									5.6
898									5.8
899									4.98
900									5.64
901									4.42
902									5.1
903									4.58
904									4.88
905	1,566,602	1,154,923	293,668	72,716		74	92		4.39
906	1,506,291	1,163,841	224,687	84,483		77	92		3.8
907	1,603,224	1,066,720	299,886	156,867		67	85		4.61
908	1,620,415	981,428	321,665	237,194		61	80		4.51
909	1,597,055	1,052,778	251,548	199,062		66	82		4.12
910	1,642,610	1,011,343	292,490	209,028		62	79		3.13
911	1,711,241	845,665	329,843	250,972	119,636	49	69	7	4.32
912	1,721,815	731,736	344,265	239,232	197,456	42	62	11	4.35
913	1,723,094	689,695	356,485	173,439	247,292	40	61	14	4.46
914	1,755,270	601,453	353,882	127,532	394,403	34	54	22	3.67
915	1,186,004	259,096	231,639	28,907	547,923	22	41	46	4.02
916	1,655,512	206,048	343,589	4,220	1,032,140	12	33	62	3.06
917	1,677,310	134,683	361,874	1,592	1,133,180	8	30	68	3.75
918	1,315,572	56,976	273,936	223	952,481	4	25	72	3.66
919	1,573,662	56,148	334,160	97	1,146,443	4	25	73	3.54
920	1,827,876	74,119	429,174	2,087	1,270,481	4	28	70	3.3
921	1,289,805	12,610	256,764	4,775	995,479	1	21	77	3.37
922	1,800,843	16,063	402,734	344	1,358,165	1	23	75	3.73
923	1,715,150	13,870	416,540	4,400	1,255,000	1	25	73	3.81
924	1,787,843	22,271	796,362		876,264	1	46	49	4.07
925	1,924,282	8,384	659,420		1,128,946	0	35	59	4.14
926	1,785,802	4,234	667,474		981,783	0	38	51	4.29
927	1,518,199	4,261	599,149		795,740	0	40	52	4.01
928	1,738,472		767,411		799,523		44	46	4.63
929	1,841,478		804,069		847,950		44	46	4.63
930	2,082,420		936,134		837,344		45	40	3.97

NOTE: Area is measured in feddans.

TABLE 3. Egyptian cotton premia

Year	FGF Sakellaridis[a]	FGF Brown or Uppers[b]	Col1/Col2
1901		14.97	
1902		22.72	
1903		22.09	
1904		17.63	
1905		23.47	
1906		24.38	
1907		21.78	
1908		20.28	
1909		31.44	
1910		24.22	
1911		20.81	
1912		19.63	
1913		20.56	
1914		19.69	
1915		19.59	
1916		63.3	
1917		46.1	
1918	42	controlled	
1919	198	48.3	4.10
1920	104.25	65.5	1.59
1921	63.1	44.35	1.42
1922	39.15	32.4	1.21
1923	52	46.85	1.11
1924	75.75	39.4	1.92
1925	46.75	33.25	1.41
1926	39.1	28.48	1.37
1927	44	31.85	1.57
1928	41.3	28	1.48
1929	35.77	23.9	1.50
1930	21.85	15.07	1.45
1931	17.15	12.26	1.40
1932	19.18	15.37	1.25
1933	17.5	13.66	1.28
1934	17.07	14.11	1.21
1935	18.37	14.62	1.26

TABLE 3 *(continued)*

Year	FGF Sakellaridis[a]	FGF Brown or Uppers[b]	Col1/Col2
1936	24.75	18.57	1.33
1937	17.6	13.17	1.34
1938	14.99		
1939	25.7		
1940	16.25		
1941	18.25		

NOTE: Prices are in "talaris"/cantar.
[a] FGF: Fully Good Fair grade of cotton. Sakellaridis: Extra-long-staple introduced in 1911.
[b] Brown: Regular Egyptian long staple; after 1920, Uppers replaces Brown.

yields, which would be the case if growers engaged in the crop shifts I suggest. Large- and small-scale Egyptian growers were extremely sensitive to price fluctuations through the channel of income per unit of area.

That growers chose a crop that maximized income per unit of area (rather than the yield per plant or per acre) was implicit in the results of Balls's research, which I have already mentioned. Even before the emergence of Sakellaridis, it had been suggested that an explanation for observed yield declines was the channel-of-income incentive:

> If we consider the yield (in money) per feddan, since the area has increased only 50 percent between 1897 and 1907, while the value of the crop has increased nearly 100 percent, the increase in money received per feddan amounts to nearly 40 percent. And if as has been suggested above, the fellah has obtained this result with diminished intensity of cultivation, that is, with a less expenditure of energy, he is doubly a gainer . . . It is doubtful how far any efforts to persuade the fellah that the yield of cotton is diminishing will meet with success, when the evidence of his purse is to the contrary effect.[23]

The interpretation of a single index number such as aggregate physical yield as a reliable indicator of changes in the Egyptian cotton crop is dangerous because it masks many changes in what was a nonhomogeneous crop. Craig suggested that the attempts to improve crop quality that were already under way by 1911 affected yields; for example, there were fewer pickings of the

..ld, and consequently less trash was processed as cotton.[24] The trans-
..nation of the Egyptian cotton crop continued throughout the twentieth century. As table 2 makes apparent, there were significant changes in
the composition of the crop, and both Mit Afifi and another strain, Joan-
novitch, disappeared before 1930. These same forces explain the disappearance of Sakel in the 1930s. Due in large part to its susceptibility to wilt
disease, Sakel yields continued to decline throughout the 1930s, but more
important, so did its price relative to other grades of cotton.[25]

The story I tell here seems novel and statistically sophisticated, but in fact
it was once the standard account. As early as 1921 Egyptians publicly linked
the extension of Sakel and the aggregate-yield decline,[26] and it remained the
standard explanation in expert Egyptian and international opinion.[27] A few
years later, Gerald Dudgeon divided aggregate-yield figures into precisely these
two categories (Sakel and non-Sakel) to explain the shift back to Ashmuni
in terms of the price differential between cotton types: "Taking the average
yield per feddan for Lower Egypt, which is roughly equivalent to the Sakellaridis area, for five years and comparing it with that of Upper Egypt, which
is nearly equivalent to the Ashmouni area, for a similar period, we arrive at
the following averages: Lower Egypt average 3.43 [cantars/feddan] . . . Upper
Egypt average: 4.26."[28] Later in the decade, Victor Mosseri[29] matter-of-factly
explained: "The excess of the falling off [of aggregate yields] since 1912 is attrib-
utable, one might say almost entirely, to the combined action of two new
factors, the one accidental, viz. the ravages of the pink boll-worm, the other
essential, viz. cultivation of Sakel. The nett yield of this new variety is indeed
constitutionally about 15 percent inferior to the cottons which it has supplanted
(Afifi, Assili, etc.)."[30] Mosseri's testimony is important because he was one
of the two rapporteurs of the 1910 Cotton Commission, created by the government to explore the reasons for the disastrous crop failure that year. The
commission's findings are often adduced to buttress the claims about
drainage. The commission's report recommended extending the drainage
system, particularly in the northernmost areas of the country, but its somewhat tentative findings were clearly oriented to resolving what its members
were convinced was a one-time problem. The later decline in yields was, as
far as Mosseri was concerned, a completely different issue.

If yields were not related to some ecological crisis, why did anyone think
they were? One reason is that the lack of drainage has always caused an ecological problem along the northern coast because of Egypt's geography,
although the effects of this crucial problem can be mitigated by investment
choices. The northern part of the Delta, where both rice and extra-long-

staple cotton were grown, is too low and too flat to drain adequately. Consequently it has long been liable to salt buildup and was seen in the late nineteenth century as an area in need of reclamation. Salt buildup in the northern Delta remains a problem today. In other words, drainage has been recognized as a constant problem for agriculture in the northern Delta for more than 150 years, but the waxing and waning of attention to this problem is more indicative of changing patterns of interest than an objective ecological crisis caused by structural, economic, or political imbalance.

The assertion that Egypt experienced an ecological crisis raises an important historiographical issue. Specifically, if there was no ecological crisis and if contemporary observers were aware that there was none, what drove the narrative of environmental disaster in later academic writing, and why did the allegation of insufficient drainage become widely accepted? Part of the problem was a misreading of the concerns about cotton voiced by Egyptians and English spinners shortly after the turn of the century. There was a persistent conflict between growers and spinners about what was called the environmental and biological *degeneration* of Egyptian cotton. For nearly forty years spinners complained about the deteriorating quality of Egyptian cotton, and some of the arguments about environmental disaster appear to echo this theme.

Even in the early twentieth century experts attempted to understand why yields were declining, and later authors adopted their explanations. Specifically, they focused on one explanation (insufficient drainage) that had been prominent around 1910 and ignored explanations that gained currency after 1920. Divergent but plausible arguments about the reasons for fluctuations in cotton yields, which had contrasting political implications at the beginning of the twentieth century, were transformed into a single, ostensibly anticolonial, argument. The most surprising aspect of the anticolonial argument that colonialism provoked an ecological crisis is that it was born as an argument put forth by colonial officials to support their continued role in Egypt. It is instructive to review quickly the core of the arguments for ecological crisis: they were (and remain) technical, intellectual, political, and institutional.

Politically, the idea that Britain has been responsible for Egyptian history is alluring to both anticolonialists and apologists for colonialism; it certainly places the British nearly alone at the center directing Egyptian life. The discourse of drainage and ecological disaster has always been a discourse about colonialism. At first it was a narrative of colonial power triumphant; later, it became a narrative of colonial power as a force of destruction.

Writing in 1892, Alfred Milner was probably the first to describe what has since been characterized as an ecological crisis in the northern Delta when he discussed at length the "marked deterioration of the soil" as the result of perennial irrigation. Although Milner's description came a decade before the claimed onset of the ecological crisis, it is important to consider. Milner alleged that agricultural "deterioration was aggravated by the unscientific manner in which summer cultivation was introduced, and especially by the neglect of the great essential of proper drainage. It was the want of drainage, which completed the ruin of the Birriya, that broad belt of land, which occupies the northern and lowest portion of the Delta, adjoining the great lakes. There are upwards of one million acres of this region, now swamp, or salt marsh, or otherwise uncultivable, which in ancient times were the garden of Egypt." The remedy he suggested was simple: "thorough washing of the land, and by the cultivation of rice, the restorative value of which crop is well known to the Egyptian agriculturalist."[31]

Milner described a farrago of technical errors committed by French engineers (misaligned and poorly regulated canals with insufficient gradients, and missing sluices) coupled with neglected drainage or drains used as irrigation channels ("it is impossible to conceive a worse sin against every sound principle of agriculture").[32] A remarkable foreshortening occurs in Milner's narrative; the pharaonic garden of Egypt was destroyed by French maladministration. The Birriya had, however, been unsuitable for agriculture for far longer.

The discourse of ecological destruction was, in its origin, an attack that sought to undercut French ambitions to replace the English in Egypt by virtue of their technological expertise. English energy and technical ability during its occupation of Egypt accomplished what neither French engineers nor Egyptian politicians could. It is therefore not surprising that one of the next authors after Milner to focus on drainage as a cause of prolonged crisis (rather than the cause of the 1910 crop debacle) was P. G. Elgood, in his triumphal account of Lord Kitchener's years as the British Resident. Writing in the later 1920s, Elgood also blamed shortsighted Egyptian peasants for overwatering, and the shortsightedness of ministries staffed by Egyptians for responding too eagerly to peasants' demands for water without planning for the future, and thereby neglecting the country's future.[33] Elgood thus sounded an old theme: British officials, and not Egyptian elite, were the true—if not always immediately responsive—friends of the peasant. Despite sounding an alarm, Elgood (like most contemporary observers) placed the issue of drainage in what was then a well-understood triple context: maintaining the quality (not quantity) of cotton produced, reclaiming waste land in the northern Delta, and recognizing that drainage was only one among many causal agents affecting the cotton yield.

Although drainage had initially been seen as one cause among many for declining quality, its centrality as a factor grew as later authors paid more attention to aggregate yield declines.[34] The identification of drainage as the primary cause of aggregate yield decline, however, emerged as a central theme only in the 1970s, in the work of Alan Richards. Richards was aware of the shifts to and then away from a lower-yielding crop,[35] but they formed only a minor part of a story told to establish the predatory and thus primarily negative nature of the economic structure of British imperial rule. Richards linked declining yields to a plausible characterization of why a rational government would provide irrigation but not drainage and wrote a powerful anti-imperialist narrative. An analysis that began as a tribute to imperial foresight and a concern with the profitability of investments by primarily foreign-owned companies turned into an attack on imperial shortsightedness, although in both instances the focus remained on the power of the colonial state as the key actor in Egyptian economic life. As taken over by Bent Hansen (for whom the British were not inherently a negative force) and by Joel Beinin (for whom they were), the politics of the narrative turned a widely recognized problem whose solution had always been well understood into an ecological crisis that neatly supplemented other crises inherent in imperial regimes.

The explicitly anti-imperialist accounts of Egyptian history exclude Egyptians from any active role in the construction of the economic and political order that lasted more than half a century. The focus on representation makes intellectuals and imperial officials far more central to the emergence of the world in which we live than they actually were and profoundly misreads the commercial, cultural, and social connections between Egypt and England.[36]

If most growers were not concerned that a drainage crisis existed and were not prepared to exert great effort to extend the drainage system, who was? Agricultural societies and individual landowners with large investments in cotton and rice in the extreme north of the Delta were certainly affected by the drainage issue and appear to have been consistent supporters of extending the network of drains and pumping stations.[37] Because hydraulic engineering was linked to British prestige, irrigation and drainage were frequently foremost in the minds of British officials.[38] Emerging sectoral interests of the Egyptian elite were also involved. Thus, Hussein Sirri, the minister of public works in several governments in 1937–38, argued for the

need to extend the drainage system beyond the 35–40 percent of agricultural land that he estimated was then currently covered. "Our aim," he said,
"is to produce real drainage in the land for every plot in Egypt from Aswan
to the sea."[39] Robert Vitalis has argued that entrepreneurs in the construction industry (canal dredging in particular) were crucial actors in the Egyptian political economy. Sirri, for example, was a close colleague of the
construction magnate Ahmad Abbud.[40] Any plan to extend irrigation far
into the south where drainage (insofar as reducing the water table was concerned) was not an issue was more likely drawn with an eye for the profits
of the construction industry than for the productivity of the peasants.

Having argued that there was no ecological crisis, why does it matter?
Predicating the history and historiography of twentieth-century Egypt on
a narrative of structural crisis is an argument about the central role of the
state in the modern world and of the perversely destructive way in which
the colonial—or indeed any nonnational—state employs its power within
the state over which it rules. So powerful, the argument goes, was the imperial state that it destroyed the society it had an obligation to protect. The
feeble resistance to state activity that the dominated population could
demonstrate was insufficient to prevent the destruction of society or the
environment. If this sounds like the story told by colonial officers of their
heroic attempts to master both society and nature for the benefit of progress,
it ought to. Our received story is, in short, the story of triumphal colonialism in reverse.

Narratives of effulgent imperial powers are ancient and widespread, but
if the narrative I discuss here is rooted in official colonial rhetoric, the counternarrative that informs Egyptian historiography has its roots in Lenin's
view of imperialism. Writing in 1917, Lenin argued that "finance capital finds
most 'convenient,' and derives the greatest profit from, a *form* of subjection
which involves the loss of political independence of the subjected countries
and peoples." Lenin distinguished twentieth-century imperialism from
earlier imperialisms and colonial policies because it was based on the quest
to monopolize raw material: "The more capitalism is developed, the more
strongly the shortage of raw materials is felt, the more intense the compe-
tition and the hunt for sources of raw materials throughout the whole world,
and the more desperate the struggle for the acquisition of colonies."[41] It is
not surprising that Lenin employed Egypt as an example of this process:

The British capitalists are exerting every effort to develop cotton growing in
their colony, Egypt (in 1904, out of 2,300,000 hectares of land under culti-

vation, 600,000 or more were under cotton); the Russians are doing the same in *their* colony, Turkestan, because in this way they will be in a better position to defeat their foreign competitors, to monopolize the sources of raw materials and form a more economical and profitable textile trust in which *all* the processes of cotton production and manufacturing will be "combined" and concentrated in the hands of one set of owners.[42]

For the socialist movement in Lenin's day, however, there was no concern that the structural characteristics of imperialism would have negative consequences for the physical environment. Colonial rule was widely understood to affect both society and the individual, but preservation of the environment was not generally a concern of the Left; if anything, conservation—especially insofar as it appears to be linked to ideas of purity—was more often a concern of the Right.

By the 1960s, however, European critiques of colonial and imperial rule more frequently invoked claims about the destruction of the environment. Thus, in 1968, Jacques Berque's monumental and influential *Egypt: Imperialism and Revolution* made an early (and possibly the earliest) case for structural destruction of the environment with the mention of "a development which seemed to challenge the most sensational successes of the past half-century . . . The yield of cotton, after increasing between the Occupation and the end of the century, now declined."[43] Berque noted in passing that yields of other crops, including the major food crops of wheat, barley, and beans, actually increased under British rule and that the value of the cotton crop per areal unit doubled during this period. Nevertheless, he used the decline of areal yields over a five-year period to draw a moral and political lesson: "It was the Victorian varieties, those connected with the economy and taste of the time, which seemed to suffer most."[44] Because Berque preferred moral pronouncement to causal argument, he simply ignored what countervailing trends might mean and did not investigate the processes that might cause a decline in yields. Rather, he invoked vague "agronomic factors" at one level but intoned that even more vague factors were really at play because "at a deeper level it [yield decline] involved those relations between man and Nature which were affected by colonization. In fact, its social and even psychological repercussions were felt sharply, and were not confined to the ruling minority or to articulate opinion."[45]

In the 1970s and 1980s, with growing concern in Europe and the United States about the environment, far more attention was placed on the negative consequences of development, capitalism, and colonial projects. The destructive consequences, especially in tropical Africa, of deforestation and the forced introduction of commercial crops became a standard measure against which to evaluate colonial rule.[46] It appears that this discourse now plays a role in the narrative of the Egyptian political economy, and it is this discursive construction that has made the assertion about ecological catastrophe widely popular, and largely unexamined, in academic circles since the 1970s.

THE MISSING CHILDREN

Concluding *Egypt: An Economic and Social Analysis*,[47] Charles Issawi considered two important problems: overpopulation and land reform. Economists remain fascinated with these issues, as one especially trenchant review of the literature on development has shown.[48] Issawi was an early exponent of the "surplus-labor hypothesis," another way of saying that countries like Egypt had too many people for too little remunerative employment. On the penultimate page, Issawi notes an estimate that Egyptian agriculture required between 370 and 390 million man-days for full production. In addition, it required nearly half again as much labor by women and children, between 125 and 198 million women- or child-days.[49]

A few years later, Mahmoud Amin Anis published an important study of Egypt's national income. He also noted the importance of women and children in the Egyptian economy, more precisely than Issawi had. Anis found statistics indicating that in 1943 about 4.1 million people were engaged in Egyptian agriculture—about 2.4 million men, 700,000 women, and 1 million boys and girls. Anis was also able to disaggregate the labor inputs of men and boys for various crops. For Egypt as a whole, boys provided about half the labor inputs of men; their work was highly concentrated. As Issawi was aware, boys were disproportionately employed in the production of cotton and rice, where they constituted a larger portion of the workforce than men, and in the production of maize and wheat, where they provided significant proportions of the overall labor.

Although it is obvious that the Egyptian cotton-export economy was based on the labor of children, it is rare to find an extensive discussion of child labor in the existing literature. It is also rare to find any discussion of the role of child labor in growing industrial sectors of Egypt during the twentieth century, although it is apparent that so-called early industrialization frequently increased the demand for the labor of children.[50] Child labor in agriculture did not disappear under Nasser. According to one study it remained, at least in some areas, a crucial part of the labor force.[51] Child labor has certainly not disappeared today, for a 1988 U.S. government survey estimated that in Egypt 1.4 million children (under the age of fourteen) were working in agriculture and industry, including some export industries. Children with significant work experience can obtain monthly incomes that are competitive with those of educated adults.[52]

When Issawi revised his 1947 book as *Egypt at Mid-Century*, he still addressed the issue of overpopulation and insufficient work, using the same figures for adult and child employment.[53] Yet neither in regard to the insufficiency of employment nor in regard to the threat of cheap labor from the countryside did he consider whether child labor itself was a problem. Writing after 1952, Issawi concluded his study of Egypt no longer with problems but, rather, with an analysis of social and political trends. Whereas Issawi had earlier seen difficulties and remedies, he now argued that the old regime was a structural failure. "The writing on the wall," he wrote, "had for many years been plain to see."[54] Issawi welcomed the land reform of the new regime and much of its other economic legislation, including the labor laws of December 1952, and paid tribute to the new-found feelings of self-respect, unity, and hopefulness that Egyptians (except for "a few *ci-devant* pashas and wealthy men") felt. When he mentioned, in passing, the role of child labor in the economy it was simply as an afterthought, far less important for him than, for example, encouraging peasant women to use birth control to slow population growth.

With few exceptions, later studies pursued the path blazed by Issawi in 1954: they defended the gains of the Nasserist revolution and argued about whether it had gone sufficiently far. In the process, they also created a crisis that never happened, while largely ignoring the role of children in the economy. Much, although not all, changed under Nasser, and it is long past time to begin anew the writing of the Egyptian political economy.

NOTES

1. Joel Beinin, "Egypt: Society and Economy, 1923–1952," in *The Cambridge History of Egypt*, ed. M. W. Daly (Cambridge: Cambridge University Press, 1999), 309–10.

2. The exception is Robert Tignor, whose history of the Egyptian economy between 1918 and 1952 is not anchored in a narrative of crisis and generally presents World War I as an exogenous shock. Tignor, *State, Private Enterprise and Economic Change in Egypt, 1918–1952* (Princeton, NJ: Princeton University Press, 1984).

3. Ellis Goldberg, *Trade, Reputation, and Child Labor in Twentieth-Century Egypt* (New York: Palgrave, 2004).

4. Robert Vitalis, *When Capitalists Collide* (Berkeley and Los Angeles: University of California Press, 1995).

5. James I. Craig, "Notes on Cotton Statistics in Egypt," *L'Egypte Contemporaine*, 1910, 166–98; International Federation of Master Cotton Spinners' and Manufacturers' Associations, *Official Report of the International Cotton Congress* (1927).

6. Joel Migdal, *Peasants, Politics and Revolution* (Princeton, NJ: Princeton University Press, 1974); Samuel Huntington, *Political Order in Changing Societies* (New Haven, CT: Yale University Press, 1968), 72; David Apter, *The Politics of Modernization* (Chicago: University of Chicago Press, 1965), 47.

7. Jacques Berque, *Egypt: Imperialism and Revolution*, trans. Jean Stewart (London: Faber, 1972).

8. Timothy Mitchell, *Colonising Egypt* (Cambridge: Cambridge University Press, 1988); Huntington, *Political Order*; Joel Migdal, *Strong Societies and Weak States* (Princeton, NJ: Princeton University Press, 1988), 93–95; Eric Wolf, *Europe and the People without History* (Berkeley: University of California Press, 1982), 311; P. J. Vatikiotis, *The Modern History of Egypt* (New York: Praeger, 1969).

9. Of course, Great Britain's *second* most important, and fastest growing, export was itself a staple: coal.

10. Lawrence Balls, "Analyses of Agricultural Yield, Part III, The Influence of Natural Environmental Factors upon the Yield of Egyptian Cotton," *Philosophical Transactions of the Royal Society of London, Series B* 208 (1918): 157–223; G. C. Dudgeon, "A Brief Revue of the Cotton Conditions in Egypt during the Past Five Years," *L'Egypte Contemporaine* 14 (1923): 517–32; M. Matteo Casoria, "Chronique Agricole de l'Année 1922," *L'Egypte Contemporaine* 70 (1922): 141–61.

11. Tignor, *State, Private Enterprise and Economic Change*; Alan Richards, *Egypt's Agricultural Development 1800–1980* (Boulder, CO: Westview Press, 1982); Bent Hansen, "Employment and Wages in Rural Egypt," *American Economic Review* 59 (1969): 298–313; Hansen, *Egypt and Turkey* (Oxford: Oxford University Press, 1991); Beinin, "Egypt."

12. Hansen, *Egypt and Turkey*.

13. Beinin, "Egypt"; Balls, "Analyses of Agricultural Yield"; John A. Todd, *The World's Cotton Crops* (London: A. and C. Black, Ltd., 1915), 266–69.

14. Balls, "Analyses of Agricultural Yield," 123.

15. Ibid., 129.

16. Ibid.

17. Egypt, Ministry of Finance, *Annuaire Statistique* (Cairo: Imprimerie Nationale, 1921); Ibrahim Ahmad and Muhammad Abd al-Rahman Hafiz, *Aswaq al-qutn wa*

tijaratuhu fi Misr (Cairo: Al-Saadah Publishers, 1937); Zvi Griliches, "Hybrid Corn: An Explanation in the Economics of Technological Change," *Econometrica* 25 (1957): 501–22.

18. However, in April 1949, ninety-five hundred growers in California, farming nearly a million acres, switched from one strain of Acala to another. See Moses S. Musoke and Alan L. Olmstead, "The Rise of the Cotton Industry in California: A Comparative Perspective," *Journal of Economic History* 42 (1982): 385–412, 390.

19. Jean Sakellaridis himself was given several monetary awards by the Egyptian government in recognition of the importance of the type.

20. John A. Todd, "The Market for Egyptian Cotton in 1909–1910," *L'Egypte Contemporain*, 1911, 1–29; Craig, "Notes on Cotton Statistics"; Richards, *Egypt's Agricultural Development*, 77–80; Hansen, *Egypt and Turkey*, 23; Beinin, "Egypt," 309–10.

21. Sakel was grown until World War II, but the areal yield remained on average about three cantars per feddan for the years 1935–39 during which no drainage problem could possibly have been obtained. See Hasan Sidki, *Al-Qutn al-Misri* (Cairo: Egyptian Renaissance Press, 1950), 260; and International Institute of Agriculture, *Agricultural Problems in Their International Aspect* (Rome: Printing Office of the International Institute of Agriculture, 1926), 177: "Thus in Upper Egypt, where Achmouni is the principal variety, the average yield is estimated at 450 pounds, while in Lower Egypt, where Sakellaridis is the principal variety, the average yield per acre was 300 pounds."

22. Leon Polier, "La question des prix du coton et de l'approvisionnement des filatures," *L'Egypte Contemporaine* 5 (1914): 323.

23. Craig, "Notes on Cotton Statistics," 182.

24. International Federation of Master Cotton Spinners' and Manufacturers' Associations, *Official Report*, 90, notes the decrease in the number of pickings.

25. International Federation of Master Cotton Spinners, *Official Report of the XVIII International Cotton Congress* (Manchester: Cloister Press, 1938), 76.

26. Yusuf Nahas, *Juhud al-Niqabah al-Zira'iyya al-Misriyya al-'Ammah fi Thalathina 'Amm* (Cairo: Dar al-Nil, 1952), 41.

27. Ahmad and Hafiz, *Aswaq al-qutn wa tijaratuhu fi Misr*, 11, 70–71; J. D. Black, "The Outlook for American Cotton," *Review of Economic Statistics* 17, no. 3 (1936): 68–78; International Institute of Agriculture, *Agricultural Problems*, 113.

28. Dudgeon, "Brief Revue," 529.

29. Mosseri was an internationally recognized expert as well as a large landowner and a member of an extremely influential family; he was president of the Egyptian Institute, a corresponding member of the Agricultural Academy of France, and a technical adviser to the Royal Agricultural Society of Egypt (International

Federation of Master Cotton Spinners' and Manufacturers' Associations, *Official Report*).

30. Ibid., 205; Yusuf Nahas, *Dhikrayat* (Cairo: Dar al-Nil, 1952), 41, gives the same overall yield difference as Mosseri (International Federation of Master Cotton Spinners, *Official Report*)—15 percent—but splits it into two parts: crop yield and ginning outturn.

31. Alfred Milner, *England in Egypt* (London: Edward Arnold, 1892), 284.

32. Ibid.

33. P. G. Elgood, *The Transit of Egypt* (London: Edward Arnold and Company, 1928), 201–2.

34. Charles Issawi, *Egypt: An Economic and Social Analysis* (London: Oxford University Press, 1947); Issawi, *Egypt at Mid-Century: An Economic Survey* (London: Oxford University Press, 1954); Issawi, *Egypt in Revolution* (London: Oxford University Press, 1963).

35. Richards, *Egypt's Agricultural Development*, 126.

36. Mitchell, *Colonising Egypt*; Beinin, "Egypt."

37. Casoria, "Chronique Agricole," 145.

38. Earl of Cromer, *Modern Egypt* (London: Macmillan and Company, 1908), 2:463–65; Lord Lloyd, *Egypt since Cromer* (London: Macmillan and Company, 1933), 1:148.

39. International Federation of Master Cotton Spinners, *Official Report* (1938), 63.

40. Vitalis, *When Capitalists Collide*, 53.

41. V. I. Lenin, "Imperialism, the Highest State of Capitalism," in *Selected Works* (Moscow: Progress Publishers, 1967), 3:740.

42. Ibid., 3:742.

43. Berque, *Egypt*, 234.

44. Ibid.

45. Ibid., 235.

46. Michael F. Lofchie and Stephen K. Commins, "Food Deficits and Agricultural Policies in Tropical Africa," *Journal of Modern African Studies* 20, no. 1 (1982): 14.

47. Issawi, *Egypt*.

48. Timothy Mitchell, *Rule of Experts* (Berkeley and Los Angeles: University of California Press, 2002).

49. Issawi, *Egypt*, 201.

50. Pamela Barnhouse Walters and Carl M. Briggs, "The Family Economy, Child Labor, and Schooling: Evidence from the Early Twentieth Century South," *American Sociological Review* 58, no. 2 (1993): 163–81.

51. Hansen, "Employment and Wages."

52. United States Department of Labor, *By the Sweat and Toil of Children* (Washington, DC: Government Printing Office, 1994), 55. This is not a conclusion drawn in the study, but it becomes clear by comparing earnings of children in the knotted carpet industry with those of government employees.

53. Issawi, *Egypt at Mid-Century.*

54. Ibid., 271.

PART IV

Emerging Voices

7

On Gender, History, . . . and Fiction

MARILYN BOOTH

ntroducing her encyclopedic dictionary of notable women through the
ages and across continents, Lebanese emigrant to Cairo Zaynab Fawwaz
(ca. 1850–1914) noted with apparent exasperation that histories of men
had been written and rewritten, while "amidst all this activity I have
observed no one . . . reserving even a single chapter in the Arabic tongue
for half the human world."[1] Had she been alive a century later, Fawwaz would
have found much to engage her attention: indeed, she would confront a ver-
itable flood of historical work on women and on gender as a socially constitutive marker of difference, in Arabic, Farsi, Turkish, English, and French.
Indisputably, academic feminist studies of the twentieth century's second
half have spurred this scholarship, but we must recognize its roots in the
earlier energies of Fawwaz and her contemporaries and, in the twentieth
century's first half, further works of "recuperation" that performed necessary groundwork, recognizing women's very presence in history and simultaneously exposing History as ideologically shaped narrativization. Some
of this early work has never been superseded. Nabia Abbott's 1940s essays
on women in the Hijaz at Islam's founding did not merely "add women and
stir"—in that famous if reductive characterization of early feminist historical work on Euro/American societies—but rather assessed the significance
of women's vocal presences to the shaping of that historical moment, a normative ideal for later Muslims. Abbott echoed a writing of earlier women's
lives, by Arab women writing in Arabic, that formed the earliest basis for
feminist scholarship on Arab societies.[2]

Now, at the start of a new century, so rich has become the production
of gender studies in and on MENA (Middle East and North Africa) that

two academic journals have emerged (*Hawwa* and *Journal of Middle East Women's Studies*) as have a metaliterature analyzing cross-disciplinary production and a literally encyclopedic ambition to capture the state of the art now, most energetically represented in the mammoth and ongoing project *Encyclopedia of Women & Islamic Cultures*. In this brief assessment, I survey some of the copious English-language specifically historical scholarship while stressing the presence and importance of publication in languages indigenous to the region and gesturing to the continuing significance of thinking across disciplines, briefly describing my current project that aspires to do so.

Challenge and accomplishment continue to shape MENA gender history. First, the obvious still bears saying: the fortunes of academic gender history are inextricably bound up in contemporary local and global politics, and at the present moment this entanglement seems especially inescapable in MENA gender history.[3] Nor should we want to escape this, for to study the work of gender categories over time is to deconstruct pasts directly productive of our present situations. Moreover, images students bring to our courses—whether images of "the Orient" or of "the Occident"—directly implicate those histories of gender as a marker of political hierarchies. Second, while the field flourishes in North America and England, the gender-sensitive study of history for the region started *in* the region, with the first historical analyses of women's status published just before the turn of the twentieth century in Lebanon, Egypt, and Turkey, as interventions in shaping nationalist narrative. It is crucial not only to engage with and honor early and ongoing work in the region but to recognize the historiographical significance of how academies are differentially placed in the global—too often an easy substitute for "Western"—production of knowledges. I believe that the center of gravity is shifting once again to West Asia and North Africa. But—my third focus—in an increasingly conservative social and political atmosphere characterized by growing popular discontent about the postcolonial state's perceived failure to perform its duty toward citizens, its consistent repression of any real opposition, and the continuing weight of neocolonialism in its shape-shifting forms, women are (yet again) bearing a double symbolic and social-political burden. Claimed by various political actors simultaneously as embodying all that is wrong with society *and* as the all-important repository of everything the society cherishes most, women may find their every articulation on gender history resonating far beyond the academy. Such circumstances have repercussions on academic work, implications for how research is framed and received, and things to say about how a far-flung scholarly community views, defines, and polices itself as well as how it is modulated by events and by other communities. Sensitivities and loud silences around gender remain at the center of the politics of the nation, and therefore, so does gender history, as it analyses, questions, and reframes earlier narratives of nation and gendered identities. Ongoing debates formulated among scholars in the Middle East, and factors outside the academic discipline of history, are leading the field in exciting and activist directions, though sometimes with troubling sideshows afforded by popular-media interventions that we ignore at our peril, for these also shape our audiences (and our world). Of course boundaries between "here" and "there," or between English-language scholarship and that presented in Arabic, Turkish, Persian, and French, are not static: in fact, issues of "where" and "how" one is situated are very much to the fore. With the growth of gender studies in/on MENA in every social science and humanities discipline, there has been a fierce, often acrimonious, contestation over situated knowledges and positionality, a constant if variably constructive reminder of the importance of activism in shaping scholarly agendas, the perceived urgency of the issues at hand, and of course the interested nature of all scholarship. That scholarship on gender in the Middle East is directly pertinent to activisms around gender and human rights (with repercussions in law reform, legislation, medical care, social safety nets, and a host of other areas with immediate impact on the lives of women, men, and children) is a remarkable and exciting responsibility for scholars.

If those of us who try to conceptualize, research, and teach Middle East gender history in North America feel we work within an ever-more highly charged political atmosphere, how much more sharply evident it is for scholars in the MENA region, who face restraints both material and political, not to mention generally difficult conditions that obtain in the region's overcrowded, underresourced public universities. Yet, centers and collectives throughout the region sustain the study of gender. The University of Sanaa in Yemen, the American Universities in Cairo and Sharjah, the Lebanese American University in Beirut, and Bir Zeit University in Palestine (to the extent it can remain open in siege conditions) have lively centers and teach women's and gender-focused history. Some of these centers have existed since the 1970s, the founding decade for the Institute for Women's Studies in the Arab World at Beirut College for Girls (later Lebanese American University) and the Women's Studies Center at Ahfad College for Girls (later Ahfad University for Women, Omdurman, Sudan). This ongoing energy in teaching and curriculum development is crucial to create a constituency of young women and young men, giving them historical narratives through or against which to think about their own lives. Yet there are strong and possibly growing deterrents to research work on gender in the region; and there remains a gulf between what is published in North America and Europe, and sometimes translated into Middle Eastern languages, and what is published in West Asian and North African capitals, and almost never translated into English.[4]

In the region particularly, the "archaeological" work of republishing, annotating, and analyzing earlier writings on gender continues. This is not only a scholarly imperative—and a slow process, for archives remain difficult to access and incomplete. It is also a political necessity for feminist scholars in the region, in the present political climate, where the biographies and writings of individuals of an earlier time are also constantly constructed in the interests of conservative gender agendas. In fact, the many popular works on women of the first and second Muslim generations that continue to be published throughout the region are eloquent evidence of how important the act of constructing gendered histories remains to contemporary and contesting political forces. If not produced deliberately as a counterweight, new Arabic-language biographies of early feminist figures, such as Nabawiyya Musa and Huda Sha'rawi, are important in offering alternative views of women's sociopolitical action. Contemporary women's collectives—Multaqa al-Mar'a wa-al-Dhakira (Women and Memory Forum) in Cairo, al-Bahithat (Researchers' Collective) in Beirut, and the editorial groups that publish the journals al-Ra'ida at Beirut University College and Nur in Cairo—are republishing early works by Arab women and early volumes of women's magazines, partly to counter accusations that feminism is alien to non-Western societies, to recognize that women's activism against gender-shaped social inequalities takes many forms. And to republish early texts is to maintain a strategy for speaking out when contemporary feminist analysis and the study of sexualities are vulnerable to official censorship and even more to "censorship of the street"—pressure from religiously self-defined activists. In fact, historians of gender who republish earlier documents are often vying with Islamist publishing houses that also republish medieval Islamic tracts focusing on gender, since—ironically, perhaps—Islamist discourse gives center stage to the body and to sexuality by focusing regulatory discourses there. Islamist writers are also publishing translations with commentaries of selected Western documents central to histories of gender discourse, thereby working, quite consciously I think, to capture Western feminism's terrain and define it for a popular audience before others can do so, much as conservative think tanks in the United States have adopted and bent the rhetoric of multiculturalism and feminism to their own political agendas. The empirical work of unearthing documents carries political valence, offering ostensibly "objective" ground on which to advance agendas through the selective, authoritative presentation of texts with new apparatuses and prefaces.

At a state-sponsored 1999 Cairo conference on gender and history that commemorated lawyer Qasim Amin's famous and explosive second book on gender relations (1899), scholars in many disciplines, fiction writers, and filmmakers brought their own work to bear on interpreting earlier moments. Cross-disciplinary work is endemic to feminist activist scholarship, and some of the most important theoretical breakthroughs and rereadings in MENA gender history have been contributed by anthropologists and sociologists: Deniz Kandiyoti on theories of patriarchy and nationalism, Fatima Mernissi on traditions of Islamic historical scholarship and the sacrality of sources as producing certain readings of early Islamic history, Suad Joseph on kinship and family organization, Annelies Moors on changing legal structures as shaped by practice, and Saba Mahmood on what piety movements mean for and to Muslim women. Scholars outside the history discipline have contributed to study of the early nationalist period in Egypt: anthropologists (Cynthia Nelson and Lila Abu-Lughod), political scientists (Mervat Hatem), and scholars of literature (Huda al-Sadda) and of Islamic studies (Omaima Abu-Bakr). Gender history has also been influenced by Women in Development work, although perhaps less so now than fifteen years ago. But historians are now at the forefront in theorizing gender as a key analytic space and reassessing dominant historiographical narratives, for example, reassessing the formation of the modern state as centrally shaped by gender: witness the work on Iran of Parvin Paidar, Afsaneh Najmabadi, and Janet Afary. Ellen Fleischmann not only incorporates women's activism into the history of the early Palestinian nationalist movement but also sees that movement as significantly shaped by concepts of "the new woman." Elizabeth Thompson argues that a "crisis of paternity" was central to Syrian elites' struggle to oppose French interwar imperial control. Mounira Charrad explores postcolonial North African states' divergent engineering of family status law according to the different status of extended kinship groups in each case and shows how family status law became central to each state's definition of itself. Julia Clancy-Smith emphasizes gender in analyzing North African colonial encounters.[5] New work is emerging so quickly that it is impossible to do it justice here.

Such work builds on historical scholarship on women's activisms and status, whether elite women's institution-building within anticolonial nationalist contexts, such as Margot Badran's work on the Egyptian Feminist Union or Ijlal Khalifa's and Amal al-Subki's books on the Egyptian feminist movement's growth or Beth Baron's book on the Egyptian women's press as an institution in formation, or on groundbreaking historical scholarship on nonelite women's work and status vis-à-vis legal systems, notably Judith Tucker's books on Egypt and Ottoman Syria and Palestine.[6] Yet, even at the start of the twenty-first century, gender-aware historical scholarship too often remains parallel or adjunct to, rather than incorporated within or constitutive of, academic MENA history wherever practiced. That recent years have seen numerous review articles and assessments of "the field" (however defined) suggests a productive tension that has marked women's and gender history in general, between, roughly, post-structuralist emphasis on the inaccessibility of experience except as a product of discourse and feminist desires to focus on the material stuff of women's lives; perhaps because Middle East gender history is a small field wherein the lure of multiple archives and untended pastures looms large, these debates have hovered but not been as central as they might be to work in this area.

Historians, in company with other MENA scholars, have grappled with the issue of "complementarity" as a marker of—and agent in—maintaining gender binaries, although it seems to me that "complementarity" has been scrutinized more in terms of a combination of legal strictures and material experience than as a hegemonic discourse with material political implications. Long a mainstay of conservative visions of Muslim-majority (as well as Christian-majority) societies, the notion that men's and women's ascribed social-political duties were "equal but different" and "complemented" each other masked the hierarchical arrangements whereby these "complementary" roles were maintained as "natural," as they could mask institutionalized violence. Deconstructing this by foregrounding the bipolar yet hierarchical distinctions that constituted the ideological work of "complementarity" was linked to understanding the particularities of patriarchal family and supra-family political organization across time and in the region, and then in investigating linkages and dissonances between notions of domesticity and gender difference.

Historians of women and gender in the Middle East took up, to discard, Western feminist formulations of public and private, contributing to a more nuanced understanding of gender and spatial distinctions in discrete historical situations. Sophisticated work on "the harem" and a burgeoning genre of Arab women's memoirs that constructed gender segregation in specific ways fed into a relatively new attention to domesticity's multiple meanings, as strategically deployed by early feminists who sought to enter public life. Questioning reified notions of patriarchy has also led to more emphasis on masculinities, specifically the positioning of younger men in hierarchies of power, an investigation that Kandiyoti and anthropologist Suad Joseph have pioneered.

Scholarship on the political work of gendered representations and on the political force of concepts such as honor and shame, particularly with reference to the elaboration of anticolonialist nationalisms and emerging postcolonial states, examines intersections among dominant discourses of gender binaries, aesthetic culture, and political activisms. Frances Hasso argues that Palestinian flight during and just after the 1948 war enacted anxieties over familial honor transferred to the larger community, while Ellen Fleischmann analyzes Palestinian women's double use of the discourse of honor to resist imperialist encroachment and to challenge their own community's gender regime. Concepts of honor have undergirded Beth Baron's investigation of elite Egyptian women's nationalist stances, and my own formulations of elite men's discourses on women's rights as veiled discourses on masculinity in British-controlled Egypt.[7] Honor was a language in which resistance to the occupier was articulated as community preservation. But the discourse of honor remains politically operative today and can be used to discredit the project of making gender constitutive to the study of history—a move that has to be deliberately contested. What I think is one of the most important books on Middle East women and gender to come out recently is not a work of history but an anthology on the politics of sexuality, *Sexuality in Muslim Societies*, published by Women for Women's Human Rights/New Ways, a collective of Turkish feminist activists and scholars whose bold denunciation of silences around sexuality includes breaking what is probably the final taboo by speaking about Muslim lesbian communities. (Yet, I was told by the editors, regretfully these essays cannot be included in the Arabic-language version of the volume![8]) Focus on masculinities has led to a more open scholarly discussion of not only the disjunctions, historically, between same-sex sexual relationships and sexual or gender identities but also the emergence in particular of gay male identities and communities. It remains crucial to recognize that recent political events, notably the Egyptian government's imprisonment and trial of fifty-two men accused of embracing gay identity, suggest that the political climate for this work is not getting more receptive—and it is a frightening enactment of how representations of sexual identity are appropriated for political purposes. But responses are fierce as well: gender activists in the region work to disseminate alternative notions of gendered social structures partly by offering alternative historical narratives. Witness the graphically rich and popularly aimed *Mudkhal ila qadaya al-mar'a fi sutur wa suwar* (Introduction to Women's Issues in Lines [of text] and Pictures) produced by the Women and Memory Collective (Cairo, 2002), which draws on historical photographs, a "graphic-novel" format, and colloquial Arabic to introduce readers to a gender-aware narrative of Egyptian history.

For there is no doubt that the greatest silence in MENA gender research in all disciplines remains that silence around sexualities. In the region, scholars who are already attacked as "Westernized" for highlighting gender are understandably reluctant to incur even greater wrath possibly awaiting those who discuss sexuality openly. Strategic self-censorship is a dilemma that the above-mentioned *Sexuality in Muslim Societies* confronts squarely while recognizing that not everyone is in a position to publish as they have done.

Yet this is not an unbroken silence in historical scholarship. Historians have studied medieval discourses on the differentiation of bodies through "liminal" categories, for these attracted considerable legal scholarship in premodern times. Shaun Marmon's work on eunuchs, Paula Sanders on hermaphrodites, and Everett Rowson on medieval homoerotic narratives and categorizations of gender and sexuality have shown how discourses on human sexuality governed social categories of the sexual when the fluidity of ethnic and religious boundaries appeared to threaten social stability.[9] Afsaneh Najmabadi's work on early modern Iran examines how the state was elaborated through not only gendered symbolism but also sexualized social categories, which twentieth-century nationalist discourses worked to contain. If more scholars focus on how received categories of sexual identity defined according to degrees of normativity work as metaphorized social boundary markers than on sexualities as constituting a central realm of human experience and self-understanding, the latter is admittedly a difficult realm for historians to access, though one of great import.

Most work on gender to date focuses on elite groups, with significant exceptions such as Tucker's work. There is little historical work on women in labor organizations, gender-class intersections, and class-modulated relations among women; I know of no studies, for example, of mistress-servant relations among Arab elites.

Despite the fine work on sexuality and social boundaries mentioned above, premodern history suffers by comparison to the modern period with regard to gender analysis except as a backdrop to later—and ongoing—debates on "Islam and gender." The first synthetic gendered history in English, Leila Ahmed's *Women and Gender in Islam: Historical Roots of a Modern Debate*, remains widely cited and adopted in classrooms. But it was not yet time for a synthesis; many of Ahmed's suppositions call for further work, though her explanation of a basic tension within Qur'anic deployments of gender usefully brings together varied strands of work and seems likely to stand the test of time.[10] Fine microanalyses trace particular discourses through time, such as Denise Spellberg's work on the changing image of 'A'isha bint Abi Bakr, spouse of the Prophet Muhammad, as reflecting and shaping shifting notions of political community, and Fatima Mernissi's imaginative work on hadith concerning women as political actors, exhilarating and thought-provoking if sometimes overwhelming in its creative originality. Leslie Peirce's magnificent study of women in the imperial Ottoman court of the seventeenth century shows their central roles in defining as well as maintaining Ottoman power, as does her recent study on a provincial Ottoman law court.[11] Scholars of more recent periods pay lip service to the notion that the state is not monolithic, but Peirce's work truly demonstrates this for one key Middle Eastern premodern imperial center. The state's ambiguous, often self-contradictory (and multiple) roles in defining and maintaining gender orders is an area that scholars whether of medieval Islamic polities or of the modern nation-state have barely begun to seriously evaluate. As Judith Tucker and Margaret Meriwether noted recently, our relative lack of knowledge for the pre-1800s means that historians of periods since tend to draw overly sharp dichotomies between earlier and later periods, echoing modernization theory's categorical distinction between "tradition" and "modernity." Where we *have* learned much about premodern women's material lives—such as their property ownership and ability to manipulate the legal system—the question remains (as Tucker and Meriwether note) whether women's access to property meant access to authority and/or to autonomy.[12]

As I argued earlier, a sense of political crisis has shaped academic work on and in the region: assessing MENA gender studies, Deniz Kandiyoti emphasized the "highly politicized and emotionally charged reflection on key political events" that frames both activist feminisms in the region and contemporary scholarship.[13] This reflection has informed the trajectory of gender scholarship and activism from the earliest moments of formulating women's history in the region, in a context of anticolonialist nationalist activism in which Arab, Turkish, and Iranian scholars were active. But defining the focus by moments of crisis and stages of political struggle may have skewed attention overly toward gender and nationalism, ideologies of representation, and specific engagements with imperial actors and structures. Crucial as these are, work on nationalism and representation needs to be matched by work in areas such as history of the family, women as economic actors in changing economies and as labor activists, gender-aware histories of labor migration and diaspora, gendered accounts of material life, and the like. Historically specific analyses of how ideologies of gender and material histories permeate and shape each other are by no means absent, as Tucker and Meriwether's volume on gendering the social history of the Middle East demonstrates, yet these difficult-to-access areas remain less explored especially with attention to internal and chronological difference.[14] Equally, we need histories of concepts that have been shaped through material experience, through social process: "honor," "family," "kinship," and "government." We need more explorations of tensions between lived lives and texts, while recognizing difficulties of access.

It was crucial first not only to engage in archaeology, or digging women out of the dust, but also to challenge some dominant and enduring stereotypes. The specific historical lines of engagement between Middle Eastern and European societies produced images for Western consumption of the Arab or Turkish or Muslim woman as erotic exhibitionist yet also as passive and concealed, as simultaneously powerful threat and helpless victim, and of course as metaphoric sign for the allegedly contained and needy East. The heavy burden of Orientalism has weighed on much scholarship concerning the Middle East, nowhere more so than in gender studies: it has been necessary to dismantle stereotypes before and as we do anything else, which of course carries a danger that one will reify stereotypes in the very process of shattering them. Early ventures into women's history concentrated on countering these reductive images by emphasizing the agency of different groups of women in Middle East economies, in culture production, and in the formation of legal culture. The accompanying stereotype of Islam as a uniformly oppressive and unchanging cultural system also channeled scholarly energies into an emphasis on secular spheres, and on secular ideological and material sources for women's generally unequal or downgraded access to public life, material resources, cultural leadership, and authority in the family. Historians recognized that "agency" and "the secular" were inadequate as explanatory frameworks for understanding either female experience or the deployment of gender categories in particular historical contexts. But an emphasis on the secular remains strong in most institutional histories of early Arab feminism, where "Islam" is represented predominantly as a set of practices and as a presence—an ineluctable marker of cultural identity—with which feminists had to contend. This is only partly explained by the elite subject focus of this work, that is, the fact that female elites who shaped early Arab, Turkish, and Iranian feminisms were often trained to look westward; for these elites were not necessarily alienated from their religion of birth as either faith or culture.

Very recently, Middle East women's and gender history has swung from this focus on the secular—emphasizing that Islam had relatively little to do with structural aspects of women's status as legal subjects, economic actors, and family members—to privileging religion not only as a legal system and social worldview but also as an explanatory framework for women's activism, both historically and at present. Some feminist scholars see this as a possibly dangerous move; sociologist Haideh Moghissi has accused scholars who study women's religiously based activism of collusion with Islamist-oriented authorities, specifically the Iranian regime.[15] Some worry that privileging religion returns scholarship to paradigms we thought had been fully discredited—to an almost uncanny convergence between Orientalist views of Islam as a timeless, uniform, and all-encompassing system that rigidly shapes the gendered organization of society, on the one hand, and, on the other, Islamist views of the ideal society as organized along what are proposed as timeless and seamless Islamic lines. Both Orientalist and Islamist perspectives have tended to see gender identities as fixed by the religion, either in a uniformly degrading and oppressive manner (if you are an Orientalist) or in a privileged space of essentialized female self-realization (if you are an Islamist). By Islamism I mean a political program that works toward a state whose structures and legal system are wholly governed by (various and contested interpretations of) "Islam," that sees the formation of one or more Islamic states as the only possible future for the region, and that (with exceptions, mostly argued by female scholars) regards Islamic doctrine as defined by the orthodox tradition of exegesis and jurisprudence over time. Variations among Islamist groups in programs and tactics make it no less crucial in defining "Islamism" to distinguish carefully and repeatedly between "Islamism" as a range of political programs and "Islam" as a historically developing faith, shaper of (varying) moral perspectives, and cultural system that many adherents through time saw as all-enveloping.

Many scholars and scholar-activists do see this new scholarly enthusiasm for the religious as a welcome acknowledgment of the diverse paths women have taken as they have exercised agency in their own communities. It does reinvigorate a debate that has been part of Middle East women's and gender historiography, and activist debate, for a very long time indeed. As Kandiyoti notes for feminist scholarship in the Middle East, "the debate on the compatibility of Islam with women's emancipation, harking back to Qasim Amin, is still on the agenda in the 1980s and 1990s" (and a decade later!).[16] It cannot be said too often that this is not just an academic debate. Any assessment of MENA gender scholarship has to take into account the impact of Islamism as the ground on which most political and social debate takes place. In other words, religion-as-politics sets the perimeters of public discourse in the region now. Even those who are opposed to an Islamist outlook find themselves obliged to situate their arguments on terrain marked out by that outlook. This above all is where the entire field of Middle East gender studies, in whatever discipline and wherever geographically situated, is shaped by immediate politics—and that is perhaps truer of gender history than of any other discipline. It is also where lay history becomes very significant in helping to shape what professional historians do, with both positive and constraining implications. Thus, gender activists are not only doing exegesis of the foundational texts of Islam but are also looking for antecedents in history, a fine demonstration of how contemporary conditions impel historical construction.

Fatima Mernissi was probably the first scholar-activist whose investigations into the sources of Islamic law and practice—the Qur'an and hadith (the Prophet's reported sayings and acts)—became widely disseminated. Mernissi's imaginative forays into early Islamic history for a contextual reading of sources and their re/production led her to question narratives of gender that over time had been deemed "Islamic." Like other Muslim scholars the world over, Mernissi claimed *ijtihad*, the believer's right to evaluate sacred sources and shape community consensus around faith and practice. This perspective emphasizes Islam's democratic component as it suggests the potential malleability of gender practices associated with Islamic doctrine. It proposes a history of Islamic discourse, not as a rigidly prescriptive discourse on gendered rights but as a dynamic discourse on social norms subject to negotiation and defined by power relations at various moments. It highlights early Muslim women's contributions to that discourse, which were then muted in practice as Islam became linked to ruling structures.[17]

Historians are positing intersections of gender and religiously defined frameworks in nuanced ways that emphasize women's assertions of agency while recognizing that religious institutions and practices justified in the name of religion are sites of power that often work against the interests of particular groups of women. One of the tasks for gender history now is to trace discontinuities and continuities in the shaping force of religious systems with regard to histories of social practices. It seems to me that studies of contemporary faith-based gender activisms in the Middle East may overplay the novelty of women's declarations of agency within Islamic frameworks; we need more historical work on Muslim women's articulations of faith-based positions as grounding for formulating their own access to social rights and resources.

At the same time, the search for Islamic roots risks overlooking the complexities of discourse positions that historical subjects managed to hold. For instance, whereas two decades ago, scholars were portraying early feminists in the Arab world as precursors to a secularist feminism that was dominant into the 1990s, now scholars search high and low for the Islamic roots of contemporary discourse, and often they find what they seek in the same writings of those same historical personages. This is not an inaccurate reading, and if it leads to a historically grounded respect for these complex discourse positions, this is all to the good; but too often one pole—whether the Islamic or the secular—seems to be emphasized at the expense of the other. Thus, as a particular group of scholars in Cairo, the Women and Memory Forum, reprints the works of early feminists such as Nabawiyya Musa and Malak Hifni Nasif and holds conferences on them, they are attacked by certain secular feminists for allegedly overplaying the Islamic component of early gender activisms in the region.[18] More dangerously, this emphasis can lead to an analytic distinction between "Islamic" or "Islamist" and "secular" that was not necessarily perceived as a meaningful distinction in the thinking or rhetoric of these historical subjects.

The search for Islamic roots comes out of a search for feminist epistemologies that are locally situated, not dependent on Western constructions of subject and object in research methodologies. Positing a faith-based feminism in an Islamic framework represents an epistemology that cannot be classed as "Western." Yet ironically if often sensibly, it is criticized as "Western" by some in the region. Provocative debate over the validity of the term *Islamic feminism* is a case in point. This term (variously defined) is championed by some and regarded by others as the latest Western import, in fact as a sort of neo-Orientalism once again adopted by elements of the local elite.[19]

A word more about this debate, for it is significant in shaping MENA gender studies, whether in history or in other disciplines. The embrace of "Islamic feminism" risks a tautological bind, whether as a contemporary

movement or as produced in discrete historical moments. For some scholars, any activism concerning women that is interpretable as "Islamic"
becomes "feminist"; any Muslim woman's intellectual and/or activist work
becomes "Islamic." Though it is crucial to distinguish between "Muslim"
as an ascribed identity and "Islamic" or "Islamist" as deliberately chosen
approaches, such distinctions are not always made. Initiatives to reread and
reinterpret Islamic law are not only important but potentially revolutionary; it seems imperative to respect the energy thereby generated and not to
deny validity to academic perspectives that do respect work done in the name
of Islam. But to label this as "Islamic feminism" and then to seek its antecedents in history risks losing sight of some important analytic distinctions.
Moreover, the label "Islamic feminism" seems to assume the primacy of
something called "Islam" and thereby may echo Orientalist views. In any
case, feminism becomes a contested and dichotomous arena between those
who see themselves as secularists and those who define their work within
an activist stance on Islam. And from downplaying religion, the pendulum
has swung back to where religion becomes the linchpin again, albeit in a
different, far more nuanced and historically specific way. To emphasize possibilities for, and historicized examples of, women's agency within Islamic
discourse and practice is a positive thing, but I worry that this will come at
the expense of other important foci, in particular class and regional vari-
ance; ironically, if this happens in gender studies, it mimics Islamist discourse, one rhetorical outcome of which is to downplay class and certainly
national or regional allegiance in favor of a faith-based unity of outlook.
Yet the focus on women's activisms within Islamic frameworks should remain
important to historians, for this gives a more urgent visibility to questions
already explored in histories of nationalism, such as that of why certain
women have chosen at certain junctures to work within movements that
apparently restrict their choices. This remains a central question for historians of women and gender, in every region of the world. When, why, and
how have which women moved between acquiescence and resistance?

One answer to this question may be through fiction, acquiescent to certain narrative forms and social patterns acceptable in the society, while—
as demonstrated by many, many novels by Arab women over at least a
century and a quarter—resistant to accepting dominant and official histories without challenge.

Feminist recognition of historical narrative as powerful and contested
is evident in the Middle East today through alternative modes of writing
history. At the same time, novelists and critics in the Arab world are debat-

ing the terms of engagement between "fiction" and "history," calling those terms, and the distinctions that underlie them, into question. Activist authors concerned with change are writing historical novels that rewrite histories from pointedly gendered perspectives, as demonstrated by Radwa Ashour's Granada Trilogy, Nadia Khost's novel set in early twentieth-century Syria, and works by many others. In other key moments—Egypt of the 1950s, for one—the historical novel surfaced as a genre that contested dominant narratives of gendered social organization: think of Latifa al-Zayyat's 1960 feminist classic, al-Bab al-Maftuh (The Open Door). These are recognized as significant interventions in today's gender debates, including the debate on feminist memory, or how earlier debates are being reconstructed, how their histories are being written—and how these become written into today's gender politics. Similarly, Arabic historical novels of late nineteenth-century reformists in Egypt and Lebanon need to be read as attempted and aware political interventions into discourses on gender that constitute part of the *material* history of that era.

If historians now widely recognize the importance of narrative form as part of the "real" that historical documentation promises, historians of the Middle East often remain reluctant to draw on fictional narrative as part of an archive available for historical research. Yet a gender-aware historical practice can garner insights about elite Arab women's and men's concepts of gender and contributions to discourse on the politics of gender through time by historicizing women's writings of historical novels, as alternative archives that challenge some of the gaps and silences in what historians have regarded as the "archive proper." Historians of the region draw on auto/biographical texts. Thus far, though, creative use of the novel—and of poetry—as a social institution that shapes human understandings and relationships has not drawn historians of the Arab world, as it has for instance those who work on domesticity and class relations in nineteenth-century North and South American and European societies—work on which some of us draw comparatively and gratefully. Gender-aware historians of Turkey have been more alert to the historical meanings of fiction. Although Arabic literary scholarship has begun to take nineteenth-century Arabic fiction more seriously, MENA historians still appear reluctant to consider fiction as part of their archives. Literary scholars are finally contesting the canonical assignment of "first Arabic novel" status to Muhammad Haykal's Zaynab (serialized, 1912; published in book form, 1914); heretofore, fictions earlier than Zaynab but that fall into the category of "novel" were claimed to be "incomplete" or poorly realized, and rather than attend to the ways they mirrored and shaped a rich and shifting cultural scene in the period of their reception, scholars bypassed them, relying on intellectual historians to trace a paradigm of cultural decline and seeing that mirrored in the prevalence of so-called bad novels in the translation lists of late nineteenth-century publishers. We may never have print-run figures or sales statistics, but we can ponder a consistent proliferation of "bad" novels that suggests there was a market for them. The canonization of the twentieth century as the age of the Arabic novel prejudges what an Arabic novel is, denying earlier fictions status as sustained imaginative works that claimed explanatory power and appeal based on implied mimesis—and that, above all, people may well have *read*.

On the first and most obvious level, to admit fiction to the archives increases the number of sources we have. And this is *qualitatively* important. Although recent scholarship does undermine an earlier view (with its own historiography) that "the woman question" was first a male debate, and that this set the terms of debate—this view continues to prevail through the circulation of widely used texts.[20] Yet, not only were there contemporaneous writings by women, published in major periodicals including daily newspapers, but—if we include novels—there were *a lot of* writings by women. These cannot be dismissed as isolated from the political debate on gender and society. Moreover, the many pre-twentieth-century novels by Arab men need to be studied in the context of the ongoing gender debates of the time. Juxtaposing fictional texts, we may locate nuances and possibilities in these novels that do not surface in more straightforward polemics of the time. Although the study of this field of fictional discourse may not overturn present understandings of the debates, it does complicate and broaden it. For instance, with regard to Leila Ahmed's claim that "the abandonment of native culture was posed as the solution for women's oppression . . . [a] rhetoric [that] became insistent and pronounced with colonial domination,"[21] what do we make of novels that insistently perform local cultures as the grounds of women's agency in changing societies? What do we make of novels where "the veil" is not particularly central—as it also was not in biographies of women written in this period—and was not a fixed image around which issues of gender and nation swirled? Is this an accidental silence? Rather than see these texts as "bad novels," we need to examine what is going on in the text as well as around it. Predictable fictions can admit new ideas and changing mores while giving readers strategies to shape these novel elements into comfortable, traditional frameworks that our minds inhabit. Perhaps something of this sort was happening in the late nineteenth-century Arabic novel, and perhaps in novels by women more

than by men, although possible reception effects of gendering the authorial signature is a question we will never be able to fully answer. Furthermore, this capacity may be one reason why so many European novels were
translated or "arabized" at the time: perhaps they allowed new gender
arrangements to be presented at a "safe" cultural distance, but perhaps they
also offered more room to play with new ideas.[22] Moreover, in and around
the early Arabic novel hovers a metadialogue, an exchange both with possibly dismissive critics and with an assumed audience, about the purposes
and forms of fiction. This level of discourse may have emerged from
author/translators' nervousness about being identified with what was considered a debased and debasing form, but it acted as a possible authoritative voice guiding new readers, and potential writers, in the consumption
of fiction.

If we examine fiction both as a cultural-political arena, a sociological fact
wherein we need to examine attitudes to reading and gender and reception
of literary genres, *and* as a literary genre, a narrative form, one of many kinds
of narrative that circulated at the time, what will it tell us about concepts
of and debates over gender? How might these narratives have appealed to
new readers, and how did they abut on and overlap with other available cultural forms, such as folk epics and other orally transmitted stories, translations, colloquial poetry, biography, and overt polemics? These sources are
significant for thinking about *how* debates on gender were carried out in a
changing field of culture production and reception. For if novels by
women—and most early novels by men—were ignored by later critics, they
did draw notice at the time. They were a recognized if unruly part of a lively
and changing cultural field. If fiction was admittedly part of an elite nationalist narrative, it was a part with perhaps wider reach than (other) polemics.

Work on the histories of Arab feminisms, especially in Egypt, has focused
on organized feminism and on nonfictional polemics in the women's press.
The intersection of female authorship, fiction, and feminist (as well as anti-
feminist) polemics at the historical moment when anti-imperialist nationalism was coalescing to a significant extent around questions of gender and
through a gendered symbolic repertoire calls for attention. How can we read
fictional narratives as historical voices in a context where ideologies of gender organization and concepts of nation formation not only were fiercely
debated but also were having material impact on lived experience? How
might fictional narratives suggest to us both the persistence of received practices of social organization and ambiguous possibilities for change? How
can we think about fiction as possibly productive of the formation of a mid-

dle class in Egypt and the maintenance—or shifts—of hierarchical class, gender, and race relations? Do early novels vocalize imperial presences, and if so, can we think about relationships between reading novels and consuming (other) political cultures? Reading literature as historical intervention is to read it within a historicizing sense of the field of culture production at the time. In Jenny Sharpe's words, "If we are to study literature for its disruption of an ideological production that prevents social change, we can no longer afford to restrict our readings to the limits of the literary text. Rather, we should regard the literature as working within, and sometimes against, the historical limits of representation."[23]

Rita Felski has argued for a lens on modernities sensitive both to how modernity has "act[ed] as a mobile and shifting category of classification that serves to structure, legitimize, and valorize varied and often competing perspectives" and to how modernity as a normative category needs to be seen in relation to constructions of the feminine, and "distinctively feminine encounters with the various facets of the modern." When one gazes at modernity through the feminine, cultural enactments "ignored, trivialized, or seen as regressive rather than authentically modern"—such as romance novels—"gain dramatically in importance. . . . Our sense of what counts as meaningful history is subtly yet profoundly altered as the landscape of the modern acquires a different, less familiar set of contours."[24] This is by now a familiar argument in historical study for some regions, but in the MENA context it still bears repeating. To think through *processes* by which feminisms and gender activisms emerged, we need to examine gender debates through the lens of historical fiction. Here, I instantiate such an attempt, briefly discussing Zaynab Fawwaz's writings in a field of discourse richly marked by the Arabic novel as a tracing of local histories.

Drawing on Arabic biographical tradition yet departing from it radically by being the female author of a "women-only" biographical dictionary, Zaynab Fawwaz represented women across vast geographical and chronological stretches as witnesses to and of her sustained polemics on the necessity of transforming the gendered organization of Arab societies. In key ways, Fawwaz departed from what was beginning to crystallize as a dominant nationalist ideal of the gendered society. Central to her formulations were her representations of female protagonists. Templates of the imagination for female readers, biographies and female fictional protagonists might sketch out parameters of a new ideal womanhood imagined by women, or at least by a few. Fawwaz's novel *Husn al-'Awaqib aw Ghadat al-Zahira* (Good Consequences, or The Lovely Young Maid of al-Zahira [Village], 1899) traces a feudal family's power struggle in south Lebanon, echoing events in Fawwaz's own natal region. I situate this novel as a commentary on gender politics, comparing it to another novel published three years earlier by journalist and novelist Jurji Zaydan (1861–1914). Fifth or sixth in his twenty-one-novel panorama of Islamic history, *Armanusa al-Misriyya* (Armanusa the Egyptian, 1896) narrated the Muslim invasion of Egypt in 640 C.E. through the focalization of Egyptian (Coptic) and Greek-Egyptian characters. If this single juxtaposition can make no claim for the entire field of Arabic fictional discourse, the interest in "female heroes" it suggests is borne out by contemporaneous novels. Fawwaz's fiction echoes and contests her biographical dictionary, published five years before; these works, as much as her newspaper essays on gender issues, are central to the feminist quality of her writings.

New to emerge on the late nineteenth-century literary scene in Egypt, the novel fast became a key contestational field for imagining Woman. Fawwaz and other early Arab novelists were engaged in constructing fictional and biographical images of women for the nation and its emerging female readers, as they simultaneously shaped a fictional discourse as a new language of national identity. In fiction and biography, "East" and "West" were produced as embodied female images, many based on historical figures. Novels embodied and narrativized the question of indigenous versus imported "values" and how each would underwrite, or undermine, the envisioned postimperial nation. Exploring what "moral" conduct meant and how this was part of a tenuous sense-in-formation of the nation, including fixing nationalism's identity boundaries through its opposition to "the West," fiction archives a collective debate and suggests how such processes of identity formation were conveyed to the nation's subjects.

Given the popularity of exemplary biographies of celebrated women in the women's press, which drew on a long and highly respectable indigenous tradition of biographical inscription, perhaps historical fiction that constructed female protagonists based on historical figures could draw on biography's multifaceted respectability. But if historical fiction offered a path away from the dangerous route of romance adventure, early historical novels were every bit as laced with melodrama and romance. Despite or perhaps because of this promise, the historical novel offered new and readable narratives of gender that could support and contest the polemics around the gendered organization that was central to emergent nationalist discourse in the 1890s.

Like other early Arabic novels, *Good Consequences'* plot turns on a clearly defined struggle between good and evil, in this case represented in a power struggle among male cousins within a feudal ruling family in south Lebanon, a barely disguised fictional treatment of a series of events that had taken place in Fawwaz's home territory some forty years before. Fawwaz gives the rivalry a gendered dimension, and women are significant to the conflict's genesis and resolution. After a complicated series of highly dramatic events (stabbings, abductions, duels, letters in the wrong hands, tribal raids, and the like), five simultaneous weddings end the narrative, a neat closure that cements individual and collective alliances in the name of a maintained but modernized gender order, for if the marriages are "arranged" by the hero's and heroine's mothers, they are done so at the behest of daughterly desire.

This novel's constitutive struggle between good and evil, realized variously as that between "honor" and deception, moral and immoral behavior, the good ruler and the tyrant, is foundationally a struggle between divergent concepts of gender relations and their relation to hierarchies of power. At issue is the young, unmarried (or, more accurately, premarried) woman's power over her future life and her ability to make choices, contingent on others' recognition of her (limited) autonomy and the degree of her education and understanding of the world, conveyed through the book as the recurring symbol of feminine presence. If reading a novel was to educate the young female subject of the late nineteenth-century Arab world—part, at least, of Fawwaz's intended audience—then reading *in* the novel was to educate other characters about the young female protagonist's exercise of agency. The book is talisman and trace. The book also orients the reader to the trope of beauty as an intellectual rather than a physical characteristic; it is the former quality that attracts Shakib to his paternal cousin, Fariʿa. In contrast, Tamir, the scheming cousin, knows only of Fariʿa's physical beauty, not of her mental prowess, a distinction that consistently separates the good guys from the bad in this novel, an image of "good masculinity" versus "outdated patriarchy." Education and the book, or intellectual refinement, are also paired with informed housekeeping, a set of images that also structure many exemplary biographies of women published in Egypt at this time and later. Biographies and this novel are shot through with assumptions about the training into modernity that young women were exhorted to have, and parents exhorted to give, at the time. Fawwaz plays with the gap between social expectations and actual exchanges, suggesting how young women *use* social conventions to their own advantage, to escape unwanted encounters. Tamir, lamenting Fariʿa's coldness, hears his sidekick

Jabir declare that it is simply a sign of her shyness, for "young women do not let their love appear immediately"; but Tamir knows better: "No, she looks at me with disgust."[25] Fariʿa and her friends draw on the expectation of female bashfulness as a ruse to deter would-be suitors. Fawwaz also makes patriarchal privilege—and its limits—central to characters' interactions. Fariʿa's elder brother, to whom Tamir goes in expectation of help, voices what is often the perspective of the "good father" or elder brother in the era's biographies of "Famous Women": "I must seek her opinion in this," he tells Tamir. "If she accepts, that will be my wish. If she objects, I cannot force her to do what you want, because she has a mind, and often I have relied on her in my own serious concerns; and the matter of marriage is important, upon it depends her life's arc." A disappointed Tamir represents obstacles female protagonists had to confront: Tamir "had hoped that ʿAziz would give the command [that she marry him] without consulting her"; in other words, that he would exercise absolute patriarchal prerogative, disregarding the sister's wishes. Further critique of forced arranged marriages ensues when Fariʿa's companion tells Tamir: "A covenant does not happen in this way. No, by God. If marriage took place by force, you would not find a single flourishing home in this world."[26]

"Good" masculinity, the novel suggests, honors women's choices and respects bodily and psychological integrity as much as it entails fair treatment of other males (inspiring followers rather than having to pay them off, treating those lower on the social hierarchy with respect, following established rules of fair play in combat, and offering infinite generosity to those of all social strata rather than only the lodging of necessary guests), distinctions made explicitly through the different behaviors of the two suitors. To enact "honor" is to respect Fariʿa and her desires, not to police her, secluding her from nonrelated men. Indeed, Fariʿa and other female characters come in repeated contact with men; it is the women themselves who preserve their "honor."

It is refusal of patriarchal right as much as aversion to unwanted lovers that the novel emphasizes; in fact, aversion is a consequence of crude claims to that right. (The number of times Fariʿa and her friends refuse marriage to various suitors is remarkable.) This particular inscription of "evil" culminates in Tamir's abandonment of all pretense of suasion. "Do you not know that I am the ruler over you, the one who has right of disposal over you as possessor?" Here, patriarchal "right" is presented as crude power but also as moral and familial authority sanctioning crude power, as Tamir's articulation of the "patriarchal bargain" as famously outlined by Kandiyoti sug-

gests: "If you submit and agree, you will find me an obedient slave that nothing will turn from his affection for you." The falseness of this "obedience"
is not lost on Fariʿa.[27]

If *Good Consequences* has been lauded for portraying "manners and customs" of the south Lebanese mountain region and Bedouin culture of the
Hawran, in its rich references to social usages of hospitality, combat, family hierarchy, and the like, what I find more significant are the gendered contours of the narrative line: not only the question of patriarchal privilege as
central, but also the privileging of women's work, of women's desires and
initiatives, and of women's conversations and actions, for aspects of the plot
depend on a network of women. Female characters, of whatever social position, are resourceful and active as well as ever eloquent. Fariʿa plans escapes,
lies to save herself and her friends, and is ready with bold responses to would-
be suitors. Just as significant are impingements of generation and social
status together on gender: on the one hand, two mothers from aristocratic
lines who impress social and familial duty on their children (and remain
within their *qasrs*); on the other, the *ʿawagiz*, elderly women, and significantly
in this case poor ones, who act in a sense as social mediators, for good or
for ill. The novel's elderly women—one aids the villain in his continuing
attempts to kidnap his cousin, and the other competently harbors escaping
women—are figures out of the Arabic oral storytelling tradition, stories that
women tell to spellbind (and to scare) their children. If formulaic, they are
not gratuitous. As social mediators they can transgress gendered boundaries between domestic and public spaces. Umm Zahida uses her age-derived
freedom to help a younger generation of women.

The novel's accumulation of detail fills out a normative gender and status regime. That Fawwaz shows this within the world of south Lebanon and
the Hawran, among the Bedouin and the princely families as well as their
retinues, might hint that she wants to show this regime not as "modern" or
"new" but rather as always already present, as inevitable, and as indigenous,
although there are elements of modernity present, such as the *assumption*
that girls read and write. This regime hinges on the desire of the young female
subject, and it is constructed within the fictional world through stipulation
of social detail. First, as noted, there is the matter of permission to enter
and speak. Who gives permission? Who asks for it? Who feels the most aversion at its transgression? Second, choice in marriage partners looms large,
and is presented strongly as female prerogative, for suitor after suitor falls
by the wayside. Third, there is the matter of initiative. The women in this
novel are without exception vocal, bold, resourceful, and strong willed, and

it is these qualities, as much as "feminine beauty," that appear to attract the "good patriarchs" of the younger generation. The novel foregrounds women's proactive resistance to control by others, while it does set them into the expectations of their time and therefore ultimately into a "reformed" patriarchal system with limits. The "good" men are those who respect women's choices and always seek permission before coming into their tents; the "bad" ones are those who force marriage on unwilling daughters or cousins, those who show no respect for privacy, those who not only abduct young women but do so as they are by the river, on the day of the week when all nearby villagers, out of respect, stay away.

Persuaded to publish her collected essays after about a dozen years of publishing in the press, Fawwaz described them thematically as "honorable studies in defense of the rights of women, on the imperative of educating them, the prohibition of bad customs, prodding women to progress and to acquire knowledge, and everything linked to the goodness of women's morals and their influence on the human world."[28] The first essay (from *Lisan al-Hal*, April 1892) attacks those who resist expansions of women's sphere. The "Eastern woman knows herself only as an instrument in a man's hand; he makes her go wherever he goes and directs her as he wishes. He exerts pressure on her through reprehensible practices, by committing the error of seclusion—shutting the doors of education and not allowing [her] to leave the home—and by prohibiting her from attending women's public gatherings: she has come to imagine that those deeds are grave offenses and to follow them would be to violate the system [guaranteeing] her honor and the law [safeguarding] her protection." Women, Fawwaz goes on to suggest, are subject to patriarchal control that draws on force and emotional ploy equally: "Her husband is able to visit his claims on her on the basis that because he loves her to distraction, he is unable to resist the jealousy arising from this love."[29] She exhorts women to take advantage of educational opportunities and to work for happiness based on perfecting moral and mental qualities. These, she suggests, are the stuff of an unblemished reputation; she leaves the reader to contrast this with an older and more rigid notion of "honor." *Good Consequences* might be seen as a dramatization of these notions, for Fariʿa's consistent worry about her reputation, and in particular about what her elder brother will think of her after this succession of abductions and escapes, proves groundless as she yokes her eloquence, loyalty, and ability to read and write letters to her own plans for her future. Yet, worrying about her brother's (and mother's) reactions causes her much anguish. The novel conveys the psychological impact of repressive gendered expectations with more power and immediacy than nonfictional polemics could perhaps attain.

Elsewhere, Fawwaz rails against social pressures to marry that convince women a bad marriage is preferable to no marriage at all, and she warns women of the consequences—loss of wealth, subjection to the "arrogance" of a "man of bad character," and "a state of permanent grief." "Why does she not prefer her original state . . . and live a most agreeable life, enjoying the delight of repose."[30] At the time, to counsel women to consider the possible advantages of remaining single all their lives was not for the fainthearted. The violence and arrogance of Tamir and his henchmen, and their disregard of women's wishes, seem to illustrate her point.

At the same time, *Good Consequences* appears more conservative than does Fawwaz as essayist, in its resolution through (consensual) marriages of all the major characters. In her essays, Fawwaz not only suggests that women consider the benefits of single life but also supports the right of women in England to make political demands, as she supports women's rights to seek employment outside the home if they need income. Though Fawwaz draws on the argument, common at the time, that the purpose of girls' education was to form knowledgeable mothers of the future, she does not privilege this argument; she distances herself from polemicists who insisted that women must limit themselves to domestic activities.

Jurji Zaydan put female figures at the titular center of several historical novels in his ambitious project to teach Islamic history fictionally. But in Zaydan's novel *Armanusa al-Misriyya*, the female lead is far more passive than is Fawwaz's Fari'a, though her wise older attendant and one-time nanny, Barbara, shows initiative. Armanusa mostly waits and weeps, a still pivot around which history and fiction swirl.

The novel chronicles Egypt's conquest by 'Amr b. al-'As, the military leader sent by the *khalifa* 'Umar, in 640 C.E., but its events turn on the oppression of local Egyptians (Coptic Christians) by the Byzantine Empire, a subjugation dramatized in marriage practices. The Byzantine Emperor requests Armanusa, daughter of the Copts' local ruler, al-Muqawqas, for his son. Enmity between Copts and Byzantine troops is manifest in the suspicions of the emperor's military delegate that al-Muqawqas has invited in "the Arabs" (the newly Islamized populace of the Arabian peninsula) to replace the Byzantines. Armanusa, loyal and loving daughter of a man who preferred to focus on raising his daughter and son rather than remarry, falls in love with Arkadius, son of the local Byzantine commander. Armanusa struggles with the issue of loyalty to her father and "nation" versus her love for Arkadius; he struggles with loyalty to the empire (and his father) versus his growing perception that the Copts are mistreated by the Byzantines. Zaydan, contrasting the respectful treatment of Coptic churches, property, and women by the invading Muslims with the destructive and humiliating treatment visited on them by the Byzantines, offers a contemporary message of Muslim-Christian unity consonant with the nationalist strand that envisioned a secular nation, a strand stronger over the next three decades and one advanced forcefully by Syrian Christians (like Zaydan) resident in Egypt and highly conscious of their double minority status.

While, as in *Good Consequences*, the issue of consensual versus forced arranged marriage is central, in *Armanusa* it does not shape the novel's progression but rather offers a conceit around which to narrate "larger" historical events—the conquest of Egypt in the context of local and regional politics. Women are portrayed as astute political observers and advisors but their role is not central. Armanusa, like Fari'a, reads and writes—Latin as well as Coptic—which literally saves one woman's life and helps Barbara to salvage the otherwise rather hapless and passive Armanusa's future.

If, in *Armanusa*, Zaydan uses fiction to offer history, in *Good Consequences*, the historical narrative is the setting and rationale for the fiction, and for the question of women's rights and desires. Yet, one can imagine that both novels might have had an impact on adolescent readers that a more straightforward polemic on marriage might not—for instance, in articulating received expectations of the marriage institution versus an emerging ideology of value, made material in the notion of companionate marriage and in an implied critique of the notion of women as war booty. Armanusa, gazing from her balcony at the Nile, unites that central symbol of polyethnic Egyptian identity with a reformist outlook that positions the "new" companionate, nuclear family at the center of national strength. Marriage as transaction is utterly implicated in the politics of the nation. Yet, it is the politics of the nation (anachronistically evoked), rather than the plight of the young woman subject to her father's wishes and her society's expectations, that holds center stage. It seems no accident that Barbara launches into castigation of the imperialist yoke under which "we natives" (*nahnu al-wataniyyin*) labor, an oppression made concrete in the next chapter as Byzantine soldiers chase out the nuns of the Hanging Church to take it over as a fortified point, wantonly smashing the icons.[31] Barbara's explanation of the status quo was surely resonant in Egypt at the time of publication, in its second decade of occupation by the British. Alluding to Armanusa's

ethnic background seems a sly reference from the author, a Syrian immi-
grant, to "outsiders" as loyal Egyptian nationalists, a possibility central to
the plot as Armanusa's father is instrumental in forming a Muslim-Coptic
alliance to defeat the Byzantines (an alliance coming, significantly, from the
east to defeat a "European Christian" power).

At the end, it is Arkadius's anguish at the defeat, and at his own feelings
of shame, of masculinity betrayed, that is central, as are Arkadius's and
Armanusa's individual senses of guilt at disobeying their fathers, and finally,
Arkadius's reluctant acknowledgment that the Arabs—who have now
become part of the "national" landscape—are showing the Copts a respect
and freedom of worship the Byzantines never allowed. The national patriarchy is reestablished as al-Muqawqas and Arkadius (now his son-in-law)
embrace. Armanusa, object of men who represent different groupings, moves
only from one palace to another, the exemplary "site" around which the
community will (re?)constitute itself. Even if, like Fari'a, she objects to a
coerced marriage, her passivity seems to make of her an atemporal cipher,
in contrast to Fawwaz's Fari'a and Fawwaz's construction of historical
figures in her biographical dictionary, where agency that creates historical
change even if minute is crucial to defining, and making possible, female
notability and its narration.

If Zaydan's didactic cast focuses on teaching the Egyptian subject her or
his national history, interpellating her or him as part of an ongoing narrative of the triumph of the Egyptian state and of a local and secularly focused
identity, Fawwaz's eye is on the gendered negotiations on which that state
of affairs hinges. For Zaydan, the romance is sugar and leavening to the
serious business of imparting History; for Fawwaz, the romance—and its
contraries—*are* history, the stuff of which are made the politics of home
and nation, the scaffoldings of collective life. Perhaps Zaydan's novel is a
more supply constructed narrative than is Fawwaz's, yet in the end, the latter is livelier. If its characterizations appear clichéd and its movements
ponderous to us now, they bring the world of the novel close to the realm
of oral folk narrative and might have been received as joyously familiar, not
as clichéd, by Fawwaz's contemporaries.

This emphasis on articulation, action and initiative, in concert with the
minute portrayal of women's interactions and venues, is one way in which
the writings on gender by Fawwaz, and possibly by other women, stand out
against those of at least some nationalist men who posed the urgency of
changes to received notions of "women's sphere" for the nation's successful consolidation. Perhaps writers, especially women, felt freer in fiction to

advance their gender agendas and their perceptions of social process. Perhaps anxieties about and hopes for shifting gender boundaries, whether consciously voiced or not, were more likely to emerge in fiction. And perhaps young readers *read* works by women differently. The specificity of "men's" and "women's" texts, notes Felski, "should not be seen as simply internal to a text; rather, it is fundamentally shaped by the particular meanings and effects which accrue to discourses publicly authored by women. The gender of authorship is a crucial factor influencing the circulation and reception of textual meaning."[32] What would it have meant for a young, economically privileged, Cairene female school graduate in the late 1890s to read Fawwaz's novel? Or Zaydan's? How might the gender of attributed authorship as well as internal contours of the narrative have affected such a reading? And what if that girl reader had read these novels after reading Fawwaz's biographies of Arab and European women who had asserted their places in the world?

Tracing different strands of positionality that have gone into gender-aware and feminist-oriented MENA scholarship, Deniz Kandiyoti remarks that "analyses of 'home-grown' genres of writing on women in Arabic, Persian, and Turkish could contribute a great deal to our understanding of the genealogies of the 'local dialects' in feminism."[33] Kandiyoti's context is more recent feminist writing but her comment holds for writings of a century ago. If, from one perspective on Arab culture at the century's turn, the novel was an imported form, from another, it was perfectly local in its narration of (and response to) received expectations for narrative rhetoric.

These novels call into question a still-prevalent assumption that the focus on domesticity was necessarily a "conservative" one that aimed to keep women at home. Domesticity as a discursive focus must be seen as responding to real challenges of material lives in sometimes unpredictable, and undeniably local, ways. This is not to assume a mimetic identity for fiction so much as it is to assume that fictional narratives are one way that we human beings make sense of our worlds. A gender-sensitive analysis of the early Arabic novel may help us to localize our understandings of both feminist discourse and fictional narrative, by tracing the specific narrative moves through which novelists wrote contemporary gender discourse into their fictions.

NOTES

An earlier version of this essay's first part appeared in the *Journal of Colonialism and Colonial History* and is republished with permission of John Hopkins University Press.

1. Zaynab Fawwaz bt. ʿAli b. Husayn b. ʿUbaydallah b. Hasan b. Ibrahim b. Muhammad b. Yusuf al-ʿAmili, *al-Durr al-manthur fi tabaqat rabbat al-khudur* (Cairo/Bulaq: al-Matbaʿa al-kubra al-amiriyya, AH 1312 [1894 C.E.]), 5–6. Translation of the longer passage in Marilyn Booth, *May Her Likes Be Multiplied: Biography and Gender Politics in Egypt* (Berkeley and Los Angeles: University of California Press, 2001), 8.

2. Nabia Abbott, "Women and the State in Early Islam," *Journal of Near Eastern Studies* 1, no. 1 (1942): 106–26, and 1, no. 3 (1942): 341–68; Abbott, "Women and the State on the Eve of Islam," *American Journal of Semitic Languages and Literatures* 58, no. 3 (1941): 259–84.

3. In this essay's earlier version I discuss the 1999 Cairo conference "One Hundred Years of the Arab Woman's Emancipation" as an instance of the political prominence and sensitivity of academic gender studies in the region today. Marilyn Booth, "Middle East Women's and Gender History: State of a Field," *Journal of Colonialism and Colonial History* 4, no. 1 (2003), http://muse.jhu.edu/journals/cch.

4. The Supreme Council for Culture published translations of English-language gender scholarship in conjunction with the 1999 conference and continues to do so. Yet, just as Arabic literature fares poorly in North American publishing, so does Arabic-language scholarship. Only scholars able to write in English are likely to be heard outside MENA.

5. Parvin Paidar, *Women and the Political Process in Twentieth-Century Iran* (Cambridge: Cambridge University Press, 1995); Afsaneh Najmabadi, *Women with Moustaches and Men without Beards: Gender and Sexual Anxieties of Iranian Modernity* (Berkeley and Los Angeles: University of California Press, 2005); Janet Afary, *The Iranian Constitutional Revolution of 1906–11: Grassroots Democracy, Social Democracy, and the Origins of Feminism* (New York: Columbia University Press, 1996); Ellen Fleischmann, *The Nation and Its "New" Women: The Palestinian Women's Movement, 1920–1948* (Berkeley and Los Angeles: University of California Press, 2003); Elizabeth Thompson, *Colonial Citizens: Republican Rights, Paternal Privilege, and Gender in French Syria and Lebanon* (New York: Columbia University Press, 1999); Mounira M. Charrad, *States and Women's Rights: The Making of Postcolonial Tunisia, Algeria, and Morocco* (Berkeley and Los Angeles: University of California Press, 2001); Julia Clancy-Smith, "Islam, Gender, and Identities in the Making of French Algeria, 1830–1962," in *Domesticating the Empire: Race, Gender, and Family Life in French and Dutch Colonialism,* ed. Julia Clancy-Smith and Frances Gouda (Charlottesville: University Press of Virginia, 1998).

6. Margot Badran, *Feminists, Islam, and Nation: Gender and the Making of Modern Egypt* (Princeton, NJ: Princeton University Press, 1995); Ijlal Khalifa, *al-Haraka al-nisaʾiyya al-haditha: Qissat al-marʾa al-ʿarabiyya ʿala ard Misr* (Cairo: al-Matbaʿa

al-'arabiyya al-haditha, 1973); Amal al-Subki, *al-Haraka al-nisa'iyya fi Misr ma bayna al-thawratayni 1919 wa-1952* (Cairo: GEBO, 1986); Beth Baron, *The Women's Awakening in Egypt: Culture, Society, and the Press* (New Haven, CT: Yale University Press, 1994); Judith Tucker, *Women in Nineteenth-Century Egypt* (Cambridge: Cambridge University Press, 1985); idem, *In the House of the Law: Gender and Islamic Law in Ottoman Syria and Palestine* (Berkeley and Los Angeles: University of California Press, 1998).

7. Frances Hasso, "Gender and Modernity in Arab Accounts of the 1948 and 1967 Defeats," *International Journal of Middle East Studies* 32 (November 2000): 491–510; Ellen Fleischmann, "Nation, Tradition, and Rights: the Indigenous Feminism of the Palestinian Women's Movement, 1929–1948," in *Women's Suffrage in the British Empire: Citizenship, Nation, and Race*, ed. Ian Christopher Fletcher, Laura E. Nym Mayhall, and Philippa Levine (London: Routledge, 2000), 138–54; Marilyn Booth, "*Woman in Islam:* Men and the 'Women's Press' in Turn-of-the-Century Egypt," *International Journal of Middle East Studies* 33, no. 2 (2001): 171–201; Beth Baron, "The Construction of National Honour in Egypt," *Gender and History* 5 (1993): 244–55.

8. Author's interview with members of the collective, Istanbul, May 2001. *Women and Sexuality in Muslim Societies*, ed. Pinar Ilkkaracan (Istanbul: Women for Women's Human Rights [WWHR], New Ways [Kadinin Insan Haklari Projesi, KIHP], 2000).

9. Shaun E. Marmon, *Eunuchs and Sacred Boundaries in Islamic Society* (Oxford: Oxford University Press, 1995); Paula Sanders, "Gendering the Ungendered Body: Hermaphrodites in Medieval Islamic Law," in *Women in Middle Eastern History: Shifting Boundaries in Sex and Gender*, ed. Nikki R. Keddie and Beth Baron (New Haven, CT: Yale University Press, 1991), 74–95; Everett K. Rowson, "Two Homoerotic Narratives from Mamluk Literature: al-Safadi's *Law'at al-shaki* and Ibn Daniyal's *al-Mutayyam*," in *Homoeroticism in Classical Arabic Literature*, ed. J. W. Wright Jr. and Everett K. Rowson (New York: Columbia University Press, 1997), 158–91; and Rowson, "The Categorization of Gender and Sexual Irregularity in Medieval Arabic Vice Lists," in *Body Guards: The Cultural Politics of Gender Ambiguity*, ed. Julia Epstein and Christina Straub (New York: Routledge, 1991), 50–79.

10. See my review of Ahmed, *Gender and History* 5, no. 1 (Spring 1993): 148–52.

11. Leslie Peirce, *The Imperial Harem: Women and Sovereignty in the Ottoman Empire* (Oxford: Oxford University Press, 1993); idem, *Morality Tales: Law and Gender in the Ottoman Court of Aintab* (Berkeley and Los Angeles: University of California Press, 2003).

12. Judith Tucker and Margaret L. Meriwether, "Introduction," in *A Social History of Women and Gender in the Modern Middle East* (Boulder, CO: Westview Press, 1999), 10.

13. Deniz Kandiyoti, "Contemporary Feminist Scholarship and Middle East Studies," in *Gendering the Middle East: Emerging Perspectives* (Syracuse, NY: Syracuse University Press, 1996), 8.

14. Kandiyoti's thoughtful essay, cited above, discusses this in terms of stages of feminist scholarship and the impact of the study of Orientalism, which emphasized representation and tended to plot "difference" along an East-West axis even as it sought to dismantle that construction of otherness.

15. Haideh Moghissi, *Feminism and Islamic Fundamentalism: The Limits of Post-modern Analysis* (London: Zed Books, 1999).

16. Kandiyoti, "Contemporary Feminist Scholarship," 9.

17. Fatima Mernissi, *The Veil and the Male Elite: A Feminist Interpretation of Women's Rights*, trans. Mary Jo Lakeland (Reading, MA: Addison-Wesley, 1991). Mernissi carries on this investigation of historical documentation and dominant narratives; see her *Forgotten Queens of Islam*, trans. Mary Jo Lakeland (Cambridge: Polity Press, 1993).

18. The Women and Memory Forum published proceedings as *Min ra'idat al-qarn al-'ishrin: Shakhsiyyat wa-qadaya* (From Pioneers of the Twentieth Century: Personalities and Issues), edited by Huda al-Sadda (Cairo: Multaqa al-mar'a wa-al-dhakira, 2001).

19. *Middle East Women's Studies Review* has featured interventions in this debate.

20. Ahmed's *Women and Gender in Islam* (New Haven, CT: Yale University Press, 1992), for instance, is a basic textbook in many syllabi. She states, "The subject of women first surfaced as a topic of consequence in the writings of Muslim male intellectuals," 128.

21. Ibid., 129.

22. Thus, it is an important task to compare Arabic versions of European novels to their "originals," to consider divergences significant to an author's "reading" of local readers.

23. Jenny Sharpe, "The Unspeakable Limits of Rape: Colonial Violence and Counter-Insurgency," *Genders* 10 (Spring 1991): 42.

24. Rita Felski, *The Gender of Modernity* (Cambridge, MA: Harvard University Press, 1995), 14–15, 22.

25. Zaynab Fawwaz, *Riwayat Husn al-'Awaqib aw Ghadat al-Zahira* (Cairo: Matba'at Hindiyya, 1899), 2 (37); reprinted as Zaynab Fawwaz, *Husn al-'Awaqib (riwaya)/ al-Hawa wa'l-wafa' (masrahiyya)*, ed. Fawziyya Fawwaz (Beruit: al-Majlis al-thaqafi li-Lubnan al-janubi, 1984). References to the republished version appear in parentheses. All translations are mine.

26. Ibid., 36 (59); 36 (60); 42 (63).

27. Ibid., 168 (147).

28. Zaynab Fawwaz, *al-Rasa'il al-zaynabiyya* (Cairo: al-Matbaʿa al-mutawassita, n.d.), 2.

29. Ibid., 3.

30. Ibid., 12, 13.

31. Jurji Zaydan, *Armanusa al-Misriyya* (Cairo: Dar al-Hilal, n.d.; first published 1896), 24.

32. Felski, *Gender of Modernity*, 33.

33. Kandiyoti, "Contemporary Feminist Scholarship," 25 n. 58.

8

Will That Subaltern Ever Speak?

Finding African Slaves in the
Historiography of the Middle East

EVE M. TROUTT POWELL

DIFFERING DEGREES OF SILENCE

For decades now, historians writing studies of African slavery in the Islamic world have adopted a tone of righteous indignation at the meagerness of secondary sources available on the subject in the Middle East. As Bernard Lewis wrote in the preface of *Race and Slavery in the Middle East*, "In time, we may hope, it will be possible for Muslim scholars to examine and discuss Islamic slavery as freely and as openly as European and American scholars have, with the cooperation of scholars from other countries, been willing to discuss this unhappy chapter in their own past."[1] Lewis and others explicitly blame this silence on Muslims' extraordinary sensitivity on the subject; implicitly, they attribute it to shame, since, as they have stated, the Qur'an does not forbid slavery.[2] In a more recent work, Ronald Segal attributed not only a historiographical silence but also a political stifling of the subject to the repressive nature of Muslim states:

Paradoxically, however, in Western societies so long deformed by racism and an ultimate totalitarianism of money, there exist, too, a constitutional secularism and democracy that allow a much larger measure of freedom to proselytize, dissent and denounce than may be found in most Islamic societies, and especially those "fundamentalist" ones governed by religious law. Such repressiveness has little to do with the spirit or even letter of the faith as communicated by the Prophet. Islam's ideal community is one of unity, justice and compassion, with specific guidance in the Qur'an to tolerance. Yet too much of Islam's history has involved coercive regimes that have had a great deal less to do with promoting unity, justice and compassion than with serv-

ing and securing the interest of corrupt, avaricious rulers, their courts, or associated elites.

Nor need one look very far to find the counterparts of these regimes in Islam
today: exploiting a nationalism whose initial development was a response to
Western imperial conquest; and even, in Mauritania and Sudan, pursuing policies with a distinct racist component.[3]

Readers of these books could easily conclude that until the late nineteenth
century there existed in Islamic Arab societies a predisposition to slavery
that only the labors of Western abolitionists could eradicate. Moreover,
although slavery also stained the history of the United States and Western
Europe, a collective shame and recognition of slavery's evil redeemed Western societies in the twentieth century; this shame, however, had no parallel in the Middle East.

Other scholars have noted other, perhaps even more disquieting silences
in the study of this particular trade in slaves—the absence of the slaves' voices
themselves. American scholars in particular, having grown up in a society
where slave narratives have been taught in elementary schools since the late
1960s, often note, as Terence Walz has, that "the best evidence—first-hand
accounts written by slaves or former slaves—is missing from modern Arabic literature."[4] Nor have stories of slavery passed down through families
been discovered. Scholars looking for communities of African slaves' descendants in the Middle East are often disappointed, writes John Hunwick,
since this "lack of what may be called a 'black voice' in the Mediterranean
lands may also be due to the relatively small number of clearly identifiable
descendants of slaves and to their depressed social status and lack of education."[5] The slaves themselves seem to have left no traces, either written
or genetic.

How then can their history be found, much less told? How can we hear
them? Or do we, as historians, resign ourselves to the sad statement that the
slave, the ultimate subaltern, cannot speak? Or if she ever did, was "made
to unspeak herself posthumously"?[6] Gayatri Spivak is referring here to the
history of Hindu women who committed suttee during the British Raj, but
I find her questions about the voices of the subaltern extremely relevant to
the study of slavery. It has become imperative for many historians of Africa
and the Middle East to retrieve the voices of slaves, an issue they discuss
passionately, sometimes with palpable anger at the layers of difficulty
involved.[7] It is informative to read, therefore, how Spivak herself has
changed her mind and reversed her statement—"the subaltern cannot

speak"—an outcry written, she says, in "the accents of passionate lament."
Addressing scholars of history, she writes that "it is important to acknowledge our complicity in the muting, in order precisely to be more effective
in the long run. Our work cannot succeed if we always have a scapegoat."
Spivak acknowledges the importance of "decipherment" for recovering
slaves' speech. Yet this is not easily done, especially regarding a topic that
invokes deep anger at slavery and sympathies with the muted slaves—the
"moot decipherment by another in an academic institution . . . many years
later must not be too quickly identified with the 'speaking' of the subaltern."[8] As I read her, the attribution of blame to explain the silence of the
slaves themselves may well have camouflaged, for many historians, other
routes toward information. I also hear in Spivak's caution an urging to
rethink the nature of the slave narrative, and the historian's narration of it.

This essay will borrow from Spivak's trajectory to explore how historians of the twentieth century have negotiated the study of African slavery
in the Middle East, given the much-lamented silence of the slaves themselves.
I question why some of the same issues confronting nineteenth-century
eyewitnesses to slavery still affect contemporary historical writings, why perspectives on the geographic heart of the question of slavery have changed
so much (i.e., in which region does the researcher look for the slaves) in the
past decades, how Islam is constructed in the debate over Middle Eastern
slavery, what a slave's narrative consists of, and, finally, how constructions
of race in Africa, the Middle East, Great Britain, and the United States have
affected this historiography.

ARCHIVAL ECHOES

Nineteenth-century European eyewitnesses to the capture and enslavement
of Africans by Arabs, and the Middle Eastern markets where they were sold,
imbued their accounts with a vivid horror. Their evocative language had a
great effect on the abolitionist movement in Great Britain. The British and
Foreign Anti-Slavery Society (BFASS), the largest organization of the abolitionist movement, collaborated closely with the explorers of the Royal Geographic Society and, armed with the information that men like David
Livingstone published about the Nile Valley, the Arabian Peninsula, and East
Africa, was able to garner influence with the British Foreign Office and, eventually, British colonial administrations.[9] The abolitionists' outrage at African
slavery was particularly uncompromising on the question of slave raids and
the harsh journeys the slaves made to their new lives of servitude. Even though

many stated that Islamic slavery was a far milder institution than the plantation slave cultures of the British Caribbean or the southern United States, the images of the transatlantic trade and institution deeply influenced how the Victorian public envisioned African slaves in the Middle East.

Given the stark and dramatic narratives of slavery published in the United States in the middle of the nineteenth century, it is little wonder why. The narratives of former slaves were published under the careful editing and supervision of white American abolitionists and were intended to convey not so much an individual as a general experience of slavery. As Frances Smith Foster has written: "If we recall that slave narratives were meant to be personal accounts of ex-slaves' struggles for freedom which were also written to expose the perfidy of slavery, the tension between the depiction of the protagonist as individual and the protagonist as every slave becomes obvious."[10] Again and again, in the more than six thousand estimated slave narratives found, there is "an overwhelming sameness" to the story of the enslaved.[11] It is the experience of slavery itself that becomes the subject of the story, while the former slave, as many scholars of African-American studies have suggested, remains the object. The slave's voice is "striking because of what it relates, but even more so because the slave's acquisition of that voice is quite possibly his only permanent achievement once he escapes and casts himself upon a new and larger landscape."[12]

Although escaping from slavery brought publicity, it did not automatically bring authorial autonomy. For many years, former slaves in the United States could not publish without the sponsorship of white benefactors, "who had strong ideas about what roles black Americans ought to play in American literary and intellectual life, as well as in their own emancipation."[13] A particular slave emerged from these highly sentimental and stylized writings. If a woman, she was often biracial (because of the frequency with which white masters fornicated with black slave women) and always sexually vulnerable. If a man, he was exposed physically to terrible beatings. The normalcy of marriage and family life could not exist because "two basic tenets of the nineteenth-century abolitionists were that slavery prevented normal family relationships and that the kind of absolute authority that slave owners legally possessed over slaves encouraged atrocities."[14] It would be fascinating to explore the impact of African-American slave narratives on the European public, particularly British audiences, as so many runaway slaves fled to England, particularly after passage of the Fugitive Slave Act in 1850. Some of these exiled former slaves were also well known for their published narratives and set themselves up as lecturers.[15]

Although these images of slavery set in the agrarian southern United States and embodied in the authentic, first-person narration of former slaves were created in strikingly different environments than that of the Ottoman Middle East, the sexual vulnerability and exposure to despotic violence certainly coincided with many of the ideas that British political administrators had about Africans enslaved in Islamic Africa and the Middle East. In the minds of many in the late nineteenth century, how else could the personal power of the slaveholder be articulated? It is interesting to note, however, that in the 1860s, when abolition was a well-established issue in Great Britain, explorers tracking Africa's great rivers or hired by the Egyptian ruler to put down the slave trade wrote very little about the slaves whose predicament they had been hired to resolve. In much of his correspondence, David Livingstone was more descriptive of the geography, the flora, and the fauna of Zambia, for instance, than he was of the many slave caravans he encountered. Samuel Baker, hired in 1869 by the Khedive Isma'il to abolish the White Nile slave trade, was also more fascinated with slave owners and traders than with the "niggers" themselves (a word employed by both Livingstone and Baker).[16]

These men and their successors, British administrators of the Foreign Office and officials in Istanbul, Khartoum, and Cairo, became the ears and eyes of slavery for historians of the twentieth century enquiring into the issue of African slavery. In a much-quoted chapter on the abolition of slavery in his study of Egyptian social history, Gabriel Baer relied heavily on British Foreign Office records for his analysis of both the trade in slaves and slaves' experiences in Egypt. When these officials cite their own actions to bring about the abolition of Egyptian slavery, Baer takes them at their word, as shown in his description of the official Della Sala, who, he writes, "devised efficient plans for fighting the caravans of slave dealers, most of which were stopped by his vigorous action."[17] Baer's only source here is correspondence from Della Sala to Edward Malet in Cairo,[18] yet there is no questioning of this account, no quotation marks placed around the adjectives "efficient" or "vigorous." When discussing the lived experience of domestic slavery, Baer reveals his strong faith in the word of British men on the spot: "Since most of the slaves were an integral part of the families in which they lived, their manumission involved a breach in the secretiveness of the Arab family, so dear a value to the Egyptian and the Arab in general: instead of being *mastura* ("covered" or "concealed"), the family would become *makshufa* and its secrets revealed to the outside world."[19] These insights are not in quotation marks, but the note suggests they may be a direct quote from Raphael Borg to Sir Charles Cookson, British consular officials in Cairo and Alexandria, respectively. The slaves themselves are glossed over by their integration into the family, whose fears of becoming "*makshufa*" may perhaps be unfounded, so hidden are they by overgeneralizing.

To his credit, Baer does turn to Ali Mubarak's *Al-Khitat al-tawfiqiya fi masr al-jadida* for information about the slave markets of Cairo and follows Mubarak's map of the journey African slaves took once they arrived in Cairo in the late nineteenth century. But when researching slave traders of the Cairo markets he resorts to the descriptions of Evliya Celebi, a seventeenth-century Ottoman traveler: to Cairo came "dark-skinned people from the districts of the Oases, Aswan and Ibrim." This process went on for generations, Baer writes (which would explain why he used a seventeenth-century source to describe a nineteenth-century phenomenon): "these people continued, *apparently*, to constitute the main element of slave dealers until the abolition of the slave trade late in the nineteenth century (emphasis added)."[20] Any change in the patterns of acquiring slaves by different tribes or kingdoms over two centuries of the slave trade along the Nile Valley is effaced with the use of the word "apparently."

Gabriel Baer was an Israeli historian researching Egyptian history in the late 1960s, so it is quite understandable that he was unable to gain access to the archives of Cairo. But his chapter demonstrates an even greater geographic distancing through its indifference, then common, to the demographics of the African slave trade. Baer exiled to other books the European officers hired by the Khedive Isma'il to abolish slavery in the Nile Valley, not only because a great deal had previously been written about them, but also because "their efforts and the results of their activities belong to the history of the Sudan rather than that of slavery in Egypt."[21] This is an example of how historiography has kept the slaves hidden and mute. By divorcing Sudanese from Egyptian history, the geographic origins of the trade, and the majority of the slaves, are removed from the map of slavery.

Unlike Baer, Bernard Lewis carefully asserts the prominence of relations between "black Africa [and] the Muslim lands."[22] Lewis's work covers a much broader subject in both geography and historical time, and *Race and Slavery in the Middle East* certainly raised the important issue of constructions of race in the Islamic world when it was published. But as in Baer's, there is also a problematically defined geographic separation in Lewis's work on slavery, this time between the West and the East. Slavery in the "one" is the obverse of slavery in the "other," so what African slavery really meant is described only in the negative. Lewis first wrote the lectures that constitute *Race and Slavery in the Middle East* in 1969, and although the 1990 edition of the book was revised, Lewis's strong distinction between "black" and "white" in Arab societies bears many influences of debates about race that took place during the decade when Afro-American studies was only just coming into its own. Perhaps that is why Lewis never succumbed to the compulsion to define the terms *black* and *white* in either an African or Middle-Eastern context. In *Race and Slavery*, the racial classifications that seem so firm to him are presented as unchanging over centuries, from pre-Islamic Arabia through the Ottoman Middle East in the late nineteenth century.

Lewis's reach extends far: law, literature, Islamic art, and poetry. He offers important examples of Arab-, Persian-, and Turkish-Muslim biases against sub-Saharan Africans and even goes so far as to include graceful translations of "black" poets' laments, as in the following lines written by Nusayb ibn Rabah (d. 726):

> Blackness does not diminish me, as long as I
> have this tongue and this stout heart,
> Some are raised up by means of their lineage; the
> verses of my poems are my lineage!
> How much better a keen-minded, clear-spoken
> black than a mute white![23]

As a historian, Lewis has often displayed formidable literary insight, and the pleasure he takes in poetry is clear. But his obvious enjoyment of the Arabic language leads him in two contradictory directions, both of which obscure the experiences of the slaves whose identities and histories he tries to uncover. He writes that "after the eighth century, there are few identifiable black poets in Arabic literature, and their blackness is not a significant poetic theme." Later African Muslims wrote poetry in their own languages, preferring to use "Arabic for scholarship." Even though African slavery in the Middle East continued, "the school of self-consciously black poets came to an end." Few slaves had the education or the cultural fluency to compose Arabic poetry, "while the few Arabic poets of African or part-African ancestry were too assimilated to see themselves as black and therefore other."[24] But his extensive footnotes offer no information about the poetry of black African Muslims writing in languages other than Arabic. The idea of blackness itself changes after the eighth century, no longer to be discussed by poets but by jurists, who argue, in Lewis's words, "that piety outweighs blackness and impiety outweighs whiteness."[25] Yet he concluded this chapter by saying, "from the literature, it is clear that a new and sometimes vicious pattern of racial hostility and discrimination had emerged within the Islamic world."[26]

This is a difficult argument, because Lewis first asserts a change in racial thinking and then asserts an unchanging pattern from the eighth century through the Ottoman and Persian empires. The slaves themselves, so deserving of Lewis's sympathy, are frozen in Nusayb's images. The changes in identities to which Lewis briefly alludes are also simultaneously effaced. None of the documents discussed in the chapter about images and stereotypes was written after 1597, and yet Lewis asserts, "what is more important is that the black is almost entirely missing from the positions of wealth, power and privilege. Medieval authors sometimes attribute this want of achievement by black slaves and freedmen to lack of capacity. The modern observer will recognize the effect of lack of opportunity."[27] Again, there is a leap across time here without what I would consider requisite information about how slavery enabled people in the Middle East to construct racial identities; instead, the reader is asked to fill in the blanks using material from his or her own experience. Nor does Lewis help the reader understand in what ways literary sources can inform modern observers about antiblack prejudice. The reader is again left up to his or her own devices to conjure up an image of the black slave from the pages of Lewis's book. Although cited by many scholars, *Race and Slavery in the Middle East* remains part of the tradition created by the British "men on the spot," whose descriptions of African slavery in the Muslim world left much to the imagination of their readers.

TURNING TOWARD AFRICA

As mentioned earlier, Bernard Lewis does assert the importance of the relationship between Africa and the Middle East, although both of these regions remain monolithic and amorphous in his pages. The places where slaves were born, and the territory they traversed to get to the Middle East—the actual map of the lands they crossed—took some time to find their way into studies of slavery within different fields of area studies. Just as Gabriel Baer left the Sudan out of his account of the Egyptian-African slave trade, so too have Africanist historians omitted mention of the Middle East when exploring the issues of Islamic slavery. Suzanne Miers and Richard Roberts, two of the most prolific historians of the African slave trade, edited a collection of essays published in 1988, *The End of Slavery in Africa*, in which not one of the seventeen articles includes a discussion of the Middle East.[28] It is an extremely valuable collection from which much can be learned about the historiography of slavery that must complement archival research with oral history and anthropology, but those tools must be drawn out and used in analogous form by the Middle Eastern specialist. That is why the broader geographical study edited by Paul Lovejoy, *The Ideology of Slavery in Africa*, is actually so useful for the study of African slaves in the Middle East. Lovejoy's own exploration of the ideological dynamics of slavery would serve well to answer some of the questions raised by Lewis; he notes, for example, that "there was a sharp distinction between how slaves were actually treated and how society perceived the institution of slavery."[29]

It is Frederick Cooper, though, who has directly confronted the Islamicist historiography of the African slave trade by asking for a reexamination of some basic assumptions: "What is Islamic about slavery in an Islamic society of Africa? This is a question that is rarely asked, least of all by Islamicists. To many scholars, the question hardly seems worth asking, for Islam in itself embodies a set of institutions and a culture. Islamic slavery is thus a given, and one can comfortably discuss its variations with the assurance that the basic nature of slavery is defined."[30] For Cooper, Lewis's work demonstrates the opacity of the Africans' experience of slavery when it is discussed in terms that neglect to address these questions. If one writes as if "the religious norms and legal standards leap away from the continuous process of social change—they develop on their own," then "religion and law become causal agents, determining the nature of a Muslim social order and the thinking of people of all strata."[31]

Because Islam represents such a totality for Lewis, who, according to Cooper, "confuses religion with the societies in which religion is practiced, he cannot go beyond a tu quo que argument: Muslims, like everyone else could be prejudiced." Cooper goes on to say that Lewis's arguments make sense when seen only as a refutation of the arguments of Islamic apologists, who try to minimize the importance of the severity of slavery or racism in Islam. Both the apologies and their refutation have the same flaw: the vain search for a universal essence of Islamic slavery or society, a quest that puts more of a burden on the significance of religion than it can possibly bear.[32]

Such a monolithic approach conceals from the researcher ways of exploring how African slaves negotiated the lived experience of religion. Cooper turns to the more personal relationships between slaves and their masters and between slaves and their own systems of belief by asking, "What did Islam mean to slaves?"[33] Like other historians of the African slave trade,

Cooper confronts this query without personal narratives from slaves. He examines, instead, the practices of naming and what the name a slave was given revealed about how his masters looked at him. In Lamu, for example, only freedmen bore Qur'anic names. The names of slaves "came from days of the week (Juma), what slaves brought to their master (Farda-profit), or even what they had cost him (Arba'ini—$40). The world of God and the world of nature were opposites."[34] But even such whimsical names (and I cringe at them) brought slaves partially into the local belief system of Islam. There needed to be great delicacy here, since the "slaves' own acquisition of religious knowledge and cultural familiarity could undermine the basis of their inferiority." Owners, therefore, brought their slaves halfway into the system. Of course,

> No documents, as far as I know, give a slave's version of Islam. Yet scholars working in different parts of the coast have been uncovering a strong tradition among the descendants of slaves which suggest the importance of two strands of thought: 1) conversion to and mastery of Islam made slaves the religious equals of their masters within the terms of coastal culture and 2) those terms were not the only valid ones, for hinterland culture and identity were also worth preserving. These strands provided alternatives for different people, and even for the same individual.[35]

Keeping traditions and keeping Islam were thus the tools used by African slaves along the Swahili coast of East Africa. While Cooper does not name the non-Islamic traditions employed by slaves in their efforts to create an autonomous identity, he does present an idea of slaves' *living* through slavery: thinking, calculating, and assessing how to exist with as much dignity and as many rights as possible. His analysis also emphasizes the double-edged power of local understandings of Islam for both master and slave. While stating that no slave subculture that could threaten society's structure emerged, "the very real potential that it might strongly influence the relations of master and slave and its partial development protected the slaves against the notion that dependence implied inferiority."[36] And the "paternalistic self-image" of the slave owner was reinforced by "the fixity and evocative power of the written word" in Islam. This power "may not have cowed a single slave, but it helped to make clear that the slave was not simply up against his master, but against a social and moral order."[37]

Cooper's essay highlights the intimacy of the relationship between the slave owner and the slave, describing it as continuous negotiations between

two mutually dependent threats of power. The slave in this work, however, remains an emblem, a potential customer bargaining for identity without ever really purchasing one. Refuting Lewis's Manichaean presentation
of race in Islam is important, and Cooper, in his epic study *Plantation Slavery on the East Coast of Africa*, demonstrates how difficult the application
of European or American racial standards to East African Islamic identities can be. For example, he writes that "the congruence of ideology and
long-standing social practices in East Africa meant that the notion of slaves
as socially inferior dependents was deeply ingrained. This ideology equipped
masters to understand why their slaves would acquiesce to a system that
defined them as inferior, without having to postulate that slaves were
different sorts of individuals from their masters."[38] There is a deep sense
of difference, but such a sense could not lie in racial ideologies, writes
Cooper, because of who the slaves and their masters were, and how closely
they were related:

> Racial lines in coastal society were blurred. The masters were ethnically mixed,
> and *waungwana* [freeborn] were not necessarily light-skinned, although all
> thought of themselves as ethnically distinct from the Africans of the inte-
> rior. . . . Even Arabs could have dark skins and Negroid features, since chil-
> dren of Arab men by black concubines were considered Arabs. Finally, the
> entourage of a powerful man, as well as a communal group, included, among
> the people from whom support was expected and who were involved in a
> network of social relations, light-skinned Arabs or Swahili, black slaves, black
> freed slaves, perhaps a few light-skinned slaves, and black clients recruited
> from nearby societies. Racial distinctions were recognized, but they were a
> rough guide to a person's status or group affiliation.[39]

The multiracial relationships of slavery, according to Cooper, did not produce formal practices of racial prejudice until the coming of the colonial
state in the late nineteenth century.[40]

But there is silence on another aspect of slave identities: the slave remains
a "he." While Cooper is able to lay out some of the interiors of this relationship, the masculinity of the category of "slave" leaves out a great deal of
information, even speculation, about how slave women coped with the
physical and legal powers of their owners. The lack of a gendered discussion here thus limits the readers' perspective on the experience of African
women who were enslaved. If Cooper's assertions are correct, as I think they
are, regarding the importance of the slave in the African Muslim slaveholding

family, then more exploration of the concept of family is needed to round out the picture.

Historians of Ottoman-era slavery have done exceptional work on the questions of gender, family, and identities created by slavery.[41] In fact, the sensitivity of the issue that piqued Bernard Lewis has inspired historians like Hakan Erdem and Ehud Toledano to explore the language and terminology with which Ottoman officials discussed the questions of slavery. Erdem has explained that this "extreme sensitivity" may come from a "paralyzing contradictory stance: acceptance of Western mind views of slavery and a desire to defend Islamic culture."[42] Toledano has looked at the framework that created these mind views of slavery and sees "an obvious gap between the prototype of American slavery and Ottoman realities":

> Members of the Ottoman elite could not but feel that what British and other European critics of the institution were talking about and what they themselves were familiar with in Ottoman society were two completely different phenomena. The fact that the horrors of the slave trade were quite similar in both cases was conveniently brushed aside—if not repressed—by the "collective mind" of the Ottoman elite, which only reinforced their view of the benign, if not benevolent, nature of Ottoman slavery. Most wealthy, urban and urbane Ottomans encountered slaves in their own houses and in those of their friends and relatives. They could pretend that this was where the story actually began and that what had happened before belonged to another world—uncivilized, unruly, beyond their control.[43]

Although Ottoman elites relegated the lands from where their slaves came to the outer reaches of their imagination, slaves occupied a tender place in these elites' sense of home. Slaves, after all, were not foreigners; they were the "mothers, wet nurses, nannies and female relatives" for many Ottomans.[44]

Erdem also explores the nuances of British reactions to Ottoman slavery, performing the kind of "decipherment" recommended by Spivak when looking through colonial archives. From such records, Erdem writes, "one can learn more than just British official policy as British officials tried to learn, as much as they could, about the legal positions of slaves and about slavery customs in the Empire."[45] But he goes further in deconstructing the correspondence sent to the Foreign Office and considers the implications of the terminology adopted by officials for "slavery" and for the "slave trade."[46] A form of amnesia developed among many British officials regarding the historical origins of slavery in general:

Often disregarding the fact that Judaism and Christianity, before Islam, had
also sanctioned slaveholding, many British officials of all levels regarded slavery as an exclusively Muslim affair. Persuaded by apologists for the institution in the Empire, many believed that slavery was a necessity under the
domestic arrangements of Muslims. There would be slavery so long as the
Harem system lived, and its abolition would require and impose profound
changes on the social organisation of the Muslims. This, in turn, was not desirable for fear of the expected social upheavals which would accompany an abo-
litionary decree and which would ultimately defeat the slow promotion of
anti-slavery sentiments in the Empire.[47]

Within this cautionary circle, who spoke for the slaves? What did they want?
As Erdem describes it, African slaves' only articulation was expressed
through their feet, that is, if they went to the many manumission bureaus
established under Lord Cromer in Egypt and other parts of the empire.
Cromer used these bureaus to gauge slaves' volition; as quoted by Erdem,
he stated that "only those slaves who did not wish to acquire their freedom,
who were otherwise unable to escape from their masters, or who did not
know by which means to acquire it, remained slaves."[48] Erdem also mentions an organization called the Care of Emancipated Slaves, "a remarkable
organization which belonged to the freed black slaves and slaves in Istanbul," whose existence was not at all pleasing to Ottoman slave owners.[49]

LEARNING IN AFRICA

Erdem's account invites more research on these slave organizations, as well
as the manumission bureaus and the Cairo Home for Freed Slave Women.
His study also reveals an interesting, circular approach that British officials
took to slavery in general and African slavery in particular. These organizations and homes notwithstanding, a detailed understanding of the lives
of African slaves does not emerge in the archives of the Public Record Office.
As demonstrated by Cromer's comment, the transition from slave to freed
slave was just about all the development British officials allowed themselves
to see in the slaves. Ahmad Alawad Sikainga studies very similar records
about British officials and Sudanese slaves in his work *Slaves into Workers:
Emancipation and Labor in Colonial Sudan*, an exploration of the fate of
ex-slaves and their descendants.[50] Unlike other historians considered in
this article, Sikainga asserts that British officials were actually dependent
on the Sudanese societal classification system for the development of a pol-

icy (or lack thereof) about slavery once the British were in control, after 1899:

> During the last two centuries, the Arabic-speaking northern Sudanese have developed genealogies upon which they claim Arab descent, and created ideologies that defined who is free and who is enslaveable. Accordingly, Arab ancestry became the main criteria for freedom while animism and darker skin were associated with servility and hard manual labor. These perceptions were adopted by British officials who brought their own conceptions, framed by the Western European intellectual tradition and the experience of slavery in the New World.[51]

The British had to work much harder at translation of local constructions of race once they were in control of a slave-trading country.

Following, in a sense, Cooper's questioning the meaning of Islam for East African slaves, Sikainga investigates slaves' and ex-slaves' conceptions of freedom, which he defines as autonomy, and which in itself held different meanings, dependent on slaves' circumstances:

> How and why particular slaves chose particular options was determined by factors such as kinship and family ties, the nature of slavery in the particular society and economic and social prospects after departure. Most significant, however, were gender differences. The main consideration for female slaves was whether or not they had children and if they could get custody. Another distinction lay between old and newly acquired slaves; it is likely that desertion was more common among the latter than the former.[52]

One gesture frequently made by newly manumitted slaves was a direct response to the kinlessness that slavery had imposed on them. For them it was important to sort out "the redefinition of identity and the construction of quasi-ethnic and quasi-kinship categories." To remedy the uprooting of slavery, people could "adopt" new kin and "reintegrate themselves into communities from their home areas and have a sense of belonging."[53] Sikainga outlines the living arrangements made by former slaves in the Khartoum Daims in the 1920s and 1930s. These neighborhoods "bore the names of ethnic groups from the slave-raiding frontiers of Dar Fur, Dar Fertit, [and the] the Nuba Mountains."[54] Sikainga uses these areas, which began as shantytowns, as an important indicator of ex-slaves' self-images: "The prevalence of ethnic labels in the Daims yields significant insights into the history of ex-slaves in the post-emancipation period. It sheds light on the way in which liberated slaves tried to rebuild their lives and create new identities. They grouped themselves ethnically, regionally and occupationally."[55]

How did former slave owners and their descendants view former slaves? Sikainga sees northern Sudanese also participating in the process of assimilating ex-slaves and their descendants, in part due to the practices of the British administration, which concentrated economic and educational resources in the north and central Sudan. In Sikainga's view, this led to neglect of the southern and western Sudan, areas that in the nineteenth century had functioned "as slave reservoirs for northern Sudan and the outside world." In the twentieth century these regions became "a backwater and a source of cheap labor."[56] In the northern Sudan, however, the vast majority of ex-slaves "became Muslims and spoke Arabic": "This was part of the process of uprooting which enslavement involved. Assimilation of ex-slaves into northern Sudanese cultural norms 'conferred' on them a rank higher than that of southern Sudanese and other non-Arab groups who were regarded with great disdain, on racial as well as cultural grounds. So if social discrimination was the common factor between ex-slaves in the northern Sudan and other non-Arabized groups, cultural factors divided them."[57]

Sikainga's research certainly fills out many of the features of the African slave, often represented as a cipher in other historical works. Another example of his close examination of communities built by ex-slaves is his affirmation of the effect slaves and ex-slaves had on slaveholding society. His discussion of postemancipation urban music is a thoughtful attempt to see (hear) legacies of the cultures that slaves and ex-slaves brought with them to Khartoum.[58] 'Umad Ahmad Hilal also traces the influence of slaves through music in his recent and monumental study *Al-raqiq fi Masr fi-l-qarn al-tasi' 'ashr* (Slavery in Nineteenth-Century Egypt). He notes, for example, that Sudanese slave regiments of the Egyptian army were famous for their musical performances and, in the 1850s, a complete musical band of slave-regiment soldiers was formed.[59] With details like these, his work traces the history of both African and Circassian slavery in Egypt, exploring many of the same themes earlier examined by Baer. Hilal provides a very thorough history of the slave trade itself, the varying prestige different kinds of slaves brought to Egyptian households, and the development of abolition, all of which is familiar to readers of any several of the works I discuss in this essay.

Hilal's work distinguishes itself for its isolation of African slaves' experiences at certain crucial historical moments, for instance, when the Khedive Isma'il opened a school for the teaching of African languages (first Ethiopian languages and then Egyptian hieroglyphs) in 1869. The first ten students were brown and black slaves. Hilal writes, "perhaps Isma'il opened this school out of his need for translators specializing in Ethiopian languages," as part of his strategy for Egyptian expansion into eastern Africa.[60] Slave women, who lived with fewer worries about their honor, did not provoke objections to their placement in early public education in Egypt, and ten women from the Sudan and Ethiopia were the first students of the Midwifery School of Egypt, established by the French doctor Clot Bey in 1832, during Muhammad Ali's reign.[61]

Perhaps the most poignant example of Hilal's careful detective work in finding the voice of slaves and their descendants is his discussion of Muhammad Imam al-'Abd, the son of Sudanese slaves, who became a poet of some renown in turn-of-the-century Cairo. Hilal singles out al-'Abd's literary achievement by considering the poet in terms of the languages most slaves used to speak with each other. Classical Arabic was alien to both Circassian and African slaves. Even after obtaining their freedom, the majority of Circassian ex-slaves were affiliated with the higher social classes in a form of semi-isolation; Turkish was the language they spoke among themselves. As for Sudanese slaves, most of who did not belong to these classes, their knowledge of Arabic was limited to 'ammiya (colloquial Arabic).[62] While I think this conclusion about slave languages needs more study (how can we be sure that Sudanese or Ethiopian dialects were not used?), it is certainly significant that this briefly educated young man was able to become a recognized poet, and a good friend and colleague of the famous Egyptian poet, Hafiz Ibrahim.[63]

Hilal's and Sikainga's studies represent important steps in bringing African slaves in the Middle East into sharper focus. By looking at the living patterns of former slaves, the musical impact slaves had on the societies in which they were enslaved, and, as in al-'Abd's case, the perspective of children of slaves, these historians have refuted the passive posture of slaves presented in some of the other historical studies discussed in this essay. Toledano has also explored the historiography of Middle Eastern slavery in several essays, and he, too, turns to Africanist historical work for clues as to how to chart the roads slaves walked.[64]

But questions remain unanswered and much more work is needed. Several of the historians discussed here look at the racial implications of the African slave trade in the Middle East—what did "race" as a concept mean for slaves? If we look for the biological descendants of African slaves in Middle Eastern societies, as Walz did, are we admitting that slaves did not remain kinless, that slave women often bore children with their owners, linking them indissolubly with the owners' families? Did the consequent miscegenation blur the rather rigid racial classifications of American scholars? Or perhaps it is more helpful to ask, as Michael A. Gomez does, how so many Africans "made the transition from ethnicity to race" in the United States, and whether an analogy can be made to Middle Eastern and African societies as well. Did the descendants of southern Sudanese living in the northern Sudan, as described by Sikainga, do what Africans in the United States may have done, Gomez wonders, "simply decide one day to eschew their ancestral heritage and become 'new Negroes'; did they simply forget as the years passed by?"[65]

We also need to look at alternative ways of representation among the communities from which the slaves came, so as not to speak for the slaves, as Spivak warns, but to hear them in an intergenerational voice. Gomez discusses this in his analysis of Works Projects Administration interviews of former slaves conducted in the United States in the 1940s. Like the slave narratives I mentioned above, there are remarkable similarities in the replies made by former slaves and the children of slaves about the capture of their ancestors. For Gomez, accounting for the tailoring of replies given to white American interviewers does not erase the power of these answers:

> The story of capture represented an intergenerational crafting by those who were actually captured and by those born on American soil. The story was not told as it actually happened but recast to convey what the African-based community perceived as the essential truth of the experience. This is critical, for the presentation of the facts alone, to the African way of thinking, cannot communicate the full meaning of an event. What physically happened and the deeper meaning of what happened are very different things. And for the sake of the African-based community, for whom these accounts were expressly designed, it was crucial that they grasp the deeper implications.[66]

NOTES

1. Bernard Lewis, *Race and Slavery in the Middle East* (London: Oxford University Press, 1990), vi. As Lewis says in his preface, the first edition of this book appeared in 1971.

2. Ibid., 9.

3. Ronald Segal, *Islam's Black Slaves: The Other Black Diaspora* (New York: Farrar, Straus and Giroux, 2001), 10–11.

4. Terence Walz, "Black Slavery in Egypt during the Nineteenth Century as Reflected in the Mahkama Archives of Cairo" in *Slaves and Slavery in Muslim Africa*, ed. John Ralph Willis (Princeton, NJ: Princeton University Press, 1985), 2:137.

5. John Hunwick, "The Same but Different: Africans in Slavery in the Mediterranean Muslim World" in *The African Diaspora in the Mediterranean Lands of Islam*, ed. John Hunwick and Eve M. Troutt Powell (Princeton, NJ: Princeton University Press, 2002), xii.

6. Gayatri Chakravorty Spivak, *A Critique of Postcolonial Reason: Toward a History of the Vanishing Present* (Cambridge, MA: Harvard University Press, 1999), 273.

7. Please see Michael A. Gomez, *Exchanging Our Country Marks: The Transformation of African Identities in the Colonial and Antebellum South* (Chapel Hill: University of North Carolina Press, 1998), and Ahmad Alawad Sikainga, *Slaves into Workers: Emancipation and Labor in Colonial Sudan* (Austin: University of Texas Press, 1996), for examples of interesting new perspectives on the experience of African slaves.

8. Spivak, *Critique*, 308–9.

9. Please see my *A Different Shade of Colonialism: Egypt, Great Britain, and the Mastery of the Sudan* (Berkeley and Los Angeles: University of California Press, 2003), particularly chap. 3.

10. Frances Smith Foster, *Witnessing Slavery: The Development of Ante-bellum Slave Narratives* (Madison: University of Wisconsin Press, 1994), 68.

11. James Olney, "'I Was Born': Slave Narratives, Their Status as Autobiography and as Literature," in *The Slave's Narrative*, ed. Charles T. Davis and Henry Louis Gates Jr. (New York: Oxford University Press, 1985), 148.

12. Robert Burns Stepto, "I Rose and Found My Voice: Narration, Authentication and Authorial Control in Four Slave Narratives," in ibid., 225.

13. Wilson Moses, "Writing Freely? Frederick Douglass and the Constraints of Racialized Writing," in ibid., 66.

14. Foster, *Witnessing Slavery*, 129.

15. Timothy B. Powell, *Ruthless Democracy: A Multicultural Interpretation of the American Renaissance* (Princeton, NJ: Princeton University Press, 2000), 148–49.

16. David Livingstone, *Letters and Documents: 1841–1872* (Bloomington: Livingstone Museum / Multimedia Zambia / Indiana University Press, 1990); Samuel W. Baker, *Ismailia* (London, 1878).

17. Gabriel Baer, *Studies in the Social History of Modern Egypt* (Chicago: University of Chicago Press, 1969), 180.

18. Foreign Office, FO 141/140, Assiout, November 8, 1880, cited in ibid.

19. Baer, *Studies*, 184.

20. Ibid., 172–73.

21. Ibid.,178.

22. Lewis, *Race and Slavery*, 50.

23. Ibid., 29.

24. Ibid., 31.

25. Ibid., 35.

26. Ibid., 36.

27. Ibid., 61.

28. Suzanne Miers and Richard Roberts, eds., *The End of Slavery in Africa* (Madison: University of Wisconsin Press, 1988).

29. Paul Lovejoy, "Slavery in the Sokoto Caliphate" in *The Ideology of Slavery in Africa*, ed. Paul Lovejoy (London: Sage Publications, 1981), 207.

30. Frederick Cooper, "Islam and Cultural Hegemony," in ibid., 271.

31. Ibid., 272.

32. Ibid., 273–74.

33. Ibid., 277.

34. Ibid., 289.

35. Ibid., 291–92.

36. Ibid., 297.

37. Ibid.

38. Frederick Cooper, *Plantation Slavery on the East Coast of Africa* (New Haven, CT: Yale University Press, 1977), 262.

39. Ibid., 267.

40. Ibid.

41. For example, Leslie Peirce, *Imperial Harem: Women and Sovereignty in the Ottoman Empire* (New York: Oxford University Press, 1993); Hakan Erdem, *Slavery in the Ottoman Empire and Its Demise* (London: Macmillan, 1996); and Ehud Toledano, *The Ottoman Slave Trade and Its Suppression: 1840–1890* (Princeton, NJ: Princeton University Press, 1983). All of these works, using Ottoman archives and court records, are able to offer substantial insights into the situation of non-African slavery throughout the Ottoman Empire, as well as how families and households were constructed around slavery. Few articles draw out the particular pressures on female slaves as well as Toledano's work on the ill-fated pregnancy of Semsigul, in his remarkable chapter "The Other Face of Harem Bondage: Abuse and Redress," in his *Slavery and Abolition in the Ottoman Middle East* (Seattle: University of Washington Press, 1997), 54–80.

42. Erdem, *Slavery in the Ottoman Empire*, xvii.

43. Toledano, *Slavery and Abolition*, 127.

44. Ibid., 123.

45. Erdem, *Slavery in the Ottoman Empire*, xviii.

46. Ibid., 71.

47. Ibid., 85.

48. Ibid., 92.

49. Ibid., 173.

50. Ahmad Alawad Sikainga, *Slaves into Workers: Emancipation and Labor in Colonial Sudan* (Austin: University of Texas Press, 1996), xii.

51. Ibid., xii–xiii.

52. Ibid., 51, 53.

53. Ibid., 80.

54. Ibid., 79.

55. Ibid.

56. Ibid., 121.

57. Ibid., 171.

58. Ibid., 163–66.

59. ʿUmad Ahmad Hilal, *Al-raqiq fi Masr fi-l-qarn al-tasiʾ ʿashr* (Cairo: Dar al-ʿArabi, 1999), 272.

60. Ibid., 263. It is important to note that Hilal found this quote in another source: Amin Sami's *Taqwim al-Nil.*

61. Hilal, *Al-raqiq fi masr fi-l-qarn al-tasiʾ ʿashr,* 264.

62. Ibid., 278.

63. Ibid., 279. For a longer discussion of Muhammad Imam al-ʿAbd, please also see my book, *A Different Shade of Colonialism,* chap. 5.

64. See his chapter "Discourses on Ottoman and Ottoman-Arab Slavery," in *Slavery and Abolition in the Middle East.* Also, Toledano's article, "The Concept of Slavery in Ottoman and Other Muslim Societies: Dichotomy or Continuum?" in *Slave Elites in the Middle East and Africa: A Comparative Study,* ed. Miura Toru and John Edward Philips (London: Kegan Paul, 2000), 172–74.

65. Gomez, 12.

66. Ibid., 199.

9

Muslim Religious Extremism in Egypt

A Historiographical Critique of Narratives

JUAN R. I. COLE

The post-Nasser offshoots of the Muslim Brotherhood have attracted a remarkably small literature in Western languages, given how important they have been to the political and social development of that country. It has not been easy for Western authors to write about them, both for reasons of Egyptian government censorship and because the movements themselves have often been clandestine and highly xenophobic. In recent years, of course, some of them have turned to random anti-Western terrorism of a sort that would put off even the most intrepid social scientists. Additionally, writing about such movements ideally requires the skills of a scholar versed in Islamics, combined with those of a contemporary social scientist. It is no great surprise that few have combined such skills. The subject has gained urgency with the rise of al-Qaeda and September 11, given that the Egyptian al-Jihad al-Islami is a key component of that organization.

Rather than attempt a dry catalog of this historiography, I prefer in what follows to engage in a limited number of soundings and to offer a critique (not just criticism) of a few selected works. I choose the works because they appear to me to put forward strong conceptual theses about the sources of what some call neofundamentalism and explicitly or implicitly to put forward strong views on the best methodologies for understanding it. I will query some basic premises often found in this literature. Is the source of fundamentalist radicalism mainly government repression? Is the picture of the radicals that emerges from mainstream works and the media in Egypt wholly inaccurate? Are these groups purely religious in origin, or do they use religion for interest politics and the advancement of the interests of their social classes? Are radical fundamentalist groups a force for pluralism and civil society in authoritarian Republican Egypt? What are the most fruitful social science tools that we could employ to understand the radical fundamentalists? How useful are phenomenology, structuralism, postmodernism, and the sociology of religion, all intellectual tools developed in Europe, in approaching these movements?[1]

Little contemporary history is written of the Middle East by historians, and social scientists wishing to treat the contemporary period must often provide historical background through their own efforts, despite their lack of training in how to weight documents and reason historically. Therefore, I would argue, it is all the more important that historians take the time to evaluate such works from a historiographical point of view. For historians to ignore the past fifty years of Middle Eastern history, simply because the archives are not open, would be unconscionable.

Gilles Kepel, in his *Muslim Extremism in Egypt*, sees himself as laboring against a tendency of Western intellectuals to view Muslim movements from the redoubt of the Enlightenment (*une rationalisme éclairé*), reducing them to a simple eruption of irrationality.[2] This latter approach could be expected from two of the major French intellectual schools, the Marxist and the neoconservative. Although writing in the early 1980s (the book was published in French in 1984), Kepel in this work declined to discuss postmodernism or Michel Foucault's critique of the Enlightenment or his overly optimistic reading of Iran's Islamic Revolution as the cry of an oppressed spirit. He does reject the Marxist contention that Muslim radicalism is nothing more than economic grievances dressed up in religious garb. Kepel announces what I see as a 1960s structuralist approach, seeking to understand how these movements "'make sense' to the Islamicist mind (*la conscience islamiste*), to the semantic system (*système sémantique*) of the bearded militants in their white gallabiehs?" He asserts hopefully that "to discover this is to reconstruct that system's grammar and lexicon (*le grammaire et lexique de ce système*), and thus also the Muslim cultural tradition from which it issued and the contemporary Third World in which it functions."[3] He adds, "Here the tasks of the orientalist and the political scientist are inevitably intertwined."[4] Note that Kepel, like several other French thinkers of the period, rejects the words *fundamentalism* and *intégrism* as inappropriate analogies from Protestantism and Catholicism. The use of *Islamism* underlines the ways in which he views the phenomenon as unique.

Where does this language about the "grammar and lexicon" of a "system" of thought come from? It recalls French structuralist anthropologist Claude Lévi-Strauss and literary theorists Roland Barthes and Julia Kristeva.[5]

In structuralist thinking, derived from Ferdinand de Saussure's linguistics, systems of thought such as mythologies are like languages, with the mythologies of more distant but related tribes being like dialects of a language (this is the approach of Lévi-Strauss, of course).[6] Lévi-Strauss argued that the myths of the native peoples of Brazil were not irrational, but rather demonstrated their own rationality in their structure, through bridging of contradictions and through contiguities. Here, Kepel asserts that if one understands the "grammar" and "lexicon" of the "Islamicist mind"—that is, its "semantic system"—then one will also have grasped the basics of the "Muslim cultural tradition" as a whole. That is, both are "generated" by the same grammar and lexicon, one being a special case of the other. In linguistic terms, the "Muslim cultural tradition" is the hypernym—the more embracing and larger term—and the particular "Islamicist mind" is the hyponym, the smaller, more specific form of the phenomenon. In Kepel's telling, the "Islamicist mind" functions according to a semantic system that is a subset of the greater Muslim cultural tradition; that is, "Islamism" is a dialect of the Muslim "language." Just as studying a dialect of a language will reveal to a linguist the main features of the language as a whole, and not just the particularities of the dialect, so the structuralist social scientist can learn about a whole cultural stream by studying one of its narrow currents.

Phenomena such as Khomeinism and the Egyptian Muslim radicals, he implies, appear "monstrous" to the European mind because the Western "semantic system" is constituted differently, is a different mythology or "language." Note that a nonstructuralist theory of Islamic extremism might see it as significantly different from the mainstream Muslim cultural tradition, not a hyponym but a sort of antonym, from the study of which one would learn a great deal about cultlike ways of thinking but very little about normative Islam. Post-structuralists such as Foucault emphasized rupture rather than system and continuity. Kepel's announced allegiance to structuralist ways of thinking has predetermined the significance he finds in the phenomenon he is studying. Ironically, given his determination to escape the dismissive attitudes of the Marxists and the neoconservatives, his approach has the unfortunate potential of essentializing Islam and normalizing extremist fundamentalism within it.

The other terms he employs to frame his project are equally revealing. He seeks to bridge the role of "orientalist" and political scientist. It is the "orientalist" training, in Arabic and Islamics, that gives one the keys to the "cultural system" of the "Islamicist mind," but it is structuralist and third worldist theories of social scientists that allow it to be analyzed. Third worldism, or *tiers-mondisme*, has been a tendency in leftist French intellectual culture of reconfiguring Marxist anti-imperialism. Whereas Marxists saw the working class of the colonized nations as the hope of an anti-imperial struggle, during and after the Algerian Revolution many began substituting the third world nation itself for the working class. From this point of view, third world countries were progressive in and of themselves, insofar as they stood against aggressive, acquisitive capitalist regimes that sought to impose colonial or neocolonial hegemony on the rest of the world.[7] Kepel seeks to reposition Muslim radicalism as a third worldist phenomenon. In French Left-Bank terms, this would actually make it potentially progressive, whereas from a strict Marxist point of view fundamentalism was inevitably reactionary.

Kepel's position has resonances with the evolution of thinking about the Middle East among leftist French intellectuals. Many European leftists had defected from the colonial consensus over Algeria. But because the French Left tended to side with Israel, because of the military nature of the Nasserist regime, and because Gamal Abdel Nasser bitterly persecuted the communists until around 1963, Nasserism was open to being castigated as a form of Bonapartism despite its anti-imperialism. *Les Temps Modernes* carried articles such as "La repression anti-démocratique en Egypte," by Adel Montasser, in its August–September 1960 issue. Leading French Marxist Jean-Paul Sartre in 1967 denounced the Arab regimes as "fascist." He later explained that he took this stance because of his opposition to war and despite his sympathy with the Palestinian people (a sympathy, the depths of which were questioned by Edward Said).[8] Foucault complained to a Tunisian acquaintance of mine in 1968 while he was in Tunis that the Palestine Liberation Organization was merely a petty bourgeois movement, an analysis, if widespread, that would help explain the coldness of the French Left toward the Arab cause.

Kepel retained the analysis of the Nasserist regime as protofascist but jettisoned the assumption that its fundamentalist foes were necessarily also mere unthinking reactionaries. Despite his critique of the fundamentalists, he bends so far over backward to be fair to them that he ends up caricaturing the Nasserist regime. He consistently casts doubt on Nasser's charges that the Muslim Brotherhood had attempted to assassinate him and was implicated in terrorist plots. After reporting the assassination attempt of October 26, 1954, he adds, "The Brethren countered the regime's charge of conspiracy by claiming that the attack had been a police provocation. But no one listened. Their headquarters were burned down, their leaders were arrested and tortured, and government agents inflamed the populace against their members. Immediately after 26 October, the state destroyed the last independent organization standing between society and itself." The rhetorical devices here are all intended to bring into question the Nasser regime's charges: "no one listened" (*ils ne sont pas entendus*), "police provocation" (*une provocation policière*).[9] Later on, Kepel speaks of the Egyptian press in the mid-1960s "taking up the old chorus [*antienne*] of 1954 about the assassinations and bombings planned by the criminals."[10] The word "*antienne*"—"chant, refrain"—is clearly intended to suggest unthinking parroting and to cast doubt on whether the charges were true, as is the placing of scare quotes around "*comploteurs*" (conspirators). Kepel says of the 1954 assassination attempt by tinsmith Mahmud 'Abd al-Latif, "whether it was a police provocation or a deliberate act, the attack gave the president the perfect excuse [literally, "dreamed-of pretext": *prétext rêvé*] for finishing off the Muslim Brethren."[11] Although his language here is somewhat even-handed, elsewhere he seems to give more credence to the "police provocation theory." But even here, rather than see Nasser's reaction to almost being killed as understandable, he calls it a "pretext." Since the Free Officers had already banned organizations like the Wafd Party, which were far more powerful than the Brotherhood, why should Nasser have needed a pretext? He could have banned the Brotherhood along with the parties as early as 1953, without any need for an excuse.

Is Kepel's approach to the assassination attempt reasonable? It is not as if the Muslim Brotherhood had been a pacifist organization or had been uninvolved in assassination attempts against Egyptian prime ministers. Egyptian historian Sa'id 'Abd al-Rahman Yusuf 'Abdullah has pulled together documentation for the Brotherhood's activities in the mid-to-late 1940s, in a book published in 1995. Of course, Kepel may not have had access to this information when he was writing, but we must take it into account in this critique. We know to a certainty that in the 1940s the Secret Apparatus of the Muslim Brotherhood was running terrorist training camps and had produced significant numbers of operatives. They bombed Jewish-owned businesses and made British and Egyptian government sites their targets. Several violent incidents occurred as early as 1946. By 1948 clashes between members of the Muslim Brotherhood and the police were becoming common. According to Egyptian government documents, the Brotherhood was conducting protection rackets against businesses in order to extort money from them. A Muslim Brother bombed the King George Hotel in Ismailia. In January of 1948 fifteen Muslim Brothers were arrested in Muqattam Hills for conducting paramilitary training. On March 22, 1948, two members of the Secret Apparatus of the Muslim Brotherhood assassinated prominent court judge Ahmad al-Khazindar Bey for having sentenced to prison a Muslim Brother who attacked British soldiers at a club in Alexandria. In the summer of 1948 there were bombings of and attacks on the Jewish quarter in Cairo, at a time when Egypt and the new state of Israel were at war. In the fall of that year, police arrested thirty Muslim Brothers of the Secret Apparatus, seizing extensive documentation from their safe house on their terrorist plans. They also discovered a cache of Secret Apparatus arms and ammunition in Ismailia. As a result, Prime Minister Mahmud Nuqrashi Pasha formally dissolved the Muslim Brotherhood on October 28, 1948. In response, the Brotherhood assassinated Nuqrashi Pasha on December 28, 1948, after he had cracked down on the organization on discovering the clandestine terror operation.[12] Muslim Brotherhood leader Hasan al-Banna was in turn assassinated in 1949, probably by government agents and in retribution for the murder of the prime minister. Some four thousand members were arrested, and the ban lasted until 1951.[13]

The remnants of the Secret Apparatus were not firmly under the control of al-Banna's successor Hasan al-Hudaybi. That they should have attempted to assassinate Nasser in hopes of provoking a Muslim Brotherhood countercoup is in this light not at all implausible in principle, quite aside for there being excellent evidence for the fact of it. The foremost historian of the Brotherhood in this stage of its existence, Richard P. Mitchell, who was in Cairo at the time, evinces not the slightest doubt that the Secret Apparatus had decided to strike at Nasser because of his signing of the evacuation treaty with the British.[14] The most judicious recent treatment of the episode by a historian, that of Joel Gordon, notes that would-be assassin 'Abd al-Latif was indisputably a Muslim Brother and suggests that "the real question is, who in the Brotherhood ordered 'Abd al-Latif to kill Nasser, and why?"[15] Gordon demonstrates that the paramilitary wing, or Special Apparatus, of the Brotherhood, headed by Yusuf Tal'at, Salah Shadi, and Abu al-Makaram 'Abd al-Hayy, "operated with relative autonomy from Hudaybi and the Guidance Council." Al-Hudaybi was closer to Tal'at than he would admit, however, and Tal'at confessed in court to giving a belt of dynamite to his Cairo section chief early that October and to having considered the assassination of Nasser desirable. The lower-level operatives implicated both Tal'at and al-Hudaybi, and Gordon concludes that "Hudaybi, however, should bear more responsibility for the ultimate recourse to violence" than Mitchell and other previous historians had laid upon him.[16] Nor was the regime's response in

banning the organization and arresting its chiefs unreasonable, despite the
questions that remain about the precise relationship of al-Hudaybi and the
members of the Secret Apparatus. Kepel's apparent conviction that the 1954
crackdown was a regime ploy derives from overreliance on the radical Muslim narrative (and perhaps on rumors, which still circulate in Arabist circles
in Washington, that the United States urged Nasser to find a pretext to crack
down on the Brotherhood).

Kepel maintains that "the state destroyed the last independent organization standing between society and itself." This assertion was made before
the big "civil society" debates of the 1990s, but it is their harbinger. Kepel's
starting point is that the Muslim Brotherhood could have been an element
in a pluralist, democratic society, but that it was pushed underground by a
grasping, tyrannical Nasserist state that employed trumped-up conspiracy
plots as a pretext massively to repress it. The assertion begs all sorts of questions. Was the Nasserist state really totalitarian, lacking all intermediary institutions? Or was it corporatist in character? Was not the Muslim Brotherhood
itself totalistic in its outlook and organization? Are all intermediary institutions of any type valuable in detracting from despotism? Would an active
Stalinist party, for instance, have helped Egypt be more democratic at that
juncture? Note that Marxists were also jailed by Nasser until 1963, but Kepel
does not so much as mention their plight. In the first half of the twentieth
century throughout the world, Stalinist parties that were allowed free reign
tended to make opportunistic alliances with their bourgeois foes and to operate in a parliamentary framework only until they could make a coup and
abolish it. Attempts to "pull them" in to democracy in places like Eastern
Europe and China ended badly for democracy. The question is, was the Muslim Brotherhood cut from similar cloth despite being ideologically on the
other side of the spectrum? Kepel never seems to countenance this question, despite the copious evidence that elements in the Brotherhood did hope
to accomplish a violent coup at various points in modern history.

The Muslim Brotherhood of the 1940s was an extremely hierarchical organization, with a supreme leader, the leadership of which could not be criticized by the rank and file, who were forbidden to belong to other political
parties. It quite self-consciously divided itself into an outer layer of sym-
pathizers, a core of true believers, and a still more secret inner sanctum of
terrorists working for organization aims through violence. It apparently
aimed at eventually imposing a theocratic dictatorship on Egypt. Such a cultlike organization would have offered Egyptians little impetus to democracy
or pluralism in the 1950s. This is not to say that a less corporatist and more

genuinely democratic and pluralist approach to politics on the part of the Free Officers might not have benefited Egypt in the 1950s. But the Brotherhood did have an opportunity to be involved in parliamentary politics in the 1940s, and it chose terrorism instead, leading to its banning in 1948. Likewise, Nasser offered the Brotherhood an olive branch in not banning it in early 1953 along with the political parties. It responded by repeatedly calling for an Islamic state, agitating against the extent of the Free Officers' land reform plans, and increasingly demanding "a commanding voice in the affairs of state."[17] When Nasser curbed it, early in 1954, he set his regime on a collision course with the organization, and elements within it appear to have made an attempt on his life later that year. The unwillingness of an organization to operate within the established governmental framework may lead to its being excluded, even when the state is willing initially to include it. Kepel in his rhetoric puts most of the blame for the exclusion on the state and tends to exonerate the ambitious, grasping, and ultraconservative Brotherhood.

Kepel likewise calls the 1965 Muslim Brotherhood conspiracy a "plot," with scare quotes to indicate he believes the charges fraudulent or overblown. He ascribes the further crackdown to jockeying for position among Egyptian intelligence agencies, each trying to convince Nasser it could better protect him. While some of the elements of the alleged plot as announced in the official media are far-fetched, it is not implausible that an organization such as the Brotherhood that had had some five hundred thousand members and a well-developed terrorist wing in the late 1940s was able to reconstitute itself secretly and to brace for further action by the mid-1960s. There were places where militants could hide out, and one of the targets the army struck was a village on the route to the Libyan Desert that had long been a refuge for smugglers and dissidents. Near there, the Muslim Brotherhood had established its terrorist training camps in the 1940s, a point Kepel mentions only in passing, as though it were irrelevant to the narrative of 1965. Had the training camps been revived?

Figures on whom suspicion fell, such as Sayyid Qutb, were known to be radicals who did not consider Nasser or his government officials Muslims, and Qutb was denounced as having gone beyond the pale even by other Muslim Brotherhood leaders. Kepel dismisses the confessions of those arrested as the products of torture. As unspeakable and intolerable as torture is, this way of proceeding begs the question of whether torture always and only elicits untruths. Skepticism about the Nasser propaganda machine and about the sometimes trumped-up charges it launched at opponents is in order, but mere skepticism is not the same as historical analysis. The effect of Kepel's rhetorical devices is to whitewash Muslim Brotherhood extremism before the late 1960s and to blame radical tendencies on Nasserist repression. That the radical Muslims themselves might be power hungry or aggressive or violent on their own accord and without any special provocation is never admitted.

Moreover, one of the memoirs that lends a certain credence to elements of the 1965 charges against the Brotherhood had already appeared when Kepel was writing and is listed in his bibliography: the memoirs of Zaynab al-Ghazzali. Since then, several further memoirs by Muslim Brothers active in the 1960s have appeared that contain even more damning information. Among the main elements of the government's case against the Muslim Brotherhood was, first, that it had reconstituted itself as a tightly knit organization (*tanzim*). (Note that such organization was forbidden.) Al-Ghazzali and the later memoirists freely admit this reorganization and the recruitment of a new generation of activists. Second, it is alleged that Sayyid Qutb had emerged as the most popular leader among the new activists. The memoirists do not dispute this proposition, though they contain no evidence that he himself plotted in a practical way to kill Nasser. It was alleged that young male Muslim Brothers received martial arts and weapons training (some had even managed to be admitted to the military academy and to become junior officers). It was charged that elements in the reorganized Brotherhood desperately wanted to assassinate Nasser. The memoirists of the 1980s and 1990s often will admit these two charges but claim that the militant, proassassination elements were a minority (and that they themselves had not belonged to those factions) and that the military-type training was for some vague future exigency.[18] It was alleged that money was coming into the reorganized Brotherhood from abroad, and some suspect that Saudi Arabia was funding it as a way of making trouble for Nasser in response to his involvement in Yemen. Finally, it should be remembered that even in U.S. law it is illegal to threaten to kill the president. The sorts of heated discussions about how and when to assassinate Nasser that are reported in some memoirs would have been provocation enough for the arrests, if they were known to the regime. This 1965–66 plot incident was nevertheless far too small, and too relatively leniently handled (three executed, a little more than two hundred sentenced to prison terms), to hang on it the radicalization of Muslim fundamentalists that took place in the 1970s and later.

The Nasserist regime in Kepel's telling had virtually no positive points. He declines to mention its industrialization program or the impressive increases in per capita income achieved during 1952–70. As we shall see, he even manages to configure the substantial advances in education achieved by the Nasserists as somehow warped. He says nothing about the regime's having carried out the first extensive land reform, transforming millions of landless laborers into an agricultural middle class. Peasants are infrequently mentioned, and when they are, typically they are being targeted by government sweeps where they are near terrorist training camps. That the regime had benefited them in any way is elided. Nasser's courage in 1956 may have been a dim memory by the early 1980s when Kepel was writing, but since authenticity and third worldism are invoked with regard to Islamism, it is strange that the anti-imperialist bona fides of the early republic are ignored.

Nasser certainly ran an intellectually repressive regime and jailed dissidents. As even subsequent Egyptian courts have found, the regime did torture Muslim Brothers.[19] There is little hard evidence, however, for the scale of this practice. The one person I knew personally who had been imprisoned by Nasser in the late 1960s was a Baha'i. He said he was not physically tortured, but psychological techniques were used. Guards would turn on the lights and wake him up several times a night, for instance. Without questioning that the regime did engage in brutal torture in many instances, we must still ask, how much of the torture alleged by lower-ranking young radical Muslims was of this psychological sort? By Kepel's own admission, Sayyid Qutb was allowed to virtually live in the prison infirmary and to publish his books from prison, which makes his situation seem less than dire. Even the scale of the arrests in the various crises is disputed by historians. Gordon, who is quite careful, speaks of a roundup of about a thousand after the 1954 assassination attempt, while others speak of several thousand. Most prisoners in any case were soon released, and only a handful were executed. After the 1965 plot was denounced, as well, "hundreds" are said to have been arrested. Three leaders were sentenced to death (including Sayyid Qutb), twenty-five to life at hard labor, eleven to between ten and fifteen years at hard labor, and about two hundred more to various shorter terms.[20] Already by 1967, Nasser had begun talking about commuting some of the harsher sentences. Most of these detainees appear to have been in jail for terms between a few months and three years, with the last small group being released by Anwar el-Sādāt in the early 1970s.

Despite the undeniable dark side of Nasserism, Kepel goes entirely too far when he speaks of Nasser's "concentration camps" (*camps de concentration*) and suggests that radical Islamism was born in them, as a result of torture.[21] Tura prison, Kepel's referent, is not a concentration camp, and the number of radical Muslims in prison in 1966 was no more than a few hundred, most of who were soon released. Only a handful were ever executed, some for attempted murder. Since there was already an extensive terrorist wing to the Muslim Brotherhood in the 1940s, and since some later radical Muslims had been arrested for alleged participation in an armed plot, it is not clear that Nasserist torture, even if it was severe, was the main reason for their violent tendencies. The phrase "concentration camps" conjures in Western languages an image of Auschwitz. Intentionally or not, Kepel transforms a fringe group of often violent cultists guilty of the worst sort of hate speech, and sometimes of aiming at revolution through terror, into innocent victims of a Nasserism reimagined in almost Nazi proportions. Ironically, the vision of Nasser as a Hitler or Mussolini, long dismissed by social scientists studying Egypt, has its genealogy in British prime minister Anthony Eden's neo-imperialism.

Kepel's own account sometimes argues against the points he is making. For instance, he admits that the Egyptian government left Shukri Mustafa's Society of Muslims (dubbed by the press al-Takfir wa al-Hijra [Excommunication and Holy Flight]) alone despite knowing about its highly unorthodox ideas, until Mustafa attempted violently to punish some dissidents for leaving the group.[22] He calls the Egyptian press's characterization of Mustafa's group as Excommunication and Holy Flight a "caricature." But since Mustafa's ideology did require seeing mainstream Sunni Muslims as infidels, and since he did urge withdrawal from society to remote areas, it is hard to see how one could fault the Egyptian journalists for this description. Kepel admits that Mustafa even married off two village girls to adherents and then refused to let them see their parents any longer, since they were "infidels." In the West, this sort of behavior is associated with religious cults. Only when Mustafa attempted to impose the violent discipline of the cult on some ex-members did the state intervene to ban the society. At that point, Mustafa ordered the kidnapping of no less than a cabinet member, who had been critical of his group, and whom they ultimately murdered. It is true that Mustafa had been briefly imprisoned by Nasser in the 1966 crackdown, but it is not clear that most of his society's members had ever been harmed by the state. Al-Takfir wa al-Hijra's odyssey demonstrates the opposite of Kepel's main thesis. Its violence preceded government intervention and was directed toward internal dissidents, as one would expect with an authoritarian cult. When the state did intervene, the group's response was highly disproportional, almost apocalyptic, in making a personal attack on a cabinet member and so threatening the political elite as a whole. The state had killed no members of this splinter group before they killed a high state officer.

Kepel's treatment of the radical Muslims in the second half of his book, when he turns to an analysis of their tactics after the break with Sādāt in 1979, is far more evenhanded, though he continues to speak perhaps too even-handedly of what he calls Shukri Mustafa's "resocialization efforts." He presents canny analyses of the radical Muslims' use of Sayyid Qutb, of their provocations in Upper Egypt against Copts, and of their use of local institutions, whether campus clubs or the arms depots of village headmen to which they had access because many of them came from that class. His chapter on Shaykh Kishk, a fiery orator but not a radical activist, seems oddly out of place in this book. It reminds one of the emphasis Kepel places in his introduction on semantics and discourse analysis. Because Kishk sometimes sounds a little like the radical groups, he is grouped with them, even though there is no evidence that he ever took direct political action (he also, by the way, alleged he had been tortured in the 1966–69 crackdown, when he was jailed for declining to denounce Qutb as an infidel; yet he did not turn to violence). Kepel's account of the assassination of Sādāt focuses only on al-Jihad al-Islami, since at the time he wrote we did not know about al-Jama'ah al-Islamiyyah and Shaykh 'Umar 'Abdu'r-Rahman's role in allying the two radical groups. Kepel errs in thinking that the failure of the popular forces to rally around assassin Khalid Islambouli indicates that the radical Muslim movement had entered a new "phase of weakness."[23] Underestimating radical Muslim fundamentalism appears to be an occupational hazard for its historians; Richard Mitchell, the foremost historian of the Muslim Brotherhood, also thought he was studying ephemera. In fact, during the 1990s the Egyptian government was able to deal with the powerful radical Muslim challenge only by jailing between twenty thousand and thirty thousand persons and killing more than fifteen hundred in street battles.

In his conclusion, Kepel maintains that he had presented a "raw form" of the material on the radical Muslims, as a way of disorienting the reader. Yet, as we have seen, his language, rhetorical devices, and conceptual framework were anything but neutral. He insists that "it is essential to find the Orient disorienting when pondering the Islamicist movement." This move, he argues, allows the observer to resist the temptation to reduce the phenomenon observed to "known categories." Thus, Kepel rejects the idea that the radical Muslims are analogous to French Catholic integralists or American Protestant fundamentalists. Kepel in contrast insists that he is engaged in "value-free" social science that avoids merely sneering at the militants as

"backward fanatical terrorists." He also rejects only attempting to understand
them through textual analysis, which might produce an overly positive evaluation of them if not coupled with an understanding of their actual behavior. He is especially insistent on not reducing these religious movements
merely to class struggles or socioeconomic protest, as Engels might have. He
cannot resist a dig at the Marxist Orientalists, who have "suffered a train of
disappointments."[24] Islamism is not merely ideology in the sense of a super-
structural phenomenon deriving from a base of social (class) discontent.

Kepel appears to be setting up the radical Muslims as an essentially "Oriental" phenomenon, not accessible to the tools of social science. But if it is
really sui generis, then it would resist any analysis at all. All we could do is
describe it and its peculiarities. It is not even clear that non-Orientals could
understand it at all. Kepel clearly is a social scientist and does want to make
some sort of generalizations about radical Islamism. Yet his insistence here
that right-wing religious violence in Egypt is completely unlike that in France
or the United States would, if taken seriously, challenge the basic principle
of social science, explained most cogently by Jürgen Habermas, of intersubjectivity. Accounts of social phenomena must be rationally comprehensible to all other social scientists.[25]

Kepel's first solution to this problem is to insist that the groups can be
understood, but only by a structural and phenomenological analysis of their
generative grammar. He presents the radical Muslims as merely attempting semiotically to reenact the early sacred history of the Muslims, with the
Prophet's flight, the holy struggle against the Meccans, and the rightly guided
caliphs (he says the Muslim fundamentalists stopped time in 661, with the
advent of Umayyad dynastic rule). These events of sacred history, he says,
are the "originating myth" for radical Muslims, as the history of the Athen-
ian republic is for Westerners. Radical Muslims reject the nation in favor
of reenacting this early Muslim utopia, attempting to obliterate interven-
ing history rather than, as most Muslims do, accommodating to it. At root,
he says, is the "aspiration for justice."[26] The Orientalist (this is his word for
himself) in Kepel therefore, rather in the manner of Henry Corbin, has situated the radical Muslims outside history, as reenactors of mythical time
in search of the Platonic ideal of justice.[27]

Kepel the political scientist acknowledges that this first move, of appeal
to phenomenology, is insufficient. The movements must also be contextualized in contemporary Egypt, as one among many forms of "dissent," along
with Sufi Brotherhoods and forms of communalism. (In the past fifty years
or so in Egypt, Sufi Brotherhoods have not actually played much of a dis-

senting role, and his grouping of them with the fundamentalists in this regard strikes me as odd). He goes on to discuss the radical Muslims as one result of the vast increase in the educated class in Egypt under the Republic, as first generation peasant intellectuals who want not only to reenact the golden age of early Islam but also to restore society to the friendly, undifferentiated gemeinschaft of village life. The "bearded" Islamists in their "gallabiehs" (traditional Egyptian robes), he says, are able to speak to this new generation of alienated intellectuals, who feel themselves "guinea pigs" in the "maladroit experiment" of the Nasserist state in mass education.[28] But now that we have identified the "social class" out of which the radical Muslims come, and specified their social discontents, have we not forsaken phenomenology for Engels once more? Are we not dealing with a new petty bourgeoisie of rural origins that finds itself blocked by Egypt's exploitative capitalist and state capitalist sectors? If this is the case, why is it so important that they happen to cast their utopia in the form of a reenactment of early Islamic mythic time? Kepel seems unaware of having reverted to a Marxist analysis at this point.

Kepel concludes by returning to Islam. He downplays radical Muslim violence against Copts on the grounds that it is really aimed against the Egyptian state, and he speaks of "pious" medieval polemics—though I would argue that medieval Islam was relatively tolerant of indigenous Christians. His final sentence is, "In the Middle East of the 1980s, largely alien to Western political categories, the message of Muhammad the Prophet threatens to become ever more insistent the greater is the execration of Pharaoh."[29] This concluding phrase is framed in the worldview of the people he is studying. Are Excommunication and Holy Flight and al-Jihad al-Islami really exemplars of "the message of the Muhammad the Prophet?" Why would an objective outsider wish to deny the assertion of Hosni Mubarak and the members of the Egyptian parliament that they themselves are believing Muslims loyal to the message of the Prophet Muhammad? And why associate the message of the Prophet with obscure cultists like Shukri Mustafa, whose idea of marriage seems closer to that of the Reverend Moon than to Islamic jurisprudence, or with assassins like Khalid Islambouli? Assassination, after all, is a form of murder (*qatl*), which is forbidden in the Qur'an, and although the Prophet Muhammad led troops to fight the Meccans (who had tried to kill him and snuff out his movement), there is no good proof that he ever assassinated anyone. In fact, he treated the conquered Meccans with great generosity.

Kepel does not refer again in his conclusion to the premises of his introduction. He does not again broach the idea that he is investigating the semi-otic system of the "Muslim mind," which is represented by its radical Mus-lim hyponym. Yet here he reveals that he does associate "the message" of Islam with the radical Muslims. They are somehow being true to Islamic semiotics, to the "Muslim mind." Nor does he refer again to third world-ism, or the possibly "progressive" role third worldist movements play in "resisting" Western neo-imperialism. Kepel Nazified the Nasserist regime, endowing it with "concentration camps" and castigating its developmen-talist devotion to making the nation literate as a "maladroit experiment" on Egyptian youth who were "guinea pigs." Yet in other places in the third world where states have promoted greater literacy, such as Turkey or Iran or Indonesia, they tend to be praised for this accomplishment. States like Pakistan that devote few resources to education are criticized for it. For Kepel, Republican Egypt can do no right. He therefore leaves in play the positions he took in his introduction, that radical Islamism is one legitimate mani-festation of the Muslim semiotic system and that it is simultaneously a form of third worldist dissent.

A nonstructuralist or post-structuralist approach could challenge these premises. Foucault's emphasis on rupture might suggest that rather than manifest "the Muslim mind" (perhaps even in pure form), radical Islamism may be a contingent departure from mainstream Muslim culture, an entirely new "episteme" or system of thought that breaks decisively with the premises of its predecessor.[30] Even just a thorough familiarity with early Islamic history and the life of the Prophet would suggest that Shukri Mus-tafa was not exactly a representative of pristine Islam.

Other social science approaches would also bring into question some of Kepel's premises. The work of the scholars assembled by Martin Marty for the American Academy of Arts and Sciences on the five-volume Funda-mentalist Project disagree with Kepel that the phenomenon he studied is sui generis, peculiarly "Oriental," "monstrous," or entirely incommensurate with fundamentalist movements in other contemporary religions.[31] This is a point to which I wish to return later. Third worldism as a movement has largely petered out with the end of the cold war and with events like the civil war in Algeria or the massacres by Africans of other Africans in the millions in places like Rwanda and Zaire/the Congo, all of which have brought sharply into question the premise that the third world nation is in and of itself pro-gressive (even for those who found this somewhat bizarre idea plausible in the first place). In his subsequent work, Kepel has self-consciously abandoned his early foray into Corbin-style phenomenology for a Marxisant approach.

He concludes that successful radical Muslim movements are a political alliance of poor urban youth, a radical Muslim counterbourgeoisie (often with Gulf-derived money), and pious Muslims.[32] (Note that he still identifies radical Islamism with "genuine" or "pious" Islam!)

Despite its brevity, the account of post-Nasser developments in Egyptian religious extremism by Nazih Ayubi is among the better in print.[33] Ayubi, a political scientist, is in no doubt as to the social and political roots of the radicals. He refers to Egyptian president Anwar el-Sādāt's use of the fundamentalists to offset the strength of the Left in post-Nasser Egypt. He finds that the movements, especially al-Jihad al-Islami, are disproportionately young, urban, and university educated, calling them a "militant" petite bourgeois phenomenon that is "quasi-fascist." Ayubi sees a difference between Excommunication and Holy Flight, which is hierarchical and had a cult of personality around Shukri Mustafa, and al-Jihad al-Islami, which is characterized by what he calls a kind of "democratic centralism." He also discusses a greater range of these shadowy movements than do most authors writing in a Western language.

Ayubi argues that what success these neofundamentalist movements have had derives from a developmental crisis in Egypt. He says that "many new social forces have been unleashed without their energies being politically absorbed and without their economic and social expectations being satisfied."[34] He instances growing social inequality, cultural alienation, and a large and restless youth culture. He notes that in the 1980s the Egyptian state replied on two fronts. It introduced more religion into legislation, in an effort to appease the fundamentalists, and it simultaneously cracked down hard with police and security. Elsewhere he notes flawed government attempts to appeal to the prurient side of the Egyptian public by putting more belly dancing and other mildly salacious fare on television. He notes that these approaches largely failed in the 1980s, in part because the fundamentalists saw the government's attempts at accommodation as a sign of weakness.

Let me now make some brief remarks about a book that follows very much in Kepel's footsteps, Denis Sullivan and Sana Abed-Kotob's *Islam in Contemporary Egypt: Civil Society vs. the State*. This slim volume is highly useful, in taking the story of Muslim fundamentalist movements up to the late 1990s. Still, its conceptual framework seems to me fundamentally flawed. The authors have a tendency to overestimate the importance of the Muslim fundamentalists in modern Egyptian history. For instance, at one point they suggest that there were two million members of the Muslim Brotherhood in the late 1940s. Mitchell, the most careful historian of this period, says that they claimed between five hundred thousand and one million in the late 1940s, and it seems clear to me that the estimate of five hundred thousand is the more likely of the two. Religious movements tend to exaggerate their numbers and influence, and one can almost never go wrong in accepting a lower such estimate. (The Nation of Islam in the United States, which sociologists put at three hundred thousand members in the 1970s, was claiming nine million then.)

Sullivan and Abed-Kotob also construct an image of Egypt under almost constant "occupation" from antiquity, transforming Cleopatra into a modern nationalist.[35] That such categories may have been meaningless in premodern times does not seem to occur to them. We are clearly being prepared, with this *tour d'horizon*, for the idea of the fundamentalists as anti-imperial and so part of modern Egypt's struggle for independence. (This position makes explicit the third worldism argument to which Kepel only alluded.) They position Hasan al-Banna in this book as an heir of the reformist Muhammad 'Abduh, even though 'Abduh was a rationalist modernist, and al-Banna was a fundamentalist. The latter is made into an icon of the struggle against the West and against "tyranny." No mention is made of the rules he instituted, that he could not be criticized, that all the Muslim Brothers had to obey him, and that the Brothers could not belong to political parties. The authors allege that King Farouk banned the Brotherhood in 1948 because it demanded the institution of Islamic law. They neglect to refer to the Secret Apparatus or the terrorist cells and operations that actually led to the ban (which was issued by the elected prime minister, not by the playboy king). They call the decision by the Muslim Brotherhood to attempt to participate in electoral politics in 1941 a hopeful sign.[36] They allege that this honorable intent was thwarted by political corruption and the decision to exclude the Brotherhood (again, eliding the actual reasons for the prohibition). That a secretive, authoritarian organization with a clandestine terrorist wing volunteered to enter politics may not have been the good news Sullivan and Abed-Kotob suggest. Nor was it a sign of good faith that the organization in the same decade developed a secret apparatus that carried out terrorist attacks and assassinations on the very officials running the system in which they declared themselves participants.

The story that Nasser's harsh crackdowns radicalized the fundamentalists is dutifully reported. (Since they never discussed the Secret Apparatus that engaged in terror in the 1940s, long before Nasser, this assertion appears plausible in the framework of their text.) Kepel reported that "hundreds" of Muslim Brothers were arrested in the aftermath of the 1965 plot, something 'Abdu'llah Imam's careful examination of the evidence supports. These authors give the figure of arrestees at an incredible twenty thousand, though they are far less skeptical that there was indeed a plot.[37]

Sullivan and Abed-Kotob are not historians, and they are on firmer ground when they turn to their real subject, the contemporary Muslim fundamentalist nongovernmental organizations (NGOs) in Egypt. They do a good job of demonstrating how varied these organizations are and that many of them have forsaken violence for a willingness to work within the Egyptian political system. They attempt to argue that these fundamentalist NGOs are part of Egyptian civil society and are a force for pluralism in an otherwise authoritarian state. This thesis, I would argue, can be upheld only if we define "civil society" in a way radically different than it was used by Locke, Hegel, and Habermas. For Habermas, the public sphere in which civil society exists is characterized by institutions that are neither under the control of the government nor private. He insists that these institutions must be forces for tolerance and communicative rationality. He points to a press and a theater free of state censorship, even coffeehouse political discussions that attract no sanctions, as examples of this public sphere.

From a Habermasian point of view, narrow religious groups cannot form part of the public sphere or civil society because they are particularistic. They tend to be intolerant or at least to insist on a monopoly over the content of the truth and to work for the implementation of values based on authority, not on reason. While many Muslim fundamentalists in contemporary Egypt are willing to avoid violence and to work for their goals civilly, their ultimate aim nevertheless includes the imposition of their interpretation of Islamic law on the whole society and the establishment of an Islamic state that is unlikely to have democratic contours.

Sullivan and Abed-Kotob (and they are hardly alone) have confused the existence of multiple groups and institutions with civil society. As noted above, having a Stalinist group in a society does not contribute to tolerance or intersubjectivity, and neither do the activities of religious fundamentalists. It may be that they can help challenge more extreme forms of governmental authoritarianism. Yet, in modern Egyptian history the basic incompatibility of their goals with the aims of the country's elite has more often reinforced authoritarian tendencies in the state than reduced them. That is, the attempts to assassinate President Mubarak, and the terrorist actions against tourists, government officials, and Copts, have provoked arrests on a massive scale and necessitated expanding the secret police and the prison system. Rather than contribute to civil society, the radical fundamentalists

have been a major reason for its suppression. That nonviolent fundamentalists form NGOs to provide health care in poor neighborhoods is perhaps
a good thing, but given that their ultimate objective is to impose a theocratic despotism on society, they are not exemplars of civil society, and this
goal is unacceptable to the country's elites. Civil society must be measured
against its ultimate outcome, and groups said to contribute to it must foster tolerance and greater open communication across subcultures. The work
of Amaney Jamal demonstrates that in authoritarian societies, grassroots
organizations often configure themselves so as to contribute to authoritarianism, rather than work against it.[38] The easy assumption of much of the
civil society literature that the mere proliferation of NGOs equals pluralism, which in turn equals greater liberty, is simply incorrect.

That Muslim fundamentalists consist of large numbers of distinct and
various subcultures, that many of them are nonviolent, and that they often
function as or support NGOs in ways that are helpful to Egyptian citizens
are important findings of Sullivan and Abed-Kotob's book. The attempt to
put these groups under the sign of "civil society" and to set up a match called
"civil society versus the authoritarian state," however, is to commit a
significant category error. It conjures a false dawn of hope, that from intolerance and authoritarian discourse democracy may emerge.

As noted above, the Fundamentalist Project approach would instead
depict the radical Muslim groups as sectarian, as departures from the mainstream characterized by greater polarization and greater exclusiveness and
quest for control over adherents. Scholars who have examined fundamentalisms have identified nine major motifs in such movements: a reaction
against the marginalization of religion, selectivity about the tradition and
about modernity, moral dualism, absolutism and inerrancy, millennialism,
an elect membership, sharp boundaries, authoritarian organization, and
strict behavioral requirements.[39] All of these motifs are present in the radical movements of Egypt. From this point of view, Muslim radicalism is
not a dialect of the unique Muslim language but rather a form of fundamentalism. Fundamentalism in turn is one typical reaction of less-favored
populations to modernity and its ramifications in societies dominated by
Abrahamic religions.

That is, modernity and consumerism challenge the puritan moral values of elites in rural or rurban societies. (Many of the fundamentalist leaders who took over the Southern Baptist convention in the course of the 1980s
were brought up on farms even if they were themselves professionals.)[40]
The ways in which modernity and consumerism affect the position of women

challenge patriarchal domination and produce a disorientation of male identity, a point made at length by Ellis Goldberg.[41] He also instances to the vastly
increased ability of the state to intervene in matters that once would have
been local or private, producing a backlash that sometimes takes a fundamentalist form. This important insight yields clues as to why the Muslim
Brotherhood should have opposed both Nasserist socialism and Sādāt's lib-
eralization. Goldberg implicitly rejects the Kepel thesis of the sui generis
nature of "Islamism," comparing Sunni radicalism directly to early Calvinism and admitting the fraught utility of the term *fundamentalism*. It is the
nature of fundamentalism to claim for itself a monopoly over its religious
tradition and to insist that it is a return to the pristine form of the religion.
Kepel's treatment gives too much credence to these claims on the whole,
seeing the radicals as revivers of the early Muslim theocracy at Mecca. This
depiction derives from them; it is how they see themselves. But it is not plausible to anyone who knows early Islamic history well, and it is hard to see
in any case how a Western social scientist can adjudicate the competing claims
to Muslim authenticity put forward by modernists in the 'Abduh tradition
and those in the radical stream.

The "high-tension" model of the sect predicts that it not only will attempt
to draw firm boundaries around itself with regard to the mainstream host
society, but it also will strive to exclude those adherents who are seen as too
accommodating to mainstream norms.[42] High tension with the outside tends
also to imply exclusivism on the inside. (Thus, it is clear that both under
al-Banna and under al-Hudaybi, Muslim Brothers who showed too much
independence of thought were ordered systematically shunned by the leadership, and adherents had to cut them off to remain members.) Movements
can move in a more sectlike or a more churchlike direction. Some elements
of the Muslim Brotherhood have certainly become more mainstream in the
past thirty years, whereas other splinter groups have come into ever-greater
tension with mainstream Egyptian society. One advantage of the Weberian
tradition is that it can accommodate analyses of ideology, social organization, and social class that are not reductive. Max Weber refused to "read
off" superstructure from base. Thus, you could have a bourgeois sect (Calvinism) or a proletarian sect (Anabaptists), a bourgeois "church" (Episcopalianism) or a proletarian "church" (later Methodism). Religious form and
social class are both variables in an overall analysis, rather than class being
the sole independent variable. Weberianism also positions groups with regard
to capitalism and the state, giving them political legibility. The opposition
of the Muslim Brotherhood to Nasser's land reform proposals can there-

fore help us identify it on a political scale, as "Right," an enterprise in which structuralism and phenomenology are not terribly useful, and which challenges its "third worldist" credentials.

The works examined here tend to focus on the Nasser period and its aftermath, the essentially military regime of Republican Egypt. The authors' underlying thesis, expressed directly or through rhetorical devices, is that fundamentalist radicalism came in reaction to state repression and torture, as a populist reaction against Nasserist protofascism. The picture that emerges from these works is of groups with a commitment to the mythic ideal of early Islamic governance, who make an entirely reasonable demand that a Muslim society be governed by Islamic law, who then run headlong into a tyrannical state that excludes them from politics and even jails and tortures them under various pretexts. In reaction to this unthinking repression, some of these groups turn, perhaps understandably, to violence. Others, however, choose peace and social service even in the face of Pharaoh's jackboot, providing needed goods to the poor and incidentally endowing an otherwise totalitarian society with an important measure of pluralism that might hope eventually to help constitute a civil society and a public sphere that contributes to greater democracy.

All of these premises seem to me to require the most severe skepticism, and most of them seem to me exaggerated or simply incorrect. Muslim fundamentalist groups in Egypt have their own agency and are hardly epiphenomena of Nasserism. They often adopted programs, including violent ones, without necessarily reacting to governmental tyranny. The Secret Apparatus and its extensive terrorist activities in the 1940s, including the assassination of a sitting prime minister, stand witness to this point. So does the plot to assassinate Nasser in 1954 (he had been far less repressive to the Muslim Brotherhood than to any other political force in Wafdist Egyptian society). So too does the very prominence of Upper Egypt in the production of Muslim radicalism, insofar as it is an area where the central state has far less authority than in the Delta.

Radical fundamentalists may resent government policies or the intrusion of the state or, from the 1970s, of commodity capitalism into their lives, but the vast majority of them before the 1990s had never been tortured or imprisoned by the state. Nor are a majority of Egyptians necessarily outraged by commodity capitalism or the impact of Western mass culture. In the mid-1980s I saw in an Egyptian newspaper the results of a poll done by Egyptian television about what programs Egyptians would like to see more of, and the most frequent answer was "American action shows." The vast popularity of American soap operas such as *Falcon Crest* was obvious to anyone living in Cairo in the late 1980s; street traffic even perceptibly lightened in the nine-to-ten nightly time spot in the middle-class sections of the city. Many of the fundamentalists' protests, moreover, center not on the tyranny of the Republican government but rather on its external policies—its peace treaty with Israel, its alliance with the United States (or in the 1960s with the Soviet Union; sometimes it was alleged that Nasser was a puppet of both superpowers simultaneously). Nativism and xenophobia of an unexamined sort seem to be more important as key issues to fundamentalists than lack of democracy. Their ideal "Islamic" state would not be a parliamentary democracy, in any case.

Kepel's notion that the fundamentalists are simply attempting to re-create the early Muslim theocratic utopia in modern Egypt, and the associated implication that any "pious" Muslim would attempt to do so in the face of the incursions of modernity, begs so many questions that one barely knows where to begin. All Muslim movements, even secularist ones such as that led by 'Ali 'Abd al-Raziq in the early twentieth century, reference the norms of early Islam for their purposes. The claims of the radicals that they have a privileged understanding of that period of sacred history should be interrogated by social scientists, not merely acquiesced in. Even Kepel is compelled to admit toward the end of his book, despite his struggle against Engels's base/superstructure reductionism, that the radicals do have specific social origins and a social context. Moreover, it is unclear why we should give their forms of religious ideology primacy in the task of explaining them over their class, regional, and educational determinants. Only about a third of Egyptians appear to be sympathetic to the Muslim fundamentalist currents, including the now mainstreamed Muslim Brotherhood. One poll of the mid-1980s suggested that fully 20 percent of Tunisians give "none" when asked about their religion, more than twice as high as U.S. citizens. Over half of Turks say they are Turks first and Muslims second. If a natural Muslim desire to re-create the Meccan Utopia primarily drove "Islamism," then why is it such a minority taste among Muslims? And why are such commitments so much rarer among persons trained as humanists, or in certain regions (e.g., the Kabylia in Algeria, or Tashkent as opposed to Fergana in Uzbekistan), or among certain social classes, than among others? They are all "Muslims," after all. Even in his first book Kepel was in the end constrained to acknowledge that a structuralist approach to the "grammar" of the Islamic system, or a Corbin-like phenomenology of Islam, insofar as such approaches are ahistorical and resist contextualized social analysis, cannot explain "Islamism" by itself. The entire structuralist project was unsustainable. In the end, "difference" would come to be more valued in most academic thinking than "system."

Finally, the argument that fundamentalist movements are forces for pluralism in an otherwise totalitarian Nasserist state seems more assertion than argument. The radical fundamentalists, insofar as they have a significant but minority social base, and insofar as they have repeatedly attempted to overthrow the state, have certainly contributed to greater authoritarianism on the part of the governmental elite. Even the distrust with which the mainstream Muslim Brotherhood was viewed by the Mubarak government impeded any opening of the system to free elections in the 1980s and 1990s. The totalism of the fundamentalists, their insistence on an Islamic state run according to their ideas of what Islam is, alienates the majority of Egyptians and makes the current elite unwilling to trust them. Without such trust, democracy is impossible. No leader of a civil state wishes to face the fate met by the Pahlavi elite in 1979, and everyone remembers the promises of democracy issued by Khomeini's circle in Paris.

If we view nonviolent Muslim fundamentalist groups as analogous to the sects of Western societies, their social welfare activities look a lot like those of the Salvation Army and many mainly African-American movements such as that of Father Divine or the Nation of Islam. It should be remembered that cults such as Jim Jones's People's Temple had such apparently liberal and social service aspects (Jones was once the civil rights commissioner for Indiana). David Koresh's Branch Davidian movement likewise was centered on community. In the light of this analogy, the notion that fundamentalist "NGOs" form part of or encourage a civil society that contributes to a democratizing public sphere cannot, at the very least, be accepted as self-evident. The Weberian tradition in the sociology of religions, as authors associated with the Fundamentalism Project have shown, can be very fruitful in the study of modern Muslim movements. That the extensive literature in the sociology of religion field should be almost entirely ignored by scholars of modern Muslim movements seems to me a sort of hubris, an insistence on reinventing the wheel. And, I would argue, it has taken the field into some conceptual dead ends.

NOTES

Presented at the conference "New Approaches to the Historiography of the Middle East," Bosporus University, Istanbul, May 2002.

1. My seminar on Islamic Radicalism at the University of Michigan in winter 2002 read these and other works, and much of my thinking about them became clarified in discussions with Murat Tezcur and Taymiya Zaman, to whom I am grateful for some of the insights in what follows. The blame for any errors in what follows lies firmly on my shoulders, of course.

2. Gilles Kepel, *Le Prophète et Pharaon* (Paris: La Découverte, 1984), 18; English translation, *Muslim Extremism in Egypt: The Prophet and the Pharaoh* (1985; Berkeley and Los Angeles: University of California Press, 1993).

3. Kepel, *Le Prophète et Pharaon*, 20–21.

4. Kepel, *Muslim Extremism*, 23–24.

5. See Claude Lévi-Strauss, *The Savage Mind* (Chicago: University of Chicago Press, 1972); and the following works of Jonathan Culler: *Structuralist Poetics: Structuralism, Linguistics, and the Study of Literature* (Ithaca, NY: Cornell University Press, 1975); *Ferdinand de Saussure* (New York: Penguin, 1977; 2nd rev. ed., Ithaca, NY: Cornell University Press, 1986); *The Pursuit of Signs: Semiotics, Literature, Deconstruction* (Ithaca, NY: Cornell University Press, 1981); and *Roland Barthes* (New York: Oxford University Press, 1983). For structuralist "generative grammar," see A. J. Greimas, *Structural Semantics: An Attempt at a Method*, trans. Daniele McDowell, Ronald Schleifer, and Alan Velie (Lincoln: University Nebraska Press, 1983); and Daniel Patte, "Greimas's Model for the Generative Trajectory of Meaning in Discourses," *American Journal of Semiotics* 1, no. 3 (1982): 59–78.

6. Claude Lévi-Strauss, *Myth and Meaning: Cracking the Code of Culture* (New York: Schocken Books, 1995).

7. Christian Comeliau, *Mythes et espoirs du tiers-mondisme* (Paris: CETRAL, 1986); Robert Malley, *The Call from Algeria: Third Worldism and the Turn to Islam* (Berkeley and Los Angeles: University of California Press, 1996).

8. Amina el-Bendary, "Of Words and Echoes," *Al-Ahram Weekly*, no. 477 (April 13–19, 2000), http://www.ahram.org.eg/weekly/2000/477/bk5_477.html; Edward Said, "My Encounter with Sartre," *London Review of Books*, vol. 22, no. 11 (June 2000), http://www.lrb.co.uk/v22/n11/said2211.htm.

9. Kepel, *Le Prophète et Pharaon*, 31.

10. Ibid., 37 (33 of the English text).

11. Ibid., 44 (41 of the English text).

12. Sa'id 'Abd al-Rahman Yusuf 'Abdu'llah, *Mahmud Fahmi al-Nuqrashi wa Dawruhu fi al-Siyasah al-Misriyyah wa Hall Jama'at al-Ikhwan al-Muslimin (1888–1948)* [Mahmud Fahmi al-Nuqrashi and His Role in Egyptian Politics and the Dissolution of the Muslim Brotherhood (1888–1948)] (Cairo: Madbouli, 1995), 621–66 (this source is archivally based and extremely well documented); Richard P. Mitchell, *The Society of Muslim Brothers* (1969; Oxford: Oxford University Press, 1993), 62–65.

13. "Politics in God's Name," *al-Ahram Weekly*, no. 247 (November 16–22, 1995), http://www.ahram.org.eg/weekly/archives/parties/muslimb/polgod.htm.

14. Mitchell, *Society*, 150–53.

15. Joel Gordon, *Nasser's Blessed Movement: Egypt's Free Officers and the July Revolution* (New York: Oxford University Press, 1992), 180.

16. Ibid., 182.

17. Mitchell, *Society*, 111.

18. A careful interrogation of the memoir literature by a partisan of Nasser is 'Abdallah Imam, *'Abd al-Nasir wa al-Ikhwan al-Muslimun* [Abdel Nasser and the Muslim Brotherhood] (Cairo: Dar al-Khayyal, 1997), 168–99; one important source on which he depends is the memoir of Ahmad 'Abd al-Majid, *al-Ikhwan wa 'Abd al-Nasir: Al-Qissah al-Kamilah li Tanzim 1965* [The Muslim Brotherhood and Abdel Nasser: The Complete Story of the 1965 Organization] (Cairo: Al-Zahra li'l-I'lam al-'Arabi, 1991).

19. "Egypt Liable over 1950s' Torture," September 27, 1999, BBC Online, http://news.bbc.co.uk/hi/english/world/middle_east/newsid_459000/459460.stm.

20. Imam, *'Abd al-Nasir wa al-Ikhwan al-Muslimun*, 185.

21. Kepel, *Muslim Extremism*, 37, 74.

22. Ibid., 77.

23. Ibid., 192.

24. Ibid., 223–25.

25. Jürgen Habermas, *The Theory of Communicative Action* (Boston: Beacon Press, 1984).

26. Kepel, *Muslim Extremism*, 231.

27. Steven M. Wasserstrom, *Religion after Religion: Gershom Scholem, Mircea Eliade, and Henry Corbin at Eranos* (Princeton, NJ: Princeton University Press, 1999).

28. Kepel, *Muslim Extremism*, 235.

29. Ibid., 240.

30. Michel Foucault, *The Archeology of Knowledge* (New York: Harper and Row, 1972).

31. Martin E. Marty and R. Scott Appleby, eds., Fundamentalism Project, 5 vols. (Chicago: University of Chicago Press, 1991–95).

32. Gilles Kepel, *Jihad: The Trail of Political Islam* (London: I. B. Tauris, 2002).

33. Nazih Ayubi, *Political Islam: Religion and Politics in the Arab World* (London: Routledge, 1991), 72–87.

34. Ibid., 86.

35. Denis Sullivan and Sana Abed-Kotob, *Islam in Contemporary Egypt: Civil Society vs. the State* (Boulder, CO: Lynne Rienner Publishers, 1999), 6.

36. Ibid., 52.

37. Ibid., 43.

38. Amaney Ahmad Jamal, "Democratic Citizens in Non-democratic Nations: Civic Participation and Associational Life in the West Bank" (PhD diss., University of Michigan, 2002).

39. Gabriel A. Almond, Emmanuel Sivan, and R. Scott Appleby, "Fundamentalism: Genus and Species," in Marty and Appleby, Fundamentalism Project, 5:399–424.

40. Nancy Ammerman, *Baptist Battles* (New Brunswick, NJ: Rutgers University Press, 1990), 128–29.

41. Ellis Goldberg, "Smashing Idols and the State: The Protestant Ethic and Egyptian Sunni Radicalism," in *Comparing Muslim Societies: Knowledge and the State in a World Civilization*, ed. Juan R. I. Cole (Ann Arbor: University of Michigan Press, 1993), 195–236.

42. Rodney Stark and William Sims Bainbridge, *The Future of Religion: Secularization, Revival, and Cult Formation* (Berkeley and Los Angeles: University of California Press, 1985), 19–24, 135; see also the same authors' *A Theory of Religion* (New Brunswick, NJ: Rutgers University Press, 1996).

10

Audiovisual Media and History
of the Arab Middle East

WALTER ARMBRUST

This essay examines two aspects of mass media in the Middle East. First is the relationship of writing to vision. Written texts were subject to a sensory reorganization, particularly as a manuscript culture predicated on oral techniques encountered the technology of printing. The shift to print was accompanied by changes in the way vision was socially deployed in communication. Walter Ong claims that writing "locks [words] into a visual field forever."[1] This is at best misleading in the context of Arabic textual practices, which involve listening in distinctive ways. But Ong's emphasis on "the technologizing of the word," is nonetheless useful. It provides a link between printed media and audiovisual media, which in the Arab Middle East were all adopted in a relatively compressed time frame.

Second, the essay examines literature on nonprint audiovisual media in the Arab Middle East in the context of how mass media have influenced music in Egypt. Like reading, music involves the senses and can therefore be related to a discussion of changes in textual practices. Music has always been in the mainstream of debates about cultural authenticity in the face of colonialism. It therefore serves well as a means of invoking issues of broad relevance to modern Middle Eastern history. Furthermore, music very clearly sits astride several technologically driven "culture industries," including the gramophone, radio, cinema, television (terrestrial and later satellite broadcasts), and mass-circulation print media. It is therefore a focal point at which the sensory practices discussed in the first part of this essay can be seen in the context of more general processes involving mass media.

I conclude by suggesting that mass media provide a crucial addition to histories of the modern Middle East that emphasize modernity as a product of colonial discipline and order. Modernity does compel certain behaviors through institutions and discourse and makes others difficult to countenance. But modernity is a product of the carrot as much as of the stick. The history of audiovisual practices provides an effective means of analyzing how agency was constructed within, or in some cases, against, the constraints imposed by disciplinary regimes.

VISUAL CULTURE

Trajectories of Western domination inform the literature relevant to visual culture in Middle Eastern studies. This concern is linked to the issue of "visualism" in Western approaches to knowledge. "Visualism" can be defined as "the reduction of all experience to the representational means available to only one sensory medium, that of sight."[2] Some argue that this is an attribute of modern Western culture generally and of epistemology.[3] In the context of the Middle East, visualism is a focal point for criticism.[4] Contestation of the Orient as an object was broadly influenced by the French critique of European visualism and has given rise to an extensive scholarship on representational issues affecting the relationship of Europe to its own constructs of opposing cultures. A smaller literature addresses the consequences of the imposition or transference of European visualist modes to the Middle East itself.[5] However, it should be emphasized at the outset that one of the problems with the criticism of *visualism* in Middle East studies is that it does not adequately suggest a path to understanding *visual culture* in the Arab Middle East.

It should be said that attributing visualism to Europe does not imply that the Middle East was somehow deficient in visual culture. All human beings have the same array of senses, just as they are endowed universally with genders. To say that Arabs "lacked visual culture" would therefore be like saying that a matrilineal kinship system lacks men. The point, of course, is that matrilineal systems order gender relations differently from patrilineal systems, not that either of them lacks men or women. Hence, to say that Europe was visualist, while the Arab Middle East was audiocentrist, does not imply that Europeans did not hear, or that Arabs did not see. Communication involving texts clearly privileges vision or hearing (as opposed to smell, taste, or touch) in various forms. What is at issue here is therefore an aspect of the social organization of both sight and hearing.

Middle Eastern visual culture consists, unsurprisingly, of long-standing practices such as architecture, painting, illustration, and decoration. These are tangential to my essay insofar as its primary purpose is expressive rather than communicative. Of course expressive and communicative cultures by necessity draw on a common repertory of practices. Nonetheless, fields such as architecture, painting, and calligraphy are well beyond my brief. Such issues are best addressed by specialists.

Caricature bridges art and media and has received some scholarly attention.[6] Much remains to be done in relating caricatures to the ways that consumers read them and the logic used by producers to relate the various elements of magazines to each other. Photography likewise bridges artistic expression and communicative practices. There is no adequate analysis of how photography was used in mass media or of the "social life of the photograph" as has been done for other regions.[7] It was not until the 1920s that substantial audiences had access to illustrated magazines at affordable prices.[8] The juxtaposition of text and image in Middle Eastern literature was not novel, but had appeared previously mainly as illustrations of scientific works or literature, much of which was meant to be read aloud.[9] By contrast, in the post-World War I illustrated magazines the link to writing was more complex. They were meant to be read visually; the beer ad was meant to be seen next to the story about movie stars, and the automobile ad next to the caricature about greedy bourgeois wives, all of it abutting the article about the prime minister's views on the Sudan. Consequently, illustrated magazines were an element in shaping cultural practices of consumption. The total object could be "correctly" consumed only by an individual reading silently. The gap between that kind of reading and precolonial textual practices could easily be as great as that between copying a manuscript through oral transcription and watching a film. How people read was as important as what they read.

WRITING AND READING

The transposition of sound to vision defines the technological divide between oral and literate cultures.[10] But cultures organize the relationship of writing to vision, hearing, and speaking differently. In precolonial Arab literary practice authoritative texts were transmitted orally, which is to say that texts were ideally embedded in a social relationship between reciter and listener.[11] By contrast, modern Arab (and Western) societies tilt toward writing as an individual activity and reading as a silent visual practice. Silent reading facilitates individual access to texts. It developed from a perceived need to retrieve complex information quickly and to train large numbers of people to do this from an early age.[12] The specific social conditions shaping demand for such techniques were found in Europe before the colonial era. The transferal of the techniques for silent reading to the Middle East occurred in the context of European domination of the region.

In Europe the printing press added momentum to the practice of silent reading,[13] which required both mass-produced texts and a repertory of techniques that predated the printing press.[14] The printing press has been described as an element of European visualist order imposed on the Arab Middle East and predicated on gridlike spatialized plans expressed in forms as diverse as city planning or bureaucratic texts.[15] Though known in the Ottoman Empire from the early eighteenth century, it was not used in Egypt until the 1820s.[16] Egypt and Lebanon were relatively quick to adopt the new technology, but it was still not until the 1870s that government control of printing was relaxed.[17] A "multiplier effect"—the literate reading to the illiterate[18]—augmented small print runs. Obviously a multiplier effect assumes audition rather than silent reading. Nonetheless silent reading was adopted. A visual layout that virtually required visual apprehension of magazines was clearly marketable by the 1920s. We know little about the mechanisms that enabled the growth of more visual styles of reading or about the relationship between silent visual reading and the growing use of the printing press.

Certain textual conventions facilitate silent reading. These include word separation,[19] a book trade autonomous from religious institutions, vernacularization, organization of texts through punctuation and indexing, and the creation of cursive scripts that facilitated rapid copying.[20] In some cases these techniques were specific to Europe. Other related developments, such as the rise of humanism, were linked to Europe's relations with the Middle East.[21] And some techniques integral to silent reading in Europe, such as cursive scripts, were used in the Middle East long before the modern period of European domination.[22] On the other hand, vernacularization—crucial in Europe for facilitating the spread of literacy—was a nonstarter in the Arab world. The crucial point is that while there may be historical reasons for developing practices like silent reading, the process of doing so is unpredictable. Some of the techniques cobbled together to produce silent reading in Europe were used in the Middle East, but it does not follow that silent reading develops the same way everywhere. Arab literary culture prior to extensive European domination emphasized face-to-face audition of authoritative texts. The fact that oral rather than visualist textual conventions dominated Arab literary culture had more to do with the primacy accorded to the concept of direct revelation, and its reiteration in authoritative textual production through persons, than it did with a technical capacity for silent reading inherent in Arabic graphic conventions.

Add to this the impact of the printing press. In Europe the relatively long development of silent reading suggests that the use of the printing press spread quickly because its invention was buttressed by a preexisting trajectory in writing and reading practices. The effect of the printing press in the Arab world needs to be looked at in comparison to this process.[23] If printing was an industrial partner of visualist reading practices that (in Europe) developed over centuries, it might then be reasonable to speak of a relatively rapid adoption of the press in the Middle East. Starting from the late nineteenth century, it took only a generation or two for it to become firmly established, and Arab reluctance to adopt new technology might not have been the most crucial factor inhibiting the spread of the new medium.

AUDIOVISUAL MEDIA: THE CASE OF MUSIC

Printed texts came to the Arab world almost simultaneously with proficient means of publishing images. Audiovisual technology also flooded the region rapidly, beginning in the early twentieth century. The near-simultaneous introduction of multiple forms of media introduces an added note of caution to any assumptions one might be inclined to make about the printed word being a natural extension of a preexisting manuscript culture. The entire field of communication changed rapidly, and changes in the written word were bound up in the introduction of audiovisual technologies.

The new technologies included the gramophone (from the turn of the century), radio broadcasting (from the 1920s in Egypt on an unregulated basis, and from 1934 as an organized national service), the cinema (silent films from the mid-1920s, talkies from 1932), television (from 1960), "small" media (audio- and videocassettes from the mid-1970s), and global media (satellite broadcasting from the early 1990s). These new technologies were both ear- and eye-centered, though the long-term trend has been toward the dominance of vision.

I briefly survey the impact of audiovisual media in the context of its effects on music in Egypt. Music provides a common touchstone for all media. It obviously involves audition, traditionally in ways distinct from textual audition; but as individual-oriented silent reading proliferated—reading tied to pleasure rather than to education in the strict sense—the line between musical and textual practices became blurred. Although academic literature on

music has little difficulty relating itself to mass media,[24] in general literature on contemporary mass media focuses much more on politics (particularly civil society) and religion (Islam in transnational context) than does
the historical literature.[25] "New media" (satellite television, and the Internet in particular) inspire a great deal of the contemporary literature. Older
"new media" (radio, cinema, and terrestrial television broadcasting) remain
understudied. Music is the preeminent instance of this kind of media production. Indeed, it would be misleading to consider the impact of mass media
on Egyptian music without contemplating the reverse. The only modern
medium that did *not* involve music at the outset was print, but even in this
medium the influence of popular music began to assert itself early on. This
is because music, particularly in modern Egypt, was a prominent part of
the economics and aesthetics of all the audio and audiovisual media. In the
print medium the pleasure of reading was often enhanced by news about
performers made famous through audiovisual media.

From the 1920s through the 1950s, many publications featured extensive
news of theatrical and musical performers, and these were among the best
sellers. For example, in 1947 *al-Ithnayn*, a lavishly illustrated variety magazine with a heavy emphasis on show business, was estimated by the British
Foreign Office to have a weekly circulation of 120,000.[26] According to the
available circulation figures compiled by Ami Ayalon, this was much higher
than any of the magazine's rivals. Although the popularity of *al-Ithnayn* cannot be attributed solely to its emphasis on popular arts—with musicians
always prominent—there is no doubt that Egyptian illustrated magazines
from the 1920s to the present have always sought to sell themselves through
association with musical personalities.

Music became an attractive element of a great deal of media production.
In societies still plagued by high rates of illiteracy at the end of the twentieth century, music demands little on the part of listeners but pulls them
into a cultural domain that they can share with more educated members of
society. Furthermore, music crosses multiple media domains. Through the
gramophone music reached mass audiences before other audiovisually mediated content; radio brought music into homes and cafes; early filmmakers
capitalized on preexisting audiences by casting famous singers in their films.

The Phonograph

Commercial catalogs of Egyptian music date from 1904, and the dominance
of records lasted until the early 1930s, when the introduction of radio and

film lessened their importance.[27] Although written information on the character of the prerecording-era Egyptian music is fragmentary, and recordings of noncommercial music essentially nonexistent, it is possible to surmise dramatic changes in musical practice deriving from recording.[28] To begin with, the phonograph removed musical performance from live audiences and, therefore, from the "ecstatic feedback" between audience and performer on which Arab musical aesthetic was based.[29] Written and oral sources, however, indicate that the live-performance repertoires of recording artists were shaped by the popularity of gramophone recordings.[30]

Recordings were fragmented as a result of the technical limitations of recording technology. Wax cylinders and ten-inch disks used before World War I imposed a limit of two to three minutes on a recording. This was quite a severe limitation in a musical culture that emphasized lengthy improvisation. Many genres simply could not be represented in the recorded archive other than in truncated or serial (over several records) form. Technical limitations on the length of recorded music became less severe by the mid-1920s, but the general tendency of audiences to have preconceived ideas about a given song based on a recording remained, as did the tendency of performers to gear live repertoires to recorded performance. By the end of the phonograph era musicians specialized in popular genres such as the *taqtuqa* and the *qasida*, tailored to recording and appreciated by audiences in their own right.[31] Records were produced by many companies, but the market was dominated by three main competitors: the Gramophone Company, Odeon, and Baidaphon (based in England, Germany, and the Middle East, respectively). The buying public consisted initially of the wealthy and public venues such as cafes. By the end of the phonograph era records were increasingly accessible to a broad middle class.

Radio

Perhaps the most dramatic effect of early recorded music was its capacity to create musical celebrities on a much wider scale than was possible by means of live performance. This capacity was greatly expanded in the 1930s with the introduction of radio and then cinema. Radio broadcasting was the most important musical medium between the end of the phonograph era (the early 1930s) and the introduction in the 1970s of more portable means of playing back recorded music.[32] The introduction of radio was marked by a widespread winnowing-out process in which some stars of the old medium proved more skillful at adapting to new media than others. Many performers had achieved wide fame among nonspecialist, nonelite audiences through the phonograph. These included such figures as 'Abd al-Hayy Hilmi, Shaykh Salama Hijazi, and Munira al-Mahdiyya. Al-Mahdiyya was famously eclipsed by both Muhammad 'Abd al-Wahhab and by Umm Kulthum.[33] Their rivalry was depicted in a 1999 historical serial titled *Umm Kulthum*, broadcast during Ramadan. 'Abd al-Wahhab and Umm Kulthum, two early phonograph celebrities, were notable for their skill in amplifying their fame through new media innovations. Dominant male and female performers, their mastery of media made them the prominent musical figures of twentieth-century Egypt and the Arabic-speaking Middle East.[34]

Radio broadcasting in Egypt began in the 1920s on an unregulated basis. After a tentative beginning due to a dearth of radio receivers in the country, radio was brought under government control and began broadcasting in 1934.[35] The Egyptian State Broadcasting (ESB) service was administered by the Ministry of Communication. The Egyptian government had signed a contract with the Marconi Company of the United Kingdom. The system was financed through license fees on receivers, which rapidly became more accessible in price as the decade wore on. The contract was maintained with Marconi until 1947, when Egypt cancelled the agreement, probably due to increasing conflict with British policy.[36] In the 1950s, after the Free Officers took power and definitively ended direct colonial presence in Egypt, the range of Egyptian radio broadcasting was greatly expanded, and its regional broadcasts reached the entire Middle East, parts of Africa, Europe, Asia, and even North America on a limited basis. By the 1970s Egypt was the sixth largest international broadcaster in terms of weekly program output.[37]

The ESB started out with two main programs, one in foreign languages and the other in Arabic. In the 1930s and 1940s the program was not oriented to politics, and as a consequence a great deal of airtime was devoted to music.[38] Programming reflected the tastes of Mustafa Rida, the director of the Arabic Music Institute, who held the title "Arabic Music Consultant" at the ESB, and Midhat Asim, the director of ESB's Arabic Music Section. Rida was considered a conservative defender of musical *turath* (tradition) in comparison to Asim, who was trained in both Arabic and Western music. As Salwa Aziz El-Shawan describes it, the goals of the ESB were to improve the quality of song texts, to encourage composers who incorporated Western musical elements into Arabic music, and to "improve" the musical taste of audiences by exposing them to a variety of styles.[39]

Initiatives to "improve the masses" lend themselves to nationalist agendas everywhere, and the Middle East is no exception. But while states sought openly to define canons of taste within which to situate varieties of musical performance, it goes without saying that the process of promoting or demoting styles of music could be controversial, and resisted or misinterpreted. Therefore, to characterize Rida as "conservative" and Asim as "modernist" is not to say that Rida was a champion of what Americans would call "classical music" (a category that evokes "tradition" but is itself a synthetic and continuously shifting construct) and Asim an advocate of either fashion-conscious popular music or an elitist avant garde. All the major figures writing about modern Egyptian music emphasize the dangers of imposing Western musical categories on Middle Eastern music.[40] At the same time, one should not underestimate the persistence of a modernist discourse that inevitably sought to order expressive culture into hierarchies of artistic value. The existence of a musical canon is a highly contentious issue, but the lack of consensus among academics over what a canon would be, or whether identifying one is even a meaningful exercise, should not cause one to lose sight of the fact that Egyptian nationalists have long seen culture as a means for carrying out their agenda. The hierarchies themselves need not be taken at face value, but understanding the process of creating them can be very productive analytically. Martin Stokes's writing on "Arabesk" music in Turkey is one of the best analyses of how nationalism constructs artistic canons.[41] In a quite different medium Sibel Bozdogan examines "a nationalist view based on a double negation" of both the Ottoman past and the Western-dominated present.[42] A similar dynamic can be seen in the Arab world.[43]

The ESB, with its official imprimatur, was an obvious venue for constructing national culture. Muhammad 'Abd al-Wahhab and Umm Kulthum, who had already established their reputations through recording and film, solidified their positions as dominant figures in the national arena through radio. Both performers had signed contracts with the ESB very soon after the service began in 1934.[44] For all performers, radio offered enormous advantages over recording technology. The length of songs was no longer circumscribed by recording technology. Live concerts could be broadcast, which enabled performers to reconnect with audiences. Umm Kulthum, for example, did not like studio performances because she felt she needed live feedback from an audience. By 1937, radio made this possible.[45] 'Abd al-Wahhab, by contrast, had less affinity for live performance. By the 1940s he found radio to be the perfect venue for long, heavily orchestrated compositions, devoid of improvisation, and usually based on texts written in classical Arabic. These "grand songs"[46] were the perfect vehicle for accomplishing the formal objectives of the ESB, which were broadly formulated around the notion of constructing a high national culture. 'Abd al-Wahhab and Umm Kulthum were given pride of place in the ESB program. Asim treated them equally, dividing the Thursday evening program between them. Umm Kulthum's performance career lasted longer than 'Abd al-Wahhab's, and eventually Thursday evening became indelibly associated with her highly anticipated performances.[47]

Between 1934 and the 1970s music broadcast on radio reached the largest number of listeners of any medium, with the minimum technical constraints on performance. Radio was, of course, an entirely government-controlled medium, which undoubtedly meant that access was restricted to certain performers and certain styles of music. This is not to say that radio music was either overtly propagandist or frozen into a sort of state-approved conservatism. Indeed, it would be entirely reasonable to argue that the 1930s through the end of the 1960s were an exceptionally creative period of artistic ferment in the field of music. Needless to say, radio broadcasts have continued; however, the post-1960s media ecology was significantly reshaped by the introduction of portable media, specifically the cassette player, which decisively compromised the ability of the state to control access by performers to very wide musical markets. It must be emphasized, though, that from the 1930s until the 1970s the creative ferment of musical culture was heavily influenced by another important medium, namely, film. In these decades, sound became increasingly linked to image, and image began to assert primacy.

Musical Films

Egypt began producing films in the 1920s. Around a dozen silent films were produced before the first talkie, Muhammad Karim's melodrama *Sons of Aristocrats* (Awlad al-dhawat) in 1932. The first musical, *Song of the Heart* (Unshudat al-fu'ad) followed immediately, in 1932. It was directed by Mario Volpi, an Italian, and starred a singer named Nadira. Because Volpi was Italian, credit for the first Egyptian musical is often given to Muhammad Karim, who directed *The White Rose* (Al-Warda al-bayda) toward the end of 1933. This film starred 'Abd al-Wahhab, who by that time had become part owner of the Baidaphon record company.[48] Clearly, musical stars were cast in Egyptian films because they facilitated box-office success.[49] It is also true that singers' salaries commanded a very large share of film budgets. Jacob Landau reported that Umm Kulthum received up to £E 18,000 to appear in films, and 'Abd al-Wahhab possibly more; the female singer Asmahan made £E 10,000 per film, and Layla Murad earned £E 10,000–£E 12,000 per film.[50] Budgets for films at this time (from the 1940s to the mid-1950s) ranged from £E 25,000 to £E 50,000.[51] Non-singing actors inevitably made less than those who could sing. By the late 1950s, well after Umm Kulthum and 'Abd al-Wahhab had retired from cinema, a calculation of film-star earnings on a per-hour basis put singer/composer Farid al-Atrash at the top, at £E 100 per hour, followed by singers Layla Murad (£E 50 per hour) and 'Abd al-Halim Hafiz (£E 41 per hour).[52] The highest-paid non-singing star in this calculation was Fatin Hamama, who averaged £E 41 per hour.

Content from one medium often formed the basis of markets for products in newer media. For many in the United States or Europe this is a familiar dynamic: television first threatened and then amplified the film business; LPs gave way to compact disks and then to additional digital formats. But understanding the effects of such a cultural/economic/technological nexus should also be a goal of modern Middle Eastern history. In the case at hand, it is important that 'Abd al-Wahhab, a megastar in the recording medium whose persona as a performer was increasingly tied to images elaborated in print media, starred in and financed his first film in 1933. At roughly the same time plans were being laid for the creation of a more extensive and independent filmmaking infrastructure. Studio Misr (Egypt Studio) was part of financier Muhammad Tal'at Harb's empire. Harb's enterprises included banking, textiles, and large infrastructure projects. The film studio was a prestige project and probably not highly profitable.[53] But many regard Studio Misr as a quasi-national institution, despite its status as a private company.[54] Studio Misr's initial purpose was to document the activities of Harb's commercial ventures. Its first full-length fiction film—and the public unveiling of its ability to make films entirely on Egyptian soil, unlike earlier films that had depended heavily on European facilities—was *Widad*, a historical romance starring Umm Kulthum made in 1936.

All of 'Abd al-Wahhab's and Umm Kulthum's films (seven and six, respectively) were well received, but by the time the film era began both stars were well advanced in their careers and, more importantly, were already famous by other mass-mediated means. By 1947 they had both ended their acting careers, except for two cameo appearances made by 'Abd al-Wahhab, one in the late 1940s and another in the early 1960s. Both remained influential for several more decades through radio, composing for others (in the case of 'Abd al-Wahhab) and giving live performances (particularly by Umm Kulthum) that were broadcast on both radio and television. In many ways the careers of 'Abd al-Wahhab and Umm Kulthum were typical in that they both became prominent through a variety of channels, including film, recording, and broadcasts of live concerts. But between the 1930s and the end of the 1960s musical film occupied a special place in the arsenal of media outlets available to performers. Some singers became particularly adept at acting and ultimately established unique screen personalities that were less dependent on other media. Film images were intrinsic to the public personae of younger singers such as Layla Murad, Farid al-Atrash, Muhammad Fawzi, Huda Sultan, and 'Abd al-Halim Hafiz.[55] During the 1940s and 1950s popular illustrated magazines such as *al-Ithnayn* and *al-Kawakib* publicized the lives of these younger performers as an extension of their film roles, whereas 'Abd al-Wahhab and Umm Kulthum by this time were often publicized as singers or, more accurately, as artists rather than film personalities.

Until the 1960s musical films were the private-sector counterpart to the state-owned radio service. The two catered to substantially overlapping audiences and featured many of the same performers. The cinema never reached as large an audience as radio, though. Indeed, for many, watching an Egyptian film might have been an exercise in discontinuity. According to Farid el-Mazzawi, by the 1960s Egyptian studios made only between ten and twenty prints of individual films (as opposed to eight hundred to one thousand prints of Hollywood films at the time).[56] The prints were shown less often in well-maintained first-run theaters than they were in cheaper, second-run theaters. Such theaters used outdated equipment that damaged the prints. A typical 35mm film was meant to be shown "for 25 weeks of projection at an average of 28 showings a week," but Egyptian film reels were screened far more than this.[57] The result was that the limited number of prints quickly deteriorated. Consequently, during the pre-television heyday of the musical, film narratives and film songs seen and heard in theaters must have often been experienced in fragments. Radio undoubtedly helped reconstruct songs that might have been victimized by bad prints or worn-out theater sound systems, but it was probably not until the advent of television that audiences were regularly able to experience film songs in the context of coherent narratives on a regular basis and under relatively favorable conditions. Egyptian television broadcasting began in 1960, and by 1969 there were almost half a million television sets in the country, a figure that has since more than doubled.[58] This means that by the end of the 1960s most Egyptians in cities and towns who wanted to watch television could do so, either at home or in a public place such as a cafe. Television has been broadcast in the Arab world for almost fifty years and is therefore undoubtedly becoming a legitimate focus of historical inquiry. But television is a frustrating object of historical study. Most academic literature on Arabic-language television is based on material broadcast during field research or available in commercial video release (a tiny portion of total television production).[59] The few exceptions are works that focus on aspects of broadcasting that demand little access to broadcast content.[60] But there is no question that for historical analysis, television and radio archives in Egypt or Lebanon, for example, would be a gold mine for research. In terms of audiences' experiences, the musical film—currently an object of nostalgia—is in some ways more often a product of television rebroadcasts than of the relative immediacy of theaters.

The movie-theater experience was also strongly gendered. In Egypt women typically feel less comfortable in public space than men; therefore it is unsurprising that movie-theater audiences are dominated by men. This has probably always been the case, though the actual proportion of men to women in a movie theater undoubtedly has varied historically by class (more expensive theaters typically accommodate greater mixing of genders) and perhaps by genre.[61]

In its entire history the Egyptian cinema has produced approximately three thousand feature-length fiction films. The most intense production of musicals took place from the mid-1940s to the early 1960s. Production of musicals began to decline in the 1960s, and by the end of the decade had practically ceased. Certain directors have attempted to revive the genre in recent years.[62] The prevalence of musicals in the Egyptian cinema is often casually exaggerated for the purpose of criticism, the point being that "too much" music was indicative of a general lack of seriousness on the part of filmmakers. Salah Ezzedine, for example, claimed that the casting of second-rank musicians in films was proof "that film producers' predilection for singing, dancing, etc. almost amounted to an obsession."[63] Ezzedine's statement is often reduced to a stereotype, namely, that "all Egyptian films are musicals." More accurate assessments suggest that during the heyday of the musical roughly a third of some 900 feature films produced were musicals. Galal al-Sharqawi identifies 38 out of 106 films (about 36 percent) made between 1939 and 1944 as musicals.[64] Viola Shafik mentions that from 1944 to 1946 50 percent of Egyptian film production consisted of musicals.[65] Ezzedine himself notes that the years from 1950 to 1955 represent "a period of superabundance" in the production of musicals.[66] However, any attempt to interpret the significance of musicals in the Egyptian cinema should note that the decade following World War II was also the most productive period for musicals in Hollywood. For example, as much as 30 percent of the films made by MGM during the period were musicals.[67] The question, then, should not be, Why was Egypt producing so many musicals? since the proportion of musicals produced in Egypt during the 1940s and 1950s was not drastically higher than in Hollywood, and when the musical began to decline in Hollywood, so too did it in Egypt. One might be tempted to redirect the question to focus on the presupposition of imitativeness rather than strictly on the sheer volume of musicals: Why do Egyptian films slavishly imitate Hollywood fashions? This criticism of derivativeness has always been leveled at Egyptian cinema, by both local critics and outsiders.[68] Musicals—particularly those made after 'Abd al-Wahhab and Umm Kulthum retired from the screen—are the prime culprits in this accusation. For example, in a 1996 referendum on the best 100 Egyptian films of all time, only about 10 percent were musicals.[69] But such criticism is highly misleading. For one thing, a nonspecialist referendum on memorable films might very well reverse the proportion of musicals to nonmusicals. This suggests that it is only in formal discourse that musicals are denigrated, while in the more culturally intimate spaces created by national culture musicals are highly valued.[70]

Furthermore, it is certainly true that many Egyptian films were adaptations of foreign genres, particularly the backstage musical but also vaudeville, French popular theater, and various forms of diegetic musicals (films in which music is part of the narrative). But if the form of these films was often adapted from foreign sources, the music itself always served to keep cinema locally meaningful. Meaning was not only a function of building on culturally rooted genres such as the *muwashshah, mawwal, qasida,* or *nashid,* all of which were represented in films. A wide variety of Western music ranging from contemporary jazz (or other forms of contemporary Western popular music), to orchestral classics was also always incorporated into Egyptian films, both as background music and in songs. Proliferation of Western music is sometimes viewed with alarm in discourses on authenticity, but there is every reason to believe that the most lasting impression of Egyptian musicals was precisely the Egyptian music. For example, anthropologist Katherine Zirbel describes an elderly informant who played in Western-style big bands during the colonial and early postcolonial periods. Film audiences had wide exposure to such music because it was often featured in films. Now Zirbel's informant feels sad nostalgia for "his" style of jazz because the only musical memories people have from the period are of Egyptian hits.[71] The cinema, together with other media, created a dialectical relation between styles of music, performers, and audiences. Pre-media forms of Arabic music would have been out of the mainstream of this dialectic as much as American popular music, but elements of both could be incorporated in the vigorously hybrid styles facilitated by the cinema.

It is, however, important to emphasize that the dialectics of mediated musical culture in this period (1930–70) were shaped by relatively centralized systems of dissemination. Both radio and the cinema were subject to cultural gatekeepers who employed different but complementary logics. In the case of radio, the public rationale behind programming choices was the improvement of taste; for the cinema it was marketability. But the two media drew substantially from the same pools of talent and catered to greatly overlapping audiences. The result was a unique blend of discrimination, responsiveness to audience tastes and incentive for innovation. This arrangement has changed greatly since the 1960s.

PORTABILITY, PIRACY, AND NEW MEDIA

By the early 1970s audiocassette technology began to be available to consumers all over the world.[72] In Egypt the effect of the new medium may not have been immediately apparent, because the late 1960s and early 1970s were a time of political and economic turmoil. In terms of media history, the introduction of the audiocassette was preceded first by widespread nationalization of print media (in the early 1960s), then by nationalization of the film industry (by 1964). The effect of nationalizing the film industry is controversial. Many feel that the mid-to-late-1960s public-sector cinema produced the best films in the history of Egyptian cinema, but such esteem is usually accorded from the perspective of the cultural gatekeeper. The most artistically successful films were often commercial failures. In terms of the thoroughly commercialized musical film, nationalization of the cinema undoubtedly hastened the end of the genre. There were a few largely unsuccessful attempts at making populist musicals during the public-sector period, but these also failed to resonate with audiences. Some of these films were strongly ideological, whereas others were nationalistic but refrained from direct engagement with ideology.[73] 'Abd al-Halim Hafiz's privately produced, and highly successful, Father Is up a Tree (Abi fawqa al-shajara) proved to be the swan song of the musical.[74] By the beginning of the 1970s the genre was moribund and ceased to be a significant factor in shaping public tastes in music. The cinema was reprivatized in 1970, at least to the extent that the state no longer directly financed film production (though it maintained ownership of the means of production), but very few musicals were made until a mini-revival of the genre in the 1990s.[75]

The radio service remained, and of course still remains, but the continual cross-fertilization between public-sector radio and commercial film music was a thing of the past. Television continually rebroadcasts musicals, as well as live concerts by approved performers (and, more recently, a somewhat less-tradition-bound selection of MTV-style music videos). But official approval became increasingly conservative, to the point that newer singers such as 'Ali al-Hajjar and Suzan Atiyya were sometimes perceived as imitating not Western style but the style of such giants of the musical film age as 'Abd al-Halim Hafiz and Umm Kulthum.[76]

The advent of affordable consumer audiocassette technology was highly significant because it provided a new commercial forum for music at a time when the state had gained substantial control over all other mass media. Aside from music, audiocassettes provide a general means of circumventing centralized media. The audiocassette medium has also been used in poetic discourse, political movements, and in sermons.[77] Like the radio, the audiocassette projected music into everyday settings that would never have been musical contexts in pre-mass-media times. The home, the automobile, public transportation, leisure space, and the workplace had all become potential sites of music consumption, and with the introduction of the audiocassette, the consumer chose the content, musical or otherwise. Commercial audiocassettes very nearly eliminated any form of cultural gatekeeper. Cassettes are easier and less expensive to produce than records, let alone musical films, and far more portable. Cassette tape piracy further shook the economics of musical production and consumption. Records cannot be easily pirated, and of course films must be watched either in a theater or on a television screen. But by the end of the 1970s almost anyone could have a cassette tape copied for very little money.

One effect of the new technology was that it became increasingly difficult for any singer to dominate the market. When radio and the cinema were the primary outlets for music, from the 1930s through the 1960s, the social capital earned from the culturally discriminating ESB could be converted to financial capital through commercial cinema. Both were relatively centralized forms of media, the radio because it was controlled by the state and the cinema because of the substantial capital required to make films.

The greatest fame could be achieved by those who had a foot in both worlds. By the 1970s there was less cross-fertilization between state-controlled and commercial media. State media was, in any case, somewhat discredited by adverse economic and political developments from the mid-1960s to the 1980s, including disastrous wars (abject defeat against Israel in 1967 followed by the destructive, although partially redemptive, October War of 1973), harsh repression of both leftists and political Islamists, and jarring economic dislocations caused by a transition from state capitalism under Gamal Abdel Nasser, to limited free markets under Anwar el-Sādāt. As a result, national institutions, an unambiguous point of pride in colonial or early postcolonial days, came to be viewed with a degree of skepticism. Conditions were ripe for audiences to tune out the radio, and for those who were so inclined cassette technology provided the means to do so.

The range of music available in the cassette medium is wide compared to what is available on radio. Old favorites by Farid al-Atrash, Asmahan, Layla Murad, and Muhammad Fawzi occupy shelf space next to newer singers who became known to their publics by means of the audiocassette. These include performers such as Hamdi Batshan, Sha'ban 'Abd al-Rahim, 'Ali Hamida, Muhammad al-Hilu, Muhammad Munir, Sahar Hamdi, Ihab Tawfiq, and Ahmad 'Adawiyya.[78] These singers come from diverse backgrounds, ranging from the relatively cerebral Muhammad Munir (whose Nubian roots and associations with European performers give him cachet in World Music circuits, as has his acting and singing in films by the celebrated director Yusuf Shahin), to the unprepossessing Sha'ban 'Abd al-Rahim (a makwagi—launderer—who has become a successful, if sometimes controversial, singer known for his commentary on social and political issues). Ahmad 'Adawiyya, a popular singer who generally eschews conventional vocal artistry, was perhaps the king of the audiocassette during its heyday.[79] Although exact sales figures are scarce and unreliable, during the 1980s he probably outsold all other contemporary singers, and he did this without recourse to the centralized mass media of earlier decades. Although there has been a diversity of musical styles in post-1970 Egyptian music, discussion of 'Adawiyya is paradigmatic of the larger discourse on music in the period. His merits (and faults) are framed by a discourse on taste. 'Adawiyya is often the target of disapproval, derided as the singer of uncouth microbus drivers, the preferred flavor of Gulf Arabs (who are often denigrated in Egypt for their alleged vulgarity), and the hero of errant youth who have not learned to appreciate the artistry of "authentic" Arab music. It has often been noted that many people who express disapproval of 'Adawiyya do so in the context of formal public discourse, while in less formal situations they may actually enjoy his music.[80]

But in the larger scheme of things the importance of 'Adawiyya is not that he stands at the head of his generation. Others, such as Muhammad Munir or, more recently, the Iraqi singer Kadhim al-Sahir, who has become popular in Egypt, have been treated more kindly by critics and are largely immune from the sort of scathing commentary leveled at 'Adawiyya. But as possibly the most commercially successful singer of the audiocassette age, 'Adawiyya encapsulates the significance of a transformation in the media ecology. The audiocassette has given the consumer greater choice; the cultural gatekeeper is absent, and therefore people have greater freedom to listen to whatever they deem pleasurable. Such choices have political implications, even when the music itself is largely free of direct political commentary.

The reverse side of the audiocassette coin is that in some ways, musicians have less choice in what they produce, because anything they sell will be pirated. Piracy lessens the economic incentive to produce finely honed performances for the audiocassette market. So if 'Adawiyya became emblematic of an age in which there were "no more giants" of the caliber of Umm Kulthum or 'Abd al-Halim Hafiz, it was also true that very few of these younger musicians had the luxury of producing the kind of intricate, highly rehearsed and brilliantly polished performances of earlier generations, even if they wanted to do so.[81] Today, a very large proportion of the music available in the Egyptian cassette market features vocalists backed not by live ensembles but by a synthesizer. The liberal use of synthesizers is a sore point for musical purists, but for most musicians the use of synthesizers in the studio is simply an economic necessity. Of course, the synthesizer can be adapted to Arabic music, just as Western instruments were incorporated into the *takht*. But the use of the synthesizer is undoubtedly a fault line for discussions of authenticity in Arabic music.

Finally, it should be noted that the dominance of the audiocassette in commercial music may soon be a thing of the past. Compact discs are making inroads in Egyptian and Arab markets, just as the technology to duplicate them is becoming widespread. Satellite television is of potentially greater importance. Popular performers such as Amr Diyab and Hakim have already begun to make a mark with MTV-style music videos, which are broadcast in Egypt on both terrestrial and satellite television. These are popular and less vulnerable to piracy than audiocassettes. The music, of course, can be copied, but because the videos are experienced by consumers with an intrinsic visual component, there may well be continual demand for the entire audiovisual package. Needless to say, videocassettes of music videos can also be copied, but the video player is a far more unwieldy device than the cassette player. Demand for music videos comes from terrestrial television (now broadcast in Egypt on at least nine channels, each of which needs at least some unique content) as well as satellite television, but in all likelihood it is the satellite companies that are driving the demand. Satellite broadcasts to the Arab world began in the early 1990s, and thus far most writing on satellite television has focused either on the business itself or on the political economy of the new medium.[82] There are now satellite broadcast companies owned or affiliated with Egypt, Saudi Arabia, Lebanon, Syria, Qatar, and the United Arab Emirates. None produces unambiguously commercial programs, which means that all are driven to some extent by the politics of their respective nation-states.[83] A satellite television operation is, however, an expensive undertaking, and therefore even state-run companies have an interest in making satellite television pay for itself. Thus far none has been able to do so. Attractive content is therefore a necessity for satellite television, and music videos financed by cassette and CD producers and mobile phone companies clearly have the potential to attract paying customers. From the musicians' point of view, satellite broadcasting creates the possibility of recapturing a more centralized and lucrative media market than had been feasible during the decentralized era of audiocassette dominance. Furthermore, satellite broadcasts are Pan-Arab. The scope of Egyptian media has always reached beyond Egypt's national borders, but the satellite age promises to be quite different—not an export market, but a transnational market. Whereas Egypt enjoyed a near monopoly of media production in certain fields (particularly the cinema), the playing field of satellite television promises to be far more level, or possibly tilted in favor of Gulf-owned stations.

CONCLUSION: HISTORIES OF PLEASURE

This is obviously not a historiographical essay in the sense that it traces conceptual debates within the field. However, if there is a historiographical aspect to the issues discussed here, it is in relation to a persistent disregard for culture within all Middle Eastern history. In this case I have focused mainly on cultural constructions of pleasure; it is pleasure that forms a common thread linking all the issues raised in the essay. Pleasure deserves to be taken seriously as a general category that ties the analysis of mass media to a number of issues including sensory practices; histories of reading, books, and textual production; and consumption and expressive culture. By leaving it out of Middle Eastern history we fundamentally fail to understand how the Middle East became modern.

On the whole, the best-elaborated analytical approach to modernity in the modern Middle East—in history and in other fields concerned with culture—focuses not on pleasure but on discipline, which forms another broad analytical category. We derive such analysis mainly from Michel Foucault, who was brought into Middle East studies largely through Edward Said's criticism of Orientalism.[84] Discipline constrains. It discursively shapes the lives of individuals, and it diffuses power through the operation of small processes that can rarely be seen strictly as the expression of ideology. There is no question that discipline-centered analyses have been productive. It is hard to imagine a literature on constructions of gender in the Middle East, for example, that rejects using "discourse" as a key category, and the primary attribute of such a technical use of the term *discourse* is constraint. Writing on institutions, concepts of the body, and of course representations would similarly be hard to imagine without a concept of discipline. Indeed, commonly made invocations of "social construction" often imply instilling disciplined practices or habits.

The problem with cultural histories predicated on understanding constraint is that the only logical alternative to structured constraint is "resistance." And yet, resistance is hard to conceptualize in a theoretical stance that discounts both ideology and individual subjectivity. In Middle Eastern studies the preponderance of discipline-centered work better explains systems of social compulsion than does subversion, resistance, or simply the capacity of individuals to effect change.

As an analytical category, pleasure has the advantage of providing a focal point for agency. In Middle East studies the high profile of Said's book perhaps gave greater impetus to a disciplinary orientation rather than to approaches that emphasized agency. In anthropology practice, resistance, and performance were some of the labels used to invoke the centrality of individual social actors.[85] There is, however, no intrinsic distinction between cultural anthropology and cultural history. The former typically relies more on live informants, the latter on textual sources, but by no means to mutual exclusion. Both require careful contextualization of diverse and complex cultural phenomena. The two categories in question—pleasure and discipline—are complementary processes in which modernity was simultaneously imposed on the Middle East and embraced by Middle Easterners. I have tried to focus here more on the embrace than on the imposition.

The history of audiovisual media in the Middle East can be approached through an ethnography of the senses. Manuscript culture was tied to audition. The print medium was important not just as a means for creating "imagined communities" but also as a harbinger of new communicative practices oriented to sight—to the silently read word and associated imagery. Subsequent accretions of new media invited greater involvement in visual cul-

ture. This was true even of music. By the end of the twentieth century the
dominant musical performers were virtually inseparable from their images.
Umm Kulthum and ʿAdawiyya occupy radically different positions in hierarchies of taste, but one can scarcely think of them without invoking their
images, even though their legacy is nominally sonic. This is perhaps unsurprising in a media ecology characterized by the interpenetration of fan magazines, recordings, video, and film.

Clearly, audiovisual culture, including the more individualized practice
of visual reading that came with printed texts, draws people into a pleasurable new world of consumption. Consumption can be a creative activity or a product of structured desires. The line between the two is not as
clear as we might have once assumed, and therein lies the productive ambiguity at the heart of audiovisual culture.

NOTES

1. Walter Ong, *Orality and Literacy: The Technologizing of the Word* (New York:
Routledge, 1982), 12.

2. Michael Herzfeld, *Anthropology: Theoretical Practice in Culture and Society*
(Oxford: Blackwell, 2001), 35.

3. Chris Jenks, "The Centrality of the Eye in Western Culture," in *Visual Culture*, ed. Chris Jenks (New York: Routledge 1995), 1–25, 3.

4. Edward Said, *Orientalism* (New York: Vintage Books, 1978).

5. Timothy Mitchell, *Colonising Egypt* (Cambridge: Cambridge University Press,
1988), 35; Brinkley Messick, *The Calligraphic State* (Berkeley and Los Angeles: University of California Press, 1993).

6. Beth Baron, "Nationalist Iconography: Egypt as a Woman," in *Rethinking
Nationalism in the Arab Middle East*, ed. Israel Gershoni and James Jankowski (New
York: Columbia University Press, 1997), 105–24; Allen Douglas and Fedwa Malti-
Douglas, *Arab Comic Strips: Politics of an Emerging Mass Culture* (Bloomington: Indiana University Press, 1994); Mohamed-Salah Omri, "Gulf Laughter Break": Cartoons
in Tunisia during the Gulf Conflict," in *Political Cartoons: Cultural Representation
in the Middle East*, ed. Fatma Müge Göçek (Princeton, NJ: Markus Weiner Publishers,
1998), 33–55; Sherifa Zuhur and Tonia Rifaey, "Visualizing Identity: Gender and
Nation in Egyptian Cartoons," in *Colors of Enchantment: Theater, Dance, Music, and
the Visual Arts of the Middle East*, ed. Sherifa Zuhur (Cairo: American University in
Cairo Press, 2001), 386–404.

7. Christopher Pinney, *Camera Indica: The Social Life of Indian Photographs* (London: Reaktion Books, 1997).

8. Ami Ayalon, *The Press in the Arab Middle East: A History* (Oxford: Oxford University Press, 1995), 148–51.

9. Robert Hillenbrand, "Literature and the Visual Arts," in *Encyclopedia of Arabic Literature*, ed. Julie Scott Meisami and Paul Starkey (New York: Routledge, 1998), 2:475–77.

10. Ong, *Orality and Literacy*, 12.

11. Messick, *The Calligraphic State*, 212; Kristina Nelson, *The Art of Reciting the Quran* (Austin: University of Texas Press, 2001), 3; Johannes Pedersen, *The Arabic Book* (Princeton, NJ: Princeton University Press, 1984), 20–36.

12. Paul Saenger, *Space between Words: The Origins of Silent Reading* (Stanford, CA: Stanford University Press, 1997), 11.

13. Elizabeth Eisenstein, *The Printing Press as an Agent of Change* (Cambridge: Cambridge University Press, 1993), 11, 129–36.

14. Paul Saenger, "Silent Reading: Its Impact on Late Medieval Script and Society," *Viator: Medieval Renaissance Studies* 13 (1982): 367–414. See also Saenger, *Space between Words*.

15. Mitchell, *Colonising Egypt*; Messick, *The Calligraphic State*, 231–50.

16. George Atiyeh, "The Book in the Modern Arab World: The Cases of Lebanon and Egypt," in *The Book in the Islamic World: The Written Word and Communication in the Middle East*, ed. George Atiyeh (Albany: State University of New York Press, 1995), 233–54, 234.

17. Juan Cole, *Colonialism and Revolution in the Middle East: Social and Cultural Origins of Egypt's ʿUrabi Movement* (Princeton, NJ: Princeton University Press, 1993), 123.

18. Ayalon, *The Press*, 154–59; Cole, *Colonialism and Revolution*, 123.

19. Saenger, *Space between Words*, 9–11.

20. Saenger, "Silent Reading."

21. George Makdisi, *The Rise of Humanism in Classical Islam and the Christian West: With Special Reference to Scholasticism* (Edinburgh: Edinburgh University Press, 1990).

22. Saenger, *Space between Words*, 257.

23. Guglielmo Cavallo and Roger Chartier eds., *A History of Reading in the West*, trans. Lydia G. Cochrane (Oxford: Polity Press, 1999); Roger Chartier, ed., *The Culture of Print: Power and the Uses of Print in Early Modern Europe*, trans. Lydia G. Cochrane (Cambridge: Polity Press, 1989); Saenger, *Space between Words*.

24. Marc Schade-Paulson, *Men and Popular Music in Algeria: The Social Significance of Raï* (Austin: University of Texas Press, 1999); Ted Swedenburg, "Saʾida Sultan/Danna International: Transgender Pop and the Polysemiotics of Sex, Nation, and Ethnicity on the Israeli-Egyptian Border," in *Mass Mediations: New Approaches*

to *Popular Culture in the Middle East and Beyond*, ed. Walter Armbrust (Berkeley and Los Angeles: University of California Press, 2000), 88–119; Katherine Zirbel, "Playing It Both Ways: Local Egyptian Performers between Regional Identity and International Markets," in Armbrust, *Mass Mediations*, 120–45.

25. Jon Anderson and Dale Eickelman, *New Media in the Muslim World: The Emerging Public Sphere*, 2nd ed. (Bloomington: Indiana University Press, 1999).

26. Ayalon, *The Press*, 150. See also Ahmad Husayn al-Tamawi, *Al-Hilal: Mi'at 'Am min al-Tahdith wa al-Tanwir, 1892–1992* (Cairo: Dar al-Hilal, 1992).

27. Ali Jihad Racy, "Musical Change and Commercial Recording in Egypt, 1904–1932" (PhD diss., University of Illinois at Urbana-Champaign, 1977).

28. Ibid., 5–9.

29. Ali Jihad Racy, "Creativity and Ambience: An Ecstatic Feedback Model from Arab Music," in *World of Music* 33, no. 3 (1991): 7–28.

30. Racy, "Musical Change," 8.

31. Ibid., 172.

32. Douglas Boyd, *Broadcasting in the Arab World: A Survey of the Electronic Media in the Middle East* (Ames: Iowa State University Press, 1999).

33. Walter Armbrust, *Mass Culture and Modernism in Egypt* (Cambridge: Cambridge University Press, 1996), 74; Virginia Danielson, *The Voice of Egypt: Umm Kulthum, Arabic Song, and Egyptian Society in the Twentieth Century* (Chicago: University of Chicago Press, 1997), 59–68.

34. Armbrust, *Mass Culture and Modernism*, 94–115; Nabil Salim Azzam, "Muhammad 'Abd al-Wahhab in Modern Egyptian Music" (PhD diss., University of California, Los Angeles, 1990); Danielson, *The Voice of Egypt*.

35. Boyd, *Broadcasting*, 16–17.

36. Ibid., 18.

37. Ibid., 30–31.

38. Salwa Aziz El-Shawan, "Al-Musika al-Arabiyyah: A Category of Urban Music in Cairo, Egypt, 1927–1977" (PhD diss., Columbia University, 1980), 111–12.

39. Ibid., 112–13.

40. See, e.g., Danielson *The Voice of Egypt*; Racy, "Musical Change"; El-Shawan, "Al-Musika al-Arabiyyah."

41. Martin Stokes, *The Arabesk Debate: Music and Musicians in Modern Turkey* (Oxford: Clarendon Press, 1992).

42. Sibel Bozdogan, *Modernism and Nation Building: Turkish Architectural Culture in the Early Republic* (Seattle: University of Washington Press, 2001), 240.

43. Armbrust, *Mass Culture and Modernism*; Christa Salamandra, "The Construction of Social Identity in Damascus" (DPh diss., University of Oxford, 2001); Jonathan Shannon, "Among the Jasmine Trees: Music, Modernity, and the Aesthetics

of Authenticity in Contemporary Syria" (PhD diss., City University of New York, 2001).

44. Danielson, *The Voice of Egypt*, 86.

45. Ibid.

46. Azzam, "Muhammad ʿAbd al-Wahhab," 192; see also Walter Armbrust, "Colonizing Popular Culture or Creating Modernity? Architectural Metaphors and Egyptian Media," in *Middle Eastern Cities, 1900–1950: Public Places and Public Spheres in Transition*, ed. Hans Christian Korsholm Nielsen and Jakob Skovgaard-Petersen (Aarhus: Aarhus University Press, 2001).

47. Danielson, *The Voice of Egypt*, 86–87.

48. Racy, "Musical Change," 113.

49. Viola Shafik, *Arab Cinema: History and Cultural Identity* (Cairo: American University in Cairo Press, 1998), 103–8.

50. Jacob Landau, *Studies in the Arab Theater and Cinema* (Philadelphia: University of Pennsylvania Press, 1958), 181.

51. Ibid.

52. Cited in Walter Armbrust, "The Golden Age before the Golden Age: Commercial Egyptian Cinema before the 1960s, in *Mass Mediations: New Approaches to Popular Culture in the Middle East and Beyond*, ed. Walter Armbrust (Berkeley and Los Angeles: University of California Press, 2000), 207.

53. Eric Davis, *Challenging Colonialism: Bank Misr and Egyptian Industrialization, 1920–1941* (Princeton, NJ: Princeton University Press, 1983), 206.

54. See, e.g., Munir Muhammad Ibrahim and Ahmad Yusuf, "Studyu Misr: Madrasat al-Sinima al-Misriyya," in *Misr, mi'at sana sinima*, ed. Ahmad Ra'fat Bahgat (Cairo: Mahrajan al-Qahira al-Sinima'i al-Dauli al-ʿIshrin, 1996), 158–66; Ahmad Yusuf, "Qira'a fi Istifta' Afdal Mi'at Film fi Tarikh al-Sinima al-Misriyya: Istifta' haula ʿAshq al-Sinima wa al-Watan," in Bahgat, *Misr, mi'at sana sinima*.

55. Joel Gordon, *Revolutionary Melodrama: Popular Film and Civic Identity in Nasser's Egypt* (Chicago: Middle East Documentation Center, 2002), 117–29; Sami Asmar and Kathleen Hood, "Modern Arab Music: Portraits of Enchantment from the Middle Generation," in *Colors of Enchantment: Theater, Dance, Music, and the Visual Arts of the Middle East*, ed. Sherifa Zuhur (Cairo: American University in Cairo Press, 2001), 297–320, 299–305; Walter Armbrust, "Manly Men on the National Stage (and the Women Who Make Them Stars)," in *Histories of the Modern Middle East: New Directions*, ed. Ursula Wokoeck, Hakan Erdem, and Israel Gershoni (Boulder, CO: Lynne Rienner Publishers, 2002), 247–78; Sherifa Zuhur, "Musical Stardom and Male Romance: Farid al-Atrash," in Zuhur, *Colors of Enchantment*, 270–96; Mahmud Qasim, *Al-Kumidiya wa-al-Ghina fi al-Film al-Misri* (Cairo: Wizarat al-Thaqafa, al-Markaz al-Qawmi lil-Sinima, 1999), *Milaffat al-Sinima*, 12–13.

56. Farid el-Mazzawi, "The U.A.R. Cinema and Its Relations with Television," in *The Cinema in the Arab Countries*, ed. Georges Sadoul (Beirut: Interarab Centre of Cinema and Television, 1966), 200–216.

57. Ibid., 210.

58. Boyd, *Broadcasting*, 51.

59. Lila Abu-Lughod, *Dramas of Nationhood: The Politics of Television in Egypt* (Chicago: University of Chicago Press, 2004); Armbrust, *Mass Culture and Modernism*, 11–36; Andreas Christmann, "Une piété inventée: Le Ramadan dans les mass media syriens," in *Ramadan et Politique*, ed. Fariba Adelkhah and François Georgeon (Paris: CNRS Éditions, 2000), 55–80; Martha Diase, "Egyptian Television Serials, Audiences, and the Family House: A Public Health Enter-Educate Serial" (PhD diss., University of Texas, Austin, 1996); Christa Salamandra, "Moustache Hairs Lost: Ramadan Television Serials and the Construction of Identity in Damascus, Syria," *Visual Anthropology* 10, nos. 2–4 (1998): 227–46; Elizabeth Seymour, "Imagining Modernity: Consuming Identities and Constructing the Ideal Nation on Egyptian Television" (PhD diss., State University of New York at Binghamton, 1999).

60. Boyd, *Broadcasting*; Naomi Sakr, *Satellite Realms: Transnational Television, Globalization and the Middle East* (London: I. B. Tauris, 2001).

61. Walter Armbrust, "When the Lights Go down in Cairo: Cinema as Secular Ritual," *Visual Anthropology* 10, nos. 2–4 (1998): 413–42.

62. Shafik, *Arab Cinema*, 106.

63. Salah Ezzedine, "The Role of Music in Arabic Films," in Sadoul, *The Cinema*, 48.

64. Galal al-Sharqawi, *Risala fi Tarikh al-Sinima al-ʿArabiyya* (Cairo: al-Maktabat al-ʿArabiyya, 1970), 98.

65. Shafik, *Arab Cinema*, 103.

66. Ezzedine, "Music in Arabic Films," 48.

67. Steven Cohan, "Feminizing the Song-and-Dance Man: Fred Astaire and the Spectacle of Masculinity in the Hollywood Musical," in *Screening the Male: Exploring Masculinities in Hollywood Cinema*, ed. Steven Cohan and Ina Rae Hark (New York: Routledge, 1993), 46–69, 61, 68 n. 11.

68. Samir Farid, "Surat al-Insan al-Misri ʿala al-Shasha: Bayna al-Aflam al-Istahlakiyya wa al-Aflam-al-Fanniyya," in *Al-Insan al-Misri ʿala al-Shasha*, ed. Hashim al-Nahhas (Cairo: GEBO, 1986), 205–14; Roy Armes, *Third World Film Making and the West* (Berkeley and Los Angeles: University of California Press, 1987), 196–203.

69. Bahgat, *Misr, miʾat sana sinima*; in particular, see Yusuf, "Qiraʾa fi Istiftaʾ Afdal Miʾat Film fi Tarikh al-Sinima al-Misriyya."

70. Roberta Dougherty, "Dance and the Dancer in Egyptian Film" (paper pre-

sented at the symposium "Dancing in the Rain: Indo-Egyptian Musical Film," organized by the Hagob Kevorkian Center for Middle East Studies at New York University, January 1999); Dougherty, "The Egyptian Musical Film: Diegesis Derailed?" (paper presented in the Mediterranean Program of the Robert Schuman Centre for Advanced Studies, Florence, Italy, March 2000).

71. Zirbel, "Playing It Both Ways," 164.

72. Peter Manuel, *Cassette Culture: Popular Music and Technology in North India* (Chicago: University of Chicago Press, 1993), 28.

73. See, e.g., Husayn Kamal, *Shay' min al-Khauf* (Cairo: al-Mu'assa al-Misriya al-'Amma lil-Sinima, 1969); 'Ali Rida, *Gharam fi al-Karnak* (Cairo: Sharikat al-Qahira lil-Intaj, 1967); Anthony Shay, *Choreographic Politics: State Folk Companies, Representation, and Power* (Hanover, NH: Wesleyan University Press, 2002); Gordon *Revolutionary Melodrama*.

74. Husayn Kamal, *Abi fauqa al-Shajara* (Cairo: Aflam Saut al-Fann, 1969).

75. Shafik, *Arab Cinema*, 105–6.

76. Danielson, *The Voice of Egypt*, 305–6.

77. Flagg Miller, "Metaphors of Commerce: Trans-valuing Tribalism in Yemeni Audiocassette Poetry," *International Journal of Middle East Studies* 34, no. 1 (2002): 29–57; Mamoun Fandy, *Saudi Arabia and the Politics of Dissent* (New York: St. Martin's Press, 1999); Annabelle Sreberny-Mohammadi and Ali Mohammadi, *Small Media, Big Revolution: Communication, Culture, and the Iranian Revolution* (Minneapolis: University of Minnesota Press, 1994); Charles Hirschkind, "Technologies of Islamic Piety: Cassette-Sermons and the Ethics of Listening" (PhD diss., Johns Hopkins University, 2000).

78. Lila Abu-Lughod, "Bedouins, Cassettes, and Technologies of Public Culture," *Middle East Report*, no. 159 (July–August 1989): 7–11; Armbrust, *Mass Culture and Modernism*; Virginia Danielson, "New Nightingales of the Nile: Popular Music in Egypt since the 1970s," *Popular Music* 15 (1996): 299–312.

79. See Armbrust, *Mass Culture and Modernism*; Danielson, *The Voice of Egypt*.

80. Danielson, *The Voice of Egypt*, 307; Armbrust *Mass Culture and Modernism*, 187–88.

81. Danielson, *The Voice of Egypt*, 127–33.

82. Jon Alterman, *New Media, New Politics? From Satellite Television to the Internet in the Arab World* (Washington, DC: Washington Institute for Near East Policy, 1998); Sakr, *Satellite Realms*.

83. Sakr, *Satellite Realms*.

84. Said, *Orientalism*.

85. Rosalind Morris, "All Made Up: Performance Theory and the New Anthropology of Sex and Gender," *Annual Review of Anthropology* 24 (1995): 567–92.

Glossary

'abqariyyat (plural of 'abqariyya) genius

al-Khulafa' al-Rashidun the first four caliphs of Islam, the rightly guided caliphs

'aql intelligence, reason

'ammiya colloquial or vernacular Arabic as opposed to the literary Arabic

'awagiz an elderly women

cantar a unit of weight measure equal to 44.93 kilograms in Alexandria

cizye (Turkish; Arabic = jizya) a head tax or poll tax, graded according to wealth, payable to the Islamic state by the members of the other monotheistic religions who were subjects

dhimmis the non-Muslim subjects of a Muslim state who were members of the other monotheistic religions

durbar the court of an Indian prince; a state reception by a native Indian ruler

effendiyya urban middle classes of Egyptian society educated in modern schools

farda profit

feddan a unit of land measure equal to 0.4046 hectares or 1.038 acres

fiqh Islamic jurisprudence

gallabiyya a traditional Egyptian robe

hadith recorded traditions of the Prophet's behavior and words

ijtihad exercise of reason by a capable scholar, the believer's right to exercise reason

Islamiyyat popular Islamic literature about early Islamic society and the exploits of Islamic founding fathers

jahili pertaining to pre-Islamic Arabia

khalifa Caliph, the Prophet's successor

makhzan central government of Morocco

makshufa revealed, uncovered

makwagi a launderer, a presser

mastura covered, concealed (females)

mawwal a form of popular song, often performed as improvisation, in which the singer shifts from one mode to another

muwashshah a sung poem in the Andalusian Arab style

nashid a song, a religious chant

qasida an ancient form of Arab poetry, the ode, maintaining a single end-rhyme throughout

qasr a palace, a mansion

qatl a murder, a killing

Sahaba companions of the Prophet Muhammad

silsila a chain of authority reaching back to the Prophet's time

Sira traditional life-story or biography of Muhammad

sürgün Ottoman forced population transfers

suttee the Hindu custom of burning a widow on the funeral pyre of her husband

şenlendirmek to populate or repopulate an area; literally, "to make it cheerful"

şeriat Islamic law, produced by the disciplined intellectual efforts of the scholars

tafsir Qur'anic commentary

takht a traditional ensemble

tanzim an organization

taqtuqa a short, simple song; a ditty

tujjar al-sultan "the royal merchants," i.e., Jewish merchants in Morocco

turath heritage or tradition

ʿulama learned Islamic scholars

ʿumda a village headman, particularly in Egypt

Contributors

WALTER ARMBRUST is the Albert Hourani Fellow of Modern Middle East Studies, St. Antony's College, University of Oxford. He is the author of *Mass Culture and Modernism in Egypt* (1996) and editor of *Mass Mediations: New Approaches to Popular Culture in the Middle East and Beyond* (2000). He is currently working on a cultural history of Egyptian cinema.

MARILYN BOOTH is an associate professor in the program in comparative and world literature at the University of Illinois at Urbana-Champaign. Her most recent book is *May Her Likes Be Multiplied: Biography and Gender Politics in Egypt* (2001), and she is working on a study of the early gender activist and writer Zaynab Fawwaz. She has translated many works of Arabic fiction into English.

JULIA CLANCY-SMITH is an associate professor of history at the University of Arizona, Tucson. She published *Rebel and Saint: Muslim Notables, Populist Protest, Colonial Encounters (Algeria and Tunisia, 1800–1904)* (1994), which received three book awards. She coedited *Domesticating the Empire: Race, Gender, and Family Life in French and Dutch Colonialism* (1998) and a special issue of *French Historical Studies*, "Writing French Colonial Histories," and edited *North Africa, Islam, and the Mediterranean World from the Almoravids to the Algerian War* (2001).

JUAN R. I. COLE is a professor of modern Middle Eastern and South Asian history at the University of Michigan. He is the author of *Sacred Space and Holy War* (2002), *Modernity and the Millennium* (1998), and *Colonialism and Revolution in the Middle East* (1993), among other works.

Y. HAKAN ERDEM teaches in the Faculty of Arts and Social Sciences of Sabancı University, Istanbul. He is the author of *Slavery in the Ottoman Empire and Its Demise, 1800–1909* (1996) and the coeditor of *Histories of the Modern Middle East: New Directions* (2002).

ISRAEL GERSHONI teaches the history of the modern Middle East in the Department of Middle Eastern and African History at Tel Aviv University. Among his recent publications are *Light in the Shade: Egypt and Fascism, 1922–1937* (1999) and, with James Jankowski, *Commemorating the Nation: Collective Memory, Public Commemoration, and National Identity in Twentieth-Century Egypt* (2004).

FATMA MÜGE GÖÇEK is an associate professor of sociology and women's studies at the University of Michigan. She is currently working on a book tentatively titled "Deciphering Denial: Turkish Historiography on the Armenian Massacres of 1915."

ELLIS GOLDBERG is a professor of political science at the University of Washington (Seattle), where he also heads the Middle East Center. His most recent book is *Trade, Reputation, and Child Labor in Twentieth-Century Egypt* (2004).

R. STEPHEN HUMPHREYS is a professor of history and Islamic studies at the University of California, Santa Barbara. He is the author of several books and numerous articles on the medieval and modern Middle East, including *Islamic History: A Framework for Inquiry* (1991) and *Between Memory and Desire: The Middle East in a Troubled Age* (1999). He was editor of the *International Journal of Middle East Studies* from 1994 to 1999 and is a past president (2001) of the Middle East Studies Association.

AMY SINGER teaches Ottoman and Turkish history in the Department of Middle Eastern and African History at Tel Aviv University. Her most recent works include *Constructing Ottoman Beneficence* (2002) and the coedited volume *Poverty and Charity in Middle Eastern Contexts* (2003).

CHARLES D. SMITH is a professor of Middle East history in the Department of Near Eastern Studies at the University of Arizona. He is the author of two books, including *Palestine and the Arab-Israeli Conflict*, now in its fifth edition, and articles on topics ranging from Egyptian secularism and Islam to nationalism to the impact of empires on the Middle East.

EVE M. TROUTT POWELL is an associate professor of history and Africana studies at the University of Pennsylvania. She is the author of *A Different Shade of Colonialism: Egypt, Great Britain, and the Mastery of the Sudan* (2003) and the coauthor, with John Hunwick, of the anthology *The African Diaspora in the Mediterranean Lands of Islam* (2002). In 2003, she was awarded a MacArthur Foundation Fellowship. Troutt Powell is now working on a book about spiritual life and the historical memory of African slavery in the Nile Valley.

Index

1948 war, 46, 184, 217
Abbasid, 23
Abbott, Nabia, 211
Abbud, Ahmad, 200
ʿAbd al-Krim, 74
ʿAbd al-Latif, Mahmud, 266, 267
ʿAbd al-Nasir, Jamal, 143, 158
ʿAbd al-Qadir, 74
ʿAbd al-Rahim, Shaʿban 304
ʿAbd al-Raziq, ʿAli 134, 137, 138, 142, 147, 148, 151, 159, 160, 171, 283; *al-Islam, wa-Usul al-Hukm* (1925), 148
ʿAbd al-Raziq, Mustafa, 136, 137
ʿAbd al-Wahhab, Muhammad, 295, 296, 298, 301; "grand songs," 296
Abdel-Malek, Anouar, 76
ʿAbduh, Muhammad, 133, 137, 138, 142, 150, 154, 157, 278, 281
Abdulhamid II, Sultan, 23
Abdullah, Amir, 48
ʿAbdullah, Saʿid ʿAbd al-Rahman Yusuf, 266
ʿAbduʾr-Rahman, Shaykh ʿUmar, 273
Abed-Kotob, Sana, 277, 278, 279, 280
abolitionists, 243, 244, 245

Abu-Bakr, Omaima, 215
Abu-Lughod, Lila, 215
Action Army, 122
Adams, Charles C., 137, 138, 154
Adas, Michael, 75
Adawiyya, Ahmad, 304, 305, 308; and audiocassette, 304; reputation of, 304–5
Aden, 40, 41
Adorno, Theodor, 102
advertising, 77
Afifi, Hafiz, 159
Afary, Janet, 215
Africa, 28, 74, 75, 77, 89, 202, 244, 276, 295; Islamic 246; and Muslims, 248, West, 86; East, 251, 252; East African Islamic identities, 252; expansion into Eastern, 257
Ageron, Charles-Robert, 82, 85
Ahfad University for Women, 213. *See also* Women's Studies Center at Ahfad College for Girls
Ahmad, Labiba, 171
Ahmed, Feroz, 51, 52
Ahmed, Leila, 219, 226

Ahmed Midhat, 78

A'isha bint Abi Bakr, 219

Al-Afghani, Jamal al-Din, 138, 142, 145, 157

Al-'Aqqad, 'Abbas Mahmud, 134, 136, 137, 143, 145, 147, 150, 151, 153, 159, 160, 161, 167, 171, 173; *'Abqariyyat,* 150, 167

Al-Atrash, Farid, 299, 304

Al-Azhar, 166

Al-Bahithat (researchers' collective), 214

Al-Banna, Hasan, 157, 267, 278, 281

Aleppo, 43

Alevis, 121

Alexandria, 80, 188, 247, 267

Al-Fasi, 'Allal, 88

Algeria, 74, 75, 80–84, 88, 89, 265, 276, 283;

Algerian War, 83; and revolution, 265

Al-Ghazali, 23

Al-Ghazzali, Zaynab, 270

Al-Hajjar, 'Ali, 303

Al-Hakim, Tawfiq, 134, 145, 148, 148, 149, 161, 171, 173; *'Awdat al-Ruh* (1933), 148; *Muhammad,* 150, 161

Al-Hilu, Muhammad, 304

Al-Hudaybi, Hasan, 267, 268, 281

Ali, Kurd, 142

Ali, Sayyid Ameer, 142

Al-Ithnayn, 293, 299

Al-Jahdi, Sulayman, 88

Al-Jama'ah al-Islamiyyah, 273

Al-Jarida, 134, 136, 137, 154

Al-Jihad al-Islami (Egypt), 262, 273, 275, 277

Al-Kawakib, 299

Al-Khazindar Bey, Ahmad, 267

Allied powers, 111–12, 113, 117

Alloula, Malek, 87

Al-Mazini, Ibrahim 'Abd al-Qadir, 134, 136, 137, 148, 171, 173

Al-Qaeda, 262

Al-Rafi'i, Mustafa Sadiq, 171

Al-Ra'ida (Beirut journal), 214

Al-Sadda, Huda, 215

Al-Sahir, Kadhim, 304

Al-Sanhuri, 'Abd al-Razzaq, 160, 172

al-Sayyid, Ahmad Lutfi, 134, 136, 137, 152, 154, 158

Al-Sharqawi, Galal, 300

Al-Siyasa, 137, 163; *Al-Siyasa al-Usbu'iyya,* 163

Al-Subki, Amal, 216

Al-Takfir wa al-Hijra (Excommunication and Holy Flight), 272, 275, 277

Al-Tha'albi, 'Abd al-Aziz, 88

Al-'Usur, 160

Al-Zayyat, Ahmad Hasan, 171

Al-Zayyat, Latifa, 225; *Al-Bab al-Maftuh,* 225

American Academy of Arts and Sciences, 276

American Historical Association, 83

American University in Cairo and Sharjah, 213

Amin, Ahmad, 134, 148, 150, 160, 162, 171, 173

Amin, Qasim, 134, 137, 154, 215, 222

'ammiya (colloquial Arabic), 257

Anabaptism, 281

Anatolia, 104, 107, 112, 113, 116, 117, 123

Anderson, Benedict, 54, 55, 75

Andrew, Christopher, 46, 50, 51

Anglo-Arab encounters, 47

Anis, Mahmoud Amin, 202

anthropology, history and, 307

anticolonial protest, 75

anti-imperialism, 22, 265, 271

anti-Zionism, 22
Antonius, George, 40, 41, 43, 54
Antun, Farah, 157
Appleby, R. Scott, 162
ʿaql, 143
Arab Middle East, 138, 155
Arab population, Palestine, 43
Arab revolt, 48
Arab Television, research on, 299–300
Arabesk, 296
Arabic Music Institute, 295
Arab-Israeli conflict, 39–40
architecture, 289, 290
Armenia, Armenians, 101, 103, 104, 109, 111, 112, 115, 117, 121, 123; diaspora, 104, 113; historiography, 103, 108; massacre, 107, 111, 122; narrative, 115
ASALA (Armenian Secret Army for the Liberation of Armenia), 117, 119
Ashour, Rawda, 225; Granada Trilogy, 225
Asia, 28, 74, 75, 77, 89, 138, 295
Asim, Midhat, 295, 296
Asmahan, 297, 304
Aswan, 200, 247
Atatürk. See Mustafa Kemal
Atiyya, Suzan, 303
Auclert, Hubertine, 89
audiocassette, 302–5; audiocassette technology, 302, 303; piracy of, 303, 304; and religious and political discourse, 303
audiovisual media, 292–93
audition. See orality
Auschwitz, 272
Austria-Hungary, 39, 81. See also Habsburg Empire
Ayalon, Ami, 293
Ayalon, David, 25

Ayubi, Nazih, 56, 277
ʿAzmi, Mahmud, 136, 171
ʿAzzam, ʿAbd al-Wahhab, 171

backstage musical, 301
Badawi, Mustafa, 160, 161
Badran, Margot, 216
Baer, Gabriel, 246, 247, 249, 256
Bahaʾism, 271
Baidaphon, 294, 297
Baker, Samuel, 246
Bakhit, Shaykh Muhammad, 157
Bakhtin, Mikhail, 55
Balandier, Georges, 74
Balfour, Arthur, 50
Balfour Declaration (1917), 39, 43, 44, 45, 46, 50, 51
Balkans, 104, 113
Balkan Wars (1912–13), 106
Balls, Lawrence, 189
Baron, Beth, 216, 217
Barrera, Giulia, 86
Barthes, Roland, 31, 263
Bartol V. V. (Wilhelm Barthold), 32
Bateson, Gregory, 84
Batshan, Hamdi, 304
Beck, Lois, 71
Becker, Carl L., 23, 133
Bedouin, 232
Beinin, Joel, 191, 199
Beirut, 213, 214
Beirut College for Girls, 213. See also Lebanese American University
Bell, Gertrude, 21, 25
Berber, 84
Bergson, Henri, 167
Berkowitz, Michael, 51
Berlin, Isaiah, 133
Berque, Jacques, 74, 83, 86, 201

Birriya, 198
Bir Zeit University, 213
Bonapartism, 265
Bonin, Hubert, 81
Booth, Marilyn, 82
Borg, Raphael, 246
Botman, Selma, 152, 153
Bourguiba, Habib, 88
Bozdogan, Sibel, 296
Branch Davidian movement, 284
Braune, E. G., 22
Brazil, 264
Bremond, Edouard, 49
British and Foreign Anti-Slavery
  Society (BFASS), 244
British Caribbean, 245
British colonialism, 169
British diplomacy, 51
British Empire, 25, 41, 56, 78, 82, 83, 87
British Foreign Office, 47, 244, 246, 253,
  293
British imperialism, 40, 41, 52, 58, 73,
  80, 81, 140, 199
British India, 71
British navy, 41
British occupation of Egypt, 183, 184
British reaction to Ottoman Slavery,
  253
Brunschvig, Robert, 25
Buenttner, Elizabeth, 79
Burke III, Edmund, 73, 75, 80, 86
Burton, Antoinette, 78
Busch, Briton Cooper, 47
Bush, George W., 41
Byzantine Empire, 23, 234, 235, 236

Cachia, Pierre, 153, 154, 159
Cahen, Claude, 25
Cain, P. J., 52

Cairo, 22, 42, 47, 75, 211, 213, 214, 222,
  237, 246, 247, 257, 267, 283; Jewish
  quarter, 267; Cairo Home for Freed
  Slave Women, 254; Cairo Univer-
  sity, 81
calligraphy, 290
Calvinism, 281
Canada, 86
Care of Emancipated Slaves, 254
caricature, 290
Çark, Y. G., 118, 119
Cassirer, Ernest, 141
Catholicism, 263, 273
Caetani, Leone, 30
Çelik, Zeynep, 78, 87
Charnay, Jean-Paul, 86
Charrad, Mounira, 88, 215
Chatterjee, Partha, 107
Chaudhuri, Nupur, 78
chieftaincy, 57; "failed," 57
child labor, 202, 203
China, 268
Christelow, Allan, 84
Christians, 275; Syrian, 235
Churchill, Winston, 44
cinema. See films
Clancy-Smith, Julia, 215
Cleopatra, 278
Cloarec, Vincent, 50
Clot Bey, 257
Cole, Juan, 81
Collingwood, R. G., 155
Collins, Patricia Hills, 102, 103
Collins, Randall, 170
Colombe, Marcel, 153
colonialism, 22, 57, 86, 90, 169
Colonna, Fanny, 83, 85
Committee of Union and Progress
  (CUP), 106, 112, 113, 115, 118, 122

concentration camps (*camps de concentration*), 271, 272
Congo. *See* Zaire
Conklin, Alice F., 86
Constantinopole, 104. *See also* Istanbul
conversion to Islam, 250
Cook, Michael, 30
Cookson, Charles, 246
Cooper Frederick, 250, 251, 252, 256
Copts, 229, 234, 235, 236, 273, 275, 279
Corbin, Henry, 274, 276, 283
cotton, Egyptian, 186–90, 192–97, 199, 202; Ashmuni, 191–94, 196; commission, 196; Joanovitch, 196; Mit Afifi, 191–94, 196; Sakellaridis (Sakel), 189–94
Cragg, Kenneth, 160
Craig, James I., 195
Credit Foncier, 81
Cromer, Lord, 23, 254
Crone, Patricia, 30
Crusades, 23
Cuno, Kenneth, 81
Curzon, Lord, 23

Dalrymple, William, 75
Damascus, 22, 43
Dar Fertit, 255
Dar Fur, 255
Darnton, Robert, 132
Dawn, C. Ernest, 54
Dayf, Ahmad, 136
De Beauvoir, Simone, 87
decolonization 74, 159
decoration, 289
Delhi, 75
Della Sala, 246
Delta, 196–99
Deringil, Selim, 52, 53

Derrida, Jacques, 31
De Saussure, Ferdinand, 264
dhimmi, 105
diaspora, history of, 220
diplomacy, 51
discipline, history of, 306–8
discourse, 44
Diyab, Amr, 305
Douchesne, Edouard Adolphe, 86
Douglas, Mary, 162
Dresch, Paul, 57
Droit des Femmes, 89
Dudgeon, Gerald, 196
Dunn, John, 131
Dunn, Ross E., 75
Dutch colonialism, 22
Dutch Empire, 72

ecstatic feedback, 294
Eden, Anthony, 272
effendiyya, 169, 185
Egger, Vernon, 160
Egypt, 23, 24, 48, 52, 71, 76, 79, 80, 82, 86, 88, 104, 134–37, 140, 143, 145–48, 151–53, 157–61, 163, 165–68, 172, 173, 183–207, 212, 215–17, 225, 227–29, 234–36, 246, 247, 257, 262–84, 288, 291–95, 297, 300, 301, 305, 306; agriculture, 184, 198, 202; Delta, 282; film industry, nationalization of, 302; Ministry of Communication, 295; nationalist movement, 185, 186; Upper, 273, 282
Egyptian Feminist Union, 216
Egyptian State Broadcasting (ESB), 295, 296, 303; and Um Kulthum and 'Abd al-Wahhab, 296–97
Egyptian studios, 299
Eickelman, Dale, 57

Eisenstadt, S. N., 162
Elgood, P. G., 198
El-Mazzawi, Farid, 299
El-Sādāt, Anwar, 271, 273, 277, 281, 304
El-Shawan, Salwa Aziz, 295
Engels, Friedrich, 274, 275, 283
England. *See* Great Britain
Enlightenment, 115, 263
Episcopalianism, 281
Erdem, Hakan, 253, 254
Eritrea, 86
Ethiopia, 257
ethnicity, 56
Europe, 114, 133, 143, 149, 156, 163, 201, 263, 268, 291, 292, 295, 298; Eastern 268; Western, 243
European Union, 123
Evliya Çelebi, 247
exceptionalism, 40
Ezzedine, Salah, 300

Fahmi, Mansur, 134, 137
Fahmy, Khaled, 81
famine, 49, 53
Fanon, Franz, 74
Faroqhi, Suraiya, 30
Farouk, King, 278
fascism, 172, 265
Father Divine, 284
Father Is Up a Tree (Abi Fawqa al-Shajara), 302
Fawwaz, Zaynab, 211, 228, 229, 230, 232–34, 236, 237; *Husn al-ʿAwaqib aw Ghadat al-Zahira* (Good Consequences, or the Lovely Young Maid of al-Zahira), 228–36
Fawzi, Husayn, 171
Fawzi, Muhammad, 299, 304

Faysal, Amir, 44, 55, 58
Felski, Rita, 228, 237
feminism, 26, 27, 87, 211, 214, 221, 223, 224, 227, 229; French, 89; Islamic, 223, 224; Turkish, 217
Feraoun, Mouloud, 74
Fergana, 283
Ferry, Jules, 83
fiction, and history, 226–28
films, 77, 292, 297–302; budget, 298; Egyptian 297, 301; musical, 297–302
Findley, Carter V., 78
fiqh, 139
Fleischmann, Ellen, 215, 217
FLN (National Liberation Front), 88
Forbes, Geraldine, 78
Foster, Frances Smith, 245
Foucault, Michel, 26, 31, 76, 90, 263, 264, 265, 276, 306–7
France, 39, 40, 44, 48, 49, 51, 72, 81, 84, 88, 89, 186, 198, 215, 263–65, 273, 274; Colonial Historical Society, 83; colonialism, 83; diplomacy, 51; empire, 25, 71, 82, 84, 85; imperialism, 40, 41, 52, 81, 89; protectorate, 88; Revolution, 106, 115, 120
Frankfurt School, 102
Free Officers, 266, 269
Friedman, Isaiah, 42, 43, 46, 47, 49, 50
Friesel, Evyatar, 51
Fromkin, David, 43–45
Fugitive Slave Act (1850), 245
fundamentalism, 281

Gallagher, John, 74
gays and lesbians, 217–18
Geertz, Clifford, 30, 31, 35

Gelvin, James, 55, 58, 86

gender, 28, 70–100, 211–41

gender analysis, 87

generative grammar, 274

genocide, 107, 110

"gentlemanly capitalism," 52

George, David Lloyd, 43, 50, 51

Germany, 122, 294; archives, 49, 53

Ghali, Mirrit Butrus, 171

ghettoization, 80

Gibb, Sir Hamilton A. R., 21, 24, 25, 135–46, 148, 150–55, 157, 161, 162, 173

Goitein, S. D., 25

Goldberg, Ellis, 281

Goldziher, Ignaz, 21, 22, 30, 33

Gomez, Michael A., 258

Gordon, Joel, 267, 271

gramophone and phonograph, 292–94

Gramophone Company, 294

Gramsci, Antonio, 107

Great Britain, 39–44, 46–50, 53, 72, 75–77, 80, 81, 89, 107, 186–88, 197, 199, 201, 212, 244–46, 254, 256, 266, 267, 294, 295

Great War. See World War I

Greater Syria, 135, 157

Greece, 119

Grey, Sir Edward, 46, 47

Griliches, Zvi, 190

Guha, Ranajit, 76, 107

Gulf, 304

Habermas, Jürgen, 103, 274, 279

Habsburg Empire, 23, 56

hadith, 139, 222

Hafiz, 'Abd al-Halim, 298, 299, 302, 303, 305

Hafiz Ibrahim, 257

Haim, Sylvia, 54

Hakim, 305

Hama, 43

Hamdi, Sahar, 304

Hamida, 'Ali, 304

Hansen, Bent, 199

Harb, Muhammad Tal'at, 298

harem, 254

Hasso, Joseph, 217

Hatem, Mervet, 215

Hawwa (acdemic journal), 212

Haydar, Rustem, 48

Haykal, Muhammad Husayn, 134, 137, 138, 142, 143, 145, 147, 149, 150–53, 159–68, 171, 173, 225; Fi Manzil al-wahy (At the Site of Revelation), 149, 167; Hayat Muhammad (The Life of Muhammad), 142, 149, 151, 160, 161, 165–67; Al-Khulafa al-rashidun, 150, 152, 167; Taghrib al-sharq, 173; Zaynab, 225

Hegel, G. W. F., 21, 155, 279

Higham, John, 133, 156

Hijaz, 49, 54, 57

Hijazi, Shaykh Salama, 295

Hilal, 'Umad Ahmad, 256, 257; Al-raqiq fi Masr fi-l-qarn al-tasi' 'ashr (Slavery in Nineteenth-Century Egypt), 256

Hilmi, 'Abd al-Hayy, 295

historicism, 22

Hitler, Adolph, 272

Hitti, Philip, 24

Hobsbawm, Eric, 75

Hobson, J. A., 73

Hodgson, Marshall G. S., 34

Hogarth, David, 42, 43, 45

Hollywood, 301

Holocaust, 102

Homs, 43

Hong Kong, 40, 41
Hopkins, A. G., 52
Hopwood, Derek, 154
Horkheimer, Max, 102
Hourani, Albert, 32, 34, 36, 48, 135, 139, 153–55, 156–59, 170
Hunswick, John, 243
Hunter, F. Robert, 80
Hurgronje, Christiaan Snouck, 21, 22, 32, 33
Husayn-McMahon Correspondence, 42, 46, 47, 57
Husayn of Mecca, Sharif, 41, 42, 43, 45–48, 55, 57
Husayn, Taha, 134, 136, 137, 142–45, 147–49, 151–55, 157–61, 165–67, 171, 173; 'Ala hamish al-sira (On the Margin of the Life of the Prophet), 144, 149, 151, 154, 159–61, 165, 166; Fi al-adab al-jahili (On Pre-Islamic Literature), 148, 165; Fi al-shi'r al-jahili (On Pre-Islamic Poetry), 136, 148, 165; Min ba'id (From Afar), 165; Mustaqbal al-thaqafa fi Misr (The Future of Culture in Egypt), 142, 143, 165; Qadat al-fikr (The Leaders of Thought), 165
Husserl, Edmond, 141
hypernym, 264

Ibn Khaldun, 23
Ibn Rabah, Nusayb, 248
Ibn Rashid, 57
Ibn Rushd, 23
Ibn Saud, 57
Ibrim, 247
ijtihad, 222
Ilbert, Robert, 80
illiteracy, 293

illustrated magazines, 290; Egyptian, 293
illustration, 289
Imam, Abdu'llah, 279
imperialism, 21, 22, 24, 40, 45, 46, 51, 82, 114, 169, 200
'Inan, Muhammad 'Abdallah, 171
India, 40, 107; colonial 75, 76, 89
Indiana, 284
India Office, 75
Indochina, 86
Indonesia, 72, 276
İnönü, İsmet, 119
Institute for Women's Studies in the Arab World, 213
intégrism, 263
Intellectual Life in the Arab East, 54
Iqbal, Muhammad, 142
Iran, 77, 82, 276
Iraq, 39, 45
Islam, 275
Islambouli, Khalid, 273, 275
Islamic Mind (la conscience islamiste), 263, 264
Islamic Revolution, 263
Islamic Spain, 25
Islamism, 214, 221, 224, 264, 271, 274, 283, 284, 303
Islamiyyat, 134, 138, 139, 143, 144, 153, 161, 166, 169, 170, 171
Ismailia, 266, 267
Israel, 39, 44, 265, 283, 303
Issawi, Charles, 183, 184, 202, 203
Istanbul, 246
Italian Empire, 86

jahiliyya, 136
Jamal, Amaney, 280
jazz, 301

Jemal Pasha, 49, 53
Jennings, Eric, 86
Jews, 84, 91, 121; organization, 53; population in Palestine, 39, 53
Jidda, 43
Johnson, Lyndon, 26
Jones, Jim, 284
Jordan, the Hashemite Kingdom of, 48, 53
Joseph, Suad, 215, 217
Journal of Middle East Women's Studies, 212
Julien Charles-André, 82, 85

Kabyle, 85; myth, 86
Kabylia, 283
Kandiyoti, Deniz, 215, 217, 219, 222, 231, 237
Kanya-Forstner, A. S., 46, 50, 51
Karim, Muhammad, 297; *Sons of Aristocrats* (Awlad al-Dhawat), 297
Karsh, Ephraim, 43, 45, 46, 53
Karsh, Inari, 45, 53
Kayali, Hasan, 52, 53
Kazdaghli, Habib, 85
Keddie, Nikki, 71
Kedourie, Elie, 42, 43, 45–50, 52, 54; "The Chatham House Version," 42, 46
Kelly, J. B., 73
Kennedy, Dane, 73
Kent, Martin, 47, 56
Kepel, Gilles, 263–66, 268–78, 281, 283; *Muslim Extremism in Egypt*, 263
Khadduri, Majid, 160
Khalid, Khalid Muhammad, 160
Khalidi, Rashid, 54, 55
Khalifa, Ijlal, 216
Khartoum, 246, 253, 256

Khedive Isma'il, 246, 247, 256–57
Khomeini, Ayatullah, 284
Khomeinism, 264
Khost, Nadia, 225
Khoury, Gerard D., 49, 50
Khoury, Philip S., 57, 58, 86
King George Hotel (Ismailia), attack on, 266
Kishk, Shaykh, 273
Kitchener, Lord, 48, 198
Köprülü, Fuat, 24
Koresh, David, 284
Kostiner, Joseph, 57
Kramer, Martin, 54
Kristeva, Julia, 263
Kurds, 121

labor migration, history of, 220
Lambton, Anne K. S., 24
Lammens, Henri, 30
Lamu, 251
Landau, Jacob, 297
Landes, David, 81
land reform, 281
languages of research, 19, 20, 24
Largueche, Dalenda and Abdelhamid, 85
Larson, Pierre, 90
Laurens, Henry, 49, 50
Lebanese American University in Beirut, 213
Lebanon, 39, 40, 45, 49, 53, 58, 79, 158, 212, 225, 229, 230, 232, 291, 300, 306
Lefebvre, Henri, 87
leftists, 303
Lenin, Vladimir, 200, 201
Lerner, Daniel, 25
Les Temps Modernes, 265
Levant, 86

Levine, Philippa, 79
Levi-Provençal, Évariste, 26
Levi-Strauss, Claude, 141, 263, 264
Lewis, Bernard, 25, 40, 41, 151, 242, 247–50, 252, 253; *Race and Slavery in the Middle East*, 242, 247–49
Liberal Constitutionalist Party, 163, 164, 166
Lieven, Dominic, 55, 56
Ligue Coloniale, 83
linguistic turn, 30, 131
Liverpool, 187
Livingstone, David, 244, 246
Locke, John, 279
London, 47, 75
Lorcin, Patricia, 86
Lovejoy, Arthur O., 133, 138, 141, 156
Lovejoy, Paul, 250
Libyan Desert, 269

Maghreb, 71, 73, 79, 80, 82, 87, 88, 90
Mahdiyya, Munira, 295
Mahmood, Saba, 215
Malcolm, Sir John, 79
Malet, Edward, 246
Mamluks, 25
mandate states, 39, 40, 58
Marconi Company, 295
Marmon, Shaun, 218
Marseilles, Jacques, 81
Marsot, Afaf Lutfi al-Sayyid, 152, 160, 162
Marty, Martin, 276
Marxism, 185, 263–65, 268, 273, 276
Marx, Karl, 21, 31
masculinity, 79, 236
Massignon, Louis, 21, 25
Mauritania, 243
mawwal, 301

Mazhar, Isma'il, 160, 171
McMahon, Sir Henry, 42, 43, 46, 47
Mecca, 274, 275, 281, 283
media, state control of, 303–4
Mediterranean Sea, 49, 52, 53, 71, 74, 80
Mehmet Ali, 183; *See also* Muhammad Ali
Memmi, Albert, 74
Meriwether, Margaret, 219, 220
Merle, Isabelle, 84
Mernissi, Fatima, 215, 219, 222
Metcalf, Barbara, 78
Methodism, 281
MGM studios, 300
Middle East Studies Association, 83, 104
Midwifery School of Egypt, 257
Migdal, Joel, 57
Milner, Alfred, 198
minorities, 105, 106, 119, 120, 121, 122
missionaries, 79
Mitchell, Richard P., 137, 267, 273, 277
Mitchell, Timothy, 80
modernism, 136–8, 143, 146, 151, 153, 154, 156, 159, 163, 167, 169, 171, 172; Egyptian, 136, 137, 151, 154
Moghissi, Haideh, 221
Monroe, Elizabeth, 47
Montasser, Adel, 265
Moors, Annelies, 215
Moreau, Odile, 85
Morocco, 74, 88
Morris, Benny, 45, 46
Mosseti, Victor, 196
Motherland Party, 123
Mubarak, Ali, 247; *Al-Khitat al-Tanfiqiya fi Masr al-Jadida*, 247
Mubarak, Hosni, 275, 279, 284
Mubarak, Zaki, 171

Muhammad Ali, 257. *See also* Mehmet Ali
Muhammad Imam al-'Abd, 257
Muhammad, Prophet 22, 134, 138, 139, 142, 151, 154, 159–61, 166, 219, 274–76
multiculturalism, 26
multiethnic empires, 55, 56
multiplier effect, 291
Munir, Muhammad, 304
Muqattam Hills, 266
Murad, Layla, 297–99, 304
murder (*qatl*), 275
Murphey, Murray G., 132
Musa, Nabawiya, 171, 214, 223
Musa, Salama, 134, 136, 159, 160, 171, 173
Musa, Sulayman, 48
music, 288, 292–306; Egyptian, 294, 296, 304; orchestral classics, 301; portability of, 294, 303; synthesizer and, 305; Western popular, 301
musicals, Egyptian, 300–301
Muslim Brotherhood, 152, 158, 262, 265, 266–73, 277, 278, 280, 282–84; Guidance Council, 267; Secret Apparatus, 266–68, 278, 282
Muslim fundamentalism, 263, 265, 276, 277, 280, 284
Muslim radicalism, 263–65, 270–77, 280–82; Egyptian, 264; Sunni, 281
Mussolini, Benito, 272
Mustafa Kemal (Atatürk), 45, 112, 116, 118, 119, 122
Mustafa, Shukri, 272, 273, 276, 277
Mutlaqa al-Mar'a wa-al-Dhakira (Women and Memory Forum), 214, 218, 223; *Mudkhal ila qadaya al-mar'a fi suture wa suwar* (Cairo, 2002), 218
muwashshah, 301

Nadira, 297
Najmabadi, Afsaneh, 215, 218
Nantes, archives, 49
Napoleon, Bonaparte, 183
narratives, 245; slave, 244, 245
nashid, 301
Nasif, Malak Hilmi, 223
Nasser, Gamal Abdel, 183, 202, 203, 262, 265–71, 281, 282, 304
Nasserism, 265, 268, 270–72, 278, 280–84
Nasserist Socialism, 281
Nation of Islam, 278, 284
National Defense Education Act (1958), 28, 29; Title VI, 28, 29, 30
nationalism, 39–42, 53, 55–57, 89–91, 106, 107, 115, 116, 120–23, 137, 143, 150, 151, 215, 217, 220, 235, 236, 296; Arab, 40–42, 53, 54, 58, 106, 143, 151; Armenian, 106, 107; ethnic, 55; and gender, 107; Greek, 106; and race, 107; Turkish, 106, 107, 117, 120, 121, 122
Nationalist Opposition, 78
nation-state, 70, 107–9, 112, 114, 118, 120
nativism, 283
Nazism, 102, 172, 276
Nelson, Cynthia, 215
neoconservatism, 263, 264
neofundamentalism, 262
neo-imperialism, 272, 276
Nettl, J. P., 162
Nevakivi, Jukka, 47, 50
New Democracy, 123
New Egyptian Civil Code (1949), 172
New Media, 393, 305–6
NGO, 279, 280, 284
Nile Valley, 188, 190, 244, 247; White Nile, 246
Nöldeke, Theodor, 21

Nora, Pierre, 85
North Africa, 25, 70, 71, 74, 79, 80, 82,
    84–88, 90, 91, 138, 211, 215
North America, 83, 133, 212, 213, 295
Nuba Mountains, 255
Nuqrashi Pasha, Mahmud, 267
Nur (Cairo, journal), 214

oases, 247
Ochsenwald, William, 57
October War (1973), 303
Oddie, Geoffrey, 90
Odeon, 294
Ong, Walter, 288
orality, 291–92
Orbay, Rauf, 119
orientalism, 22–25, 30–32, 73, 76, 133,
    134, 140, 158, 159, 161, 166, 220, 221,
    223, 224, 264, 273, 274, 307
Ottoman Empire, 23, 24, 39–42, 45,
    48, 51–54, 56–58, 78, 81, 85, 86, 101,
    103–8, 110–12, 115–18, 120, 122, 216,
    219, 246, 248, 249, 253, 291, 296; Arab
    Lands of, 40–42, 49, 51, 54; archives,
    52, 108; Armenians, 105, 108, 110;
    "bourgeoisie," 105; court, 219; Greeks,
    105; historiography, 52; investigative
    narrative, 110; Jews, 105; minorities,
    105, 106, 120–22; monetary policies,
    52; Muslin bourgeoisie, 106; narra-
    tives, 110; sources, 104; Westerniza-
    tion, 104
Oulebsir, Nabila, 87
Owen, Roger, 56, 81, 154, 155
Oxford, 155
Özal, Turgut, 123

Pahlavi, 284
Paidar, Parvin, 215

painting, 289, 290
Pakistan, 276
Palestine, 39, 42–45, 47, 55, 77, 213, 216,
    217, 265; Mandate, 39
Palestine Liberation Organization,
    265
Palestinian nationalist movement, 215
Palestinian-Israeli conflict, 39–40
Pamuk, Şevket, 52
pan-Arabism, 143
Paris, 75, 284
Pears, Edwin, 23
Peirce, Leslie, 219
People's Temple, 284
Perkins, Kenneth J., 80
Persian Empire, 249
pharaoh, 275, 282
phenomenology, 263, 282, 283
phonography, 77, 290, 293–94
Pichon, Jean, 49
Piterberg, Gaby, 154
Planel, Anne-Marie, 85
Plantation Slavery on the East Coast
    of Africa, 252
pleasure, history of, 306–8
Pocock, J.G.A., 131
political economy, 183–207
poll tax (*cizye*), 105
Pollard, Lisa, 82
population exchange, Greek-Turkish,
    123
population transfer (*sürgün*), 104, 107;
    See also şenlendirmek
postcolonialism, 22, 26, 30, 107
postmodernism, 30, 263
postnationalism, 110, 123
postnationalist critical narrative, 110
poststructuralism, 131, 276
Powell, Eve M. Troutt, 79

printing and printing press, 291–93;
   in Europe, 291
Prochaska, David, 85
professionalization, 29
Protestantism, 263, 273
protofascism, 282
Public Record Office, 254

qasida, 294, 301
Qatar, 306
Quai d'Orsay (French Foreign Office),
   50, 81; archives, 50
Qur'an, 219, 222, 242, 251, 275
Qutb, Sayyid, 269, 270, 271, 273

race, racism, 78, 79, 244, 248, 257; racial
   ideologies, 252
radio, 293–97, 298, 299, 302, 303; and
   Free Officers, 295
Raj, 76, 78
Ramusack, Barbara, 79
Ranger, Terence, 74, 75
recording technology, 296
records, 293, 294
Red Sea, 49
reform, land, 271
reformism, 225
Reid, Donald M., 81, 154
Reimer, Michael J., 80
Reinharz, Jehuda, 51
religion, sociology of, 263
religious law (şeriat), 105
Republican People's Party (RPP), 119
Richards, Alan, 199
Rida, Mustafa, 295, 296
Rida, Rashid, 138, 142, 150, 154, 157
Robinson, Ronald, 74
Rogan, Eugene, 52, 53, 86
Roman Empire, 23

romanticism, 139, 140, 146, 151
Roshwald, Aviel, 55, 56
Rowson, Everett, 218
Royal Geographic Society, 244
Russel, Malcolm B., 58
Russell, Mona, 82
Russia, 39, 56, 81, 113
Rwanda, 276
Rycaut, Paul, 23

Safran, Nadav, 141, 147–52, 159–61, 165,
   169
Sahaba, 144
Said, Edward, 22, 23, 26, 31, 32, 71, 76,
   132, 265, 307; Orientalism, 32, 71, 76,
   78, 132
Saint, Lucien, 88
Salvation Army, 284
Sanders, Paula, 218
Sartre, Jean-Paul, 265
satellite broadcasting, 305–6
Saudi Arabia, 57, 270, 306
Saul, Samir, 81
Schacht, Joseph, 24, 25
Schilcher, Linda Schatkowski, 49, 53
Schroeter, Daniel J., 84
Scott, James E., 75
Segal, Ronald, 242
semantic system (système sémantique),
   263, 264
şenlendirmek, 104
September 11, 2001, 41
settlers, European, 74, 79, 85
sexuality, 79, 80, 87, 214, 217
Sha'rawi, Huda, 214
Shadi, Salah, 267
Shafik, Viola, 300
Shahin, Yusuf, 304
Sharett, Moshe, 44

Sharpe, Jenny, 228
Shils, Edward, 162
Shorrock, William I., 51, 52
Shumayyil, Shibli, 157
Sidqi, Isma'il, 166
Sikainga, Ahmad Alawad, 254–57
silent reading, 290, 292, 307
silsila, 139
Singapore, 40, 41
Sinha, Mrinalini, 79
Sira, 160
Sirri, Hussein, 199, 200
Sivan, Emanuel, 85
Sivers, Peters von, 75
Skinner, Quentin, 131, 162
slaveholding, 252
slavery, 242–58; African, 242–48, 250, 251, 254–57; African experience of, 250; American, 253; Circassian, 256, 257; end of in Africa, 249; historiography of Middle Eastern, 257; ideology of in Africa, 250; Islamic, 242, 245; Nile Valley, 247; Ottoman, 253, 254; slave's version of Islam, 251; Sudanese, 254
slave trade: African, 247, 249, 250, 253; White Nile, 246
Smith, Charles D., 153, 157, 161–70
Smith, Dorothy, 102, 103
Smith, Margaret, 25
Smith, Wilfred Cantwell, 141, 144–47, 150, 171
Society of Muslims, 272. See also al-Takfir wa al-Hijra
Sonbol, Amira, 81
Song of the Heart (Unshudat al-Fu'ad), 297
Southern Baptists, 280
Soviet Union, 283

Spagnolo, John, 51
Spain, 81
Spellberg, Denise, 219
Spivak, Gayatri, 79, 107, 243, 244, 253, 258
Sputnik, 26, 28
Stalinism, 268
state formation, 39, 56
Stokes, Martin, 296
Stoler, Ann, 79
Strobel, Margaret, 78
structuralism, 263, 264, 282, 284
Studio Misr (Egypt Studio), 298
subaltern studies, 79
Sub-Saharan Africa, 74
Sudan, 79, 213, 243, 249, 255–57, 290
Sufism, 274
Sullivan, Denis, 277–80
Sultan, Huda, 299
Sunna, 272, 281
Suny, Ronald Grigor, 103
Swahili, 252
Swahili Coast, 251
Sykes, Sir Percy, 79
Sykes-Picot Agreement (May 1916), 42, 46, 47, 49
Syria, 39, 40, 44, 45, 49, 53, 55, 58, 79, 215, 216, 225, 235

tafsir, 139
Tal'at, Yusuf, 267
taqtuqa, 294
Taraud, Cristelle, 87
Tashkent, 283
Tauber, Eliezer, 54
Tawfiq, Ihab, 304
Taymur, Mahmud, 161
Teitelbaum, Joshua, 57
television broadcasting, 298, 299, 303

theory, 29–31

Third Republic (France), 84

Third World, 263; Third Worldism (*Tiers-mondisme*), 264–65, 271

Thobie, Jacques, 51, 52, 81

Thompson, Elizabeth, 53, 58, 86, 215

Tibawi, Abd al-Latif, 47

Tignor, Robert, 81

Tillion, Germaine, 86–87

Tilly, Charles, 55

Toledano, Ehud, 253, 257

Transjordan, 53, 58

Treaty of Lausanne, 112–14, 123

Treaty of Sèvres, 111–14

Trumpener, Ulrich, 51, 52

Tucker, Judith, 82, 216, 218, 219, 220

Tunisia, 81, 88, 91, 265

Tura Prison, 272

Turkey, 39, 45, 81, 101–23, 212, 225, 276, 296; bourgeoisie, 106; historiography, 101, 103, 104, 108, 110; narrative, 115

Turkish Democratic Party, 119, 123

Turkish Independent Movement, 117

Turkish Progressive Republican Party, 123

Turkish Republican defensive narrative, 110, 116

Turkish War of Independence, 112–14, 118

ʿulama, 166, 167

ʿUmar, Khalifa, 234

Umayyad dynasty, 274

Umayyads, 22

ʿumda, 158, 162

Umm Kulthum, 295–98, 301, 303, 305, 308; "Thursday concerts," 297

United Arab Emirates, 306

United Kingdom. *See* Great Britain

United States, 26, 28, 40, 41, 46, 47, 53, 189, 201, 203, 243, 245, 246, 257, 268, 270, 273, 274, 278, 283, 279, 298

universities, 26–28; European, 20, 21, 25, North American, 25; Turkish state, 108, 109; Western, 27

University of Sanaa, 213

Uras, Esat, 118, 119

urbanization, 77

USSR, 28. *See also* Soviet Union

Uzbekistan, 283

Uzunçarşılı, İsmail Hakkı, 24

Van Berchem, Max, 21, 23, 33

Vasiliev, Alexander, 23

Vatican, 53

Vatikiotis, P. J., 151

Verete, Mayir, 51

vernacularization, 291

Vietnam, 26, 28

visual culture, 289–90

visualism, 289

Vital, David, 51

Vitalis, Robert, 200

Volpi, Mario, 297

Von Grunebaum, Gustave E., 141–46, 153, 157, 161

Wafd Party, 266, 282

Wajdi, Farid, 146–47

Wallerstein, Immanuel, 31

Walz, Terence, 243, 258

Wansbrough, John, 30

Washington, D.C., 268

"weak state," 57

Weber, Max. 31, 281, 284

Weizmann, Chaim, 50, 51

Wellhausen, Julius, 21, 30, 33

Wessels, Antoine, 161

White Nile, 246

White, Hayden, 131

White, Owen, 79

White Rose, The (Al-Warda al-Bayda), 297

Widad, 298

Wilson, Jeremy, 50

Wilson, Mary C., 58

Wittek, Paul, 24

Wolf, Lucien, 51

women, 19, 21, 24, 27, 28, 70–100, 171, 211–41, 243; Algerian, 87; Arab, 224; and development, 215; and education 89; Egyptian, 217, 300; Hindu, 243; and labor, 202; and magazines, 214; North African, 86–89; Palestinian, 217; and sexuality, 87; South Asian, 75, 76; South-East Asian, 79; Syrian, 86; Tunisian, 88

Women for Women's Human Rights/ New Ways, 217; and *Sexuality in Muslim Societies* 217, 218

Women's Studies Center at Ahfad College for Girls, 213

Works Projects Administration, 258

World War I, 21, 22, 24, 39–42, 45–49, 51–58, 74, 136, 185, 186, 190, 191

World War II, 28, 74, 88, 102, 119, 151, 300

World's Fairs, 77

Wright, Gwendolyn, 87

writing and reading, 290–92

xenophobia, 283

Yapp, Malcolm, 79

Yemen, 57, 213, 270

Young Egypt, 152

Young Turks, 106, 120

Zaghloul, Sa'ad, 74

Zaire (Congo), 276

Zayd, Amir, 48

Zaydan, Jurji, 229, 234–37; *Armanusa al-Misriyya* (Armanusa the Egyptian), 229–36

Zeine, Zeine N., 48, 54

Zionism, 40–46, 50, 58

Zipperstein, Steven, 51

Zirbel, Katherine, 301

Printed in the United States
200062BV00004B/88-315/A